Plato at Syracuse

THE HERITAGE OF WESTERN GREECE

The cultural and intellectual heritage of Western Greece—the coastal areas of Southern Italy and Sicily settled by Hellenes in the 8th and 7th centuries BCE—is sometimes overlooked in academic studies. Yet evidence suggests that poets, playwrights, philosophers, and other maverick intellectuals found fertile ground here for the growth of their ideas and the harvesting of their work. The goal of this series is to explore the distinctive heritage of Western Greece from a variety of disciplinary perspectives including art history, archaeology, classical literature, drama, epigraphy, history, philosophy, and religion.

Philosopher Kings and Tragic Heroes
Edited by Heather L. Reid and Davide Tanasi
2016 ISBN 978-1942495079

Politics and Performance in Western Greece
Edited by Heather L. Reid, Davide Tanasi, and Susi Kimbell
2017 ISBN 978-1942495185

The Many Faces of Mimēsis
Edited by Heather L. Reid and Jeremy C. DeLong
2018 ISBN 978-1-942495-22-2

Looking at Beauty to Kalon *in Western Greece*
Edited by Heather L. Reid and Tony Leyh
2019 ISBN 978-1-942495-33-8

Plato at Syracuse

Essays on Plato in Western Greece
with a new translation of the *Seventh Letter*
by Jonah Radding

edited by
Heather L. Reid
and Mark Ralkowski

Parnassos Press
2019

Copyright © 2019 Fonte Aretusa LLC
Individual authors retain their copyright to their articles, which are printed here by permission. All rights reserved. This book or any portion thereof may not be reproduced or used in any manner whatsoever without the express written permission of the author and publisher except for the use of brief quotations in a book review or scholarly journal.

First Printing: 2019
ISBN 978-1-942495-28-4 (paperback)
ISBN 978-1-942495-31-4 (e-book)

Parnassos Press
Fonte Aretusa Organization
Sioux City, IA USA
www.fontearetusa.org

Cover illustration: Head of Plato. Marble, apparently around 340-300 BC. Archaeological Museum of Syracuse, Inv. N. 742. Modified from original image by Zdenek Kratochvil. Creative Commons License https://creativecommons.org/licenses/by-sa/3.0/deed.en

Epigraph

δάκρυα μὲν Ἑκάβῃ τε καὶ Ἰλιάδεσσι γυναιξὶ
Μοῖραι ἐπέκλωσαν δὴ τότε γεινομέναις,
σοὶ δέ, Δίων, ῥέξαντι καλῶν ἐπινίκιον ἔργων
δαίμονες εὐροίας ἐλπίδας ἐξέχεαν.
κεῖσαι δ' εὐρυχόρῳ ἐν πατρίδι τίμιος ἀστοῖς,
ὦ ἐμὸν ἐκμήνας θυμὸν ἔρωτι Δίων.

The fates spun out tears, as they came into life,
for Hekabe and the women of Troy,
but Dion, for you and your glorious deeds,
the gods poured out hopes for flourishing times.
Esteemed all throughout your vast land you now lie,
Oh Dion, who sparked mad love in my heart.

Epitaph on Dion's Tomb attributed to Plato
Translated by Jonah Radding

Acknowledgments

The editors are grateful to all the participants of the seminar on Plato at Syracuse held just before the Fourth Interdisciplinary Symposium on the Heritage of Western Greece in 2018. They included Lee Coulson, Christos Evangeliou, Filippo Forcignanò, Andrew Hull, Tony Leyh, Mary McHugh, Gudrun Von Tevenar, William Wians, Marija Rodriguez, Matteo Duque, and Elliot Domagola. Their comments and criticisms were valuable to the authors, editors, and translator alike. Aron Reppmann also assisted in the early stages of the project. The Greek text of the *Seventh Letter* is reprinted from the Loeb edition with permission from Harvard University Press and essays published in the conference proceedings are reprinted with the permission of Parnassos Press. Harvard's Center for Hellenic Studies and the Fulbright Commission helped to support Prof. Reid during the editing phases of the book. We would also like to thank Susi Kimbell and the Exedra Mediterranean Center of Siracusa for their help and hospitality.

Table of Contents

Epigraph v

Acknowledgments vi

Heather L. Reid and Mark Ralkowski
Introduction ix

Jonah Radding
Translator's Note xix

Translation of the *Seventh Letter* 1

Historical Context

Carolina Araújo
What was Plato up to in Syracuse? 77

Marina Marren
The Historical Background of the *Seventh Letter*:
Political Philosophy in Context 91

Marion Theresa Schneider
Success Against All Odds, Failure Against All Logic:
Plutarch on Dion, Timoleon, and the Liberation of Sicily 105

Philosophical Concepts

Robert Metcalf
Plato's Discovery in Sicily:
Philosophy and Life-Structuring Practices in the *Seventh Letter* 129

Filippo Forcignanò
What is a philosophical πεῖρα?
Some reflections on Plato's *Seventh Letter* 340b-341b 149

Mary R. McHugh
Plato's Timaeus and Time 167

Political Context

Christos C. Evangeliou
Plato and Sicilian Power Politics:
Between Dion and Dionyisus II 187

Tony Leyh
Friendship and Politics in the *Seventh Letter* 201

Andrew Hull
Sleepless in Syracuse:
Plato and the Nocturnal Council 215

Philosophical Reception

Karen Sieben
Plato and Diogenes in Syracuse 233

Jill Gordon
Power/Knowledge in Syracuse or
Why the Digression in the *Seventh Letter* is Not a Digression 247

Francisco J. Gonzalez
Did Heidegger go to Syracuse? 265

Epilogue

Nickolas Pappas
Toward and from Philosophy 293

General Index 305

Index of Topics/Passages in the *Seventh Letter* 309

About the Editors and Translator 312

Heather L. Reid and Mark Ralkowski
Introduction

This book is born from a desire to understand the distinctive culture of Western Greece, the Hellenic settlements in Sicily and Southern Italy that thrived from the 6th century BCE, through the Roman Empire. That desire led to the founding of Fonte Aretusa, an organization dedicated to the link between ancient Italy and Greece, and spawned an interdisciplinary conference on the subject in 2015, which attracted several scholars to Siracusa. The specific question of what Plato was doing in Western Greece, and how he influenced and was influenced by local philosophers became an unofficial theme in subsequent conferences. In 2018, we organized a seminar on Plato at Syracuse in the days before the regular conference, in which a small group of scholars discussed a new translation of the *Seventh Letter* and essays on the topic that had been presented in previous conferences as well as new papers submitted for consideration.

The seminar was intense but friendly, having attracted a diverse group of scholars that ranged from graduate students to senior professors, hailing from at least three different continents, and representing a variety of academic specialties. We tried to create a book that would invite further study of the topic by identifying new questions to be asked, as well as addressing enduring issues. The essays consider the historical, political, and philosophical implications of Plato's involvement in Syracuse. They also look at the reception of his voyage among fellow philosophers, ancient and modern. The translation, meanwhile, aims to capture both the meaning and the tone of the letter in vibrant, contemporary English. We present it on facing pages with the Greek text.

Many studies of the *Seventh Letter* have focused on the question of authenticity.[1] Others have considered its doctrinal relationship

---

[1] The authenticity of the *Seventh Letter* was taken for granted until modern times. Among others, Cicero, Plutarch, Dionysius of Halicarnassus, Aristophanes of Byzantium (third century BCE), and Thrasyllus (first century BCE) each thought Plato wrote it. See Glenn R. Morrow's *Plato's Epistles: A Translation with*

with Plato's dialogues, and some have focused on its historical and philosophical veracity in light of its apologetic aims. Because one of its primary goals is to justify Plato's involvements in fourth-century Syracusan politics, some have questioned its historical, biographical, and philosophical reliability: Plato may have lied or distorted the truth about some or all of these subjects in the service of his own reputation.[2] These questions about authenticity and reliability are emphasized for a good reason: if the *Seventh Letter* is a reliable source, it is the only place where Plato speaks in the first person about his philosophy and his life, and he tells us many important things that we don't learn anywhere else, some of which raise hard questions about a late development in his thought.[3]

One of the most important things the *Seventh Letter* tells us about is Plato's life, especially his coming of age in war-torn Athens. Most of the other ancient biographies of Plato are a mixture of myth, gossip, and creative appropriations of ideas from his dialogues, such as the story of the young Plato standing outside of the Theater of Dionysus in Athens and burning his tragedy manuscripts after

---

Critical Essays and Notes (New York: The Bobbs-Merrill Company, 1962), 5-6. On the other hand, Aristotle did not seem to be aware of the letter, and he also seemed to be unaware of Plato's trips to Syracuse and involvements in Syracusan politics (*Pol.* 1312a4-7, 33-38, b16-17). Today the letter's authenticity is a live issue. Morrow (3-16, 44-60) and Ludwig Edelstein (*Plato's Seventh Letter* [Leiden: E.J. Brill, 1966], 1-15, 56-69) present classic cases for and against authenticity, respectively. The now definitive argument against authenticity is in Myles Burnyeat and Michael Frede, *The Pseudo-Platonic Letter*, edited by D. Scott (Oxford: Oxford University Press, 2015). For a critical review of Burnyeat and Frede, see Kahn's Review of *The Pseudo-Platonic Seventh Letter*, by Burnyeat, M and M. Frede (*Notre Dame Philosophical Reviews*, http://ndpr.nd.edu/news/the-pseudo-platonic-seventh-letter/, 2015).

[2] See V. Bradley Lewis, "The *Seventh Letter* and the Unity of Plato's Political Philosophy, *The Southern Journal of Philosophy* 38 (2000a): 247 n. 8, and V. Bradley Lewis, "The Rhetoric of Philosophical Politics in Plato's 'Seventh Letter,'" *Philosophy and Rhetoric* 33:1 (2000b): 23.

[3] See Terrence Irwin, "The Inside Story of the Seventh Platonic Letter: A Sceptical Introduction," *Rhizai: A Journal for Ancient Philosophy and Science* 6, no. 2 (2009): 152-53.

meeting Socrates.⁴ Unlike these apocryphal stories, the *Seventh Letter* provides us with original details about Plato's intellectual formation. It discusses the trial and death of Socrates, for example, and it tells us how they were the final straw in Plato's flirtation with Athenian politics, how they turned him decisively toward philosophy, and how they underscored for him the unparalleled justice in Socrates's character (*Ep. VII* 324b-326b). These views help us understand both the historical context in which Plato made pivotal life decisions, as well as the motivations behind and the long development of his political philosophy, which are less clear in the dialogues on their own, without the perspective provided by the *Letter*.⁵

The *Seventh Letter* also tells us important things about Plato's philosophy. Most famously, it argues that philosophical insight cannot be expressed verbally (Plat. *Ep. VII* 341 c-d). Many scholars have thought these passages in the *Seventh Letter* can serve as a skeleton key for interpreting many of Plato's dialogues and even his oral teaching, which may not appear anywhere in the dialogues.⁶ A less-emphasized aspect of the *Letter* is its portrait of Plato as a political thinker, activist, and advisor. When this part of the letter is discussed, commentators often assume that Plato was trying to bring about some version of the *Kallipolis* in Syracuse, or it is suggested that Plato's failed encounters with Dionysius I and II led him to replace

---

⁴ This tantalizing story is most likely an extrapolation from the *Republic's* discussion of an "ancient quarrel" between philosophy and poetry (*R.* 607b). See Alice Swift Riginos, *Platonica: The Anecdotes Concerning the Life and Writings of Plato* (Leiden: E.J. Brill, 1976), 43-48.

⁵ As Charles H. Kahn says, the opening pages of the *Seventh Letter* are "most plausibly read as Plato's own self-portrayal of the events that led to the composition of the *Gorgias*" (*Plato and the Socratic Dialogue: The Philosophical Use of a Literary Form* [Cambridge University Press, 1996], 48).

⁶ For an excellent discussion of the *Letter's* philosophical significance, see Francisco J. Gonzalez, *Dialectic and Dialogue: Plato's Practice of Philosophical Inquiry* (Evanston, IL: Northwestern University Press, 1998), 245-74.

the *Republic's* ideal of the philosopher king with the *Laws'* ideal of a mixed regime based on the rule of law.[7]

Whatever the case may be about the development of Plato's political theory, the *Seventh Letter* presents us with a very different kind of Platonic thought. His most substantial political dialogues, the *Republic*, *Statesman*, and *Laws*, present visions of the good life and can be read plausibly as critiquing fifth- and fourth-century politics.[8] But in the *Seventh Letter* we get both meaningful discussions of political principles and information about concrete political advice that Plato offered in a variety of specific situations.[9] This information—Plato's advice and actions in Syracuse—needs to be thought about in connection with his political theory, and his political theory needs to be rethought in light of what he actually did and advised while he was in Syracuse and after he returned to Athens.

Several ancient sources present the facts of Plato's involvement in Syracuse.[10] They differ in their accounts of the details, but the general picture of what happened is clear enough. Plato's first trip to Syracuse was prompted by an invitation from Dionysius I, who thought of himself as a writer, and wanted to surround himself with famous intellectuals and poets, "men of repute," who could instruct him and revise his poems (Diod. Sic. 15.6.1). Others say Plato's first trip to Syracuse was motivated by an interest in visiting Mt. Etna.[11]

---

[7] Lewis (2000a: 245 n. 1), rejects this view, and argues that the *Seventh Letter* advocates for both teachings—the rule of philosophy and the rule of law.

[8] See Harvey Yunis's *Taming Democracy: Models of Political Rhetoric in Classical Athens* (Ithaca, NY: Cornell University Press, 1996).

[9] See Irwin (2009: 128-29).

[10] In addition to the *Seventh Letter*, see the lives of Dion by Plutarch and Nepos, Plutarch's *Timoleon*, Diogenes Laertius's life of Plato, and a few passages from Diodorus of Sicily. Morrow (1962: 145-80) and P. A. Brunt (*Studies in Greek History and Thought* [New York: Oxford University Press, 1993], 314-30) reconstruct the story as fully as possible. The use of these sources is complicated by the fact that "some of our extant sources (or their sources) rely on the letter as a contemporary source" (Irwin 2009: 131).

[11] This version of the story is reported in Hegesander of Delphi (Athenaeus 11.507b), Diogenes Laertius (3.18), Apuleius (I.4), Olympiodorus (*In Alcib.* 2.94-96 and *In Gorg.* 41.7), and the *Anon. Proleg.* (4.11-13). Plato mentions Mt. Etna in the *Phaedo* (111e). See Riginos (1976: 73).

Whatever the motive for the trip, Plato and Dionysius I did not become friends, perhaps because Plato was too honest in his criticism of the tyrant's poetry or politics, and so Plato eventually returned to Athens that same year, after being sold by Dionysius I as a slave for twenty minas on the island of Aegina (Diod. Sic. 15.7.1; cf. Plut. *Dion* 5.1-7 and Diog. Laert. 3.19). It was during this first trip to Sicily that Plato met Dion, Dionysius I's brother-in-law, and thus began a friendship that kept Plato tied to Syracuse and directly involved in its political affairs for more than twenty-five years.

When Dionysius I died, his son, Dionysius II, inherited the rule of Syracuse and made Dion one of his closest advisors. Dionysius II initially showed promise: he cut taxes and released political prisoners, and he showed a "keen and even frenzied passion for the teachings and companionship of Plato" (Plut. *Dion* 11.1). This was what prompted Dion to invite Plato to return to the island of Sicily: better than anyone else, he could teach the young tyrant to value justice and moderation; he could "come get control of a youthful soul now tossed about on a sea of great authority and power, and steady it by his reasonings" (Plut. *Dion* 11.2). Plato was hesitant to return (Plat. *Ep. VII* 328b), but in 367 he decided to reunite with Dion and begin working with Dionysius II, believing that the "purification of one man" could "cure Sicily of all her distempers" (Plut. *Dion* 11.3; cf. Plat. *Ep. VII* 327c-e). It didn't take long for Plato's presence in Syracuse to arouse suspicion, however. Dion had powerful political enemies in the city who envied his influence over Dionysius II and worried that Plato was a genuine threat to their own (Plut. *Dion* 11.4-13.5). In time, they stirred up a conflict between Dion and Dionysius II, which resulted in Dion's exile and Plato's temporary house arrest in the citadel (Plat. *Ep. VII* 329e). Dion was allowed to take his wealth with him to the Peloponnese, while Plato stayed in Sicily with the unfortunate job of flattering Dionysius II's ego. Plato was later allowed to return to Athens on the condition that he did not plot a revolution with Dion (Plat. *Ep. VII* 346b).

Plato's third trip to Syracuse was motivated by concern for Dion's life. Dionysius II sent messengers to Athens to request that Plato return to Syracuse. They reported that Dionysius II had made great progress in his philosophical studies (Plat. *Ep. VII* 338b-c), while Dionysius II himself wrote to Plato, promising that "no mercy would be shown to Dion unless Plato were persuaded to come to Sicily; but if he were persuaded, every mercy" (Plut. *Dion* 18.7-8; cf. Plat. *Ep. VII* 339c-d). And so, Plato returned to Syracuse in 362, "that he might once more measure back his way to fell Charybdis" (Hom. *Od.* 12.428). Unfortunately, like his first two trips, Plato's third trip to Syracuse quickly became embroiled in court intrigue and ended in failure. He eventually returned to Athens and reported on his travels to Dion while attending the Olympics of 360 (Plat. *Ep. VII* 350b). The message was clear: Dionysius II was incorrigible and dangerous.

Dion immediately began plotting to invade Syracuse and seek revenge against Dionysius II (*Ep. VII* 350c), who had taken his money and land, and married his wife to another man while he was banished from Syracuse. He felt compelled to attack in retaliation (*Ep. VII* 350e). In 357, with the help of Speusippus and several other members of Plato's Academy—though not Plato because of his age and his firm stance against vengeance (*Ep. VII* 350d)—Dion landed in Syracuse and succeeded in conquering the city while Dionysius II was away on his own military campaign in Italy (Plut. *Dion* 26.1). Dion's grip on power in Syracuse did not last long, however. He quickly found himself in a conflict with a populist leader named Heracleides, who took advantage of the Syracusans' distrust of Dion (Plut. *Dion* 33.5). Over the next two years, Dion was driven into exile for a second time, and then recalled back to Syracuse when, to the horror of most Syracusans, Dionysius II and his soldiers attempted to regain power in 355. After an unusually destructive battle in the city, Dion succeeded in defeating Dionysius II for a second time, and in doing so he endeared himself to the Syracusans as never before (Plut. *Dion* 46.1). However, thanks to continued factionalism in Syracuse and the imperiousness of Dion's rule (Plut. *Dion* 52.5-6), Dion's supporters quickly abandoned him, and he was assassinated by Callipus, a member of Plato's Academy. Syracuse was "continually exchanging one tyrant for another" (Plut. *Tim.* 1.2). This was when Dion's remaining followers fled to Leontini and wrote to Plato for his political advice. The *Seventh Letter* is Plato's response.

Plato's involvements in Syracusan politics must have been puzzling for anyone who knew about them, but especially for Dion's followers, who would have wondered why Plato stayed in Syracuse after Dionysius II banished Dion, why he returned to Syracuse for a third visit even though Dion had not yet been recalled, why he stayed in Syracuse after Dionysius II took Dion's property and revenues from him, why Plato didn't join Dion's plot against Syracuse in 357, why Plato never criticized Dionysius II openly, and why Dion's assassin was a member of Plato's Academy. Did Plato betray Dion?[12] In answering these questions, Plato provides a detailed account of his three trips to Sicily: their motivations and goals, his complicated relationship with Dionysius II, his friendship with Dion, the principles he acted on, and much more. It is a treasure trove of information, and yet it leaves us with many interpretive questions even if we assume that all of it is reliable: what exactly was Plato doing in Syracuse? Did he hope to implement the *Republic's* ideal of philosophical rule, or were his aims less ambitious and more focused on establishing the rule of law? What does the letter teach us about Plato's views on friendship, education, and philosophy itself?

Plato at Syracuse does not provide us with definitive answers to these questions, but it helps us get more clarity about what we do and don't know. If it is true that, "the name Syracuse has come to stand as an emblem of the problematic relationship between philosophy and politics," the authors of *Plato at Syracuse* try to tell us what we can still learn from that emblem.[13]

The first section of essays deal with the political context of Plato's trips to Sicily. Carolina Araújo leads off by arguing that Plato went to Syracuse in an attempt to put into practice a government and constitution based on self-control. He discovered not only that Dionysius II lacked the self-control to lead such a government, but also that his protégé Dion's self-control would be eroded by events to the point that not even he could be supported as an ideal leader. The second essay, by Marina Marren, focuses on the historical context

---

[12] See Irwin (2009: 132-36).
[13] Lewis (2000b: 23).

of the *Seventh Letter*, arguing that its warning against apparently benign passions that ultimately perpetuate tyranny can be understood through philosophical consideration of the contemporary political contingencies. Marion Theresa Schneider's essay closes the section with an ancient analysis of the political context. Comparing Plutarch's account of Timoleon's surprising success in liberating Sicily with Dion's illogical failure, Schneider observes that the author's Platonism may have influenced his fatalistic explanation.

The second section, on philosophical concepts, begins with Robert Metcalf's analysis of the *Seventh Letter's* connection between writings (*syngrammata*), as criticized in the *Phaedrus* and *Statesman*, with life-structuring practices (*epitēdeumata*) as discussed in *Republic*. He concludes that the *Seventh Letter* makes Plato's positions in these issues clearer, since it demonstrates that philosophy must be a life-structuring practice rather than any text. In the next essay, Filippo Forcignanò explores the *Seventh Letter's* conception of a philosophical "test" (*peira*). He argues that the *peira* is an aptitude test, similar to the tryout for a sports team, and that Dionysius II failed it. This conception of the *peira* also informs the *Seventh Letter*'s suggestions that philosophy cannot be written and that the moment of philosophical enlightenment comes from "communion" with ideas. In the next essay, Mary McHugh draws a fascinating thread that connects Plato's cosmology as reported in *Timaeus* with contemporary thinkers in Magna Graecia, on to Archimedes's astronomical innovations, and even into the mathematical and scientific discoveries of the Islamic world. The essay shows how Plato's trips to Syracuse had a huge impact not only on the development of philosophy, but also science and technology.

The third section of the book examines the political context of Plato at Syracuse from a variety of viewpoints. Christos Evangeliou begins by trying to reconstruct the political challenge from Plato's personal point of view. He sees the philosopher as inextricably caught between his own political ideals and the tricky realities of Sicilian power politics. In the next essay, Tony Leyh examines the special relationship between friendship and politics in the *Seventh*

Letter. Distinguishing between strong and weak friendships in the letter, he shows that politics and philosophy not only depend on strong friendships, such friendships may entail going beyond one's philosophical and political concerns – as illustrated by Plato's own behavior in Syracuse. Andrew Hull takes on the thorny question, raised by Michael Frede's argument against the *Seventh Letter's* authenticity, of whether the mature Plato still believed in philosopher-kings. Arguing that the *Laws'* nocturnal council consists of philosophers in all but name, Hull finds sufficient philosophical consistency between the *Letter* and the *Laws* to believe that Plato saw in Dion some sort of philosophical ruler.

The reception of Plato's involvement in Syracuse, by ancient and modern authors both, is the subject of the fourth section. Karen Sieben begins by considering the perspective of Plato's contemporary, Diogenes of Sinope, and endorsing his criticism. She claims that Plato can rightly be accused of duplicity with respect to his activity in Syracuse and Diogenes was right to point that out. In the next essay, Jill Gordon uses Michel Foucault's 20th century CE insights into knowledge and power to argue that the so-called digression of the *Seventh Letter* is, in fact, part of a continuous whole. The entire letter, she concludes, is a battle against false *logoi*. Francisco Gonzalez concludes the section with an analysis of the comparison between Martin Heidegger's involvement with National Socialism in the 1930s and Plato's trip to Syracuse.

The volume concludes with an essay by Nickolas Pappas, which focuses on the educational lesson embedded in the *Seventh Letter*, "How does one first come to study, let alone to value the study of philosophy?" His response connects beauty with vision and learning in a way that resonates with many of Plato's dialogues and his pedagogical project at the Academy, but it leaves the question open of how and why we become philosophers.

Translator's Note

The process of translation begins, naturally, with the attempt to reproduce the meaning of a text with the greatest precision possible. But this consists of far more than simply choosing words whose meanings match in two languages, particularly with a literary text (as opposed to, say, a technical manual). Transmitting another author's tone, style, and register presents a different set of challenges. To begin, the criteria for measuring these things is far less objective: to understand the meaning of a word, one may consult a dictionary; to perceive an author's style, on the other hand, is by and large a sensory process, one for which we do not have solidly defined standards. At the same time, a translation addresses itself to readers who differ from the original audience in almost every meaningful way – the manner in which we perform the act of reading, our relationship to the author, and our corresponding expectations regarding the manner in which we will be addressed (among many other things). English language readers in the 21st century will neither find themselves in the same position nor take the same approach to Plato's *Seventh Letter* as addressees in mid-fourth century BCE Syracuse. (The contested question of authorship becomes somewhat less relevant for the translator, since even if it is a forgery, it was presumably written with an eye towards evoking the same response that a Syracusan audience would reserve for a Platonic adviser).

Nevertheless, a translation should at least attempt to convey a similar set of impressions to the new audience as those which would have struck the original readers. This is not to claim that I am somehow able to imagine, with any degree of precision, the original readers' reception of Plato's *Seventh Letter*, nor indeed to insist that modern readers approach the letter as if they too had solicited the advice contained within. But a good translation should evoke at least some of the sensations that the original provoked, and to the extent that I was able, that has been my goal.

I began my reflection on how to transmit the style, tone, and register of the *Seventh Letter* with a re-examination of Demetrius's observations on what he calls the plain style (ὁ ἰσχνὸς χαρακτήρ), in which he includes precepts on letter-writing (cf. *On Style*, 190-239). Here Demetrius singles out several elements that are integral to this style of writing: vividness (ἐνάργεια), clarity (τὸ σαφές), and the use of ordinary language (συνήθεια). Additionally, Demetrius suggests that a letter should in some way "express the author's character" (227: "ἐχέτω τὸ ἠθικόν").

Of course, these prescriptions present their own problems. First of all, the elements that Demetrius recommends – vividness, clarity, "the expression of character" – are neither measurable nor constant. What is clear to one reader may not be clear to another, and the likelihood that two readers will perceive the same text differently surely increases across the vast distances of space and time that separate contemporary readers from the ancient Greek world. Moreover, Demetrius singles out Plato's longer letters for criticism, primarily because, in their extreme length, they become more like treatises. Certainly this objection may be made about the *Seventh Letter*, as it contains not only personal reflections and narratives, but also discourses on philosophy and political theory. In fact, shifts in register and tone are perceptible throughout the letter, often in conjunction with changes of topic.

Nevertheless, some of Demetrius's advice may be applied. It is likely that the author of the letter did in fact wish to be understood by his audience, regardless of the true intentions that lay behind writing this letter. It is also likely that any potential readers would have been highly educated individuals with some experience in dealing with (at least basic) philosophical concepts and political discussions. As such, we may presume that the author has attempted to write a letter in a style that would have been clear and vivid to his audience, even if at times it appears less clear to us. It is also evident that the author used "ordinary language": the entire letter presents only one *hapax* (συντατέον, 340c), and according to the *TLG*, the five most statistically "over-represented" *lemmata* in the collection of letters are λέγω, γίγνομαι, πᾶς, ἐμός, and ἄλλος. All of this suggests that the author of the letter follows, at least to a degree, the criteria that Demetrius would later posit.

I have attempted to juggle all of these factors in order to create a translation that reflects the complexity and shifts in register that exists throughout the letter, yet remains uniform throughout in its accessibility to a contemporary reader. To the extent that I have been successful, much credit is due to all those who participated in the seminar on "Plato at Syracuse" hosted by *Fonte Aretusa* in June 2018, each of whom took the time to go over and advise on numerous passages. I am particularly grateful to Tony Leyh, Marija Rodriguez, and Filippo Forcignanò, whose keen insight prevented a handful of grievous errors from creeping into the final draft. Heather Reid not only provided her advice on the text and translation, but also organized the seminar at which such productive discussions could take place, and has worked with me extensively in assembling and editing the final version. Ryan Platte graciously took time to consult on some particularly thorny textual problems, and to talk through adequate ways of dealing with corrupted and ambiguous passages. Charles Radding and Ashley Telman went over both early and later drafts of the translation to check for consistency and naturalness of tone and style. This translation is immeasurably better for all the input I have received from these various parties, to whom I am, and will always be, most thankful.

Jonah Radding
Northwestern University

Translation of the *Seventh Letter*

Jonah Radding

Πλάτων τοῖς Δίωνος οἰκείοις τε καὶ ἑταίροις εὖ πράττειν.[1]

ἐπεστείλατέ μοι νομίζειν δεῖν τὴν διάνοιαν ὑμῶν εἶναι τὴν αὐτὴν ἣν εἶχεν καὶ Δίων, καὶ δὴ καὶ κοινωνεῖν διεκελεύεσθέ [324a] μοι, καθ᾽ ὅσον οἷός τέ εἰμὶ ἔργῳ καὶ λόγῳ. ἐγὼ δέ, εἰ μὲν δόξαν καὶ ἐπιθυμίαν τὴν αὐτὴν ἔχετε ἐκείνῳ, ξύμφημι κοινωνήσειν, εἰ δὲ μή, βουλεύσεσθαι πολλάκις. τίς δ᾽ ἦν ἡ ἐκείνου διάνοια καὶ ἐπιθυμία, σχεδὸν οὐκ εἰκάζων ἀλλ᾽ ὡς εἰδὼς σαφῶς εἴποιμ᾽ ἄν. ὅτε γὰρ κατ᾽ ἀρχὰς εἰς Συρακούσας ἐγὼ ἀφικόμην, σχεδὸν ἔτη τετταράκοντα γεγονώς, Δίων εἶχε τὴν ἡλικίαν ἣν τὰ νῦν Ἱππαρῖνος γέγονε, καὶ ἣν ἔσχε [324b] τότε δόξαν, ταύτην καὶ διετέλεσεν ἔχων, Συρακοσίους οἴεσθαι δεῖν ἐλευθέρους εἶναι, κατὰ νόμους τοὺς ἀρίστους οἰκοῦντας· ὥστε οὐδὲν θαυμαστὸν εἴ τις θεῶν καὶ τοῦτον εἰς τὴν αὐτὴν δόξαν περὶ πολιτείας ἐκείνῳ γενέσθαι σύμφρονα ποιήσειε.

τίς δ᾽ ἦν ὁ τρόπος τῆς γενέσεως αὐτῆς, οὐκ ἀπάξιον ἀκοῦσαι νέῳ καὶ μὴ νέῳ, πειράσομαι δὲ ἐξ ἀρχῆς αὐτὴν ἐγὼ πρὸς ὑμᾶς διεξελθεῖν· ἔχει γὰρ καιρὸν τὰ νῦν. νέος ἐγώ ποτε ὢν πολλοῖς δὴ ταὐτὸν ἔπαθον· ᾠήθην, εἰ θᾶττον ἐμαυτοῦ γενοίμην κύριος, ἐπὶ τὰ κοινὰ τῆς πόλεως [324c] εὐθὺς ἰέναι. καί μοι τύχαι τινὲς τῶν τῆς πόλεως πραγμάτων τοιαίδε παρέπεσον. ὑπὸ πολλῶν γὰρ τῆς τότε πολιτείας λοιδορουμένης μεταβολὴ γίγνεται, καὶ τῆς μεταβολῆς εἷς καὶ πεντήκοντά τινες ἄνδρες προύστησαν ἄρχοντες, ἕνδεκα μὲν ἐν ἄστει, δέκα δ᾽ ἐν Πειραιεῖ, περί τε ἀγορὰν ἑκάτεροι τούτων ὅσα τ᾽ ἐν τοῖς ἄστεσι διοικεῖν ἔδει, τριάκοντα δὲ πάντων [324d] ἄρχοντες κατέστησαν αὐτοκράτορες. τούτων δὴ τινες οἰκεῖοί τε ὄντες καὶ γνώριμοι ἐτύγχανον ἐμοί, καὶ δὴ καὶ παρεκάλουν εὐθὺς ὡς ἐπὶ προσήκοντα πράγματά με. καὶ ἐγὼ θαυμαστὸν οὐδὲν ἔπαθον ὑπὸ νεότητος· ᾠήθην γὰρ αὐτοὺς ἔκ τινος ἀδίκου βίου ἐπὶ δίκαιον τρόπον ἄγοντας διοικήσειν δὴ τὴν πόλιν, ὥστε αὐτοῖς σφόδρα προσεῖχον τὸν νοῦν, τί πράξοιεν.

---

[1] With the exception of the occasional paragraph break, or where otherwise noted, the Greek text printed is that which can be found in the most recent Loeb edition. i.e. Henderson ed., *Plato IX: Timaeus, Critias, Cleitophon, Menexenus, Epistles* (Cambridge, MA: Harvard University Press, 2014).

The Seventh Letter

Plato sends his best to the friends and companions of Dion

You have written to say that I should consider your intentions to be the same as Dion's, and in fact you have insisted that I stand with you [**324a**], to the extent that I am able, with both my words and actions. For my part, if indeed you do have the same opinions and motivations as Dion, I will agree to stand with you, but if you do not, I will have to consider the matter at length. Now, concerning Dion's intentions and motivations, I can speak not through conjecture but as one who knows the matter well. For when I first arrived in Syracuse at about the age of forty, Dion was the same age as Hipparinos is now, and he held [**324b**] then the same opinion that he maintained till the very end, namely that the Syracusans ought to be free and to live in accordance with the best of laws. So it would not be at all surprising if one of the gods were to make Hipparinos hold the same views on politics and feel the same way as Dion.

It is, however, worthwhile for young and old alike to hear how all this began, so I will try to go over it from the beginning for you, since the present circumstances call for it. When I was a young man, I felt the same way that many others surely do: I believed that as soon as I became master of my destiny, I would get involved in the politics of the city. [**324c**] Unfortunately for me, the city suffered the following fate: a revolution occurred, since the government at the time was much maligned, and fifty-one men emerged as leaders of this revolution: eleven in the city and ten in the Piraeus, with each of these regulating the business of the marketplace and whatever needed managing in the urban areas; and thirty men [**324d**] who were put in charge and given full authority over everything. Now, some of these men happened to be relations and acquaintances of mine, and, more to the point, they immediately recruited me, as if these matters concerned me. Given my youth, my feelings were not surprising, for I believed that they were going to govern the city by leading it out of a sort of unjust existence into a just one, so I eagerly turned my attention to them and to what they were doing.

καὶ ἑώρων δή που τοὺς ἄνδρας ἐν χρόνῳ ὀλίγῳ χρυσῆν ἀποδείξαντας τὴν ἔμπροσθεν πολιτείαν, τά τε ἄλλα καὶ φίλον [324e] ἄνδρα ἐμοὶ πρεσβύτερον Σωκράτη, ὃν ἐγὼ σχεδὸν οὐκ ἂν αἰσχυνοίμην εἰπὼν δικαιότατον εἶναι τῶν τότε, ἐπί τινα τῶν πολιτῶν μεθ' ἑτέρων ἔπεμπον, βίᾳ ἄξοντα ὡς ἀποθανούμενον, [325a] ἵνα δὴ μετέχοι τῶν πραγμάτων αὐτοῖς, εἴτε βούλοιτο εἴτε μή· ὁ δ' οὐκ ἐπείθετο, πᾶν δὲ παρεκινδύνευσε παθεῖν πρὶν ἀνοσίων αὐτοῖς ἔργων γενέσθαι κοινωνός· ἃ δὴ πάντα καθορῶν καὶ εἴ τιν' ἄλλα τοιαῦτα οὐ σμικρά, ἐδυσχέρανά τε καὶ ἐμαυτὸν ἐπανήγαγον ἀπὸ τῶν τότε κακῶν.

χρόνῳ δὲ οὐ πολλῷ μετέπεσε τὰ τῶν τριάκοντά τε καὶ πᾶσα ἡ τότε πολιτεία. πάλιν δὲ βραδύτερον μέν, εἷλκε δέ με ὅμως ἡ [325b] περὶ τὸ πράττειν τὰ κοινὰ καὶ πολιτικὰ ἐπιθυμία. ἦν οὖν καὶ ἐν ἐκείνοις, ἅτε τεταραγμένοις, πολλὰ γιγνόμενα ἅ τις ἂν δυσχεράνειε, καὶ οὐδέν τι θαυμαστὸν ἦν τιμωρίας ἐχθρῶν γίγνεσθαί τινων τισι μείζους ἐν μεταβολαῖς· καί τοι πολλῇ γε ἐχρήσαντο οἱ τότε κατελθόντες ἐπιεικείᾳ.

κατὰ δέ τινα τύχην αὖ τὸν ἑταῖρον ἡμῶν Σωκράτη τοῦτον δυναστεύοντές τινες εἰσάγουσιν εἰς δικαστήριον, ἀνοσιωτάτην αἰτίαν ἐπιβαλλόντες [325c] καὶ πάντων ἥκιστα Σωκράτει προσήκουσαν· ὡς ἀσεβῆ γὰρ οἱ μὲν εἰσήγαγον, οἱ δὲ κατεψηφίσαντο καὶ ἀπέκτειναν τὸν τότε τῆς ἀνοσίου ἀγωγῆς οὐκ ἐθελήσαντα μετασχεῖν περὶ ἕνα τῶν τότε φευγόντων φίλων, ὅτε φεύγοντες ἐδυστύχουν αὐτοί.

σκοποῦντι δή μοι ταῦτά τε καὶ τοὺς ἀνθρώπους τοὺς πράττοντας τὰ πολιτικά, καὶ τοὺς νόμους γε καὶ ἔθη, ὅσῳ μᾶλλον διεσκόπουν ἡλικίας τε εἰς τὸ πρόσθε προὔβαινον, τοσούτῳ χαλεπώτερον ἐφαίνετο ὀρθῶς εἶναί μοι τὰ πολιτικὰ [325d] διοικεῖν· οὔτε γὰρ ἄνευ φίλων ἀνδρῶν καὶ ἑταίρων πιστῶν οἷόν τ' εἶναι πράττειν,—οὓς οὔθ' ὑπάρχοντας ἦν εὑρεῖν εὐπετές, οὐ γὰρ ἔτι ἐν τοῖς τῶν πατέρων ἤθεσι καὶ ἐπιτηδεύμασιν ἡ πόλις ἡμῶν διῳκεῖτο, καινούς τε ἄλλους ἀδύνατον ἦν κτᾶσθαι μετά τινος ῥᾳστώνης.

The Seventh Letter

As it happened, I soon saw them making the former government look like gold. Among other things, they took [**324e**] my old friend Socrates, who I would not be ashamed to say was practically the most just of all men at that time, and they sent him off, along with other men, to drag another citizen off to his death [**325a**] so that Socrates might be an accomplice to their crimes, whether he wanted to or not. He, however, did not obey, choosing instead to run the risk of facing any punishment whatsoever rather than be associated with their unholy enterprises. When I saw all of this, and some other similarly nasty things, I was appalled, and I extracted myself from that awful business.

Not long afterwards, the regime of the Thirty and the entire government collapsed, and before I knew it, the desire to engage [**325b**] with public and political matters began to lure me in again. To be sure, in that period of chaos many things were happening that one might find appalling, and it is not at all surprising that in these revolutionary times, certain people were exacting excessive vengeance against their enemies. Still, those who had returned to the city acted with great prudence.

As chance would have it though, certain individuals in power brought my friend Socrates to trial, laying on him a charge that was of the utmost sacrilege, [**325c**] and which he deserved least of all men. Indeed, they charged Socrates with impiety, while others condemned and killed him – the same man who had previously refused to take part in the unholy arrest of a friend of the very men who were unfortunate enough to be in exile at that time.

As I considered these things – both the laws and customs and the men who were engaged in politics – the more that I assessed the situation and advanced into adulthood, the more it seemed to me to be difficult to engage in politics in a reasonable manner. [**325d**] For one cannot do anything without trusted friends or associates, and it was hard to find such individuals around in those days, since our city was not being governed in accordance with the customs and manners of our forefathers, and it was also impossible to acquire new ones with any ease.

τά τε τῶν νόμων γράμματα καὶ ἔθη διεφθείρετο καὶ ἐπεδίδου θαυμαστὸν ὅσον, ὥστε με, [325e] τὸ πρῶτον πολλῆς μεστὸν ὄντα ὁρμῆς ἐπὶ τὸ πράττειν τὰ κοινά, βλέποντα εἰς ταῦτα καὶ φερόμενα ὁρῶντα πάντη πάντως, τελευτῶντα ἰλιγγιᾶν, καὶ τοῦ μὲν σκοπεῖν μὴ ἀποστῆναι πῆ ποτὲ ἄμεινον ἂν γίγνοιτο περί τε αὐτὰ ταῦτα καὶ [326a] δὴ καὶ περὶ τὴν πᾶσαν πολιτείαν, τοῦ δὲ πράττειν αὖ περιμένειν ἀεὶ καιρούς, τελευτῶντα δὲ νοῆσαι περὶ πασῶν τῶν νῦν πόλεων ὅτι κακῶς ξύμπασαι πολιτεύονται· τὰ γὰρ τῶν νόμων αὐταῖς σχεδὸν ἀνιάτως ἔχοντά ἐστιν ἄνευ παρασκευῆς θαυμαστῆς τινος μετὰ τύχης· λέγειν τε ἠναγκάσθην, ἐπαινῶν τὴν ὀρθὴν φιλοσοφίαν, ὡς ἐκ ταύτης ἔστι τά τε πολιτικὰ δίκαια καὶ τὰ τῶν ἰδιωτῶν πάντα κατιδεῖν· κακῶν οὖν οὐ [326b] λήξειν τὰ ἀνθρώπινα γένη, πρὶν ἂν ἢ τὸ τῶν φιλοσοφούντων ὀρθῶς γε καὶ ἀληθῶς γένος εἰς ἀρχὰς ἔλθῃ τὰς πολιτικὰς ἢ τὸ τῶν δυναστευόντων ἐν ταῖς πόλεσιν ἔκ τινος μοίρας θείας ὄντως φιλοσοφήσῃ.

ταύτην δὴ τὴν διάνοιαν ἔχων εἰς Ἰταλίαν τε καὶ Σικελίαν ἦλθον, ὅτε πρῶτον ἀφικόμην. ἐλθόντα δέ με ὁ ταύτῃ λεγόμενος αὖ βίος εὐδαίμων, Ἰταλιωτικῶν τε καὶ Συρακουσίων τραπεζῶν πλήρης, οὐδαμῇ οὐδαμῶς ἤρεσε, δίς τε τῆς ἡμέρας ἐμπιμπλάμενον ζῆν καὶ μηδέποτε κοιμώμενον μόνον νύκτωρ, [326c] καὶ ὅσα τούτῳ ἐπιτηδεύματα συνέπεται τῷ βίῳ· ἐκ γὰρ τούτων τῶν ἐθῶν οὔτ' ἂν φρόνιμος οὐδείς ποτε γενέσθαι τῶν ὑπὸ τὸν οὐρανὸν ἀνθρώπων ἐκ νέου ἐπιτηδεύων δύναιτο,—οὐχ οὕτω θαυμαστῇ φύσει κραθήσεται,—σώφρων δὲ οὐδ' ἂν μελλῆσαι ποτὲ γενέσθαι, καὶ δὴ καὶ περὶ τῆς ἄλλης ἀρετῆς ὁ αὐτὸς λόγος ἂν εἴη. πόλις τε οὐδεμία ἂν ἠρεμῆσαι κατὰ νόμους οὐδ' οὑστινασοῦν ἀνδρῶν οἰομένων ἀναλίσκειν μὲν δεῖν [326d] πάντα ἐς ὑπερβολάς, ἀργῶν δὲ εἰς ἅπαντα ἡγουμένων αὖ δεῖν γίγνεσθαι πλὴν εἰς εὐωχίας καὶ πότους καὶ ἀφροδισίων σπουδὰς διαπονουμένας· ἀναγκαῖον δὲ εἶναι ταύτας τὰς πόλεις εἰς τυραννίδας τε καὶ ὀλιγαρχίας καὶ δημοκρατίας μεταβαλλούσας μηδέποτε λήγειν, δικαίου δὲ καὶ ἰσονόμου πολιτείας τοὺς ἐν αὐταῖς δυναστεύοντας μηδ' ὄνομα ἀκούοντας ἀνέχεσθαι.

The Seventh Letter

Meanwhile, our customs and written laws were both in the process of being corrupted, and this had progressed to such a remarkable degree that, [325e] even though I had first been moved by a strong impulse to take part in public affairs, as I watched and saw everything always being pulled this way and that, I wound up with my head spinning. Nevertheless, I did not shy away from considering how there might be some improvement in these matters, [326a] and indeed in the entire government, and I remained ever vigilant for an opportune moment to act. Ultimately, however, I came to this conclusion about the cities of our time: they are all governed poorly, for without some sort of incredible intervention and a certain amount of luck, their laws are basically unsalvageable. And I was forced to say, in praise of the true love of wisdom, that it is through this that it is possible to understand all things just, both in politics and in the private sphere. As a result, humanity will not desist [326b] from evil until either those who truly and properly pursue philosophy come into power, or those who hold power in our cities, by some sort of divine fate, actually pursue philosophy.

I still maintained this line of thought when I first arrived in Italy and Sicily. And upon my arrival I was not at all pleased with what the Italians and Sicilians call the blessed life, one laden with feasts, spent stuffing oneself twice a day, never going to bed alone at night, [326c] and all the other things that go hand-in-hand with this lifestyle. With such habits, nobody under the sun who had followed this path since childhood could ever develop any sense – no one is tempered by so admirable a nature – nor would anyone ever be likely to become moderate. Of course, the same reasoning would apply to every other kind of virtue, and no city would find peace under laws of any kind, as long as men thought it necessary to squander everything to the extreme, and believed that they should [326d] be lazy about everything except feasting, drinking, and the avid pursuit of sexual pleasure. On the contrary, it is inevitable that such cities constantly rotate between tyranny, oligarchy, and democracy, and that those ruling such cities are unable to bear the very mention of a just government based on equality under the law.

ταῦτα δὴ πρὸς τοῖς πρόσθε διανοούμενος εἰς Συρακούσας [326e] διεπορεύθην, ἴσως μὲν κατὰ τύχην, ἔοικε μὴν τότε μηχανωμένῳ τινὶ τῶν κρειττόνων ἀρχὴν βαλέσθαι τῶν νῦν γεγονότων πραγμάτων περὶ Δίωνα καὶ τῶν περὶ Συρακούσας· δέος δὲ μὴ καὶ πλειόνων ἔτι, ἐὰν μὴ νῦν ὑμεῖς ἐμοὶ πείθησθε τὸ δεύτερον συμβουλεύοντι.

πῶς οὖν δὴ λέγω πάντων [327a] ἀρχὴν γεγονέναι τὴν τότε εἰς Σικελίαν ἐμὴν ἄφιξιν; ἐγὼ συγγενόμενος Δίωνι τότε νέῳ κινδυνεύω, τὰ δοκοῦντα ἐμοὶ βέλτιστα ἀνθρώποις εἶναι μηνύων διὰ λόγων καὶ πράττειν αὐτὰ ξυμβουλεύων, ἀγνοεῖν ὅτι τυραννίδος τινὰ τρόπον κατάλυσιν ἐσομένην μηχανώμενος ἐλάνθανον ἐμαυτόν. Δίων μὲν γὰρ δὴ μάλ' εὐμαθὴς ὢν πρός τε τἆλλα καὶ πρὸς τοὺς τότε ὑπ' ἐμοῦ λόγους λεγομένους οὕτως ὀξέως ὑπήκουσε [327b] καὶ σφόδρα, ὡς οὐδεὶς πώποτε ὧν ἐγὼ προσέτυχον νέων, καὶ τὸν ἐπίλοιπον βίον ζῆν ἠθέλησε διαφερόντως τῶν πολλῶν Ἰταλιωτῶν τε καὶ Σικελιωτῶν, ἀρετὴν περὶ πλείονος ἡδονῆς τῆς τε ἄλλης τρυφῆς ἠγαπηκώς· ὅθεν ἐπαχθέστερον τοῖς περὶ τὰ τυραννικὰ νόμιμα ζῶσιν ἐβίω μέχρι τοῦ θανάτου τοῦ περὶ Διονύσιον γενομένου.

μετὰ δὲ τοῦτο διενοήθη μὴ μόνον ἐν αὑτῷ ποτ' ἂν γενέσθαι ταύτην τὴν διάνοιαν, ἣν [327c] αὐτὸς ὑπὸ τῶν ὀρθῶν λόγων ἔσχεν, ἐγγιγνομένην δ' αὐτὴν καὶ ἐν ἄλλοις ὁρῶν κατενόει, πολλοῖς μὲν οὔ, γιγνομένην δ' οὖν ἔν τισιν, ὧν καὶ Διονύσιον ἡγήσατο ἕνα γενέσθαι τάχ' ἂν ξυλλαμβανόντων θεῶν, γενομένου δ' αὖ τοῦ τοιούτου τόν τε αὑτοῦ βίον καὶ τὸν τῶν ἄλλων Συρακοσίων ἀμήχανον ἂν μακαριότητι συμβῆναι γενόμενον. πρὸς δὴ τούτοις ᾠήθη δεῖν ἐκ παντὸς τρόπου εἰς Συρακούσας ὅ τι τάχιστα ἐλθεῖν ἐμὲ [327d] κοινωνὸν τούτων, μεμνημένος τήν τε αὑτοῦ καὶ ἐμὴν συνουσίαν, ὡς εὐπετῶς ἐξειργάσατο εἰς ἐπιθυμίαν ἐλθεῖν αὐτὸν τοῦ καλλίστου τε καὶ ἀρίστου βίου· ὃ δὴ καὶ νῦν εἰ διαπράξαιτο ἐν Διονυσίῳ ὡς ἐπεχείρησε, μεγάλας ἐλπίδας εἶχεν ἄνευ σφαγῶν καὶ θανάτων καὶ τῶν νῦν γεγονότων κακῶν βίον ἂν εὐδαίμονα καὶ ἀληθινὸν ἐν πάσῃ τῇ χώρᾳ κατασκευάσαι.

The Seventh Letter

With these things in mind, along with those referred to earlier, I crossed over to Syracuse, [**326e**] perhaps by chance, but more likely by some superior power's contrivance to lay the foundation for the things that have now befallen Dion and Syracuse. And I fear that still more will arise, if you do not now defer to me as I advise you for the second time.

Why, therefore, do I say [**327a**] that my arrival in Sicily was the beginning of all these things? As I spent time with Dion, then a young man, and revealed in conversation what I thought to be best for people, advising him to act accordingly, I dared to ignore the possibility that I could be in some way engineering, unwittingly, the eventual dissolution of the tyranny. For in fact Dion was an astute student of all things, including the arguments that I presented at the time, and he listened with such extraordinary [**327b**] acumen, like no other young man I've ever met, and he desired to live the remainder of his life differently from the majority of Italians and Sicilians, loving virtue more than pleasure or any other extravagance. As a result, he began to pass his time in a way that was obnoxious to those who were living according to the customs of the tyranny up until the death of Dionysius.

Afterwards, Dion began to think that he was not the only one to think this way, which [**327c**] he had acquired through proper reasoning, and he thought he saw it in a few others – not many, but some – and he believed that with the gods' assistance, Dionysius could soon become one of those people, and that if Dionysius did become such a man then life for both him and the rest of the Syracusans would in turn become extra-ordinarily blessed. On top of this, he thought that I should come to Syracuse as quickly as possible [**327d**] to be his partner in this venture, recalling the time he and I had spent together and how easily he had learned to desire the best and most beautiful of lives. Moreover, if he could now also bring this about in Dionysius, as he was endeavoring, he held the lofty hope of creating a happy and genuine existence throughout the entire land, one without slaughters and murders and all the current atrocities.

ταῦτα Δίων ὀρθῶς διανοηθεὶς ἔπεισε μεταπέμπεσθαι Διονύσιον ἐμέ, καὶ αὐτὸς ἐδεῖτο πέμπων ἥκειν ὅ τι τάχιστα ἐκ [327e] παντὸς τρόπου, πρίν τινας ἄλλους ἐντυχόντας Διονυσίῳ ἐπ' ἄλλον βίον αὐτὸν τοῦ βελτίστου παρατρέψαι. λέγων δὲ τάδε ἐδεῖτο, εἰ καὶ μακρότερα εἰπεῖν. "τίνας γὰρ καιρούς," ἔφη, "μείζους περιμενοῦμεν τῶν νῦν παραγεγονότων θείᾳ τινὶ τύχῃ;" καταλέγων δὲ τήν τε ἀρχὴν τῆς Ἰταλίας καὶ Σικελίας [328a] καὶ τὴν αὑτοῦ δύναμιν ἐν αὐτῇ, καὶ τὴν νεότητα καὶ τὴν ἐπιθυμίαν τὴν Διονυσίου, φιλοσοφίας τε καὶ παιδείας ὡς ἔχοι σφόδρα, λέγων, τούς τε αὐτοῦ ἀδελφιδοῦς καὶ τοὺς οἰκείους ὡς εὐπαράκλητοι εἶεν πρὸς τὸν ὑπ' ἐμοῦ λεγόμενον ἀεὶ λόγον καὶ βίον, ἱκανώτατοί τε Διονύσιον συμπαρακαλεῖν, ὥστε, εἴπερ ποτέ, καὶ νῦν ἐλπὶς πᾶσα ἀποτελεσθήσεται τοῦ τοὺς αὐτοὺς φιλοσόφους τε καὶ πόλεων ἄρχοντας μεγάλων [328b] συμβῆναι γενομένους.

τὰ μὲν δὴ παρακελεύματα ἦν ταῦτά τε καὶ τοιαῦτα ἕτερα πάμπολλα, τὴν δ' ἐμὴν δόξαν, τὸ μὲν περὶ τῶν νέων ὅπῃ ποτὲ γενήσοιτο, εἶχε φόβος—αἱ γὰρ ἐπιθυμίαι τῶν τοιούτων ταχεῖαι καὶ πολλάκις ἑαυταῖς ἐναντίαι φερόμεναι—, τὸ δὲ Δίωνος ἠπιστάμην τῆς ψυχῆς πέρι φύσει τε ἐμβριθὲς ὂν ἡλικίας τε ἤδη μετρίως ἔχον. ὅθεν μοι σκοπουμένῳ καὶ διστάζοντι πότερον εἴη πορευτέον καὶ ὑπακουστέον ἢ πῶς, ὅμως ἔρρεψε δεῖν, εἴ ποτέ τις τὰ διανοηθέντα [328c] περὶ νόμων τε καὶ πολιτείας ἀποτελεῖν ἐγχειρήσοι, καὶ νῦν πειρατέον εἶναι· πείσας γὰρ ἕνα μόνον ἱκανῶς πάντα ἐξειργασμένος ἐσοίμην ἀγαθά.

ταύτῃ μὲν δὴ τῇ διανοίᾳ τε καὶ τόλμῃ ἀπῆρα οἴκοθεν, οὐχ ᾗ τινες ἐδόξαζον, ἀλλ' αἰσχυνόμενος μὲν ἐμαυτὸν τὸ μέγιστον, μὴ δόξαιμί ποτε ἐμαυτῷ παντάπασι λόγος μόνον ἀτεχνῶς εἶναί τις, ἔργου δὲ οὐδενὸς ἄν ποτε ἑκὼν ἀνθάψασθαι, κινδυνεύσειν δὲ προδοῦναι πρῶτον [328d] μὲν τὴν Δίωνος ξενίαν τε καὶ ἑταιρείαν ἐν κινδύνοις ὄντως γεγονότος οὐ σμικροῖς.

The Seventh Letter

It was with such virtuous intentions that Dion convinced Dionysius to send for me, and Dion himself summoned me and implored me to come as quickly as possible [327e] and by whatever means, before Dionysius should fall in with anyone else who might steer him towards a lifestyle other than the best one. He implored me with the following words, though they are rather long to repeat: "what more opportune moment," he said, "are we waiting for than the one that is now at hand by some divine providence?" He described the realm of Italy and Sicily [328a] and his own power within it, mentioning the youth of Dionysius and his great eagerness for education and philosophy. And he spoke of his own nephews and relatives, how they would be easily influenced by the reasoning and lifestyle that I advocated, and in turn most capable of motivating Dionysius, so that now, if ever, all our hopes of the same people being both philosophers and leaders of great cities [328b] would come into fruition.

These were the exhortations he made, along with many others of this sort. As for my own opinion, I feared for the young people involved and what would become of them, for their desires are fleeting and often contradictory, though regarding Dion's character, I knew that his spirit was by nature serious and had already matured in due measure. Therefore, as I pondered the situation and vacillated about whether or not to listen to him and make the crossing, I was ultimately inclined to think that if ever one were to try to accomplish the things I had in mind [328c] about laws and government, it had to be attempted now. For if I could adequately convince a single person, I would accomplish something of absolute good.

It was with such intentions and convictions, then, that I left home, not with those that some have surmised. On the contrary, I felt within myself great trepidation at the thought that I might find myself to be nothing more than a voice, pure and simple, incapable of taking on any concrete action, and that I would risk betraying first of all [328d] the hospitality and friendship of Dion, who was, in reality, in no small amount of danger.

εἴτ' οὖν πάθοι τι, εἴτ' ἐκπεσὼν ὑπὸ Διονυσίου καὶ τῶν ἄλλων ἐχθρῶν ἔλθοι παρ' ἡμᾶς φεύγων καὶ ἀνέροιτο εἰπών "ὦ Πλάτων, ἥκω σοι φυγὰς οὐχ ὁπλιτῶν δεόμενος οὐδὲ ἱππέων ἐνδεὴς γενόμενος τοῦ ἀμύνασθαι τοὺς ἐχθρούς, ἀλλὰ λόγων καὶ πειθοῦς, ᾗ σὲ μάλιστα ἠπιστάμην ἐγὼ δυνάμενον ἀνθρώπους νέους ἐπὶ τὰ ἀγαθὰ καὶ τὰ δίκαια προτρέποντα εἰς φιλίαν τε καὶ ἑταιρείαν ἀλλήλοις [328e] καθιστάναι ἑκάστοτε· ὧν ἐνδείᾳ κατὰ τὸ σὸν μέρος νῦν ἐγὼ καταλιπὼν Συρακούσας ἐνθάδε πάρειμι. καὶ τὸ μὲν ἐμὸν ἔλαττον ὄνειδός σοι φέρει· φιλοσοφία δέ, ἣν ἐγκωμιάζεις ἀεὶ καὶ ἀτίμως φῂς ὑπὸ τῶν λοιπῶν ἀνθρώπων φέρεσθαι, πῶς οὐ προδέδοται τὰ νῦν μετ' ἐμοῦ μέρος ὅσον ἐπὶ σοὶ γέγονεν; [329a] καὶ Μεγαροῖ μὲν εἰ κατοικοῦντες ἐτυγχάνομεν, ἦλθες δή που ἄν μοι βοηθὸς ἐφ' ἅ σε παρεκάλουν, ἢ πάντων ἂν φαυλότατον ἡγοῦ σαυτόν· νῦν δ' ἄρα τὸ μῆκος τῆς πορείας καὶ τὸ μέγεθος δὴ τοῦ πλοῦ καὶ τοῦ πόνου ἐπαιτιώμενος οἴει δόξαν κακίας ἀποφευξεῖσθαί ποτε; πολλοῦ καὶ δεήσει."

λεχθέντων δὲ τούτων τίς ἂν ἦν μοι πρὸς ταῦτα εὐσχήμων ἀπόκρισις; οὐκ ἔστιν. ἀλλ' ἦλθον μὲν κατὰ λόγον ἐν δίκῃ τε, [329b] ὡς οἷόν τε ἄνθρωπον μάλιστα, διὰ τὰ τοιαῦτα καταλιπὼν τὰς ἐμαυτοῦ διατριβάς, οὔσας οὐκ ἀσχήμονας, ὑπὸ τυραννίδα δοκοῦσαν οὐ πρέπειν τοῖς ἐμοῖς λόγοις οὐδὲ ἐμοί· ἐλθών τε ἐμαυτὸν ἠλευθέρωσα Διὸς ξενίου[2] καὶ τῆς φιλοσόφου ἀνέγκλητον μοίρας παρέσχον, ἐπονειδίστου γενομένης ἂν εἴ τι καταμαλθακισθεὶς καὶ ἀποδειλιῶν αἰσχύνης μετέσχον κακῆς.

ἐλθὼν δέ, οὐ γὰρ δεῖ μηκύνειν, εὗρον στάσεως τὰ περὶ Διονύσιον μεστὰ ξύμπαντα καὶ διαβολῶν [329c] πρὸς τὴν τυραννίδα Δίωνος πέρι. ἤμυνον μὲν οὖν καθ' ὅσον ἠδυνάμην, σμικρὰ δ' οἷός τ' ἦν, μηνὶ δὲ σχεδὸν ἴσως τετάρτῳ Δίωνα Διονύσιος αἰτιώμενος ἐπιβουλεύειν τῇ τυραννίδι, σμικρὸν εἰς πλοῖον ἐμβιβάσας, ἐξέβαλεν ἀτίμως.

---

[2] The Zeus who oversees bonds of "guest-friendship" (*xenia*), the type of relationship that Plato and Dion shared.

The Seventh Letter

In any case, if he were to come to me – either because something bad had happened to him or because he had been exiled by Dionysius and his other enemies – and if he were to inquire of me in the following words: "Plato, I come to you as an exile, not to beg for hoplites or horsemen with which to protect myself against my enemies, but in need of the words and persuasiveness with which I know that you, above all, bring young people around to what is good and just, and are most capable of creating feelings of friendship and comradery [**328e**] among them. It is for want of these things, something for which you share some blame, that I have left Syracuse and am now here. You bear less blame for my own situation, but is it not your responsibility to see to it that philosophy – which you always praise and say is treated disgracefully by other men – not be betrayed along with me? [**329a**] If I were living in Megara, you would have doubtless come to help me in the matters to which I summoned you, or else considered yourself the worst of all men. As it is, however, do you really think you can avoid the reputation of a scoundrel by complaining of the length of the journey and of the magnitude of the travel and work involved? You will need a much better excuse than that."

What decent response could I give to such words? There is none. So I came, following both reason and justice [**329b**] (as much as a person can), and on these grounds I set aside my own studies, which were not insignificant, and I came to live under a tyranny that was suitable neither for myself nor for my words. And in coming, I freed myself of my obligation to Zeus *Xenios*, and I gave no grounds for reproach to the order of philosophy, which would have shouldered the blame if, worn down and cowed, I had engaged in such disgraceful behavior.

To make a long story short, when I arrived I found that everything around Dionysius was in a state of discord, and that numerous false accusations [**329c**] against Dion had been brought before the tyrant. I defended him as much I could, little as that was, but about three months later Dionysius accused Dion of plotting against the tyranny, and after putting him on board a small boat, he banished him in a most dishonorable fashion.

οἱ δὴ Δίωνος τὸ μετὰ τοῦτο πάντες φίλοι ἐφοβούμεθα μή τινα ἐπαιτιώμενος τιμωροῖτο ὡς συναίτιον τῆς Δίωνος ἐπιβουλῆς· περὶ δ' ἐμοῦ καὶ διῆλθε λόγος τις ἐν Συρακούσαις, ὡς τεθνεὼς εἴην ὑπὸ Διονυσίου ὡς τούτων ἁπάντων τῶν τότε [**329d**] γεγονότων αἴτιος. ὁ δὲ αἰσθανόμενος πάντας ἡμᾶς οὕτω διατεθέντας, φοβούμενος μὴ μεῖζον ἐκ τῶν φόβων γένοιτό τι, φιλοφρόνως πάντας ἀνελάμβανε, καὶ δὴ καὶ τὸν ἐμὲ παρεμυθεῖτό τε καὶ θαρρεῖν διεκελεύετο καὶ ἐδεῖτο πάντως μένειν·ἐγίγνετο γὰρ οἱ τὸ μὲν ἐμὲ φυγεῖν ἀπ' αὐτοῦ καλὸν οὐδέν, τὸ δὲ μένειν, διὸ δὴ καὶ σφόδρα προσεποιεῖτο δεῖσθαι·

τὰς δὲ τῶν τυράννων δεήσεις ἴσμεν, ὅτι μεμιγμέναι ἀνάγκαις [**329e**] εἰσίν· ὃ δὴ μηχανώμενος διεκώλυέ μου τὸν ἔκπλουν, εἰς ἀκρόπολιν ἀγαγὼν καὶ κατοικίσας ὅθεν οὐδ' ἂν εἷς ἔτι με ναύκληρος μὴ ὅτι κωλύοντος ἐξήγαγε Διονυσίου, ἀλλ' οὐδ' εἰ μὴ πέμπων αὐτὸς τὸν κελεύοντα ἐξαγαγεῖν ἐπέστελλεν, οὔτ' ἂν ἔμπορος οὔτε τῶν ἐν ταῖς τῆς χώρας ἐξόδοις ἀρχόντων οὐδ' ἂν εἷς περιεῖδέ με μόνον ἐκπορευόμενον, ὃς οὐκ ἂν συλλαβὼν εὐθέως παρὰ Διονύσιον πάλιν ἀπήγαγεν, ἄλλως τε καὶ διηγγελμένον ἤδη ποτὲ τοὐναντίον ἢ [**330a**] τὸ πρότερον πάλιν, ὡς Πλάτωνα Διονύσιος θαυμαστῶς ὡς ἀσπάζεται.

τὸ δ' εἶχε δὴ πῶς; τὸ γὰρ ἀληθὲς δεῖ φράζειν. ἠσπάζετο μὲν ἀεὶ προϊόντος τοῦ χρόνου μᾶλλον κατὰ τὴν τοῦ τρόπου τε καὶ ἤθους συνουσίαν, ἑαυτὸν δὲ ἐπαινεῖν μᾶλλον ἢ Δίωνα ἐβούλετό με καὶ φίλον ἡγεῖσθαι διαφερόντως μᾶλλον ἢ 'κεῖνον, καὶ θαυμαστῶς ἐφιλονείκει πρὸς τὸ τοιοῦτον. ᾗ δ' ἂν οὕτως ἐγένετο, εἴπερ ἐγίγνετο, κάλλιστα, ὤκνει [**330b**] ὡς δὴ μανθάνων καὶ ἀκούων τῶν περὶ φιλοσοφίαν λόγων οἰκειοῦσθαι καὶ ἐμοὶ συγγίγνεσθαι, φοβούμενος τοὺς τῶν διαβαλλόντων λόγους, μή πῃ παραποδισθείη καὶ Δίων δὴ πάντα εἴη διαπεπραγμένος. ἐγὼ δὲ πάντα ὑπέμενον, τὴν πρώτην διάνοιαν φυλάττων ᾗπερ ἀφικόμην, εἴ πως εἰς ἐπιθυμίαν ἔλθοι τῆς φιλοσόφου ζωῆς. ὁ δ' ἐνίκησεν ἀντιτείνων.

The Seventh Letter

Of course, after this those of us who were friends with Dion were all afraid that we would be accused of and punished for being in league with Dion's conspiracy. In my particular case, word got around Syracuse that I had been executed by Dionysius as the one responsible for [**329d**] everything that had happened. But Dionysius perceived how we all felt, and, afraid that something larger might arise from our fears, he received us all most warmly. What is more, he expressly reassured me and encouraged me to keep my spirits high, and he implored me to remain by all means. Indeed, my fleeing from him would have been not at all good for him, whereas my remaining… Well, it was for this reason that Dionysius pretended to need it so desperately.

As we know, however, the requests of tyrants are compounded by [**329e**] coercion. And to engineer my permanence he simply prevented my departure: he brought me to the acropolis and put me up in a place from which not a single captain would have taken me away – not without Dionysius himself sending someone with instructions to give me passage, let alone if he expressly forbade it. And there was no merchant, no official in the country's ports of exit, not a single person who saw me leaving on my own who would not have arrested me immediately and taken me back to Dionysius. Especially because by now it had been broadcast, in contrast to [**330a**] earlier reports, that Dionysius was marvelously pleased with Plato!

But how did things really stand? Truth be told, as time went by, in sharing my habits and my way of life he became more and more pleased. But he constantly wanted me to praise him more and to consider him more of a friend than Dion, and he was absolutely determined to win that battle. At the same time, he shied away from the best means by which that could be achieved, if indeed it ever could be, [**330b**] which is to say by learning and listening to my discourses on philosophy, spending time and being friendly with me; he feared the gossip of scandal-mongers, worried that he might somehow get tripped up and that Dion would achieve all his ends. I myself abided and maintained the same intentions with which I first arrived, in the hopes that he might come around to a yearning for the philosophical life. But his resistance won out.

καὶ ὁ πρῶτος δὴ χρόνος τῆς εἰς Σικελίαν ἐμῆς ἐπιδημήσεώς [**330c**] τε καὶ διατριβῆς διὰ πάντα ταῦτα ξυνέβη γενόμενος. μετὰ δὲ τοῦτο ἀπεδήμησά τε καὶ πάλιν ἀφικόμην πάσῃ σπουδῇ μεταπεμπομένου Διονυσίου· ὧν δὲ ἕνεκα καὶ ὅσα ἔπραξα, ὡς εἰκότα τε καὶ δίκαια, ὑμῖν πρῶτον μὲν ξυμβουλεύσας ἃ χρὴ ποιεῖν ἐκ τῶν νῦν γεγονότων, ὕστερον τὰ περὶ ταῦτα διέξειμι, τῶν ἐπανερωτώντων ἕνεκα τί δὴ βουλόμενος ἦλθον τὸ δεύτερον, ἵνα μὴ τὰ πάρεργα ὡς ἔργα μοι ξυμβαίνῃ λεγόμενα.

λέγω δὴ τάδε ἐγώ. τὸν συμβουλεύοντα ἀνδρὶ κάμνοντι καὶ δίαιταν διαιτωμένῳ [**330d**] μοχθηρὰν πρὸς ὑγίειαν ἄλλο τι χρὴ πρῶτον μὲν αὐτὸν μεταβάλλειν τὸν βίον, καὶ ἐθέλοντι μὲν πείθεσθαι καὶ τἆλλα ἤδη παραινεῖν; μὴ ἐθέλοντι δέ, φεύγοντα ἀπὸ τῆς τοῦ τοιούτου ξυμβουλῆς ἄνδρα τε ἡγοίμην ἂν καὶ ἰατρικόν, τὸν δὲ ὑπομένοντα τοὐναντίον ἄνανδρόν τε καὶ ἄτεχνον.

ταὐτὸν δὴ καὶ πόλει, εἴτε αὐτῆς εἷς εἴη κύριος εἴτε καὶ πλείους, εἰ μὲν κατὰ τρόπον ὀρθῇ πορευομένης ὁδῷ τῆς πολιτείας ξυμβουλεύοιτό [**330e**] τι τῶν προσφόρων, νοῦν ἔχοντος τὸ τοῖς τοιούτοις ξυμβουλεύειν· τοῖς δ' ἔξω τὸ παράπαν βαίνουσι τῆς ὀρθῆς πολιτείας καὶ μηδαμῇ ἐθέλουσιν αὐτῆς εἰς ἴχνος ἰέναι, προαγορεύουσι δὲ τῷ ξυμβούλῳ τὴν μὲν πολιτείαν ἐᾶν καὶ μὴ [**331a**] κινεῖν, ὡς ἀποθανουμένῳ ἐὰν κινῇ, τὰ δὲ βουλήσεσι καὶ ἐπιθυμίαις αὐτῶν ὑπηρετοῦντα ξυμβουλεύειν κελεύουσι τίνα τρόπον γίγνοιτ' ἂν ῥᾷστά τε καὶ τάχιστα εἰς τὸν ἀεὶ χρόνον, τὸν μὲν ὑπομένοντα ξυμβουλὰς τοιαύτας ἡγοίμην ἂν ἄνανδρον, τὸν δ' οὐχ ὑπομένοντα ἄνδρα.

And so it turned out that I spent the period of my first stay in Sicily [**330c**] engaged in all these things. After this I departed and then came back again after Dionysius summoned me most urgently. For those of you who ask what I wished to accomplish in coming a second time, I will address later the things that I did and on what account, and why they were reasonable and justified. But only after I have first advised you as to what must be done in the present circumstances, otherwise my second order of business may end up the focus.

This, then, is what I have to say: shouldn't someone advising a man who is struggling and leading a degenerate [**330d**] sort of life suggest first of all that he change his lifestyle, and only make other recommendations if this man is willing to listen? And if he is not willing to do so, well, I would consider someone who gets out of advising such a person to be courageous and skilled in the art of medicine, and someone who stays on to be unskilled and cowardly.

The same thing holds true with regard to a city, whether one person or many be in charge of it: if, on the one hand, the government is being guided down a straight path, and an adviser is sought concerning [**330e**] some suitable course of action, it is proper for a sensible person to give advice in this situation. Conversely, when those seeking advice tread well outside the boundaries of proper governance and in no way wish to fall back into line; if they tell their adviser to first of all let the government be and not to [**331a**] disturb it in any way, on penalty of death; and if they insist that he give advice as to how that which caters to their passions and desires might most quickly and easily become permanent; well, I would consider someone who stayed on for such consultations to be a coward, and someone who refused to do so to be courageous.

ταύτην δὴ τὴν διάνοιαν ἐγὼ κεκτημένος, ὅταν τίς μοι ξυμβουλεύηται περί τινος τῶν μεγίστων περὶ τὸν αὑτοῦ βίον, οἷον περὶ χρημάτων κτήσεως [331b] ἢ περὶ σώματος ἢ ψυχῆς ἐπιμελείας, ἂν μέν μοι τὸ καθ' ἡμέραν ἔν τινι τρόπῳ δοκῇ ζῆν ἢ συμβουλεύσαντος ἂν ἐθέλειν πείθεσθαι περὶ ὧν ἀνακοινοῦται, προθύμως ξυμβουλεύω καὶ οὐκ ἀφοσιωσάμενος μόνον ἐπαυσάμην.

ἐὰν δὲ μὴ ξυμβουλεύηταί μοι τὸ παράπαν ἢ συμβουλεύοντι δῆλος ᾖ μηδαμῇ πεισόμενος, αὐτόκλητος ἐπὶ τὸν τοιοῦτον οὐκ ἔρχομαι ξυμβουλεύσων, βιασόμενος δὲ οὐδ' ἂν υἱὸς ᾖ μου. δούλῳ δὲ ξυμβουλεύσαιμ' ἂν καὶ μὴ ἐθέλοντά γε προσβιαζοίμην. [331c] πατέρα δὲ ἢ μητέρα οὐχ ὅσιον ἡγοῦμαι προσβιάζεσθαι μὴ νόσῳ παραφροσύνης ἐχομένους· ἐὰν δέ τινα καθεστῶτα ζῶσι βίον, ἑαυτοῖς ἀρέσκοντα, ἐμοὶ δὲ μή, μήτε ἀπεχθάνεσθαι μάτην νουθετοῦντα μήτε δὴ κολακεύοντά γε ὑπηρετεῖν αὐτοῖς, πληρώσεις ἐπιθυμιῶν ἐκπορίζοντα ἃς αὐτὸς ἀσπαζόμενος οὐκ ἂν ἐθέλοιμι ζῆν.

ταὐτὸν δὴ καὶ περὶ πόλεως αὑτοῦ διανοούμενον χρὴ ζῆν τὸν ἔμφρονα· λέγειν μέν, εἰ μὴ [331d] καλῶς αὐτῷ φαίνοιτο πολιτεύεσθαι, εἰ μέλλοι μήτε ματαίως ἐρεῖν μήτε ἀποθανεῖσθαι λέγων, βίαν δὲ πατρίδι πολιτείας μεταβολῆς μὴ προσφέρειν, ὅταν ἄνευ φυγῶν καὶ σφαγῆς ἀνδρῶν μὴ δυνατὸν ᾖ γίγνεσθαι τὴν ἀρίστην, ἡσυχίαν δὲ ἄγοντα εὔχεσθαι τὰ ἀγαθὰ αὑτῷ τε καὶ τῇ πόλει.

Indeed, this is the attitude that I maintain whenever anyone consults me about something important in his life, such as about the acquisition of wealth, [**331b**] or about caring for his body or soul. If this person seems to be living his daily life in a reasonable manner, or to be willing to listen to the things shared by the person who is consulted, then I advise eagerly and do not give up after I have made only a token effort.

But if a person does not consult me at all, or if it is clear that he will not listen to his adviser, I will neither give unsolicited advice to such a person nor coerce him, not even if he were my own son. Now, I would advise a slave and would use force if he were unwilling, [**331c**] but I do not think it is permissible to use force with a father or a mother, unless they are sick and in a state of delirium. On the other hand, if they are living a settled sort of life that is satisfying to them, though not to me, it is not up to me to alienate them in vain by rebuking them, nor to minister to them with flattery, nor to provide them with the satisfaction of desires in the clutches of which I myself would not want to live.

Surely, a sensible person must lead his life keeping the same thing in mind when it comes to his own city: he should speak up if [**331d**] he thinks his city is governed poorly, as long as he would neither speak in vain nor die for his words. But whenever it is impossible for a city to become excellent without banishments and massacres, he should not employ violence against his fatherland for the sake of a political revolution; instead, he should keep his peace and pray for the best things both for himself and for the city.

κατὰ δὴ τοῦτον τὸν τρόπον ἐγώ ὑμῖν τ' ἂν ξυμβουλεύοιμι, ξυνεβούλευον δὲ καὶ Διονυσίῳ μετὰ Δίωνος, ζῆν μὲν τὸ καθ' ἡμέραν πρῶτον, ὅπως ἐγκρατὴς αὐτὸς αὑτοῦ ὅ τι μάλιστα [331e] ἔσεσθαι μέλλοι καὶ πιστοὺς φίλους τε καὶ ἑταίρους κτήσεσθαι, ὅπως μὴ πάθοι ἅπερ ὁ πατὴρ αὐτοῦ, ὃς παραλαβὼν Σικελίας πολλὰς καὶ μεγάλας πόλεις ὑπὸ τῶν βαρβάρων ἐκπεπορθημένας, οὐχ οἷός τ' ἦν κατοικίσας πολιτείας ἐν ἑκάσταις καταστήσασθαι πιστὰς ἑταίρων ἀνδρῶν, οὔτε ἄλλων δὴ [332a] ποθεν ὀθνείων οὔτε ἀδελφῶν, οὓς ἔθρεψέ τε αὐτὸς νεωτέρους ὄντας ἔκ τε ἰδιωτῶν ἄρχοντας καὶ ἐκ πενήτων πλουσίους ἐπεποιήκει διαφερόντως.

τούτων κοινωνὸν τῆς ἀρχῆς οὐδένα οἷός τ' ἦν πειθοῖ καὶ διδαχῇ καὶ εὐεργεσίαις καὶ ξυγγενείαις ἀπεργασάμενος ποιήσασθαι, Δαρείου δὲ ἑπταπλασίῳ φαυλότερος ἐγένετο, ὃς οὐκ ἀδελφοῖς πιστεύσας οὐδ' ὑφ' αὑτοῦ τραφεῖσι, κοινωνοῖς δὲ μόνον τῆς τοῦ Μήδου τε [332b] καὶ εὐνούχου χειρώσεως, διένειμέ τε μέρη μείζω ἕκαστα Σικελίας πάσης ἑπτὰ καὶ πιστοῖς ἐχρήσατο τοῖς κοινωνοῖς καὶ οὐκ ἐπιτιθεμένοις οὔτε αὐτῷ οὔτε ἀλλήλοις, ἔδειξέ τε παράδειγμα οἷον χρὴ τὸν νομοθέτην καὶ βασιλέα τὸν ἀγαθὸν γίγνεσθαι· νόμους γὰρ κατασκευάσας ἔτι καὶ νῦν διασέσωκε τὴν Περσῶν ἀρχήν.

ἔτι δὲ Ἀθηναῖοι πρὸς τούτοις, οὐκ αὐτοὶ κατοικίσαντες πολλὰς τῶν Ἑλλήνων πόλεις ὑπὸ βαρβάρων ἐμβεβλημένας[3] [ἀλλ' οἰκουμένας] παραλαβόντες, ὅμως [332c] ἑβδομήκοντα ἔτη διεφύλαξαν τὴν ἀρχὴν ἄνδρας φίλους ἐν ταῖς πόλεσιν ἑκάσταις κεκτημένοι. Διονύσιος δὲ εἰς μίαν πόλιν ἀθροίσας πᾶσαν Σικελίαν ὑπὸ σοφίας πιστεύων οὐδενὶ μόγις ἐσώθη· πένης γὰρ ἦν ἀνδρῶν φίλων καὶ πιστῶν, οὗ μεῖζον σημεῖον εἰς ἀρετὴν καὶ κακίαν οὐκ ἔστιν οὐδέν, τοῦ ἔρημον ἢ μὴ τοιούτων ἀνδρῶν εἶναι.

---

[3] I diverge here from Henderson (op. cit.), who prefers ἐκβεβλημένας. Both readings are present in the manuscripts, though ἐμβεβλημένας appears to be a later correction.

The Seventh Letter

It is according to this principle that I would advise you, and that I advised Dionysius along with Dion: first of all to live his daily life so as to become, as much as possible, [**331e**] master of himself, and also to acquire dependable friends and companions, so as to avoid suffering the things that his father did. For his father, after taking many of the great cities of Sicily that had previously been sacked by barbarians, was not able to settle and establish in each one administrations of reliable associates, neither of strangers [**332a**] of any origin nor indeed of brothers whom he himself had raised from a young age and had variously turned from private citizens into leaders, from poor men into exceptionally rich ones.

Not by persuasion, instruction, benefaction, or kinship was he able to make any of these men a partner to his rule. Rather, he was seven times worse off than Darius who, not trusting his kin, not even the ones he himself had raised, but only those who had been partners in his conquest of the Mede [**332b**] and the Eunuch, distributed among these seven lots, each one bigger than all of Sicily, and provided himself with reliable partners who made attempts neither against him nor each other. He thus created the model of how a good king and lawmaker should act, for he established laws that even now help preserve the Persian empire.

Beyond that example, the Athenians have also taken numerous Greek cities that they did not settle themselves, but which had been invaded by barbarians, and they have nevertheless [**332c**] maintained this empire for eighty years and acquired in each of these cities men that are well-disposed to them. Dionysius,[4] on the other hand, lumped all of Sicily into a single polity, and as a result of his prudence he trusted no one, and barely survived. For he was poor in men who were friendly or loyal, and there is no greater sign of virtue or depravity than whether or not one is bereft of such men.

---

[4] Referring here to Dionysius I, father of Dionysius II and brother-in-law of Dion.

ἃ δὴ καὶ Διονυσίῳ ξυνεβουλεύομεν ἐγώ καὶ Δίων ἐπειδὴ τὰ παρὰ πατρὸς [332d] αὐτῷ ξυνεβεβήκει οὕτως ἀνομιλήτῳ μὲν παιδείας, ἀνομιλήτῳ δὲ συνουσιῶν τῶν προσηκουσῶν γεγονέναι, πρῶτον ἐπὶ ταῦτα ὁρμήσαντα φίλους ἄλλους αὑτῷ τῶν οἰκείων ἅμα καὶ ἡλικιωτῶν καὶ συμφώνους πρὸς ἀρετὴν κτήσασθαι, μάλιστα δ' αὐτὸν αὑτῷ, τούτου γὰρ αὐτὸν θαυμαστῶς ἐνδεᾶ γεγονέναι, λέγοντες οὐκ ἐναργῶς οὕτως, οὐ γὰρ ἦν ἀσφαλές, αἰνιττόμενοι δὲ καὶ διαμαχόμενοι τοῖς λόγοις ὡς οὕτω μὲν πᾶς ἀνὴρ αὑτόν τε καὶ ἐκείνους ὧν ἂν ἡγεμὼν γίγνηται σώσει, [332e] μὴ ταύτῃ δὲ τραπόμενος τἀναντία πάντα ἀποτελεῖ·

πορευθεὶς δὲ ὡς λέγομεν, καὶ ἑαυτὸν ἔμφρονά τε καὶ σώφρονα ἀπεργασάμενος, εἰ τὰς ἐξηρημωμένας Σικελίας πόλεις κατοικίσειε νόμοις τε ξυνδήσειε καὶ πολιτείαις, ὥστε αὑτῷ τε οἰκείας καὶ ἀλλήλαις εἶναι πρὸς τὰς τῶν βαρβάρων βοηθείας, οὐ [333a] διπλασίαν τὴν πατρῴαν ἀρχὴν μόνον ποιήσοι, πολλαπλασίαν δὲ ὄντως· ἕτοιμον γὰρ εἶναι τούτων γενομένων πολὺ μᾶλλον δουλώσασθαι Καρχηδονίους τῆς ἐπὶ Γέλωνος αὐτοῖς γενομένης δουλείας, ἀλλ' οὐχ ὥσπερ νῦν τοὐναντίον ὁ πατὴρ αὐτοῦ φόρον ἐτάξατο φέρειν τοῖς βαρβάροις.

This, then, is what Dion and I advised Dionysius, seeing as his father's affairs [**332d**] had left him without either an education or suitable social connections: first, that he try to acquire for himself other friends who were in tune with virtue, both from among his relatives and from others his age; and above all that he be such a person himself, for in this he was remarkably lacking. Now, we were not entirely frank in our discussions – indeed it would not have been safe. Instead, we intimated and conveyed through argumentation that this is the way that every man saves both himself and whomever he leads, [**332e**] while by not taking this course one accomplishes the complete opposite.

Moreover, if he pursued the path that we suggested and made himself both wise and prudent, and if he settled the abandoned cities of Sicily and bound them together under laws and constitutions, so that they would be united both with him and each other against the forces of the barbarians, he would not only [**333a**] double his father's kingdom but in fact multiply it. For if all this happened, he would be ready to make the Carthaginians subject to the same yoke they had been under in the time of Gelon, unlike now, conversely, where his father had agreed to pay tribute to the barbarians.

ταῦτα ἦν τὰ λεγόμενα καὶ παρακελευόμενα ὑφ' ἡμῶν τῶν ἐπιβουλευόντων Διονυσίῳ, ὡς πολλαχόθεν ἐχώρουν οἱ τοιοῦτοι λόγοι, οἳ δὴ καὶ κρατήσαντες παρὰ Διονυσίῳ ἐξέβαλον μὲν Δίωνα, ἡμᾶς [333b] δ' εἰς φόβον κατέβαλον. ἵνα δ' ἐκπεράνωμεν οὐκ ὀλίγα πράγματα [τὰ] ἐν ὀλίγῳ χρόνῳ, ἐλθὼν ἐκ Πελοποννήσου καὶ Ἀθηνῶν Δίων ἔργῳ τὸν Διονύσιον ἐνουθέτησεν. ἐπειδὴ δ' οὖν ἠλευθέρωσέ τε καὶ ἀπέδωκεν αὐτοῖς δὶς τὴν πόλιν, ταὐτὸν πρὸς Δίωνα Συρακόσιοι τότε ἔπαθον, ὅπερ καὶ Διονύσιος, ὅτε αὐτὸν ἐπεχείρει παιδεύσας καὶ θρέψας βασιλέα τῆς ἀρχῆς ἄξιον οὕτω κοινωνεῖν αὐτῷ τοῦ βίου παντός, ὁ δὲ τοῖς [333c] διαβάλλουσιν ‹ὑπήκουσεν› καὶ λέγουσιν ὡς ἐπιβουλεύων τῇ τυραννίδι Δίων πράττοι πάντα ὅσα ἔπραττεν ἐν τῷ τότε χρόνῳ, ἵνα ὁ μὲν παιδείᾳ δὴ τὸν νοῦν κηληθεὶς ἀμελοῖ τῆς ἀρχῆς ἐπιτρέψας ἐκείνῳ, ὁ δὲ σφετερίσαιτο καὶ Διονύσιον ἐκβάλοι ἐκ τῆς ἀρχῆς δόλῳ. ταῦτα τότε ἐνίκησε καὶ τὸ δεύτερον ἐν Συρακοσίοις λεγόμενα, καὶ μάλα ἀτόπῳ τε καὶ αἰσχρᾷ νίκῃ τοῖς τῆς νίκης αἰτίοις.

οἷον γὰρ γέγονεν, ἀκοῦσαι χρὴ τοὺς [333d] ἐμὲ παρακαλοῦντας πρὸς τὰ νῦν πράγματα. ἦλθον Ἀθηναῖος ἀνὴρ ἐγώ, ἑταῖρος Δίωνος, σύμμαχος αὐτῷ, πρὸς τὸν τύραννον, ὅπως ἀντὶ πολέμου φιλίαν ποιήσαιμι· διαμαχόμενος δὲ τοῖς διαβάλλουσιν ἡττήθην. πείθοντος δὲ Διονυσίου τιμαῖς καὶ χρήμασι γενέσθαι μετ' αὐτοῦ ἐμέ, μάρτυρά τε καὶ φίλον πρὸς τὴν εὐπρέπειαν τῆς ἐκβολῆς τῆς Δίωνος αὐτῷ γίγνεσθαι, τούτων δὴ τὸ πᾶν διήμαρτεν.

The Seventh Letter

    These were the things that we expressed and urged, though the rumors seeping in from all sides had it that we were plotting against Dionysius. And in the end, by prevailing upon Dionysius, these rumors served to banish Dion and [**333b**] to set off terror among us. To make a long story short, Dion left the Peloponnese and Athens and forcefully rebuked Dionysius. But when he had twice freed and returned the city to them, the Syracusans still felt the same way about Dion as Dionysius who, when Dion was trying to instruct and encourage him to be a king worthy of his reign and to thus be a partner in his life's work, had listened to those [**333c**] who were disparaging Dion and saying that everything he was doing in that time he was doing so that Dionysius would be so entranced by education that he would lose interest in ruling and turn things over to Dion, letting him then usurp the throne and banish Dionysius from the kingdom by treachery. These accusations won over the Syracusans a second time, and for those responsible it was a disgusting and shameful victory.

    As for what transpired next, those of you [**333d**] who are summoning me to give advice concerning your present circumstances must hear about it. I came to the tyrant as an Athenian citizen, as an associate of Dion and an ally to him, and with the intention of forming a friendship rather than making war. But in my fight against the slanderers I was defeated. Dionysius, moreover, utterly failed in his attempt to persuade me, with money and honors, to remain with him as both a friend and a witness to the dignity of Dion's exile.

ὕστερον δὲ δὴ κατιὼν οἴκαδε [333e] Δίων ἀδελφὼ δύο προσλαμβάνει Ἀθήνηθεν, οὐκ ἐκ φιλοσοφίας γεγονότε φίλω, ἀλλ' ἐκ τῆς περιτρεχούσης ἑταιρείας ταύτης τῆς τῶν πλείστων φίλων, ἣν ἐκ τοῦ ξενίζειν τε καὶ μυεῖν καὶ ἐποπτεύειν πραγματεύονται.[5] καὶ δὴ καὶ τούτω τὼ ξυγκαταγαγόντε αὐτὸν φίλω ἐκ τούτων τε καὶ ἐκ τῆς πρὸς τὴν κάθοδον ὑπηρεσίας ἐγενέσθην ἑταίρω· ἐλθόντες [334a] δὲ εἰς Σικελίαν, ἐπειδὴ Δίωνα ᾔσθοντο διαβεβλημένον εἰς τοὺς ἐλευθερωθέντας ὑπ' αὐτοῦ Σικελιώτας ὡς ἐπιβουλεύοντα γενέσθαι τύραννον, οὐ μόνον τὸν ἑταῖρον καὶ ξένον προὔδοσαν, ἀλλ' οἷον τοῦ φόνου αὐτόχειρες ἐγένοντο, ὅπλα ἔχοντες ἐν ταῖς χερσὶν αὐτοὶ τοῖς φονεῦσι παρεστῶτες ἐπίκουροι.

καὶ τὸ μὲν αἰσχρὸν καὶ ἀνόσιον οὔτε παρίεμαι ἔγωγε οὔτε τι λέγω· πολλοῖς γὰρ καὶ ἄλλοις ὑμνεῖν ταῦτα ἐπιμελὲς [334b] καὶ εἰς τὸν ἔπειτα μελήσει χρόνον· τὸ δὲ Ἀθηναίων πέρι λεγόμενον, ὡς αἰσχύνην οὗτοι περιῆψαν τῇ πόλει, ἐξαιροῦμαι· φημὶ γὰρ κἀκεῖνον Ἀθηναῖον εἶναι ὃς οὐ προὔδωκε τὸν αὐτὸν τοῦτον, ἐξὸν χρήματα καὶ ἄλλας τιμὰς πολλὰς λαμβάνειν. οὐ γὰρ διὰ βαναύσου φιλότητος ἐγεγόνει φίλος, διὰ δὲ ἐλευθέρας παιδείας κοινωνίαν, ᾗ μόνῃ χρὴ πιστεύειν τὸν νοῦν κεκτημένον μᾶλλον ἢ ξυγγενείᾳ ψυχῶν καὶ σωμάτων· ὥστε οὐκ ἀξιῶ [334c] ὀνείδους γεγόνατον τῇ πόλει τὼ Δίωνα ἀποκτείναντε, ὡς ἐλλογίμω πώποτε ἄνδρε γενομένω.

---

[5] The reference here is to the Eleusinian mysteries, about which we have relatively little evidence. It appears that by the 4th century BCE participants had been divided into two groups: *mystai*, initiated into the rites for the first time, and *epoptai*, who had been initiated previously and witnessed the initiation of the *mystai*. Evidently, Dion had done this with two companions, one of whom was named Callippus (cf. Plut. *Dion* 54-58). See K. Clinton, "Stages of Initiation in the Eleusinian and Samothracian Mysteries," in *Greek Mysteries: The Archaeology of Ancient Greek Secret Cults*, ed. M.B. Cosmopoulos (London: Routledge, 2005), 50-78.

Later, while returning home from Athens, [333e] Dion was accompanied by two brothers who had become his friends not through the pursuit of philosophy, but from the sort of relationship that many friends have and that one develops through entertaining and by becoming initiands into and then witnesses to the Mysteries together. It was above all from these experiences that these two men became Dion's friends and accompanied and assisted him on his journey home. But when they [334a] arrived in Sicily, and when they understood that Dion was being falsely accused by the Sicilians – whom he had freed – of plotting to become tyrant, they not only betrayed their host and companion, they actually became the very agents of his murder, standing by with weapons in hand as accomplices to his murderers.

Now, I neither pass over nor speak at length about the shameful and unholy nature of all this – it is and will be up to others to spin [334b] those tales in the future. But I will address what is said about the two Athenians, namely that they brought shame to their city. For I dare say that it was also an Athenian who did *not* betray that same man, even though he could have gotten money and many other honors. For it was not because of some vulgar affection that he became his friend, but through the communion shared in the course of the education of a free person, the only thing a sensible person should trust more than kinship of soul and body. So I do not believe that [334c] the two killers of Dion should be a cause for reproach for the city, as if they were men who had ever been held in any regard.

ταῦτα εἴρηται πάντα τῆς ξυμβουλῆς ἕνεκα τῶν Διωνείων φίλων καὶ ξυγγενῶν· ξυμβουλεύω δὲ δή τι πρὸς τούτοις τὴν αὐτὴν ξυμβουλὴν καὶ λόγον τὸν αὐτὸν λέγων ἤδη τρίτον τρίτοις ὑμῖν· μὴ δουλοῦσθαι Σικελίαν ὑπ' ἀνθρώποις, δεσπόταις, μηδὲ ἄλλην πόλιν, ὅ γ' ἐμὸς λόγος, ἀλλ' ὑπὸ νόμοις· οὔτε γὰρ τοῖς δουλουμένοις οὔτε τοῖς δουλωθεῖσιν ἄμεινον, [334d] αὐτοῖς καὶ παισὶ παίδων τε ἐκγόνοις, ἀλλ' ὀλέθριος πάντως ἡ πεῖρα, σμικρὰ δὲ καὶ ἀνελεύθερα ψυχῶν ἤθη τὰ τοιαῦτα ἁρπάζειν κέρδη φιλεῖ, οὐδὲν τῶν εἰς τὸν ἔπειτα καὶ εἰς τὸν παρόντα καιρὸν ἀγαθῶν καὶ δικαίων εἰδότα θείων τε καὶ ἀνθρωπίνων.

ταῦτα πρῶτον μὲν Δίωνα ἐγὼ ἐπεχείρησα πείθειν, δεύτερον δὲ Διονύσιον, τρίτους δὲ ὑμᾶς νῦν. καί μοι πείθεσθε Διὸς τρίτου σωτῆρος χάριν, εἶτα εἰς Διονύσιον βλέψαντες καὶ Δίωνα, ὧν ὁ μὲν μὴ πειθόμενος ζῇ τὰ νῦν [334e] οὐ καλῶς, ὁ δὲ πειθόμενος τέθνηκε καλῶς· τὸ γὰρ τῶν καλλίστων ἐφιέμενον αὐτῷ τε καὶ πόλει πάσχειν ὅ τι ἂν πάσχῃ πᾶν ὀρθὸν καὶ καλόν. οὔτε γὰρ πέφυκεν ἀθάνατος ἡμῶν οὐδείς, οὔτ' εἴ τῳ ξυμβαίη, γένοιτο ἂν εὐδαίμων, ὡς δοκεῖ τοῖς πολλοῖς. κακὸν γὰρ καὶ ἀγαθὸν οὐδὲν λόγου ἄξιόν [335a] ἐστι τοῖς ἀψύχοις, ἀλλ' ἢ μετὰ σώματος οὔσῃ ψυχῇ τοῦτο ξυμβήσεται ἑκάστῃ ἢ κεχωρισμένῃ.

The Seventh Letter

All this I have said for the purpose of advising Dion's friends and relatives. But I will provide you with some advice in addition to this, and say for the third time something I've already told two others: neither Sicily nor any other polity should be enslaved to human masters, but rather to laws. This at any rate is my idea. For it is better neither for the enslavers nor for the enslaved themselves, [**334d**] their children, or their children's children. On the contrary, the attempt itself is totally destructive, and the dispositions of souls that are wont to snatch at such gains are small-minded and servile, and know nothing of the benefits conferred in the present and future by both divine and human justice and goodness.

I tried first to persuade Dion of these things, later Dionysius, and now, third of all, you. And for the sake of Zeus *Sōtēr* of the third libation,[6] listen to me, and look at Dionysius and Dion: the former did not listen to me and now lives [**334e**] poorly, while the latter did listen and died nobly. Indeed, it is altogether right and good for one who aspires to the best of things, both for himself and his city, to endure whatever he may endure, since none of us is immortal, nor, contrary to what many believe, would we be happy if we turned out to be. For the soul-less have nothing of either bad or good [**335a**] that is worth mentioning, while these things will be visited upon the soul whether it is with or separated from its body.

---

[6] On the order of libation offerings at banquets, the third of which would be dedicated to Zeus *Sōtēr* ("Zeus the Saviour"), see esp. D. Tolles, *The Banquet-Libations of the Greeks* (Ann Arbor: Edwards Brothers, 1943), 55-68.

πείθεσθαι δὲ ὄντως ἀεὶ χρὴ τοῖς παλαιοῖς τε καὶ ἱεροῖς λόγοις, οἳ δὴ μηνύουσιν ἡμῖν ἀθάνατον ψυχὴν εἶναι δικαστάς τε ἴσχειν καὶ τίνειν τὰς μεγίστας τιμωρίας, ὅταν τις ἀπαλλαχθῇ τοῦ σώματος. διὸ καὶ τὰ μεγάλα ἁμαρτήματα καὶ ἀδικήματα σμικρότερον εἶναι χρὴ νομίζειν κακὸν πάσχειν ἢ δρᾶσαι. ὧν ὁ φιλοχρήματος [335b] πένης τε ἀνὴρ τὴν ψυχὴν οὔτε ἀκούει, ἐάν τε ἀκούσῃ, καταγελῶν, ὡς οἴεται, πανταχόθεν ἀναιδῶς ἁρπάζει πᾶν ὅ τι περ ἂν οἴηται, καθάπερ θηρίον, φαγεῖν ἢ πιεῖν ἢ περὶ τὴν ἀνδραποδώδη καὶ ἀχάριστον, ἀφροδίσιον λεγομένην οὐκ ὀρθῶς, ἡδονὴν ἐκπορειῖν αὑτῷ τοὐμπίμπλασθαι, τυφλὸς ὢν καὶ οὐχ ὁρῶν, οἷα ξυνέπεται [τῶν ἁρπαγμάτων] ἀνοσιουργία, κακὸν ἡλίκον, ἀεὶ μετ' ἀδικήματος ἑκάστου, ἣν ἀναγκαῖον τῷ ἀδικήσαντι συνεφέλκειν ἐπί τε γῇ στρεφομένῳ καὶ ὑπὸ γῆς [335c] νοστήσαντι πορείαν ἄτιμόν τε καὶ ἀθλίαν πάντως πανταχῇ.

Δίωνα δὴ ἐγὼ λέγων ταῦτά τε καὶ ἄλλα τοιαῦτα ἔπειθον, καὶ τοῖς ἀποκτείνασιν ἐκεῖνον δικαιότατ' ἂν ὀργιζοίμην ἐγὼ τρόπον τινὰ ὁμοιότατα καὶ Διονυσίῳ· ἀμφότεροι γὰρ ἐμὲ καὶ τοὺς ἄλλους, ὡς ἔπος εἰπεῖν, ἅπαντας τὰ μέγιστα ἔβλαψαν ἀνθρώπους, οἱ μὲν τὸν βουλόμενον δικαιοσύνῃ χρῆσθαι διαφθείραντες, ὁ δὲ οὐδὲν ἐθελήσας χρήσασθαι δικαιοσύνῃ [335d] διὰ πάσης τῆς ἀρχῆς, μεγίστην δύναμιν ἔχων, ἐν ᾗ γενομένη φιλοσοφία τε καὶ δύναμις ὄντως ἐν ταὐτῷ διὰ πάντων ἀνθρώπων Ἑλλήνων τε καὶ βαρβάρων λάμψασ' ἂν ἱκανῶς δόξαν παρέστησε πᾶσι τὴν ἀληθῆ, ὡς οὐκ ἄν ποτε γένοιτο εὐδαίμων οὔτε πόλις οὔτ' ἀνὴρ οὐδεὶς ὃς ἂν μὴ μετὰ φρονήσεως ὑπὸ δικαιοσύνῃ διαγάγῃ τὸν βίον, ἤτοι ἐν αὑτῷ κεκτημένος ἢ ὁσίων ἀνδρῶν ἀρχόντων ἐν ἤθεσι τραφείς τε καὶ παιδευθεὶς [335e] ἐνδίκως.

The Seventh Letter

We must truly trust in the ancient and sacred precepts that reveal to us that a soul is immortal, that it contains within it judges, and that it pays the harshest penalties whenever it is set free from its body. Therefore, we must also believe that it is a lesser evil to suffer the greatest wrongs and injustices than it is to commit them, a notion that the man who is money-loving [**335b**] but soul-poor either does not hear, or if he does hear it he mocks it – so he thinks – all the while snatching from every corner, like a wild animal, whatever he intends to eat or drink, or whatever slavish and graceless pleasure, falsely called an object of love, he wishes to provide himself and gorge upon. He is blind and does not see the company that such wickedness keeps, an abomination ever equal to each act of injustice which the wrongdoer must drag along with himself as he wanders upon the earth and when he goes back below the earth [**335c**] on a journey that is sordid and miserable at every turn.

Now, I persuaded Dion when I explained these and other such things to him, and so I am justifiably angry with those who killed him, and likewise with Dionysius. For they all caused the gravest harm to me and to practically all of humanity: the murderers by destroying a person who wished to advance justice, Dionysius by having no desire whatsoever to advance justice [**335d**] throughout his entire kingdom. And this despite the fact that he had the utmost power in a place where, if philosophy and power had truly been united within the same individual, it would have shone forth through all peoples, Greeks and Barbarians alike, and demonstrated to everyone the truth of the idea that no city or man can ever be happy except by leading a life based on wisdom and subordinate to justice, regardless of whether this capacity is acquired independently or through a proper upbringing and education that conforms to the morals of men who are conscientious [**335e**] rulers.

ταῦτα μὲν Διονύσιος ἔβλαψε· τὰ δὲ ἄλλα σμικρὰ ἂν εἴη πρὸς ταῦτά μοι βλάβη. ὁ δὲ Δίωνα ἀποκτείνας οὐκ οἶδε ταὐτὸν ἐξειργασμένος τούτῳ. Δίωνα γὰρ ἐγὼ σαφῶς οἶδα, ὡς οἷόν τε περὶ ἀνθρώπων ἄνθρωπον διισχυρίζεσθαι, ὅτι τὴν ἀρχὴν εἰ κατέσχεν, ὡς οὐκ ἄν ποτε ἐπ' ἄλλο γε [336a] σχῆμα ἀρχῆς ἐτράπετο ἢ ἐπὶ τὸ Συρακούσας μὲν πρῶτον τὴν πατρίδα τὴν ἑαυτοῦ, ἐπεὶ τὴν δουλείαν αὐτῆς ἀπήλλαξε [καὶ] φαιδρύνας ἐλευθερίῳ δ' ἐν σχήματι κατέστησε, τὸ μετὰ τοῦτ' ἂν πάσῃ μηχανῇ ἐκόσμησε νόμοις τοῖς προσήκουσί τε καὶ ἀρίστοις τοὺς πολίτας, τό τε ἐφεξῆς τούτοις προυθυμεῖτ' ἂν πρᾶξαι, πᾶσαν Σικελίαν κατοικίζειν καὶ ἐλευθέραν ἀπὸ τῶν βαρβάρων ποιεῖν, τοὺς μὲν ἐκβάλλων, τοὺς δὲ χειρούμενος ῥᾶον Ἱέρωνος· τούτων δ' αὖ γενομένων δι' ἀνδρὸς [336b] δικαίου τε καὶ ἀνδρείου καὶ σώφρονος καὶ φιλοσόφου τὴν αὐτὴν ἀρετῆς ἂν πέρι γενέσθαι δόξαν τοῖς πολλοῖς ἥπερ ἄν, εἰ Διονύσιος ἐπείσθη, ‹πάντα› παρὰ πᾶσιν ἂν ὡς ἔπος εἰπεῖν ἀνθρώποις ἀπέσωσε γενομένη.

νῦν δὲ ἤ πού τις δαίμων ἤ τις ἀλιτήριος ἐμπεσὼν ἀνομίᾳ καὶ ἀθεότητι καὶ τὸ μέγιστον τόλμαις ἀμαθίας, ἐξ ἧς πάντα κακὰ πᾶσιν ἐρρίζωται καὶ βλαστάνει καὶ εἰς ὕστερον ἀποτελεῖ καρπὸν τοῖς γεννήσασι πικρότατον, αὕτη πάντα τὸ δεύτερον ἀνέτρεψέ τε καὶ [336c] ἀπώλεσε.

νῦν δὲ δὴ εὐφημῶμεν χάριν οἰωνοῦ τὸ τρίτον. ὅμως δὲ μιμεῖσθαι μὲν συμβουλεύω Δίωνα ὑμῖν τοῖς φίλοις τήν τε τῆς πατρίδος εὔνοιαν καὶ τὴν τῆς τροφῆς σώφρονα δίαιταν, ἐπὶ λῳόνων δὲ ὀρνίθων τὰς ἐκείνου βουλήσεις πειρᾶσθαι ἀποτελεῖν· αἳ δὲ ἦσαν, ἀκηκόατε παρ' ἐμοῦ σαφῶς·

The Seventh Letter

This is the damage that Dionysius has done, and compared to this, the rest would be but a small injury for me. The man who killed Dion did just as much harm as Dionysius, though he does not know it. For I know well, to the extent that one person can vouch for another, that if Dion had come into power, he would never have molded the city in any form [**336a**] other than this: first of all, after he had brought joy to Syracuse, his own fatherland, by delivering it from slavery and fashioning it in the form of freedom, he would have used any means necessary to equip it with laws that were the best and most beneficial to the citizens; and after this he would have set his sights on settling all of Sicily and rendering it free from the barbarians, pushing some of them out, subduing others more easily than Hieron did. Furthermore, if all these things had been done by a man [**336b**] who was just, courageous, prudent, and a philosopher, virtue would have acquired the same reputation among most people as it would have among practically everyone, if Dionysius had been persuaded, and all would have been saved.

In the end, however, some deity or, perhaps, some avenging spirit barged in bringing lawlessness, godlessness, and above all the insolence of ignorance out of which all evil sets roots and blossoms and finally produces the most bitter of fruits for those who have sown them, and this upended and ruined everything for the [**336c**] second time.

But now, so as not to jinx it,[7] let us speak this third time in auspicious terms. I still advise you to emulate Dion and his goodwill towards his fatherland and his prudent manner of living, and to try and fulfill under better auspices those plans of his that you have now heard clearly from me.

---

[7] Special thanks to Tony Leyh for providing this excellent suggestion for the translation of οἰωνοῦ, and for making me aware of the ornithological aspects shared by both the English and Greek terms.

τὸν δὲ μὴ δυνάμενον ὑμῶν Δωριστὶ ζῆν κατὰ τὰ [336d] πάτρια, διώκοντα δὲ τόν τε τῶν Δίωνος σφαγέων καὶ τὸν Σικελικὸν βίον, μήτε παρακαλεῖν μήτε οἴεσθαι πιστὸν ἄν τι καὶ ὑγιὲς πρᾶξαί ποτε· τοὺς δὲ ἄλλους παρακαλεῖν ἐπὶ πάσης Σικελίας κατοικισμόν τε καὶ ἰσονομίαν ἔκ τε αὐτῆς Σικελίας καὶ ἐκ Πελοποννήσου ξυμπάσης, φοβεῖσθαι δὲ μηδὲ Ἀθήνας· εἰσὶ γὰρ καὶ ἐκεῖ πάντων ἀνθρώπων διαφέροντες πρὸς ἀρετὴν ξενοφόνων τε ἀνδρῶν μισοῦντες τόλμας

εἰ δ' οὖν ταῦτα μὲν ὕστερα γένοιτ' ἄν, κατεπείγουσι δὲ ὑμᾶς αἱ τῶν [336e] στάσεων πολλαὶ καὶ παντοδαπαὶ φυόμεναι ἑκάστης ἡμέρας διαφοραί, εἰδέναι μέν που χρὴ πάντα τινὰ ἄνδρα, ᾧ καὶ βραχὺ δόξης ὀρθῆς μετέδωκε θεία τις τύχη, ὡς οὐκ ἔστι παῦλα κακῶν τοῖς στασιάσασι, πρὶν ἂν οἱ κρατήσαντες μάχαις καὶ ἐκβολαῖς ἀνθρώπων καὶ σφαγαῖς μνησικακοῦντες [337a] καὶ ἐπὶ τιμωρίας παύσωνται τρεπόμενοι τῶν ἐχθρῶν, ἐγκρατεῖς δὲ ὄντες αὐτῶν, θέμενοι νόμους κοινοὺς μηδὲν μᾶλλον πρὸς ἡδονὴν αὑτοῖς ἢ τοῖς ἡττηθεῖσι κειμένους, ἀναγκάσωσιν αὐτοὺς χρῆσθαι τοῖς νόμοις διτταῖς οὔσαις ἀνάγκαις, αἰδοῖ καὶ φόβῳ, φόβῳ μὲν διὰ τὸ κρείττους αὐτῶν εἶναι δεικνύντες τὴν βίαν, αἰδοῖ δὲ αὖ διὰ τὸ κρείττους φαίνεσθαι περί τε τὰς ἡδονὰς καὶ τοῖς νόμοις μᾶλλον ἐθέλοντές τε καὶ δυνάμενοι δουλεύειν. ἄλλως δὲ οὐκ ἔστιν ὡς ἂν ποτε κακῶν λῆξαι [337b] πόλις ἐν αὑτῇ στασιάσασα, ἀλλὰ στάσεις καὶ ἔχθραι καὶ μίση καὶ ἀπιστίαι ταῖς οὕτω διατεθείσαις πόλεσιν αὐταῖς πρὸς αὑτὰς ἀεὶ γίγνεσθαι φιλεῖ.

The Seventh Letter

And when it comes to those who are unable to live according to [**336d**] your ancestral ways in the Dorian fashion, those who aspire to the way of life of the Sicilians, such as Dion's murderers, I urge you neither to send for people such as these nor to think that they could ever do anything reasonable or dependable. Instead, to assist in the settlement of all of Sicily and the establishment of equality under the law, you should send for other men from both Sicily itself and from the entire Peloponnese; nor should you shy away from summoning men from Athens, for there too one may find individuals who surpass all others in virtue and despise the insolence of men who murder their friends.

If, however, these things should only occur later, and if you feel upon you the strain of the [**336e**] many and constant disagreements of ever-flourishing factions, then every man upon whom some divine fortune has bestowed a small measure of proper thinking must in some way understand that those who engage in civil wars will never see an end to their problems until the people in power stop perpetuating malice with fighting, banishments, and slaughter, [**337a**] and refrain from punishing their enemies. When they exercise restraint, and when they have passed laws that are impartial and established no more for their own satisfaction than for the defeated parties, then they will force others to regard the laws with these two crucial attitudes: respect and fear. Fear of men who show themselves to be superior when it comes to force; respect because those same men appear to be stronger than their own pleasures and because they are willing and able to subjugate themselves to the laws. Otherwise, there is no city that will ever put an end to its troubles [**337b**] when it is at war with itself. On the contrary, discord, hostility, loathing, and mistrust tend to always exist in cities that are set up along lines of internal antagonisms.

τοὺς δὴ κρατήσαντας ἀεὶ χρή, ὅτανπερ ἐπιθυμήσωσι σωτηρίας, αὐτοὺς ἐν αὑτοῖς ἄνδρας προκρῖναι τῶν Ἑλλήνων οὓς ἂν πυνθάνωνται ἀρίστους ὄντας, πρῶτον μὲν γέροντας, καὶ παῖδας καὶ γυναῖκας κεκτημένους οἴκοι καὶ προγόνους αὑτῶν ὅ τι μάλιστα πολλούς τε καὶ ὀνομαστοὺς καὶ κτῆσιν κεκτημένους πάντας [337c] ἱκανήν· ἀριθμὸν δὲ εἶναι μυριάνδρῳ πόλει πεντήκοντα ἱκανοὶ τοιοῦτοι. τούτους δὲ δεήσεσι καὶ τιμαῖς ὅ τι μεγίσταις οἴκοθεν μεταπέμπεσθαι, μεταπεμψαμένους δὲ ὀμόσαντας δεῖσθαι καὶ κελεύειν θεῖναι νόμους, μήτε νικήσασι μήτε νικηθεῖσι νέμειν πλέον, τὸ δὲ ἴσον καὶ κοινὸν πάσῃ τῇ πόλει.

τεθέντων δὲ τῶν νόμων ἐν τούτῳ δὴ τὰ πάντα ἐστίν. ἂν μὲν γὰρ οἱ νενικηκότες ἥττους αὑτοὺς τῶν νόμων [337d] μᾶλλον τῶν νενικημένων παρέχωνται, πάντ' ἔσται σωτηρίας τε καὶ εὐδαιμονίας μεστὰ καὶ πάντων κακῶν ἀποφυγή· εἰ δὲ μή, μήτ' ἐμὲ μήτ' ἄλλον κοινωνὸν παρακαλεῖν ἐπὶ τὸν μὴ πειθόμενον τοῖς νῦν ἐπεσταλμένοις. ταῦτα γάρ ἐστιν ἀδελφὰ ὧν τε Δίων ὧν τ' ἐγὼ ἐπεχειρήσαμεν Συρακούσαις εὖ φρονοῦντες συμπρᾶξαι, δεύτερα μήν· πρῶτα δ' ἦν ἃ τὸ πρῶτον ἐπεχειρήθη μετ' αὐτοῦ Διονυσίου πραχθῆναι πᾶσι κοινὰ ἀγαθά, τύχη δέ τις ἀνθρώπων κρείττων διεφόρησε. [337e] τὰ δὲ νῦν ὑμεῖς πειρᾶσθε εὐτυχέστερον αὐτὰ ἀγαθῇ πρᾶξαι μοίρᾳ καὶ θείᾳ τινὶ τύχῃ.

The Seventh Letter

To be sure, whenever they aspire towards preservation, those in power must select from among themselves whichever men of Greek origin they discover are the best. First of all they should find men who are old, and who have wives and children at home and whose ancestors are as numerous and renowned as possible, and they should all be men of [**337c**] adequate means – fifty such men should be sufficient for a city of ten-thousand people. They should summon these men from their homes with pleas and as many honors as possible, and after they have been summoned and oaths have been sworn, they should urge and implore them to set laws, and to cater no more to either the victors or the vanquished, but rather in an equal and impartial manner to the entire city.

Once the laws have been established, everything will depend on the following: if the victors yield to the laws [**337d**] more than the vanquished do, then a refuge from all evil and a full share of salvation and happiness will be provided. If they do not, however, you should not call on either myself or anyone else to deal with those who do not follow the instructions I have now given. For this is closely related to what Dion and I both, out of care for Syracuse, attempted to do, and it is the second-best course of action. The best is what we tried to do at first with Dionysius himself, namely to confer a set of benefits for everyone alike. But fortune, a force far stronger than humans, crushed that attempt. [**337e**] And now you all must try to achieve this with greater success, aided by good luck and some divine fortune.

ξυμβουλὴ μὲν δὴ καὶ ἐπιστολὴ εἰρήσθω καὶ ἡ παρὰ Διονύσιον ἐμὴ προτέρα ἄφιξις· ἡ δὲ δὴ ὑστέρα πορεία τε καὶ πλοῦς ὡς εἰκότως τε ἅμα καὶ ἐμμελῶς γέγονεν, ᾧ μέλει ἀκούειν ἔξεστι τὸ μετὰ τοῦτο. ὁ μὲν γὰρ δὴ πρῶτος χρόνος [338a] τῆς ἐν Σικελίᾳ διατριβῆς μοι διεπεράνθη, καθάπερ εἶπον, πρὶν συμβουλεύειν τοῖς οἰκείοις καὶ ἑταίροις τοῖς περὶ Δίωνα· τὸ μετ᾽ ἐκεῖνα δ᾽ οὖν ἔπεισα ὅπῃ δὴ ποτ᾽ ἐδυνάμην Διονύσιον ἀφεῖναί με, εἰρήνης δὲ γενομένης, ἦν γὰρ τότε πόλεμος ἐν Σικελίᾳ ξυνωμολογήσαμεν ἀμφότεροι, Διονύσιος μὲν [ἔφη] μεταπέμψεσθαι Δίωνα καὶ ἐμὲ πάλιν καταστησάμενος τὰ περὶ τὴν ἀρχὴν ἀσφαλέστερον ἑαυτῷ, Δίωνα δὲ ἠξίου [338b] διανοεῖσθαι μὴ φυγὴν αὑτῷ γεγονέναι τότε, μετάστασιν δέ· ἐγὼ δ᾽ ἥξειν ὡμολόγησα ἐπὶ τούτοις τοῖς λόγοις. γενομένης δὲ εἰρήνης μετεπέμπετ᾽ ἐμέ, Δίωνα δὲ ἐπισχεῖν ἔτι ἐνιαυτὸν ἐδεῖτο, ἐμὲ δὲ ἥκειν ἐκ παντὸς τρόπου ἠξίου. Δίων μὲν οὖν ἐκέλευέ τέ με πλεῖν καὶ ἐδεῖτο· καὶ γὰρ δὴ λόγος ἐχώρει πολὺς ἐκ Σικελίας ὡς Διονύσιος θαυμαστῶς φιλοσοφίας ἐν ἐπιθυμίᾳ πάλιν εἴη γεγονὼς τὰ νῦν, ὅθεν ὁ Δίων συντεταμένως ἐδεῖτο ἡμῶν τῇ μεταπέμψει μὴ ἀπειθεῖν.

ἐγὼ δὲ ᾔδη μέν που [338c] κατὰ τὴν φιλοσοφίαν τοῖς νέοις πολλὰ τοιαῦτα γιγνόμενα, ὅμως δ᾽ οὖν ἀσφαλέστερόν μοι ἔδοξε χαίρειν τότε γε πολλὰ καὶ Δίωνα καὶ Διονύσιον ἐᾶν, καὶ ἀπηχθόμην ἀμφοῖν ἀποκρινάμενος ὅτι γέρων τε εἴην καὶ κατὰ τὰς ὁμολογίας οὐδὲν γίγνοιτο τῶν τὰ νῦν πραττομένων.

ἔοικε δὴ τὸ μετὰ τοῦτο Ἀρχύτης τε παρὰ Διονύσιον ἀφικέσθαι—, ἐγὼ γὰρ πρὶν ἀπιέναι ξενίαν καὶ φιλίαν Ἀρχύτῃ καὶ τοῖς ἐν [338d] Τάραντι καὶ Διονυσίῳ ποιήσας ἀπέπλεον—, ἄλλοι τέ τινες ἐν Συρακούσαις ἦσαν Δίωνός τε ἄττα διακηκοότες καὶ τούτων τινὲς ἄλλοι, παρακουσμάτων τινῶν ἔμμεστοι τῶν κατὰ φιλοσοφίαν· οἳ δοκοῦσί μοι Διονυσίῳ πειρᾶσθαι διαλέγεσθαι πῶς περὶ τὰ τοιαῦτα, ὡς Διονυσίου πάντα διακηκοότος ὅσα διενοούμην ἐγώ.

The Seventh Letter

This advice and message, along with the earlier one about my first arrival at Dionysius's court, should suffice. But after this, anyone who is so inclined can hear about my later journey across the sea, and how fitting and reasonable it was. As I said, I have told the whole story of the first part [**338a**] of my sojourn in Sicily, the period before I advised Dion's friends and companions. After that I attempted to persuade Dionysius, by whatever means possible, to let me go. Since there was a war in Sicily at the time, we both agreed that Dionysius would call me and Dion back when there was peace and when he had made things more secure for himself in his kingdom, and he asked Dion [**338b**] to conceive of his situation not so much as an exile, but rather as a relocation. I agreed that I would come under these terms, and when peace had come, Dionysius summoned me, but he asked Dion to wait for another year, even though he insisted that I come anyway. Dion, for his part, urged and implored me to set sail, for reports kept arriving from Sicily that Dionysius had once again become tremendously infatuated with philosophy. Dion therefore eagerly begged me not to reject Dionysius's summons.

For my part, I knew that [**338c**] philosophy has often had such an effect on young men, but all the same I thought it safer by far to forget about both Dion and Dionysius, and I irritated both of them when I responded that I was old and that the current situation did not meet the standards of the agreement at all.

It appears that after this, Archytas arrived at Dionysius's court – before sailing away I had managed to forge a bond of friendship and hospitality between Archytas and the people of [**338d**] Tarentum and Dionysius – and that there were some others in Syracuse who had studied some under Dion, and still others who had studied under these and who were thus quite full of misconceptions about philosophy; I believe that they were trying to have discussions with Dionysius on such topics, as if Dionysius had thoroughly absorbed all my thinking.

ὁ δὲ οὔτε ἄλλως ἐστὶν ἀφυὴς πρὸς τὴν τοῦ μανθάνειν δύναμιν φιλότιμός τε θαυμαστῶς· ἤρεσκέ τε οὖν ἴσως αὐτῷ τὰ λεγόμενα ἠσχύνετό τε φανερὸς γιγνόμενος [338e] οὐδὲν ἀκηκοὼς ὅτ' ἐπεδήμουν ἐγώ, ὅθεν ἅμα μὲν εἰς ἐπιθυμίαν ᾔει τοῦ διακοῦσαι ἐναργέστερον, ἅμα δ' ἡ φιλοτιμία κατήπειγεν αὐτόν· δι' ἃ δὲ οὐκ ἤκουσεν ἐν τῇ πρόσθεν ἐπιδημίᾳ, διεξήλθομεν ἐν τοῖς ἄνω ῥηθεῖσι νυν δὴ λόγοις. ἐπειδὴ οὖν οἴκαδέ τ' ἐσώθην καὶ καλοῦντος τὸ δεύτερον ἀπηρνήθην, καθάπερ εἶπον νυν δή, δοκεῖ μοι Διονύσιος παντάπασι φιλοτιμηθῆναι μή ποτέ τισι δόξαιμι καταφρονῶν [339a] αὐτοῦ τῆς φύσεώς τε καὶ ἕξεως ἅμα καὶ τῆς διαίτης ἔμπειρος γεγονώς, οὐκέτ' ἐθέλειν δυσχεραίνων παρ' αὐτὸν ἀφικνεῖσθαι.

δίκαιος δὴ λέγειν εἰμὶ τἀληθὲς καὶ ὑπομένειν, εἴ τις ἄρα τὰ γεγονότα ἀκούσας καταφρονήσει τῆς ἐμῆς φιλοσοφίας, τὸν τύραννον δὲ ἡγήσεται νοῦν ἔχειν. ἔπεμψε μὲν γὰρ δὴ Διονύσιος τρίτον ἐπ' ἐμὲ τριήρη ῥᾳστώνης ἕνεκα τῆς πορείας, ἔπεμψε δὲ Ἀρχέδημον, ὃν ἡγεῖτό με τῶν ἐν [339b] Σικελίᾳ περὶ πλείστου ποιεῖσθαι, τῶν Ἀρχύτῃ ξυγγεγονότων ἕνα, καὶ ἄλλους γνωρίμους τῶν ἐν Σικελίᾳ· οὗτοι δὲ ἡμῖν ἤγγελλον πάντες τὸν αὐτὸν λόγον, ὡς θαυμαστὸν ὅσον Διονύσιος ἐπιδεδωκὼς εἴη πρὸς φιλοσοφίαν.

ἔπεμψε δὲ ἐπιστολὴν πάνυ μακράν, εἰδὼς ὡς πρὸς Δίωνα διεκείμην καὶ τὴν αὖ Δίωνος προθυμίαν τοῦ ἐμὲ πλεῖν καὶ εἰς Συρακούσας ἐλθεῖν· πρὸς γὰρ δὴ πάντα ταῦτα ἦν παρεσκευασμένη τὴν ἀρχὴν ἔχουσα ἡ ἐπιστολή, τῇδέ πη φράζουσαν· "Διονύσιος [339c] Πλάτωνι"· τὰ νόμιμα ἐπὶ τούτοις εἰπὼν οὐδὲν τὸ μετὰ τοῦτο εἶπε πρότερον ἢ ὡς "ἂν εἰς Σικελίαν πεισθεὶς ὑφ' ἡμῶν ἔλθῃς τὰ νῦν, πρῶτον μέν σοι τὰ περὶ Δίωνα ὑπάρξει ταύτῃ γιγνόμενα ὅπῃπερ ἂν αὐτὸς ἐθέλῃς· θελήσεις δὲ οἶδ' ὅτι τὰ μέτρια, καὶ ἐγὼ συγχωρήσομαι· εἰ δὲ μή, οὐδέν σοι τῶν περὶ Δίωνα ἕξει πραγμάτων οὔτε περὶ τἆλλα οὔτε περὶ αὐτὸν κατὰ νοῦν γιγνόμενα." ταῦθ' οὕτως εἶπε, τἆλλα δὲ [339d] μακρὰ ἂν εἴη καὶ ἄνευ καιροῦ λεγόμενα.

The Seventh Letter

Now, Dionysius is by no means bereft of a natural faculty for learning, and he is tremendously ambitious. As such, he was perhaps pleased by these discussions, and also ashamed when it became obvious [**338e**] that he had not studied at all during my visit. As a result, he came around to a desire to study more attentively, while at the same time his ambition pushed him to do so as well. (I have already explained, in my account above, why he had not paid attention during my earlier visit.) So when I had reached the safety of my home and rejected his second invitation – which I also explained above – it seems Dionysius became obsessed with making sure that no one believe that, once I had gotten to know his lifestyle, [**339a**] I regarded his natural abilities and his habits with disdain, and that in my disgust I was no longer willing to come to him.

It is only fair that I tell the truth and to be patient if anyone who has just heard these accounts should look down on my philosophy and believe instead that it was the tyrant who was sensible. In any case, this third time Dionysius sent for me with a trireme, so as to make the voyage easy, and he also sent Archedemus, one of Archytas's pupils, whom he thought I regarded most highly of everyone in [**339b**] Sicily, along with some other acquaintances of mine from there. All these men brought to me the same report, namely that Dionysius had progressed quite impressively with regards to philosophy.

He also sent a very long letter, knowing how I felt about Dion and about Dion's own desire for me to make the voyage and come to Syracuse. To be sure, his letter was prepared with an eye to all these things, having as it did a preface that went something like this: "Dionysius [**339c**] to Plato" – after which he said all the customary things but nothing else before – "if you should now be persuaded to come to me in Sicily, first and foremost Dion's situation will be arranged in whatever manner you wish, for I know that your wishes will be reasonable, and that I will agree to them. Otherwise, however, none of Dion's affairs will work out in the way that you want, neither as regards the person himself nor anything else you might have in mind." So he said, and the rest [**339d**] is too long and pointless to repeat.

ἐπιστολαὶ δὲ ἄλλαι ἐφοίτων παρά τε Ἀρχύτου καὶ τῶν ἐν Τάραντι, τήν τε φιλοσοφίαν ἐγκωμιάζουσαι τὴν Διονυσίου καὶ ὅτι, ἂν μὴ ἀφίκωμαι νῦν, τὴν πρὸς Διονύσιον αὐτοῖς γενομένην φιλίαν δι' ἐμοῦ οὐ σμικρὰν οὖσαν πρὸς τὰ πολιτικὰ παντάπασι διαβαλοίην. ταύτης δὴ τοιαύτης γενομένης ἐν τῷ τότε χρόνῳ τῆς μεταπέμψεως, τῶν μὲν ἐκ Σικελίας τε καὶ Ἰταλίας ἑλκόντων, τῶν δὲ Ἀθήνηθεν ἀτεχνῶς μετὰ δεήσεως οἷον [339e] ἐξωθούντων με, καὶ πάλιν ὁ λόγος ἧκεν ὁ αὐτός, τὸ μὴ δεῖν προδοῦναι Δίωνα μηδὲ τοὺς ἐν Τάραντι ξένους τε καὶ ἑταίρους· αὐτῷ δέ μοι ὑπῆν ὡς οὐδὲν θαυμαστὸν νέον ἄνθρωπον παρακούοντα ἀξίων λόγου πραγμάτων, εὐμαθῆ, πρὸς ἔρωτα ἐλθεῖν τοῦ βελτίστου βίου· δεῖν οὖν αὐτὸ ἐξελέγξαι σαφῶς, ὁποτέρως ποτὲ ἄρα σχοίη, καὶ τοῦτ' αὐτὸ μηδαμῇ προδοῦναι μηδ' ἐμὲ τὸν αἴτιον γενέσθαι τηλικούτου ἀληθῶς ὀνείδους, [340a] εἴπερ ὄντως εἴη τῳ ταῦτα λελεγμένα.

πορεύομαι δὴ τῷ λογισμῷ τούτῳ κατακαλυψάμενος, πολλὰ δεδιὼς μαντευόμενός τε οὐ πάνυ καλῶς, ὡς ἔοικεν. ἐλθὼν δ' οὖν τὸ τρίτον τῷ σωτῆρι τοῦτό γε οὖν ἔπραξα ὄντως· ἐσώθην γάρ τοι πάλιν εὐτυχῶς, καὶ τούτων γε μετὰ θεὸν Διονυσίῳ χάριν εἰδέναι χρεών, ὅτι πολλῶν βουληθέντων ἀπολέσαι με διεκώλυσε καὶ ἔδωκέ τι μέρος αἰδοῖ τῶν περὶ ἐμὲ πραγμάτων.

[340b] ἐπειδὴ δὲ ἀφικόμην, ᾤμην τούτου πρῶτον ἔλεγχον δεῖν λαβεῖν, πότερον ὄντως εἴη Διονύσιος ἐξημμένος ὑπὸ φιλοσοφίας ὥσπερ πυρός, ἢ μάτην ὁ πολὺς οὗτος ἔλθοι λόγος Ἀθήναζε. ἔστι δή τις τρόπος τοῦ περὶ τὰ τοιαῦτα πεῖραν λαμβάνειν οὐκ ἀγεννὴς ἀλλ' ὄντως τυράννοις πρέπων, ἄλλως τε καὶ τοῖς τῶν παρακουσμάτων μεστοῖς, ὃ δὴ κἀγὼ Διονύσιον εὐθὺς ἐλθὼν ᾐσθόμην καὶ μάλα πεπονθότα.

Other letters also poured in, both from Archytas and others in Tarentum, extolling Dionysius's love of wisdom and saying that, if I didn't come now, I would scuttle their friendship with Dionysius, which I had arranged and which was no trivial thing when it came to political matters. Such were the summons that I received at that time, and with the Sicilians and Italians drawing me in, and with the Athenians basically driving me out with their harassment, [339e] so to speak, the same consideration kept coming back to me: that I shouldn't betray Dion or my friends and companions in Tarentum. It also occurred to me that it did not defy belief that a sharp young man might hear snatches of discussions of lofty subjects and become enamored of the best sort of life, and that it was thus necessary to definitively investigate how these things stood, and to neither betray this ideal nor to be responsible for something truly disgraceful, [340a] if in fact things really were as they said.

After casting this veil of reasoning over myself I set out, although I was quite fearful and had a sensation that was not altogether good, as was appropriate. In any case, in coming I truly experienced this "third one for the savior," for I was fortunate to get back safely, and for this I must, after god, acknowledge a debt of gratitude to Dionysius, for although there were many who wished to destroy me, he prevented this from happening and granted some measure of respect to our dealings.

[340b] When I arrived, I thought I should first of all conduct an evaluation as to whether or not philosophy had truly lit a fire under Dionysius, or whether that great trail of reports that had come to Athens was false. Now, there is a certain way of trying to conduct such an evaluation that is not sordid, but in fact quite suitable for tyrants, particularly for ones that are full of misconceptions, which, when I arrived, I immediately perceived was the case with Dionysius.

δεικνύναι δὴ δεῖ τοῖς τοιούτοις ὅ τι ἔστι πᾶν τὸ πρᾶγμα οἷόν τε **[340c]** καὶ δι' ὅσων πραγμάτων καὶ ὅσον πόνον ἔχει. ὁ γὰρ ἀκούσας, ἐὰν μὲν ὄντως ᾖ φιλόσοφος οἰκεῖός τε καὶ ἄξιος τοῦ πράγματος θεῖος ὤν, ὁδόν τε ἡγεῖται θαυμαστὴν ἀκηκοέναι ξυντατέον τε εἶναι νῦν καὶ οὐ βιωτὸν ἄλλως ποιοῦντι· μετὰ τοῦτο δὴ ξυντείνας αὑτόν τε καὶ τὸν ἡγούμενον τὴν ὁδὸν οὐκ ἀνίησι πρὶν ἂν ἢ τέλος ἐπιθῇ πᾶσι ἢ λάβῃ δύναμιν ὥστε αὐτὸς αὑτὸν χωρὶς τοῦ δείξαντος μὴ ἀδύνατος εἶναι ποδηγεῖν.

[340d] ταύτῃ καὶ κατὰ ταῦτα διανοηθεὶς ὁ τοιοῦτος ζῇ, πράττων μὲν ἐν αἷς τισιν ἂν ᾖ πράξεσι, παρὰ πάντα δὲ ἀεὶ φιλοσοφίας ἐχόμενος καὶ τροφῆς τῆς καθ' ἡμέραν, ἥτις ἂν αὐτὸν μάλιστα εὐμαθῆ τε καὶ μνήμονα καὶ λογίζεσθαι δυνατὸν ἐν αὑτῷ νήφοντα ἀπεργάζηται· τὴν δὲ ἐναντίαν ταύτῃ μισῶν διατελεῖ. οἱ δὲ ὄντως μὲν μὴ φιλόσοφοι, δόξαις δ' ἐπικεχρωσμένοι, καθάπερ οἱ τὰ σώματα ὑπὸ τοῦ ἡλίου ἐπικεκαυμένοι, ἰδόντες τε ὅσα μαθήματά ἐστι καὶ ὁ πόνος **[340e]** ἡλίκος καὶ δίαιτα ἡ καθ' ἡμέραν ὡς πρέπουσα ἡ κοσμία τῷ πράγματι, χαλεπὸν ἡγησάμενοι καὶ ἀδύνατον αὑτοῖς, οὔτε δὴ **[341a]** ἐπιτηδεύειν δυνατοὶ γίγνονται· ἔνιοι δὲ αὐτῶν πείθουσιν αὑτοὺς ὡς ἱκανῶς ἀκηκοότες εἰσὶ τὸ ὅλον καὶ οὐδὲν ἔτι δέονταί τινων πραγμάτων. ἡ μὲν δὴ πεῖρα αὕτη γίγνεται ἡ σαφής τε καὶ ἀσφαλεστάτη πρὸς τοὺς τρυφῶντάς τε καὶ ἀδυνάτους διαπονεῖν, ὡς μηδέποτε βαλεῖν ἐν αἰτίᾳ τὸν δεικνύντα ἀλλ' αὐτὸν αὑτόν, μὴ δυνάμενον πάντα τὰ πρόσφορα ἐπιτηδεύειν τῷ πράγματι.

Basically, it is necessary to show such individuals what the entire matter consists of [**340c**] and how substantial it is, how much work it involves, and how many things it entails. For if the person is truly a lover of philosophy and is suited to and worthy of the endeavor and is inspired by the gods, then upon hearing all this he will believe the path spoken of is a marvelous one, that he must direct all his energy towards it, and that to do otherwise would not be a worthwhile existence. And in fact, after this he applies all of his own energy and that of his guide, and he does not let up until he either fulfills his purpose, or until he acquires enough power that he is able to find his way without his guide.

[**340d**] Such a person lives in this way and according to these principles in whatever business he happens to be engaged, always clinging first and foremost to philosophy and to a daily regimen that makes him sharpest, most mindful, and most able to reason with himself in a sober manner, and he consistently despises the opposite way of life. On the other hand, those who are not true lovers of philosophy, but who are merely colored by certain notions like those who have been burned by the sun – when they see how much there is to learn, what sort of work [**340e**] there is to do, and that the daily lifestyle that suits the endeavor is a moderate one, they consider the task difficult, even [**341a**] impossible for themselves. And in the end, they are not able to pursue it, and some of them convince themselves that they have learned enough about the whole thing and need know nothing more about certain matters. The experiment itself thus becomes a clear and most reliable evaluation of people who are pampered and unable to work hard, since they can never cast blame upon their guide, rather than upon themselves personally, when they are not able to fully apply themselves to the matter.

οὕτω δὴ καὶ Διονυσίῳ τότ' ἐρρήθη τὰ ῥηθέντα. πάντα μὲν οὖν οὔτ' ἐγὼ διεξῆλθον οὔτε [341b] Διονύσιος ἐδεῖτο· πολλὰ γὰρ αὐτὸς καὶ τὰ μέγιστα εἰδέναι τε καὶ ἱκανῶς ἔχειν προσεποιεῖτο διὰ τὰς ὑπὸ τῶν ἄλλων παρακοάς. ὕστερον δὲ καὶ ἀκούω γεγραφέναι αὐτὸν περὶ ὧν τότε ἤκουσε, συνθέντα ὡς αὑτοῦ τέχνην, οὐδὲν τῶν αὐτῶν ὧν ἀκούοι· οἶδα δὲ οὐδὲν τούτων· ἄλλους μέν τινας οἶδα γεγραφότας περὶ τῶν αὐτῶν τούτων· οἵτινες δέ, οὐδ' αὐτοὶ αὑτούς. τοσόνδε γε μὴν περὶ πάντων ἔχω φράζειν τῶν γεγραφότων [341c] καὶ γραψόντων, ὅσοι φασὶν εἰδέναι περὶ ὧν ἐγὼ σπουδάζω, εἴτ' ἐμοῦ ἀκηκοότες εἴτ' ἄλλων εἴθ' ὡς εὑρόντες αὐτοί· τούτους οὐκ ἔστι κατά γε τὴν ἐμὴν δόξαν περὶ τοῦ πράγματος ἐπαΐειν οὐδέν. οὔκουν ἐμόν γε περὶ αὐτῶν ἔστι σύγγραμμα οὐδὲ μήποτε γένηται· ῥητὸν γὰρ οὐδαμῶς ἐστιν ὡς ἄλλα μαθήματα, ἀλλ' ἐκ πολλῆς συνουσίας γιγνομένης περὶ τὸ πρᾶγμα αὐτὸ καὶ τοῦ συζῆν ἐξαίφνης, οἷον ἀπὸ πυρὸς [341d] πηδήσαντος ἐξαφθὲν φῶς, ἐν τῇ ψυχῇ γενόμενον αὐτὸ ἑαυτὸ ἤδη τρέφει.

καίτοι τοσόνδε γε οἶδα, ὅτι γραφέντα ἢ λεχθέντα ὑπ' ἐμοῦ βέλτιστ' ἂν λεχθείη· καὶ μὴν ὅτι γεγραμμένα κακῶς οὐχ ἥκιστ' ἂν ἐμὲ λυποῖ. εἰ δέ μοι ἐφαίνετο γραπτέα θ' ἱκανῶς εἶναι πρὸς τοὺς πολλοὺς καὶ ῥητά, τί τούτου κάλλιον ἐπέπρακτ' ἂν ἡμῖν ἐν τῷ βίῳ ἢ τοῖς τε ἀνθρώποισι μέγα ὄφελος γράψαι καὶ τὴν φύσιν εἰς φῶς [341e] πᾶσι προαγαγεῖν; ἀλλ' οὔτε ἀνθρώποις ἡγοῦμαι τὴν ἐπιχείρησιν περὶ αὐτῶν γενομένην ἀγαθόν, εἰ μή τισιν ὀλίγοις, ὁπόσοι δυνατοὶ ἀνευρεῖν αὐτοὶ διὰ σμικρᾶς ἐνδείξεως· τῶν τε δὴ ἄλλων τοὺς μὲν καταφρονήσεως οὐκ ὀρθῆς ἐμπλήσειεν ἂν οὐδαμῇ ἐμμελῶς, τοὺς δὲ ὑψηλῆς καὶ χαύνης ἐλπίδος, ὡς [342a] σέμν' ἄττα μεμαθηκότας.

This is what I said then to Dionysius. Granted, I did not go over everything thoroughly, nor did [**341b**] Dionysius inquire. For he purported to know many of the most important things himself and to be fully competent based on what he had overheard from others. Later I heard that he had written about what he learned then, framing them as if they were a product of his own creation and not at all of things he had heard. But I know nothing of this. I do know that some others have written about these same questions, though even they do not know who they are. At any rate, this is what I can say about all those who have written and [**341c**] will write on the subject, and all those who claim to know about what I work on, whether they have heard about it from me, or from others, or whether they have figured it out on their own: it is not possible, in my opinion at least, for these men to have any knowledge of the matter. There is certainly no treatise of mine on it, nor will there ever be. For unlike other sciences, this one can in no way be communicated by means of words. On the contrary, it is only through a prolonged communion with the subject, by living with it, that, like a light that is kindled [**341d**] by a flickering flame, it begins to suddenly nourish itself within one's soul.

And I know this much as well: if it is to be written or related at all, it would be best related by me, and if it was written poorly, it would cause me no small amount of pain. Moreover, if it seemed to me that these things could be adequately written and expressed to the masses, what finer thing could I do in life than to set down in writing something that would be a great boon for humanity and to illuminate [**341e**] for everyone the nature of things? But I do not believe that the attempt to do so would be good for people, except for a certain few who are able to work it out for themselves with just a little bit of guidance. As for the rest, such writings would fill some with an improper and altogether unsuitable disdain, and others with the high but empty hope that [**342a**] they had learned something truly important.

ἔτι δὲ μακρότερα περὶ αὐτῶν ἐν νῷ μοι γέγονεν εἰπεῖν· τάχα γὰρ ἂν περὶ ὧν λέγω σαφέστερον ἂν εἴη τι λεχθέντων αὐτῶν. ἔστι γάρ τις λόγος ἀληθὴς ἐναντίος τῷ τολμήσαντι γράφειν τῶν τοιούτων καὶ ὁτιοῦν, πολλάκις μὲν ὑπ' ἐμοῦ καὶ πρόσθεν ῥηθείς, ἔοικε δ' οὖν εἶναι καὶ νῦν λεκτέος. ἔστι τῶν ὄντων ἑκάστῳ, δι' ὧν τὴν ἐπιστήμην ἀνάγκη παραγίγνεσθαι, τρία· τέταρτον δ' αὐτή· πέμπτον δ' αὐτὸ [342b] τιθέναι δεῖ ὃ δὴ γνωστόν τε καὶ ἀληθές ἐστιν· ὧν ἓν μὲν ὄνομα, δεύτερον δὲ λόγος, τὸ δὲ τρίτον εἴδωλον, τέταρτον δὲ ἐπιστήμη.

περὶ ἓν οὖν λαβὲ βουλόμενος μαθεῖν τὸ νῦν λεγόμενον, καὶ πάντων οὕτω πέρι νόησον. κύκλος ἐστί τι λεγόμενον, ᾧ τοῦτ' αὐτό ἐστιν ὄνομα ὃ νῦν ἐφθέγμεθα. λόγος δ' αὐτοῦ τὸ δεύτερον, ἐξ ὀνομάτων καὶ ῥημάτων συγκείμενος· τὸ γὰρ ἐκ τῶν ἐσχάτων ἐπὶ τὸ μέσον ἴσον ἀπέχον πάντῃ, λόγος ἂν εἴη ἐκείνου ᾧπερ στρογγύλον καὶ περιφερὲς [342c] ὄνομα καὶ κύκλος. τρίτον δὲ τὸ ζωγραφούμενόν τε καὶ ἐξαλειφόμενον καὶ τορνευόμενον καὶ ἀπολλύμενον· ὧν αὐτὸς ὁ κύκλος, ὃν πέρι πάντ' ἐστὶ ταῦτα, οὐδὲν πάσχει τούτων ὡς ἕτερον ὄν.

τέταρτον δὲ ἐπιστήμη καὶ νοῦς ἀληθής τε δόξα περὶ ταῦτ' ἐστίν· ὡς δὲ ἓν τοῦτο αὖ πᾶν θετέον, οὐκ ἐν φωναῖς οὐδ' ἐν σωμάτων σχήμασιν ἀλλ' ἐν ψυχαῖς ἐνόν, ᾧ δῆλον ἕτερόν τε ὂν αὐτοῦ τοῦ κύκλου τῆς φύσεως τῶν [342d] τε ἔμπροσθεν λεχθέντων τριῶν. τούτων δὲ ἐγγύτατα μὲν ξυγγενείᾳ καὶ ὁμοιότητι τοῦ πέμπτου νοῦς πεπλησίακε, τἆλλα δὲ πλέον ἀπέχει.

The Seventh Letter

Nevertheless, I have it in mind to say a little more about this, for in speaking, what I am talking about will soon become clearer. There is a certain argument that is true and that stands in opposition to the man who writes anything at all about such things, something I have often spoken of before and which, it appears, I must now repeat: everything that exists has three elements through which one must approach the knowledge of that thing; the fourth element is knowledge itself, and the fifth, [**342b**] one must posit, is that which is in fact knowable and true. The first of these is "name," the second is "definition," the third is "image," and the fourth is knowledge.

If you wish to understand what I am saying, take a single example and reflect on everything else in the same way. There is something called a circle, the name of which is the same thing I have just pronounced. Its definition is the second thing, and it is composed of nouns and verbs: "that which is completely equal from every extremity to the middle" would be the definition of that thing that is called "round," "spherical," [**342c**] and "circle." The third element (the image) may be painted and expunged, lathed and destroyed, but the circle itself, which all these things represent, undergoes none of these changes, since it is something other than these things.

The fourth element is knowledge and understanding and a true conception of these things. And since we must establish that these are all a single thing – something that resides not in sounds or shapes of bodies but within souls – it is clear that it differs both from the nature of the circle itself and from [**342d**] the three elements mentioned above. And of these, understanding comes closest to the fifth in likeness and affinity, while all the others remain quite far off.

ταὐτὸν δὴ περί τε εὐθέος ἅμα καὶ περιφεροῦς σχήματος καὶ χρόας, περί τε ἀγαθοῦ καὶ καλοῦ καὶ δικαίου, καὶ περὶ σώματος ἅπαντος σκευαστοῦ τε καὶ κατὰ φύσιν γεγονότος, πυρὸς ὕδατός τε καὶ τῶν τοιούτων πάντων, καὶ ζώου ξύμπαντος πέρι καὶ ἐν ψυχαῖς ἤθους [καὶ] περὶ ποιήματα καὶ παθήματα ξύμπαντα· οὐ γὰρ ἂν τούτων **[342e]** μή τις τὰ τέτταρα λάβῃ ἁμῶς γέ πως, οὔποτε τελέως ἐπιστήμης τοῦ πέμπτου μέτοχος ἔσται. πρὸς γὰρ τούτοις ταῦτα οὐχ ἧττον ἐπιχειρεῖ τὸ ποῖόν τι περὶ ἕκαστον δηλοῦν **[343a]** ἢ τὸ ὂν ἑκάστου διὰ τὸ τῶν λόγων ἀσθενές· ὧν ἕνεκα νοῦν ἔχων οὐδεὶς τολμήσει ποτὲ εἰς αὐτὸ τιθέναι τὰ νενοημένα, καὶ ταῦτα εἰς ἀμετακίνητον, ὃ δὴ πάσχει τὰ γεγραμμένα τύποις.

τοῦτο δὲ πάλιν αὖ τὸ νῦν λεγόμενον δεῖ μαθεῖν. κύκλος ἕκαστος τῶν ἐν ταῖς πράξεσι γραφομένων ἢ καὶ τορνευθέντων μεστὸς τοῦ ἐναντίου ἐστὶ τῷ πέμπτῳ· τοῦ γὰρ εὐθέος ἐφάπτεται πάντῃ. αὐτὸς δέ, φαμέν, ὁ κύκλος οὔτε τι σμικρότερον οὔτε μεῖζον τῆς ἐναντίας ἔχει ἐν αὑτῷ φύσεως. ὄνομά τε αὐτῶν φαμεν οὐδὲν οὐδενὶ **[343b]** βέβαιον εἶναι, κωλύειν δ' οὐδὲν τὰ νῦν στρογγύλα καλούμενα εὐθέα κεκλῆσθαι τά τε εὐθέα δὴ στρογγύλα, καὶ οὐδὲν ἧττον βεβαίως ἕξειν τοῖς μεταθεμένοις καὶ ἐναντίως καλοῦσι.

καὶ μὴν περὶ λόγου γε ὁ αὐτὸς λόγος, εἴπερ ἐξ ὀνομάτων καὶ ῥημάτων σύγκειται, μηδὲν ἱκανῶς βεβαίως εἶναι βέβαιον. μυρίος δὲ λόγος αὖ περὶ ἑκάστου τῶν τεττάρων, ὡς ἀσαφές· τὸ δὲ μέγιστον, ὅπερ εἴπομεν ὀλίγον ἔμπροσθεν, ὅτι δυοῖν ὄντοιν, τοῦ τε ὄντος καὶ τοῦ ποιοῦ τινός, οὐ τὸ **[343c]** ποιόν τι, τὸ δὲ τί ζητούσης εἰδέναι τῆς ψυχῆς, τὸ μὴ ζητούμενον ἕκαστον τῶν τεττάρων προτεῖνον τῇ ψυχῇ λόγῳ τε καὶ κατ' ἔργα, αἰσθήσεσιν εὐέλεγκτον τό τε λεγόμενον καὶ δεικνύμενον ἀεὶ παρεχόμενον ἕκαστον, ἀπορίας τε καὶ ἀσαφείας ἐμπίπλησι πάσης ὡς ἔπος εἰπεῖν πάντ' ἄνδρα.

The Seventh Letter

To be sure, the same thing holds true for a straight line and a rounded shape and a color, and for the good and beautiful and just, and for an entire body whether it be artificially or naturally formed – fire and water and all such things – and for every living thing, and the dispositions within souls towards everything one creates or endures. For unless [342e] one can somehow grasp the first four of these, one will never fully partake in the knowledge of the fifth. In addition, because of the deficiency of language, these elements [343a] attempt to signify as much the quality of each thing as its essence. As a result, no one with any sense will ever dare to capture this understanding in words, especially in an inalterable form, which is what written characters endure.

Once again, we must go back so you understand what I am saying. Each circle that is in actuality drawn or even lathed is full of that which is opposed to the fifth, since it possesses straightness at every angle. But the circle itself, as I say, has no part either small or large of its opposite nature within itself. And the names of these things, I assert, have nothing that is [343b] constant unto themselves, and there is nothing to prevent that which is now called "round" from being called "straight" and the "straight" "round," and those things that are changed and called by their opposites will be no less constant.

The same reasoning certainly applies to the "definition," for if it is composed of nouns and verbs, then nothing constant can ever be sufficiently constant. An infinite discussion may be held about the uncertainty of each of the four things, but the most important thing, the one we mentioned a short time ago, is that although there exists an essence and a quality, when the soul is seeking to know something [343c] it searches for its essence, not its quality. And each of the four elements offers the soul, by means of discourse and according to facts, that which is not sought; everything presents itself in a form that is easy to show and to express and to refute with one's senses, and it fills just about every man with a sense of confusion and uncertainty.

ἐν οἷσι μὲν οὖν μηδ' εἰθισμένοι τὸ ἀληθὲς ζητεῖν ἐσμὲν ὑπὸ πονηρᾶς τροφῆς, ἐξαρκεῖ δὲ τὸ προταθὲν τῶν εἰδώλων, οὐ καταγέλαστοι γιγνόμεθα ὑπ' ἀλλήλων, οἱ ἐρωτώμενοι ὑπὸ [**343d**] τῶν ἐρωτώντων, δυναμένων δὲ τὰ τέτταρα διαρρίπτειν τε καὶ ἐλέγχειν· ἐν οἷς δ' ἂν τὸ πέμπτον ἀποκρίνασθαι καὶ δηλοῦν ἀναγκάζωμεν, ὁ βουλόμενος τῶν δυναμένων ἀνατρέπειν κρατεῖ, καὶ ποιεῖ τὸν ἐξηγούμενον ἐν λόγοις ἢ γράμμασιν ἢ ἀποκρίσεσι τοῖς πολλοῖς τῶν ἀκουόντων δοκεῖν μηδὲν γιγνώσκειν ὧν ἂν ἐπιχειρῇ γράφειν ἢ λέγειν, ἀγνοούντων ἐνίοτε ὡς οὐχ ἡ ψυχὴ τοῦ γράψαντος ἢ λέξαντος ἐλέγχεται, ἀλλ' ἡ τῶν τεττάρων φύσις ἑκάστου, πεφυκυῖα [**343e**] φαύλως. ἡ δὲ διὰ πάντων αὐτῶν διαγωγή, ἄνω καὶ κάτω μεταβαίνουσα ἐφ' ἕκαστον, μόγις ἐπιστήμην ἐνέτεκεν εὖ πεφυκότος εὖ πεφυκότι· κακῶς δὲ ἂν φυῇ, ὡς ἡ τῶν πολλῶν ἕξις τῆς ψυχῆς εἴς τε τὸ μαθεῖν εἴς τε τὰ λεγόμενα ἤθη [**344a**] πέφυκε, τὰ δὲ διέφθαρται, οὐδ' ἂν ὁ Λυγκεὺς ἰδεῖν ποιήσειε τοὺς τοιούτους.

ἑνὶ δὲ λόγῳ, τὸν μὴ ξυγγενῆ τοῦ πράγματος οὔτ' ἂν εὐμαθία ‹μαθεῖν› ποιήσειέ ποτε οὔτε μνήμη· τὴν ἀρχὴν γὰρ ἐν ἀλλοτρίαις ἕξεσιν οὐκ ἐγγίγνεται· ὥστε ὁπόσοι τῶν δικαίων τε καὶ τῶν ἄλλων ὅσα καλὰ μὴ προσφυεῖς εἰσι καὶ ξυγγενεῖς, ἄλλοι δὲ ἄλλων εὐμαθεῖς ἅμα καὶ μνήμονες, οὐδ' ὅσοι ξυγγενεῖς, δυσμαθεῖς δὲ καὶ ἀμνήμονες, οὐδένες τούτων μήποτε μάθωσιν ἀλήθειαν ἀρετῆς εἰς [**344b**] τὸ δυνατὸν οὐδὲ κακίας. ἅμα γὰρ αὐτὰ ἀνάγκη μανθάνειν καὶ τὸ ψεῦδος ἅμα καὶ ἀληθὲς τῆς ὅλης οὐσίας, μετὰ τριβῆς πάσης καὶ χρόνου πολλοῦ, ὅπερ ἐν ἀρχαῖς εἶπον·

The Seventh Letter

Given this state of affairs, and thanks to our miserable upbringing, we are unaccustomed to seeking the truth, and at the same time we are satisfied by the images placed before us, nor do we make each other seem ridiculous by asking [343d] and answering questions, even though we are capable of seeing through and refuting the four things. And if we force someone to distinguish and explain the fifth, whoever is willing and able to upend the argument wins, and he makes the one who is offering a full interpretation through speech, writing, or actual answers appear, to most of his audience, to know nothing of the things about which he is trying to write or speak, since the audience is sometimes unaware that it is not the soul of the writer or speaker that is being refuted, but rather the nature of each of the four things, which is inherently [343e] flawed. Nevertheless, the thorough examination of all these problems, going up and down and over each one with great effort, imparts knowledge of a good thing unto a person of a good nature. If one's nature is bad, however, as is the condition of most souls with respect both to learning and to what are called 'morals,' [344a] all these things wither and die, and not even Lynceus would be able to make such men see.

In a word, neither memory nor a sharp mind can make anything of a person who has no affinity for the matter, for a seed cannot germinate in hostile terrain. Hence all those who have no natural connection or affinity with the ways of justice and all other beautiful things, and other individuals who are at once well-versed in and cognizant of other issues, nor indeed those who do share an affinity but whose minds and memories are not sharp – none of these will ever learn the truth of virtue [344b] or of depravity to the full extent possible. For it is necessary to study these things together, along with what is true and untrue of all existence, dedicating to these questions ample time and all one's energy, as I said at the beginning.

μόγις δὲ τριβόμενα πρὸς ἄλληλα αὐτῶν ἕκαστα, ὀνόματα καὶ λόγοι ὄψεις τε καὶ αἰσθήσεις, ἐν εὐμενέσιν ἐλέγχοις ἐλεγχόμενα καὶ ἄνευ φθόνων ἐρωτήσεσι καὶ ἀποκρίσεσι χρωμένων, ἐξέλαμψε φρόνησις περὶ ἕκαστον καὶ νοῦς, συντείνοντι ὅ τι [344c] μάλιστ' εἰς δύναμιν ἀνθρωπίνην. διὸ δὴ πᾶς ἀνὴρ σπουδαῖος τῶν ὄντως σπουδαίων πέρι πολλοῦ δεῖ μὴ γράψας ποτὲ ἐν ἀνθρώποις εἰς φθόνον καὶ ἀπορίαν καταβαλῇ.

ἑνὶ δὴ ἐκ τούτων δεῖ γιγνώσκειν λόγῳ, ὅταν ἴδῃ τίς του συγγράμματα γεγραμμένα εἴτε ἐν νόμοις νομοθέτου εἴτε ἐν ἄλλοις τισὶν ἅττ' οὖν, ὡς οὐκ ἦν τούτῳ ταῦτα σπουδαιότατα, εἴπερ ἔστ' αὐτὸς σπουδαῖος, κεῖται δέ που ἐν χώρᾳ τῇ καλλίστῃ τῶν τούτου· εἰ δὲ ὄντως αὐτῷ ταῦτ' ἐσπουδασμένα ἐν γράμμασιν [344d] ἐτέθη, "ἐξ ἄρα δή τοι ἔπειτα," θεοὶ μὲν οὔ, βροτοὶ δὲ "φρένας ὤλεσαν αὐτοί."[8]

τούτῳ δὴ τῷ μύθῳ τε καὶ πλάνῳ ὁ ξυνεπισπόμενος εὖ εἴσεται, εἴτ' οὖν Διονύσιος ἔγραψέ τι τῶν περὶ φύσεως ἄκρων καὶ πρώτων εἴτε τις ἐλάττων εἴτε μείζων, ὡς οὐδὲν ἀκηκοὼς οὐδὲ μεμαθηκὼς ἦν ὑγιὲς ὧν ἔγραψε κατὰ τὸν ἐμὸν λόγον· ὁμοίως γὰρ ἂν αὐτὰ ἐσέβετο ἐμοί, καὶ οὐκ ἂν αὐτὰ ἐτόλμησεν εἰς ἀναρμοστίαν καὶ ἀπρέπειαν ἐκβάλλειν. οὔτε γὰρ ὑπομνημάτων χάριν αὐτὰ ἔγραψεν· οὐδὲν γὰρ [344e] δεινὸν μή τις αὐτὸ ἐπιλάθηται, ἐὰν ἅπαξ τῇ ψυχῇ περιλάβῃ, πάντων γὰρ ἐν βραχυτάτοις κεῖται· φιλοτιμίας δὲ αἰσχρᾶς, εἴπερ, ἕνεκα, εἴθ' ὡς αὑτοῦ τιθέμενος εἴθ' ὡς παιδείας δὴ μέτοχος ὤν, ἧς οὐκ ἄξιος ἦν ἀγαπῶν δόξαν τὴν [345a] τῆς μετοχῆς γενομένης.

---

[8] From Hom. *Il.* 7.360, 12.234.

The Seventh Letter

And when all of these things – names, definitions, appearances, and perceptions – have been painstakingly elaborated in relation to each other and examined through thoughtful argumentation by people who ask questions and provide answers without malice, only then is it that the light of knowledge and understanding of each element shines forth unto a person who has applied himself **[344c]** as much as humanly possible. As a result, any man who is serious about truly serious subjects must absolutely avoid writing about them and making them sources of envy and embarrassment for humanity.

To summarize briefly, then, whenever we look at a written composition, whether it be the laws of a lawmaker or anything else whatsoever, we must recognize that the author's most serious ideas do not reside within this text, even if the author himself is serious, but that those ideas remain lodged in the most beautiful part of his soul. And if his most seriously elaborated ideas have in fact been set down **[344d]** in writing, then "it is most certainly" not the gods but mortal men "who have destroyed his mind."

Whoever has followed me on this meandering narrative will understand that, following this logic, whether it was Dionysius himself who wrote something about the first and loftiest aspects of nature, or whether it was a lesser or greater man, this person has neither learned nor understood properly anything that he has written. For he would have respected these ideas just as I do, and he would not have dared to banish them to a state of disharmony and disrepute. Nor did he write them down in order to remember them better, for no one **[344e]** can forget something so powerful once he has grasped it with his entire soul, since it is set down in the most compact of formulations. On the contrary, this person wrote out of shameful ambition, whether he attributed the work to himself or to his affiliation with a school, and by delighting in the reputation that came with this affiliation, he proved himself **[345a]** to be unworthy of it.

Εἰ μὲν οὖν ἐκ τῆς μιᾶς συνουσίας Διονυσίῳ τοῦτο γέγονε, τάχ' ἂν εἴη· γέγονε δ' οὖν ὅπως, "ἴττω Ζεύς," φησὶν ὁ Θηβαῖος· διεξῆλθον μὲν γὰρ ὡς εἶπόν τότε ἐγὼ καὶ ἅπαξ μόνον, ὕστερον δὲ οὐ πώποτε ἔτι. ἐννοεῖν δὴ δεῖ τὸ μετὰ τοῦτο, ὅτῳ μέλει τὸ περὶ αὐτὰ γεγονὸς εὑρεῖν, ὅπῃ ποτὲ γέγονε, τίνι πότ' αἰτίᾳ τὸ δεύτερον καὶ τὸ τρίτον πλεονάκις τε οὐ διεξῇμεν· πότερον Διονύσιος ἀκούσας μόνον [345b] ἅπαξ οὕτως εἰδέναι τε οἴεται καὶ ἱκανῶς οἶδεν, εἴτε αὐτὸς εὑρὼν ἢ καὶ μαθὼν ἔμπροσθεν παρ' ἑτέρων, ἢ φαῦλα εἶναι τὰ λεχθέντα, ἢ τὸ τρίτον οὐ καθ' αὑτόν, μείζονα δέ, καὶ ὄντως οὐκ ἂν δυνατὸς εἶναι φρονήσεώς τε καὶ ἀρετῆς ζῆν ἐπιμελούμενος.

εἰ μὲν γὰρ φαῦλα, πολλοῖς μάρτυσι μαχεῖται τὰ ἐναντία λέγουσιν, οἳ περὶ τῶν τοιούτων πάμπολυ Διονυσίου κυριώτεροι ἂν εἶεν κριταί. εἰ δὲ εὑρηκέναι ἢ μεμαθηκέναι, ἄξια δ' οὖν εἶναι πρὸς παιδείαν ψυχῆς ἐλευθέραν, [345c] πῶς ἂν μὴ θαυμαστὸς ὢν ἄνθρωπος τὸν ἡγεμόνα τούτων καὶ κύριον οὕτως εὐχερῶς ἠτίμασέ ποτ' ἄν;

πῶς δ' ἠτίμασεν ἐγὼ φράζοιμ' ἄν. οὐ πολὺν χρόνον διαλιπὼν τὸ μετὰ τοῦτο, ἐν τῷ πρόσθεν Δίωνα ἐῶν τὰ ἑαυτοῦ κεκτῆσθαι καὶ καρποῦσθαι χρήματα, τότε οὐκέτ' εἴα τοὺς ἐπιτρόπους αὐτοῦ πέμπειν εἰς Πελοπόννησον, καθάπερ ἐπιλελησμένος τῆς ἐπιστολῆς παντάπασιν· εἶναι γὰρ αὐτὰ οὐ Δίωνος ἀλλὰ τοῦ υἱέος, ὄντος μὲν ἀδελφιδοῦ [345d] αὐτοῦ κατὰ νόμους ἐπιτροπεύοντος. τὰ μὲν δὴ πεπραγμένα μέχρι τούτου ταῦτ' ἦν ἐν τῷ τότε χρόνῳ, τούτων δὲ οὕτω γενομένων ἑωράκειν τε ἐγὼ ἀκριβῶς τὴν ἐπιθυμίαν τὴν Διονυσίου φιλοσοφίας, ἀγανακτεῖν τε ἐξῆν εἴτε βουλοίμην εἴτε μή. ἦν γὰρ θέρος ἤδη τότε καὶ ἔκπλοι τῶν νεῶν.

Certainly, if Dionysius had acquired this through a single interaction, such as it may be, then how he acquired it "only Zeus knows," as a Theban would say. As I said, only once did I go over these things with him, and never again after that. Moreover, whoever cares to discover the origins and development of these issues must understand what came afterwards, and why I did not go over these things a second or third time with him, or even more. I do not know whether Dionysius believes that after hearing [**345b**] everything a single time he understood it all sufficiently, or whether he figured it out for himself or learned it beforehand from others, or whether perhaps he believes that the things I said were worthless, or conversely that they are not meant for him, that they were beyond him and that he would never really be able to lead a life directed at wisdom and virtue.

Now, if he thinks they are worthless, then he is lining up against a great number of individuals who attest the opposite, people who would be far better judges of such things than Dionysius. Conversely, if he says that he discovered or learned these things beforehand (and by extension that they are a worthwhile part of the education of a free soul), [**345c**] how then, unless he is a truly astonishing person, could he have so callously mistreated the leading authority on these questions?

As for how he mistreated me, I will now explain. Not much time had passed before Dionysius, who had previously allowed Dion to hold onto his possessions and use the income from his estates, forbade his trustees from sending anything to the Peloponnese. It was as if he had completely forgotten about his earlier letter, for he claimed that those things belonged not to Dion but to his son, Dionysius's nephew, [**345d**] who according to statute was his ward. This is how far things had progressed at this point in time, and given this state of affairs, I was able to see quite clearly the 'desire' that Dionysius had for philosophy. Whether I wanted to be or not, I was justifiably vexed, for it was already summer at that point and ships were leaving port.

ἐδόκει δὴ χαλεπαίνειν μὲν οὐ δεῖν ἐμὲ Διονυσίῳ μᾶλλον ἢ ἐμαυτῷ τε καὶ τοῖς βιασαμένοις ἐλθεῖν ἐμὲ τὸ [345e] τρίτον εἰς τὸν πορθμὸν τὸν περὶ τὴν Σκύλλαν, "ὄφρ' ἔτι τὴν ὀλοὴν ἀναμετρήσαιμι Χάρυβδιν,"[9] λέγειν δὲ πρὸς Διονύσιον ὅτι μοι μένειν ἀδύνατον εἴη Δίωνος οὕτω προπεπηλακισμένου. ὁ δὲ παρεμυθεῖτό τε καὶ ἐδεῖτο μένειν, οὐκ οἰόμενός οἱ καλῶς ἔχειν ἐμὲ ἄγγελον αὐτὸν τῶν τοιούτων ἐλθεῖν ὅ τι τάχος· οὐ πείθων δὲ αὐτός μοι πομπὴν [346a] παρασκευάσειν ἔφη.

ἐγὼ γὰρ ἐν τοῖς ἀποστόλοις πλοίοις ἐμβὰς διενοούμην πλεῖν, τεθυμωμένος πάσχειν τε οἰόμενος δεῖν, εἰ διακωλυοίμην, ὁτιοῦν, ἐπειδὴ περιφανῶς ἠδίκουν μὲν οὐδέν, ἠδικούμην δέ. ὁ δὲ οὐδέν με τοῦ καταμένειν προσιέμενον ὁρῶν μηχανὴν τοῦ μεῖναι τὸν τότε ἔκπλουν μηχανᾶται τοιάνδε τινά.

τῇ μετὰ ταῦτα ἐλθὼν ἡμέρᾳ λέγει πρός με πιθανὸν λόγον· "ἐμοὶ καὶ σοὶ Δίων," ἔφη, "καὶ τὰ Δίωνος [346b] ἐκποδὼν ἀπαλλαχθήτω τοῦ περὶ αὐτὰ πολλάκις διαφέρεσθαι· ποιήσω γὰρ διὰ σέ," ἔφη, "Δίωνι τάδε. ἀξιῶ ἐκεῖνον ἀπολαβόντα τὰ ἑαυτοῦ οἰκεῖν μὲν ἐν Πελοποννήσῳ, μὴ ὡς φυγάδα δέ, ἀλλ' ὡς αὐτῷ καὶ δεῦρο ἐξὸν ἀποδημεῖν, ὅταν ἐκείνῳ τε καὶ ἐμοὶ καὶ ὑμῖν τοῖς φίλοις κοινῇ ξυνδοκῇ· ταῦτα δ' εἶναι μὴ ἐπιβουλεύοντος ἐμοί· τούτων δὲ ἐγγυητὰς γίγνεσθαι σέ τε καὶ τοὺς σοὺς οἰκείους καὶ τοὺς ἐνθάδε Δίωνος, ὑμῖν δὲ τὸ βέβαιον ἐκεῖνος παρεχέτω. τὰ χρήματα δὲ ἃ ἂν λάβῃ, [346c] κατὰ Πελοπόννησον μὲν καὶ Ἀθήνας κείσθω παρ' οἷς τισιν ἂν ὑμῖν δοκῇ, καρπούσθω δὲ Δίων, μὴ κύριος δὲ ἄνευ ὑμῶν γιγνέσθω ἀνελέσθαι. ἐγὼ γὰρ ἐκείνῳ μὲν οὐ σφόδρα πιστεύω τούτοις χρώμενον ἂν τοῖς χρήμασι δίκαιον γίγνεσθαι περὶ ἐμέ· οὐ γὰρ ὀλίγα ἔσται· σοὶ δὲ καὶ τοῖς σοῖς μᾶλλον πεπίστευκα. ὅρα δὴ ταῦτα εἴ σοι ἀρέσκει, καὶ μένε ἐπὶ τούτοις τὸν ἐνιαυτὸν τοῦτον, εἰς δὲ ὥρας ἄπιθι [346d] λαβὼν τὰ χρήματα ταῦτα· καὶ Δίων εὖ οἶδ' ὅτι πολλὴν χάριν ἕξει σοι διαπραξαμένῳ ταῦτα ὑπὲρ ἐκείνου."

---

[9] Hom. *Od.* 12.428.

The Seventh Letter

Still, it seemed to me that I should be no angrier with Dionysius than with myself and with those who had coerced me into coming [**345e**] for the third time to the strait of Scylla, "to cross over again the dread Charybdis," and that I should tell Dionysius that it was impossible for me to remain now that Dion's reputation had been tarred in this way. He, however, tried to reassure me, and he begged me to stay, thinking that it would not be good for him to have me hurrying to deliver such news myself; and when he did not convince me he said that he would provide [**346a**] transportation for me himself.

In fact, my intention was to board a dispatch vessel for the journey. I was furious and believed I needed to do whatever it took should I be impeded, since I was quite obviously doing nothing wrong but was instead being wronged myself. Dionysius, however, when he saw that I was not moved to remain, devised a plot to get me to stay through the sailing season, which went something like this.

He came to me on the following day and presented me with a specious argument: "Dion and his affairs," he said, "must be eliminated [**346b**] as a regular source of tension between the two of us. So on your behalf," he said, "I will do the following for Dion. I expect him to take his belongings and go live in the Peloponnese, not as an exile but under the pretense that he can travel here any time that he and I and you, his friends, approve of it together. But this depends on him not plotting against me, and on you and your companions and Dion's relations here guaranteeing that pledge, while he should give you his assurance. Whatever possessions he takes [**346c**] shall remain in the Peloponnese and in Athens in the hands of whomever you think fit, and Dion can use the income from these, but he shall not be able to take charge of them without you. For I do not particularly trust him to be fair to me if he has full access to his funds – and these will not be paltry – while I do trust you and your companions. Think about it and see if these terms satisfy you, remain under them for this year, and come spring [**346d**] take his money and leave. I am certain that Dion will be most grateful to you for taking care of these things on his behalf."

τοῦτον δὴ ἐγὼ τὸν λόγον ἀκούσας ἐδυσχέραινον μέν, ὅμως δὲ βουλευσάμενος ἔφην εἰς τὴν ὑστεραίαν αὐτῷ περὶ τούτων τὰ δόξαντα ἀπαγγελεῖν. ταῦτα ξυνεθέμεθα τότε. ἐβουλευόμην δὴ τὸ μετὰ ταῦτα κατ' ἐμαυτὸν γενόμενος, μάλα συγκεχυμένος· πρῶτος δ' ἦν μοι τῆς βουλῆς ἡγούμενος ὅδε [346e] λόγος· "φέρε, εἰ διανοεῖται τούτων μηδὲν ποιεῖν Διονύσιος ὧν φησίν, ἀπελθόντος δ' ἐμοῦ ἐὰν ἐπιστέλλη Δίωνι πιθανῶς αὐτός τε καὶ ἄλλοις πολλοῖς τῶν αὑτοῦ διακελευόμενος, ἃ νῦν πρὸς ἐμὲ λέγει, ὡς αὐτοῦ μὲν ἐθέλοντος, ἐμοῦ δὲ οὐκ ἐθελήσαντος ἃ προὔκαλεῖτό με δρᾶν, ἀλλ' ὀλιγωρήσαντος τῶν ἐκείνου τὸ παράπαν πραγμάτων, πρὸς δὲ καὶ τούτοισιν ἔτι μηδ' ἐθέλη με ἐκπέμπειν αὐτὸς τῶν ναυκλήρων [347a] μηδενὶ προστάττων, ἐνδείξηται δὲ πᾶσι ῥᾳδίως ὡς ἀβουλῶν ἐμὲ ἐκπλεῖν, ἆρά τις ἐθελήσει με ἄγειν ναύτην ὁρμώμενον ἐκ τῆς Διονυσίου οἰκίας;"(ᾤκουν γὰρ δὴ πρὸς τοῖς ἄλλοισι κακοῖς ἐν τῷ κήπῳ τῷ περὶ τὴν οἰκίαν, ὅθεν οὐδ' ἂν ὁ θυρωρὸς ἤθελέ με ἀφεῖναι μὴ πεμφθείσης αὐτῷ τινος ἐντολῆς παρὰ Διονυσίου.) "ἂν δὲ περιμείνω τὸν ἐνιαυτόν, ἕξω μὲν Δίωνι ταῦτα ἐπιστέλλειν, ἐν οἷς τ' αὐτ' εἰμὶ καὶ ἃ πράττω. καὶ ἐὰν μὲν δὴ ποιῇ τι Διονύσιος ὧν φησιν, οὐ [347b] παντάπασιν ἔσται μοι καταγελάστως πεπραγμένα· τάλαντα γὰρ ἴσως ἐστὶν οὐκ ἔλαττον, ἂν ἐκτιμᾷ τις ὀρθῶς, ἑκατὸν ἡ Δίωνος οὐσία· ἂν δ' οὖν γίγνηται τὰ νῦν ὑποφαίνοντα, οἷα εἰκὸς αὐτὰ γίγνεσθαι, ἀπορῶ μὲν ὅ τι χρήσομαι ἐμαυτῷ, ὅμως δὲ ἀναγκαῖον ἴσως ἐνιαυτόν γ' ἔτι πονῆσαι καὶ ἔργοις ἐλέγξαι πειρᾶσθαι τὰς Διονυσίου μηχανάς."

ταῦτά μοι δόξαντα εἰς τὴν ὑστεραίαν εἶπον πρὸς Διονύσιον ὅτι "δέδοκταί [347c] μοι μένειν. ἀξιῶ μήν," ἔφην, "μὴ κύριον ἡγεῖσθαί σε Δίωνος ἐμέ, πέμπειν δὲ μετ' ἐμοῦ σὲ παρ' αὐτὸν γράμματα τὰ νῦν δεδογμένα δηλοῦντα, καὶ ἐρωτᾶν εἴτε ἀρκεῖ ταῦτα αὐτῷ, καὶ εἰ μή, βούλεται δὲ ἄλλ' ἄττα καὶ ἀξιοῖ, καὶ ταῦτα ἐπιστέλλειν ὅ τι τάχιστα, σὲ δὲ νεωτερίζειν μηδέν πω τῶν περὶ ἐκεῖνον." ταῦτ' ἐρρήθη, ταῦτα ξυνωμολογήσαμεν, ὡς νῦν εἴρηται σχεδόν.

The Seventh Letter

When I heard these words I was in fact quite annoyed, but all the same I said that I would consider the matter until the next day and then tell him what I thought. That was how we left it then. Afterwards of course, when I was considering the matter on my own, I was deeply troubled. The first line of thought that came to me was [346e] the following: "come on, if Dionysius has no intention of doing what he says, and if I leave and he himself sends specious reports to Dion (and directs many others here to do so as well) about the things he just said to me, and how he was willing while I was unwilling to do what he was urging me to do, and that instead I totally neglected his interests, and if on top of all this he no longer wishes to allow me to leave and does not send the order [347a] to any of the captains, well, he will easily demonstrate to everyone that he does not wish for me to set sail, and then will anyone want to bring me on as a passenger when I set out from Dionysius's house?" (Indeed, on top of all my other problems I was staying in the orchard next to his residence, from which not even the door keeper would have been inclined to let me leave without some order sent to him by Dionysius.) "On the other hand, if I remain for the year I will be able to send a message to Dion about the situation in which I find myself and how I'm doing. And if Dionysius does any of the things he's promising, my [347b] actions will not end up being entirely ridiculous, as Dion's property is probably worth no less than a hundred talents, if it's estimated properly. Conversely, if it turns out that these faint signs are exactly what they seem, well, I don't know what I'll do with myself, but all the same it is perhaps necessary to suffer for a year longer and try to expose Dionysius's plot."

These were my thoughts, and on the next day I said to Dionysius, "I have decided [347c] to stay. But of course I insist," I said, "that you not think of me as Dion's guardian, but that you and I send him a letter in which we specify the terms we have just agreed upon, and that you ask him whether these satisfy him. If they don't, and he desires or insists upon something else, he should let us know as soon as possible, but you must at no point come up with any new sanctions against him." This is what I said, and this is what we agreed upon, just about exactly as I have stated it.

ἐξέπλευσε δὴ τὰ πλοῖα μετὰ τοῦτο, καὶ οὐκέτι μοι δυνατὸν ἦν πλεῖν, ὅτε δή μοι καὶ [347d] Διονύσιος ἐμνήσθη λέγων ὅτι τὴν ἡμίσειαν τῆς οὐσίας εἶναι δέοι Δίωνος, τὴν δ' ἡμίσειαν τοῦ υἱέος· ἔφη δὴ πωλήσειν αὐτήν, πραθείσης δὲ τὰ μὲν ἡμίσεα ἐμοὶ δώσειν ἄγειν, τὰ δ' ἡμίσεα τῷ παιδὶ καταλείψειν αὐτοῦ· τὸ γὰρ δὴ δικαιότατον οὕτως ἔχειν. πληγεὶς δ' ἐγὼ τῷ λεχθέντι πάνυ μὲν ᾤμην γελοῖον εἶναι ἀντιλέγειν ἔτι, ὅμως δ' εἶπον ὅτι χρείη τὴν παρὰ Δίωνος ἐπιστολὴν περιμένειν ἡμᾶς καὶ ταῦτα πάλιν αὐτὰ ἐπιστέλλειν. ὁ δὲ ἑξῆς τούτοις πάνυ νεανικῶς [347e] ἐπώλει τὴν οὐσίαν αὐτοῦ πᾶσαν, ὅπῃ τε καὶ ὅπως ἤθελε καὶ οἷσ τισί, πρὸς ἐμὲ δὲ οὐδὲν ὅλως ἐφθέγγετο περὶ αὐτῶν, καὶ μὴν ὡσαύτως ἐγὼ πρὸς ἐκεῖνον αὖ περὶ τῶν Δίωνος πραγμάτων οὐδὲν ἔτι διελεγόμην· οὐδὲν γὰρ ἔτι πλέον ᾤμην ποιεῖν.

μέχρι μὲν δὴ τούτων ταύτῃ μοι βεβοηθημένον ἐγεγόνει φιλοσοφίᾳ καὶ φίλοις· τὸ δὲ μετὰ ταῦτα ἐζῶμεν ἐγὼ καὶ [348a] Διονύσιος, ἐγὼ μὲν βλέπων ἔξω, καθάπερ ὄρνις ποθῶν ποθὲν ἀναπτέσθαι, ὁ δὲ διαμηχανώμενος τίνα τρόπον ἀνασοβήσοι με μηδὲν ἀποδοὺς τῶν Δίωνος. ὅμως δὲ ἐφάνημεν ἑταῖροί γε εἶναι πρὸς πᾶσαν Σικελίαν.

τῶν δὴ μισθοφόρων τοὺς πρεσβυτέρους Διονύσιος ἐπεχείρησεν ὀλιγομισθοτέρους ποιεῖν παρὰ τὰ τοῦ πατρὸς ἔθη, θυμωθέντες δὲ οἱ στρατιῶται ξυνελέγησαν ἀθρόοι καὶ οὐκ ἔφασαν ἐπιτρέψειν. ὁ δ' ἐπεχείρει [348b] βιάζεσθαι κλείσας τὰς τῆς ἀκροπόλεως πύλας, οἱ δ' ἐφέροντο εὐθὺς πρὸς τὰ τείχη, παιῶνά τινα ἀναβοήσαντες βάρβαρον καὶ πολεμικόν· οὗ δὴ περιδεὴς Διονύσιος γενόμενος ἅπαντα συνεχώρησε καὶ ἔτι πλείω τοῖς τότε συλλεχθεῖσι τῶν πελταστῶν.

The Seventh Letter

After this the ships set sail and it was no longer possible for me to depart. Only then did Dionysius [**347d**] remember to mention to me that Dion was entitled to only half his estate, and his son the other half. Moreover, he said that he was going to sell the estate, and that when this was done he would give me one half to bring to Dion and leave the other half here for his son, on the grounds that it would be fairest this way. I was shocked by what he said, and though I thought it would be totally ridiculous for me to keep arguing, I said we ought to wait for a letter from Dion and then write back to him with these updates. Right after this, however, Dionysius went ahead [**347e**] and sold Dion's entire estate most brazenly, wherever, however, and to whomever he wished, and he said absolutely nothing about all this to me. Likewise, I certainly did not bring up Dion's affairs with him anymore, for I thought there was nothing more I could do.

Up till now I had been providing assistance to philosophy and to my friends in this manner. Afterwards, however, we lived, Dionysius [**348a**] and I, with myself gazing outwards like a bird longing to take flight, and with him scheming up some way to scare me off without returning anything of Dion's. Nevertheless, to all of Sicily we appeared to be friends.

At this point, and in contrast to his father's practice, Dionysius attempted to reduce the wages of his more seasoned mercenaries. The soldiers became angry and convened en masse and said that they would not back down. Dionysius then tried [**348b**] to break them by closing the gates to the acropolis, after which they immediately came up to the city walls and burst into some sort of warlike, barbarian paean. Dionysius then grew very afraid and conceded to all the demands, and then some, of the peltasts that had convened.

λόγος δή τις ταχὺ διῆλθεν ὡς Ἡρακλείδης αἴτιος εἴη γεγονὼς πάντων τούτων. ὃν ἀκούσας ὁ μὲν Ἡρακλείδης ἐκποδὼν αὐτὸν ἔσχεν ἀφανῆ, Διονύσιος [348c] δὲ ἐζήτει λαβεῖν. ἀπορῶν δέ, Θεοδότην μεταπεμψάμενος εἰς τὸν κῆπον· ἔτυχον δ' ἐν τῷ κήπῳ καὶ ἐγὼ τότε περιπατῶν· τὰ μὲν οὖν ἄλλα οὔτ' οἶδα οὔτ' ἤκουον διαλεγομένων, ἃ δὲ ἐναντίον εἶπε Θεοδότης ἐμοῦ πρὸς Διονύσιον, οἶδά τε καὶ μέμνημαι. "Πλάτων γάρ," ἔφη, "Διονύσιον ἐγὼ πείθω τουτονί, ἐὰν ἐγὼ γένωμαι δεῦρο Ἡρακλείδην κομίσαι δυνατὸς ἡμῖν εἰς λόγους περὶ τῶν ἐγκλημάτων αὐτῷ τῶν νῦν γεγονότων, ἂν ἄρα μὴ δόξῃ δεῖν αὐτὸν οἰκεῖν ἐν Σικελίᾳ, τόν τε υἱὸν λαβόντα καὶ τὴν γυναῖκα ἀξιῶ εἰς [348d] Πελοπόννησον ἀποπλεῖν, οἰκεῖν τε βλάπτοντα μηδὲν Διονύσιον ἐκεῖ, καρπούμενον δὲ τὰ ἑαυτοῦ. μετεπεμψάμην μὲν οὖν καὶ πρότερον αὐτόν, μεταπέμψομαι δὲ καὶ νῦν, ἄν τ' οὖν ἀπὸ τῆς προτέρας μεταπομπῆς ἄν τε καὶ ἀπὸ τῆς νῦν ὑπακούσῃ μοι. Διονύσιον δὲ ἀξιῶ καὶ δέομαι, ἄν τις ἐντυγχάνῃ Ἡρακλείδῃ ἐάν τ' ἐν ἀγρῷ ἐάν τ' ἐνθάδε, μηδὲν ἄλλο [348e] αὐτῷ φλαῦρον γίγνεσθαι, μεταστῆναι δ' ἐκ τῆς χώρας, ἕως ἂν ἄλλο τι Διονυσίῳ δόξῃ. "ταῦτα," ἔφη, "συγχωρεῖς;" λέγων πρὸς τὸν Διονύσιον. "συγχωρῶ· μηδ' ἂν πρὸς τῇ σῇ," ἔφη, "φανῇ οἰκίᾳ, πείσεσθαι φλαῦρον μηδὲν παρὰ τὰ νῦν εἰρημένα."

τῇ δὴ μετὰ ταύτην τὴν ἡμέραν δείλης Εὐρύβιος καὶ Θεοδότης προσηλθέτην μοι σπουδῇ τεθορυβημένω θαυμαστῶς, καὶ ὁ Θεοδότης λέγει, "Πλάτων," ἔφη, "παρῆσθα χθὲς οἷς περὶ Ἡρακλείδου Διονύσιος ὡμολόγει πρὸς ἐμὲ καὶ σέ;" "πῶς δὲ οὔκ;" ἔφην. "νῦν τοίνυν," ἦ δ' ὅς, "περιθέουσι πελτασταὶ λαβεῖν Ἡρακλείδην ζητοῦντες, ὁ δὲ εἶναί πῃ ταύτῃ κινδυνεύει. ἀλλ' ἡμῖν," ἔφη, [349a] "συνακολούθησον πρὸς Διονύσιον ἁπάσῃ μηχανῇ." ᾠχόμεθα οὖν καὶ εἰσήλθομεν παρ' αὐτόν, καὶ τὼ μὲν ἐστάτην σιγῇ δακρύοντε, ἐγὼ δὲ εἶπον "οἵδε πεφόβηνται μή τι σὺ παρὰ τὰ χθὲς ὡμολογημένα ποιήσῃς περὶ Ἡρακλείδην νεώτερον· δοκεῖ γάρ μοι ταύτῃ πῃ γεγονέναι φανερὸς ἀποτετραμμένος."

The Seventh Letter

Word then spread quite quickly that Heracleides was responsible for all this. Heracleides heard this and made himself scarce, and Dionysius [**348c**] set about trying to catch him, and when he was unable to do so, he summoned Theodotes to the orchard. I happened to be walking around the orchard at that moment, and while I did not listen to the whole conversation and do not know everything else that was said, I remember well what Theodotes said to Dionysius in front of me: "Plato," he said, "I am trying to nudge Dionysius towards this course of action: if I am able to bring Heracleides back here to discuss the accusations that have been made against him, and if it is resolved that he should not reside in Sicily, then I think that he should take his wife and son and [**348d**] sail away to the Peloponnese and live there without causing Dionysius any harm, while reaping the benefits of his assets. I summoned him earlier and I will summon him again now, and perhaps he will accept one invitation or the other. But I ask and insist that Dionysius see to it that, if anyone should stumble upon Heracleides, either here or in the countryside, he will face [**348e**] no further consequence beyond being banished from the country, until Dionysius should decide otherwise. "Do you agree to this?" he asked Dionysius. "I agree," he said, "that even if he is spotted at your house he shall not meet with any consequences aside from those you have just mentioned."

The following afternoon Eurybius and Theodotes both came to me with the utmost urgency, tremendously worked up, and Theodotes began speaking: "Plato," he asked, "were you there yesterday for the agreements that Dionysius made with you and me about Heracleides?" "Of course," I said. "Well now," said Theodotes, "peltasts are running around trying to catch Heracleides, and I'm afraid he might be somewhere around here! [**349a**] You absolutely must come with us to Dionysius!" We set out and came upon him, and while those other two stood by shedding tears in silence, I said: "these men are afraid that somehow, contrary to the agreement that we made yesterday, you are devising a new punishment for Heracleides. For it seems that he has been spotted returning to these parts."

ὁ δὲ ἀκούσας ἀνεφλέχθη τε καὶ παντοδαπὰ χρώματα ἧκεν, οἷα ἂν θυμούμενος ἀφείη· προσπεσὼν δ' αὐτῷ [349b] ὁ Θεοδότης, λαβόμενος τῆς χειρὸς ἐδάκρυσέ τε καὶ ἱκέτευε μηδὲν τοιοῦτον ποιεῖν. ὑπολαβὼν δ' ἐγὼ παραμυθούμενος, "θάρρει, Θεοδότα," ἔφην· "οὐ γὰρ τολμήσει Διονύσιος παρὰ τὰ χθὲς ὡμολογημένα ἄλλα ποτὲ δρᾶν." καὶ ὃς ἐμβλέψας μοι καὶ μάλα τυραννικῶς, "σοί," ἔφη, "ἐγὼ οὔ τέ τι σμικρὸν οὔτε μέγα ὡμολόγησα." "νὴ τοὺς θεούς," ἦν δ' ἐγώ, "σύ γε ταῦτα ἃ σοῦ νῦν οὗτος δεῖται μὴ ποιεῖν." καὶ εἰπὼν ταῦτα ἀποστρεφόμενος ᾠχόμην ἔξω.

τὸ μετὰ [349c] ταῦτα ὁ μὲν ἐκυνήγει τὸν Ἡρακλείδην, Θεοδότης δὲ ἀγγέλους πέμπων Ἡρακλείδῃ φεύγειν διεκελεύετο. ὁ δὲ ἐκπέμψας Τισίαν καὶ πελταστὰς διώκειν ἐκέλευε· φθάνει δέ, ὡς ἐλέγετο, Ἡρακλείδης εἰς τὴν Καρχηδονίων ἐπικράτειαν ἐκφυγὼν ἡμέρας σμικρῷ τινι μέρει. τὸ δὴ μετὰ τοῦτο ἡ πάλαι ἐπιβουλὴ Διονυσίῳ τοῦ μὴ ἀποδοῦναι τὰ Δίωνος χρήματα ἔδοξεν ἔχθρας λόγον ἔχειν ἂν πρός με πιθανόν, καὶ πρῶτον μὲν ἐκ τῆς ἀκροπόλεως ἐκπέμπει με, εὑρὼν [349d] πρόφασιν ὡς τὰς γυναῖκας ἐν τῷ κήπῳ ἐν ᾧ κατῴκουν ἐγὼ δέοι θῦσαι θυσίαν τινὰ δεχήμερον· ἔξω δή με παρ' Ἀρχεδήμῳ προσέταττε τὸν χρόνον τοῦτον μεῖναι.

ὄντος δ' ἐμοῦ ἐκεῖ Θεοδότης μεταπεμψάμενός με πολλὰ περὶ τῶν τότε πραχθέντων ἠγανάκτει καὶ ἐμέμφετο Διονυσίῳ· ὁ δ' ἀκούσας ὅτι παρὰ Θεοδότην εἴην εἰσεληλυθώς, πρόφασιν [349e] αὖ ταύτην ἄλλην τῆς πρὸς ἐμὲ διαφορᾶς ποιούμενος, ἀδελφὴν τῆς πρόσθεν, πέμψας τινὰ ἠρώτα με εἰ ξυγγενοίμην ὄντως μεταπεμψαμένου με Θεοδότου. κἀγὼ "παντάπασιν" ἔφην· ὁ δέ, "ἐκέλευε τοίνυν," ἔφη, "σοὶ φράζειν ὅτι καλῶς οὐδαμῇ ποιεῖς Δίωνα καὶ τοὺς Δίωνος φίλους ἀεὶ περὶ πλείονος αὐτοῦ ποιούμενος." ταῦτ' ἐρρήθη, καὶ οὐκέτι μετεπέμψατό με εἰς τὴν οἴκησιν πάλιν, ὡς ἤδη σαφῶς Θεοδότου μὲν ὄντος μου καὶ Ἡρακλείδου φίλου, αὐτοῦ δ' ἐχθροῦ, καὶ οὐκ εὐνοεῖν ᾤετό με, ὅτι Δίωνι τὰ χρήματα ἔρρει παντελῶς.

The Seventh Letter

When Dionysius heard this his temper flared and his face turned all sorts of colors, as happens when one gets angry. Theodotes then [349b] fell before him, took his hand, and began to weep and beg him to do nothing of the sort, but I drew him away and tried to reassure him: "don't worry, Theodotes," I said, "Dionysius would never dare to do anything contrary to the agreement we made yesterday." Then Dionysius, looking at me most tyrannically, said: "with you I never made any agreement either small or large." "By the gods you did," I said, "namely not to do precisely what this man is begging you not to!" And having said this, I turned around and left.

After [349c] this, Dionysius continued to try and hunt down Heracleides, while Theodotes was sending messengers to him urging him to flee. Dionysius then sent out Tisias and his peltasts with orders to pursue Heracleides, but Heracleides, as the story goes, escaped and beat them to the Carthaginians' territory by just a few hours. After this, Dionysius's old plot not to return any of Dion's property seems to have provided him plausible grounds for a feud with me, and at first he sent me away from the acropolis, proffering [349d] as an excuse that the women in the orchard in which I was living needed to perform some sort of ten-day-long sacrifice; so he ordered me to stay with Archedemus during this time. While I was there, Theodotes sent for me and made it clear that he was greatly displeased about what had happened and that he blamed Dionysius. And when Dionysius heard that I had gone to Theodotes, he made of this [349e] yet another pretext for a dispute with me, one related to the previous one, and he sent someone to ask me if I had really gone to meet Theodotes when he had sent for me. "Certainly," I said, to which the other responded: "well then, he ordered me to tell you that you are behaving quite badly by always holding Dion and Dion's friends in higher regard than him." This was the conversation, and he never invited me back to his residence again, since it was by now clear that I was a friend of Theodotes and Heracleides, and an enemy to him, and he believed that I was not pleased that Dion's assets had been definitively liquidated.

[350a] ᾤκουν δὴ τὸ μετὰ τοῦτο ἔξω τῆς ἀκροπόλεως ἐν τοῖς μισθοφόροις· προσιόντες δέ μοι ἄλλοι τε καὶ οἱ τῶν ὑπηρεσιῶν ὄντες Ἀθήνηθεν, ἐμοὶ πολῖται, ἀπήγγελλον ὅτι διαβεβλημένος εἴην ἐν τοῖς πελτασταῖς καί μοί τινες ἀπειλοῖεν, εἴ που λήψονταί με, διαφθερεῖν. μηχανῶμαι δή τινα τοιάνδε σωτηρίαν· πέμπω παρ' Ἀρχύτην καὶ τοὺς ἄλλους φίλους εἰς Τάραντα, φράζων ἐν οἷς ὢν τυγχάνω· οἱ δὲ πρόφασίν τινα πρεσβείας πορισάμενοι παρὰ τῆς πόλεως πέμπουσι [350b] τριακόντορόν τε καὶ Λαμίσκον αὐτῶν ἕνα, ὃς ἐλθὼν ἐδεῖτο Διονυσίου περὶ ἐμοῦ, λέγων ὅτι βουλοίμην ἀπιέναι, καὶ μηδαμῶς ἄλλως ποιεῖν. ὁ δὲ ξυνωμολόγησε καὶ ἀπέπεμψεν ἐφόδια δούς· τῶν Δίωνος δὲ χρημάτων οὔτ' ἐγώ τι ἀπῄτουν οὔτε τις ἀπέδωκεν.

ἐλθὼν δὲ εἰς Πελοπόννησον εἰς Ὀλυμπίαν, Δίωνα καταλαβὼν θεωροῦντα, ἤγγελλον τὰ γεγονότα. ὁ δὲ τὸν Δία ἐπιμαρτυράμενος εὐθὺς παρήγγελλεν ἐμοὶ καὶ τοῖς ἐμοῖς [350c] οἰκείοις καὶ φίλοις παρασκευάζεσθαι τιμωρεῖσθαι Διονύσιον, ἡμᾶς μὲν ξεναπατίας χάριν, οὕτω γὰρ ἔλεγέ τε καὶ ἐνόει, αὐτὸν δ' ἐκβολῆς ἀδίκου καὶ φυγῆς.

ἀκούσας δ' ἐγὼ τοὺς μὲν φίλους παρακαλεῖν ἐκέλευον, εἰ βούλοιντο· "ἐμὲ δ'," εἶπον ὅτι, "σὺ μετὰ τῶν ἄλλων βίᾳ τινὰ τρόπον σύσσιτον καὶ συνέστιον καὶ κοινωνὸν ἱερῶν Διονυσίῳ ἐποίησας, ὃς ἴσως ἡγεῖτο διαβαλλόντων πολλῶν ἐπιβουλεύειν ἐμὲ μετὰ σοῦ ἑαυτῷ καὶ τῇ τυραννίδι, καὶ ὅμως οὐκ ἀπέκτεινεν, [350d] ᾐδέσθη δέ. οὔτ' οὖν ἡλικίαν ἔχω συμπολεμεῖν ἔτι σχεδὸν οὐδενί, κοινός τε ὑμῖν εἰμί, ἄν ποτέ τι πρὸς ἀλλήλους δεηθέντες φιλίας ἀγαθόν τι ποιεῖν βουληθῆτε· κακὰ δὲ ἕως ἂν ἐπιθυμῆτε, ἄλλους παρακαλεῖτε."

The Seventh Letter

[**350a**] After all this I was living outside the acropolis among the mercenaries. Some men came to me, including some attendants who were from Athens – my fellow citizens – and they reported that I was being disparaged among the peltasts and that certain individuals were threatening to kill me if they ever got their hands on me. So I hatched the following plan to save myself: I sent word to Archytas and my other friends in Tarentum, explaining the situation I was in. They in turn fashioned some pretext for an embassy from their city and sent [**350b**] Lamiscus, one of their own, on a thirty-oared ship. When he arrived, he pleaded with Dionysius on my behalf, saying that I wished to leave and that he should not refuse. Dionysius agreed, and he sent me on my way after giving me supplies for the journey. About Dion's assets, however, I never asked, nor did anyone hand them over.

When I reached the Peloponnese at Olympia, I found Dion watching the games, and I reported what had happened. Calling Zeus as his witness, he immediately demanded that my friends [**350c**] and companions and I get ready to exact retribution from Dionysius, us because he had cheated his guests (this is what he said, and he believed it), and himself on account of his unjust banishment and exile.

When I heard this, I encouraged him to call on my friends, if they were willing. "As for me, however," I said that, "you, along with some others, coerced me into sharing my meals, a roof, and religious rites with Dionysius, who probably thought that I was plotting against him and his tyranny with you, as many people accused me of doing, and despite that he was merciful [**350d**] and did not kill me. Moreover, I am no longer of the age to join anyone in waging war, and I remain connected to you both, in case you should require each other's friendship and wish to do something good. But as long as your heart is set on destruction, call on others."

ταῦτα εἶπον μεμισηκὼς τὴν περὶ Σικελίαν πλάνην καὶ ἀτυχίαν. ἀπειθοῦντες δὲ καὶ οὐ πειθόμενοι ταῖς ὑπ' ἐμοῦ διαλλάξεσι πάντων τῶν νῦν γεγονότων κακῶν αὐτοὶ αἴτιοι ἐγένοντο αὑτοῖς, ὧν, εἰ Διονύσιος [350e] ἀπέδωκε τὰ χρήματα Δίωνι ἢ καὶ παντάπασι κατηλλάγη, οὐκ ἄν ποτε ἐγένετο οὐδέν, ὅσα γε δὴ τἀνθρώπινα· Δίωνα γὰρ ἐγὼ καὶ τῷ βούλεσθαι καὶ τῷ δύνασθαι κατεῖχον ἂν ῥᾳδίως· νῦν δὲ ὁρμήσαντες ἐπ' ἀλλήλους κακῶν πάντα ἐμπεπλήκασι.

[351a] καί τοι τήν γε αὐτὴν Δίων εἶχε βούλησιν ἥνπερ ἂν ἐγὼ φαίην δεῖν ἐμὲ καὶ ἄλλον, ὅστις μετρίως περί τε τῆς αὑτοῦ δυνάμεως καὶ φίλων καὶ περὶ πόλεως τῆς αὑτοῦ διανοοῖτ' ἂν εὐεργετῶν ἐν δυνάμει καὶ τιμαῖσι γενέσθαι τὰ μέγιστα ἐν ταῖς μεγίσταις. ἔστι δὲ οὐκ ἄν τις πλούσιον ἑαυτὸν ποιήσῃ καὶ ἑταίρους καὶ πόλιν ἐπιβουλεύσας καὶ ξυνωμότας συναγαγών, πένης ὢν καὶ ἑαυτοῦ μὴ κρατῶν, ὑπὸ δειλίας τῆς πρὸς τὰς ἡδονὰς ἡττημένος, [351b] εἶτα τοὺς τὰς οὐσίας κεκτημένους ἀποκτείνας, ἐχθροὺς καλῶν τούτους, διαφορῇ τὰ τούτων χρήματα καὶ τοῖς συνεργοῖς τε καὶ ἑταίροις παρακελεύηται ὅπως μηδεὶς αὐτῷ ἐγκαλεῖ πένης φάσκων εἶναι· ταὐτὸν δὲ καὶ τὴν πόλιν ἂν οὕτω τις εὐεργετῶν τιμᾶται ὑπ' αὐτῆς, τοῖς πολλοῖς τὰ τῶν ὀλίγων ὑπὸ ψηφισμάτων διανέμων, ἢ μεγάλης προεστὼς πόλεως καὶ πολλῶν ἀρχούσης ἐλαττόνων τῇ ἑαυτοῦ πόλει τὰ τῶν σμικροτέρων [351c] χρήματα διανέμῃ μὴ κατὰ δίκην. οὕτω μὲν γὰρ οὔτε Δίων οὔτε ἄλλος ποτὲ οὐδεὶς ἐπὶ δύναμιν ἑκὼν εἶσιν ἀλιτηριώδη ἑαυτῷ τε καὶ γένει εἰς τὸν ἀεὶ χρόνον, ἐπὶ πολιτείαν δὲ καὶ νόμων κατασκευὴν τῶν δικαιοτάτων τε καὶ ἀρίστων, ὅ τι δι' ὀλιγίστων θανάτων καὶ φυγῶν γιγνομένην.

The Seventh Letter

So I said, full of hatred for my Sicilian wandering and misfortune. They, however, did not listen, and by rejecting my attempts to reconcile them they are themselves to blame for their current problems, which never would have happened, as far one can tell with human affairs, if Dionysius [**350e**] had returned Dion's assets and simply come to terms with him. Indeed, between my desire and my capacity, I would have easily restrained Dion. But as it is, by pitting themselves against each other they have ruined everything.

[**351a**] And yet, with regard to his own power and with regard to his friends and city, Dion had the very same aspirations that I would say are necessary for me or for any other person who might have the reasonable goal of holding power and political office while conferring the greatest of benefits in the most important places. Conversely, no one enriches himself, his friends, and his city by plotting and putting together conspiracies, not if he himself is poor and unable to control himself, if in his cowardice he yields to his pleasures, [**351b**] or if he kills those who own property, calling them enemies, plundering their assets, and egging on his accomplices and companions to do the same so that no one may take issue with him by claiming to be poor. The same thing goes for anyone who is honored by the city by benefitting it in this way, by distributing to the many, by popular decree, the possessions of the few, or anyone who sits at the head of a great city that rules over many lesser ones and unfairly distributes the possessions [**351c**] of those smaller ones to his own city. As such, neither Dion nor anyone else will ever willingly strive for a power that would be a plague unto himself and his people for all eternity, but rather for the purpose of making a government and a body of laws that are the best and most just, created through the fewest possible exiles and executions.

ἃ νῦν δὴ Δίων πράττων, προτιμήσας τὸ πάσχειν ἀνόσια τοῦ δρᾶσαι πρότερον, διευλαβούμενος δὲ μὴ παθεῖν, ὅμως ἔπταισεν ἐπ' ἄκρον ἐλθὼν τοῦ περιγενέσθαι τῶν [351d] ἐχθρῶν, θαυμαστὸν παθὼν οὐδέν. ὅσιος γὰρ ἄνθρωπος ἀνοσίων πέρι, σώφρων τε καὶ ἔμφρων, τὸ μὲν ὅλον οὐκ ἄν ποτε διαψευσθείη τῆς ψυχῆς τῶν τοιούτων πέρι, κυβερνήτου δὲ ἀγαθοῦ πάθος ἂν ἴσως οὐ θαυμαστὸν εἰ πάθοι, ὃν χειμὼν μὲν ἐσόμενος οὐκ ἂν πάνυ λάθοι, χειμώνων δὲ ἐξαίσιον καὶ ἀπροσδόκητον μέγεθος λάθοι τ' ἂν καὶ λαθὸν κατακλύσειε βίᾳ. ταὐτὸν δὴ καὶ Δίωνα ἔσφηλε [δι' ὀλιγίστων]· κακοὶ μὲν γὰρ ὄντες αὐτὸν σφόδρα οὐκ ἔλαθον οἱ σφήλαντες, ὅσον δὲ ὕψος ἀμαθίας [351e] εἶχον καὶ τῆς ἄλλης μοχθηρίας τε καὶ λαιμαργίας, ἔλαθον, ᾧ δὴ σφαλεὶς κεῖται, Σικελίαν πένθει περιβαλὼν μυρίῳ.

[352a] τὰ δὴ μετὰ τὰ νῦν ῥηθέντα ἃ ξυμβουλεύω, σχεδὸν εἴρηταί τέ μοι καὶ εἰρήσθω· ὧν δ' ἐπανέλαβον ἕνεκα τὴν εἰς Σικελίαν ἄφιξιν τὴν δευτέραν, ἀναγκαῖον εἶναι ἔδοξέ μοι ῥηθῆναι δεῖν διὰ τὴν ἀτοπίαν καὶ ἀλογίαν τῶν λεγομένων. εἰ δ' ἄρα τινὶ τὰ νῦν ῥηθέντα εὐλογώτερα ἐφάνη καὶ προφάσεις πρὸς τὰ γενόμενα ἱκανὰς ἔχειν ἔδοξέ τῳ, μετρίως ἂν ἡμῖν καὶ ἱκανῶς εἴη τὰ νῦν εἰρημένα.

The Seventh Letter

To be sure, Dion was doing just that, preferring to endure unholy acts rather than commit them, though still wary of suffering them, and all the same he was tripped up just as he came to the very point of overcoming his [351d] enemies; yet what he suffered was not at all incredible. Indeed, a conscientious, wise, and prudent man who is surrounded by deviants can never completely deceive his soul about such people, but it should come as no surprise if he suffers the same fate as that good helmsman who would certainly not be ignorant of an oncoming storm, but who might be caught off guard by its extraordinary and unexpected magnitude, and swept away by its violence. Dion too was brought down in this way. For he was not ignorant of the fact that the men who brought him down were very wicked indeed, but he did not realize [351e] the depths of their ignorance and general depravity and greed, for which he lies defeated, girding Sicily with boundless grief.

[352a] After everything I have just told you, my advice to you has essentially been given, and should suffice. Because of the absurd and unreasonable nature of the reports, it seemed necessary for me to repeat the reasons that I came to Sicily a second time. And if anyone thinks that what I have said just now is somewhat reasonable and provides an adequate explanation of what happened, then I have spoken enough, and with due measure.

Jonah Radding
Northwestern University

Historical Context

Carolina Araújo[1]
What was Plato up to in Syracuse?

The accusation:

What was the need to sail to Syracuse?
Wasn't Attica producing olives then? (Diog. Laert. 6.25).

This jest from Diogenes of Sinope, only apparently on olives, expresses a frequent criticism of Plato in Antiquity: why Syracuse? Why wouldn't Attica offer fertile ground for his political ideas? Why would he put so much effort into Syracuse and yet, for instance, refuse to formulate the laws of Megapolis (Diog. Laert. 3.22), a colony that would offer him an opportunity similar to the founding of Magnesia in the *Laws*? Diogenes, who generally reproaches Plato for his vanity, in this case accuses him of flattering the tyrant (Diog. Laert. 6.58, 69).[2] Diogenes Laertius seems to be replying to the charge when he explains that Plato was not concerned with politics while in Syracuse, for he knew that citizens there were accustomed to a different *politeía*, a lifestyle resistant to both philosophy and the stability of laws (Diog. Laert. 3.23). However, if political action was not on his agenda, was he there for fun? But then, why would the moderate philosopher leave Athens on a long and risky journey to spend his days in a court famous for festivals, luxury and waste?

When one has these attacks in mind, it is easier to accept the thesis that, regardless of the vexed question about its authorship, the *Seventh Letter* must be read within the apologetic purpose typical of

---

[1] Carolina Araújo is professor of Ancient Philosophy at the Universidade Federal do Rio de Janeiro and Researcher at the Brazilian National Research Council (CNPq). Her research focuses on Ancient Political Philosophy, Psychology and Metaphysics. In addition to several articles, she published Da Arte: uma leitura do Górgias de Platão (UFMG: 2008) and edited Verdade e Espetáculo: Platão e a questão do ser (Faperj / 7 Letras: 2014). She is president of the Latin American Association of Ancient Philosophy (ALFA) and member of the Brazilian Network of Women in Philosophy (Rede Brasileira de Mulheres na Filosofia).

[2] Diogenes Laertius reports that the same accusation is made of Aristippus by Metrocles (Diog. Laert. 2.68, 102). He also quotes Apollonius Mollon as a critic of the Platonic attitude (Diog. Laert. 3.34).

the genre of pseudo-epigraphy. It is an open document aiming at clarifying Plato's reasons to go to Syracuse and defending, against a reasonable accuser, the coherence of his political actions.[3] Its intricate style has the mark of a skillful author who seeks a way out from a labyrinth of factual evidence against him. He cannot ignore this evidence, but he can twist it to his best interest. In taking this approach, this paper aims to analyze the *Letter's* text and subtext, arguments, omissions and ambiguities, in order to show that Plato[4] had strong reasons to go to Syracuse and to regret it.

I shall begin by presenting some textual evidence for the claim that Plato's political project since the death of Socrates was the empowerment of a philosophical party. The aim of this party was to promote a *politeia* based on the self-control of the citizens through the engagement of many virtuous leaders in the regime. The project, though, would have to wait for the development of such partisans. Meanwhile, Plato traveled. I shall proceed by answering the title question as follows: Plato's first visit to Syracuse aimed at nothing but tourism and yet it happened that there he met a true philosopher and supporter of the project: Dion. His second trip aimed at empowering Dion's philosophical party by having Dyonisius join it. However, Plato failed in his rhetorical admonitions to change the tyrant's character. The third trip aimed merely at aiding Dion and failed in this regard. But the *Letter* shows evidence of a further failure of Plato, this time regarding the events after the third trip: he was mistaken in his assessment of Dion's commitment to a philosophical government. When he seized power, Dion neglected the kernel idea of the constitution based on self-control and proved Plato to be wrong in his expectations.

The philosophical party:

As said before, the *Seventh Letter* is an apology for Plato's political ideas. On a first reading it seems to justify Plato's going to

---

[3] See P. Butti de Lima, "Introduzione," in: Platone. *L'utopia del potere* (Venezia: Marsilio, 2015), 29.

[4] Here Plato always refers to the character of the narrative of the *Seventh Letter*, not necessarily to its real author.

Syracuse purely on the grounds of an opportunity to put a certain idea into practice (see διάνοια in 323e9, 326b5, 327b7, 328c2, 330b5). This practical purpose (δόξαν καὶ ἐπιθυμίαν, 324a2, see 327d1) consists in associating philosophy and government (326c7-b4). Philosophical power, as I shall call it, receives in the *Letter* a brief justification, followed by two methods for its implementation. The justification consists in defining philosophy as a skill that allows us to understand what is right in politics and in individuals (τά τε πολιτικὰ δίκαια καὶ τὰ τῶν ἰδιωτῶν πάντα κατιδεῖν - 326a6-7) and therefore to make the best political choices. But these choices depend on power in order to be realized and the *Letter* explicitly mentions two ways in which this empowerment can happen. The first is philosophers taking over government (326b1-2), so a revolution may occur, in which case a lot of effort and risk on the part of the agents is involved. The second is the gods conferring philosophical skills to someone who was already in power (326b3-4). Human agency is minimal in this providential alternative, limited to ensuring the proper development of the ruler's philosophical potential. Although these are the two options explicitly mentioned in the text, I would like to argue that a third route is also present there: the creation and empowering of a growing philosophical party, which would seize the power without revolutions. The first evidence of this alternative lies in the purpose of the *Letter* itself: its addressees are simply called "friends" of Plato and Dion, and the reason for this friendship is not mere affection, but sharing in Plato's cause (323e9-10).

This partisanship also marks the *Seventh Letter*'s singular description of Socrates.[5] In contradistinction to Plato's dialogues,[6] he is never mentioned as a philosopher; he was simply "the fairest of men" and, most of all, he was Plato's *philos* and *hetairos* (324d8, 325b6). These two terms have the strict meaning mentioned above:

---

[5] L. Edelstein, *Plato's Seventh Letter* (Leiden: Brill, 1966), 7-15; and T. Irwin, "Introdução à Carta VII, de Platão," Platão. *Carta VII* (São Paulo: Loyola, 2013), 18-20.

[6] Compare with *Phd.* 118a17, where being just is associated with being wise.

the sharing of some political beliefs.[7] This emphasis on the political beliefs allows the *Letter* to connect Socrates's death penalty with the episode of Leon of Salamis (324d7-325a3). As narrated in Plato's *Apology* (32c3-d8), the Thirty asked Socrates to go to Salamis to get Leon to be murdered,[8] a command to which Socrates did not listen and returned home. In describing the case, the *Seventh Letter* blames the democratic accusers of impiety for not reciprocating Socrates's protection of one of their *philoi* (325c1-5). This seemed to Plato enough to state that the important lesson he learnt from his association with Socrates was that it is not possible to act politically without trusted friends and supporters (325d1-2); that the political action of a single philosopher is suicidal if he does not have the support of a group of faithful friends who share his principles of action.

This lesson, the *Letter* suggests, remains firm and indelible in Plato's thought, explaining, in response to Diogenes of Sinope's jest, his distance from Athenian politics. Not only Athens, but cities in general suffered from the corruption of their citizens' character. Their political behavior (see πολιτεύονται, 326a3) would preclude the association of reliable friends (326a2-3). This can also be taken as the reason why Diogenes Laertius claimed that Plato was not interested in Syracusan politics: because the character of its citizens was incompatible with prudence (326c1-3), it necessarily followed that the city was doomed to continual change in its laws, alternating between tyrannical, oligarchic and democratic regimes according to successive coups (326d3-6).

The letter goes on to spell out the conditions the prudent man must observe before giving his advice to an ill-ruled city: (i) that this

---

[7] See, for example how Leon of Salamis is a *philos* of Socrates's accusers (325c4), i.e., a fellow democrat.

[8] Xenophon describes Leon as a man of excellent reputation (*Hellenics*, II). W. J. McCoy, "The identity of Leon." *American Journal of Philology*, 96 (1975): 187-199, argues for his connection with the Battle of Arginusae, which suggests a democratic interpretation for another relevant political episode in the life of Socrates, when judging the commanders in charge during the battle (see Plato, *Apology*, 32b1-c3).

advice shall not put him to death; (ii) that it shall not be in vain, i.e., have no effect in the city; (iii) that it shall not bring death and exile to the citizens; i.e., start a revolution (331c7-d5). Under these conditions, Plato would save himself and wait for the right opportunity (τοῦ δὲ πράττειν αὖ περιμένειν ἀεὶ καιρούς - 326a1-2), i.e., the cooperation of trusted friends and possibility of forming a philosophical party (παρασκευῆς θαυμαστῆς τινος μετὰ τύχης - 326a5-6).

The *politeia* of self-control:

In the previous section I argued that Plato thought that his political ideas depended on the empowerment of a philosophical party in order to be realized. I shall now argue that the *Seventh Letter* describes the constitution to be so implemented as a government based on the self-control of the citizens. It says that the philosophical party is expected to free the city from slavery and establish laws that are good for citizens (336a4-5).[9] It is emphatic that the justice of a city depends on its policy of being subjected not to individuals, but to laws (334c6-7). As long as political power depends on the individuals that hold it, the cycle of revenge and sedition will be unstoppable (337b1-3). Justice depends on stable laws, and these depend on self-controlled men (337a1-2). In general, rulers who seize power in a revolution have as their first priority to expel and kill their enemies. This is an action to ensure their survival, for otherwise their enemies will certainly organize themselves to resume power and take revenge (336e3-337a1). In contrast, Plato suggests that a ruler who comes to power must have as a priority to fight, not his enemies, but the cycle of revenge itself. The basic reason is that he should fear the outcome of an impending revolution. His action should be guided by reverence for the laws (337a6-7), hoping that, no matter who is in power, all of those ruled will be safe (337a5-6).

Good laws for citizens, however, are not good in a general way. They must be committed to the propagation throughout the population of a particular lifestyle, described in the letter as Doric (336c6), and basically consisting of self-control. While not every citizen is expected to become a philosopher, self-control is a

---

[9] This was explicitly Dion's purpose before he met Plato (324b1-2).

requirement for all, even if in most cases this means simply plain obedience to the law (335d5-e1). The problem with this idea is that it still seems pretty revolutionary, since the philosophical party would then set itself the unrealistic task of changing the lives of all citizens. Fortunately, the letter is not so naive. The promulgation of new legislation needs to rely on cooperative work with relevant social channeling, guaranteeing root support for the government. This is why certain social exponents, individuals recognized for their virtue, are crucial to the legislative procedure. The letter suggests a selection of the best men in the city in a proportion of 50 for every 10 thousand inhabitants (337b3-c6), selected for their renowned nobility in terms of genealogy, reputation, and family. Their task would be to write the laws under oath so that neither winners nor losers would have any advantage and the law would promote equality throughout the city (337c3-6).[10]

The first trip:

Ancient sources differ greatly as to the purposes and the consequences of Plato's first trip to Syracuse. Nonetheless, the best tradition attests that it was not motivated by an invitation from Dionysius I, and that Plato was doing tourism.[11] The *Seventh Letter*

---

[10] This same tone of conciliation guides the advices in the *Eighth Letter* (356c4-e5). On the antidemocratic principles of the two letters and their relation to the death of Dion, see. H.D. Westlake, "Dion and Timoleon," in: D. M. Lewis, J. Boardman, S. Hornblower, M. Ostwald, eds., *The Cambridge Ancient History*, v. VI (Cambridge: Cambridge University Press, 1994) 693-722, 704-05.

[11] Diogenes Laertius says that the purpose of the first trip was purely to visit the island and the craters (Diog. Laert. 3.18), a version attested by Olympiodorus (*In Alcibiades*, 2. 94–96 and *In Gorgias*, 41. 7), Apuleius (De Platone, 1.4), and the Anonimus *Prolegomena*, 4, 11-13, see also B. Caven, *Dionysius I: War-lord of Sicily* (New Haven: Yale University Press, 1990), 168-69. D. Nails points out the difficulty of explaining the encounter with Dion without an official invitation in *The people of Plato: a prosopography of Plato and other Socratics* (Indianapolis: Hackett, 2002), 247. I do not find it unlikely that an Athenian traveller with philosophical interests would be greeted by people of the same interest. Both Olympiodorus and Diogenes Laertius combine the tourist motivation with the personal quarrel with Dionysius himself.

itself supports this position by stating that the visit was casual (κατὰ τύχην - 326e1). It also discredits Plato's interest in the court by emphasizing his repugnance for what the Syracusans regarded as the good life (326b6-c1). On the other hand, it omits the disastrous events that late sources attribute to the end of this trip: a quarrel with Dionysius I, who would have sent Plato to Aegina to be assassinated or sold as a slave.[12] Since the episode is a recurring motive in intellectual biographies, the fact that the letter does not mention it should be considered a strong reason for dismissing it as an anecdote created by a later tradition.

If we are to take the letter as a source for the first trip, we should conclude that nothing else matters about it besides being introduced to Dion. Endowed with philosophical potential, he was the most extraordinary young man Plato had ever met (327b1). By spending time with him, Plato helped to turn this potential into a righteous, courageous and temperate philosopher (336a8-b1). Dion eventually also became an enthusiast of the idea of philosophical power and started to gather supporters (327c1-3). The friendship with Dion turned the casual trip into a deep involvement with Syracusan political affairs. In sum, on his first trip, Plato was neither up to flattery nor to meddling in politics, but chance interfered and introduced him to Dion. After that, Syracuse became a far more interesting place for his political action than Attica.

The second trip:

Dion's exhortation of Plato to come back is the sole motivation for the second trip (328d3-329a5).[13] According to his report, Dionysius II was about to become a member of the philosophical party (327c3-4). Dion's expectation was that, once associated with

---

[12] See Plutarch, *Dion*, 4-5; Diog. Laert. 3.18-21 and Diodorus Siculus (XV, 7). Lewis considers all these stories pure myths, see D.M. Lewis, "Sicily, 413-368 BC" in, D. M. Lewis, J. Boardman, S. Hornblower, M. Ostwald, eds., *The Cambridge Ancient History*, v. VI (Cambridge: Cambridge University Press, 1994), 154.

[13] Diogenes Laertius (3.21) says that the purpose of the second trip was Dionysius's promise to provide territory in order to build a city according to Plato's principles. The promise was not fulfilled. The story seems to date from a later source and clashes with the *Seventh Letter*.

Plato, he would improve his own life and that of the Syracusans. This would be a way out of the deaths and evils that raged at Syracuse (327d4-6). There is no doubt that Dion's aspiration was of "making the ruler and philosopher the same" (328a6-b1). However, he failed to mention which of the methods he was referring to. Tradition in general understood that Dion's hope was the alternative I called providential, i.e., the philosophical education of Dionysius. I would like to argue in favor of the opposite view. The recurring occurrence of claims on friendship (for instance: εἰς φιλίαν τε καὶ ἑταιρίαν ἀλλήλοις καθιστάναι ἑκάστοτε - 328d8-e1) suggests the strategy to be the strengthening of the philosophical party, and therefore the empowerment of its leader, i.e., Dion.

My best evidence is textual: the divine opportunity to which Dion refers (327e4-5) is that of forming a community of friends. It is quite true that Dion emphasized Dionysius's interest in philosophy and culture in general (328a1-2), but he knew it to be rather superficial. There is plenty of evidence of Dionysius's unstable character (328b1-5), his pretentiousness (φιλοτιμία, 338d6-7, e1-2, e7) and the threat he could pose to the project (335d1-3). On the other hand, the power Dion enjoyed in Syracuse mattered a lot in this case (328a1); in fact, it was the decisive factor for Plato's decision to sail back there (328b5-6). Plato never relied on Dionysius being a philosopher; he estimated that the idea could be put into practice because he had sufficiently persuaded one person (328c2-3), Dion, not because he hoped to persuade a second one. Even if he had the best of intentions, Plato's motivation for his second trip matches the accusations of his opponents (333b7-c5)[14]: he was up to plotting against Dionysius.[15]

Syracuse was, however, far from meeting Plato's requirements for philosophical political action. Even in his highly exhortative tone,

---

[14] See also Plutarch, *Dion*, XIV. For the truth of the detractor's speeches, see Westlake, "Dion and Timoleon," 696.

[15] This is how I interpret the statement that the agency of a higher power (326e1-3), i.e. the casual meeting of Dion during the first trip, explains how Plato, unknowingly ended up plotting against the regime (327a4-5), on his second trip.

What was Plato up to in Syracuse?

Dion makes it very clear that Dionysius was also under the influence of other parties (327e1-2). The power of the association of trusted friends was not granted and some audacity was required (328c2-4). However, Dion put the case in such a way that Plato was trapped: not supporting Dion meant not supporting philosophy (τὰ νῦν μετ 'ἐμοῦ - 328e5) and not to return to Syracuse would amount to a partisan betrayal in circumstances of danger (328c7-d2).

The first failure:

If I am right about the motivation for the second trip, no one should say that it failed due to a misjudgment of Dionysius's capacities. It failed due to a miscalculation of Dion's power. His opponents' accusations eventually caused his exile. This was a risk Plato knew well he was taking. He was familiar with the intrigue, slander, and dissension that made both Syracuse and its tyrant intrinsically unstable (329b2, 7c1). I would like to argue that Plato fails, rather, in another respect.

Plato's task in the whole plan was to persuade Dionysius, and for this he could only rely on his rhetorical skills (μὴ δόξαιμί ποτε ἐμαυτῷ παντάπασι λόγος μόνον ἀτεχνῶς εἶναι τίς - 328c5-6, see also λόγων καὶ πειθοῦς in 328d6). The lessons he gave the tyrant were not about mathematics, dialectics, physics, and logic. They were not even similar to those he gave to Dion (335c2), in which he would argue that we are mortal beings with immortal souls and that it is better to suffer injustice than to commit it (334e3-335c1). Dionysius's classes were rather exhortative, with no demonstrations involved. They consisted in admonitions about the importance of friendship (331e1, 332d3-6) with arguments such as the following: to prevent committing the same political mistakes his father made (331e1-332a2, c2-6); to follow the models of Darius (332a5-b5) and Athens (332b6-c2); to ensure the government's longevity through a Sicilian confederation to combat the Carthaginians (332e3-333a5). Through all of this, Plato had to formulate carefully what he should say and to phrase his arguments enigmatically because the danger of losing the student and failing the cause was great (332d6-7).

Carolina Araújo

Plato failed in his appraisal of the power of his own rhetoric. His speeches were not able to persuade Dionysius to take part in the association that would ultimately protect his political actions. Plato knew well that philosophical advice is vain for unstable men or cities, and still he thought he could make it. Why? Because he was relying on other kinds of forces. I understand the issue as follows: advice is only useful for those who have control over their lifestyle (331b1-2), otherwise the change can only happen through violence. Plato goes to Syracuse with the task of producing in Dionysius self-control (331d8) and once Dionysius resisted the exhortations, Plato refused to use force (331b7, 333d3).

Dion's exile eventually turned what was already a delicate situation into a trap. The impossible task of gaining Dionysius's trust became a condition for assuring the return and the integrity of Dion. Plato was under constant suspicion of plotting against the regime. This was when Dionysius showed he actually cared about Plato. It may be argued that all that mattered to him was his personal image, since Plato was by then well known in the Greek world. Nonetheless the fact is that Dionysius did not want him to leave Sicily under any impression of lack of hospitality (329d1-6, 333d4-6). He decided to simulate an interest in philosophy (329d6) in order to prevent Plato from having worse luck than Dion (330a7-b4). The false philosophical lesson was Dionysius's strategy to reverse the situation created by Dion's exile and eventually to guarantee Plato's physical integrity.

The third trip:

The failure of the second trip would have been reason enough for Plato never to make plans for Syracuse again, were it not for the insistence of two of his greatest philosopher friends, Dion and Archytas. In a letter quoted by the author of the *Seventh Letter*, Dionysius states that Plato should come to Syracuse foremost (πρῶτος) so that Dion could retrieve his goods and eventually return to Sicily (339c2-7). Some similar threat also seems to hang on Archytas. In commending Dionysius's devotion to philosophy, he makes it clear that Plato's presence at Syracuse would be decisive for his political relations with Tarentum (339d5). Plato was receiving supplications (μετὰ δεήσεως – 339d8), not invitations. He returned to Syracuse with fear (340a1-2). At every moment he was trying to persuade himself that there was some hope. Maybe, as it may well occur to the young men, Dionysius would have come to love the contemplative life (339e3-5). But this was no longer about strengthening the philosophical party; it was just a motivational fiction that he would tell himself as he was about to face risks on behalf of his friends (340a4-8).

Dionysius's interest in philosophical reputation – rather than philosophical practice – was enough to protect Plato, but of course not to change Dionysius's character or his way of ruling (344e2-3). The *Letter* says they had only one meeting (345a1-2), in which Plato decided to test Dionysius's capacity for effort and perseverance (340b1-3). This was enough for both: Dionysius heard what he needed for his philosophical career (345a7-b1), which included the publication of a book that would show his wisdom to the world (341b3-5). Plato verified that he was once again trapped. Dionysius did not comply with his promise, and did not allow Dion's fortune to be restored to him in the Peloponnese (345c4-d1). The reason was the old revenge cycle: he feared that, with money, Dion would organize an attack against the regime (346b5-8), which was exactly what Dion was about to do (350b7-c3). Dionysius's strategy was very reasonable: to make Plato the depositary of Dion's wealth and to hold him accountable should it be used against Syracuse (346b7-c6).[16] While Plato awaited Dion's instructions, Dionysius set about spending the money (347d8-e2) and keeping Plato under his control. The situation ended with Archytas rescuing Plato (350a5-b3) and Dion remaining without his possessions (350b3-5).

---

[16] There is further detail: after Plato agreed to stay in Syracuse to secure Dion his property, Dionysius announced that he was referring only to half of his wealth. The other half belonged to the son of Dion, nephew of Dionysius, who was in Syracuse. Such values should remain in the city under Dionysius's tutelage (347c8-d2, cf. 345c8-d1).

Carolina Araújo

The second failure:

Upon his return to mainland Greece, Plato met Dion at Olympia during the games. In telling him what had happened, he came to know of Dion's plan to attack Syracuse. Plato's response was full of anger (μεμισηκώς - 350d4). He accused Dion of having in some way used force (βία τινὰ τρόπον - 350c5) to make him join Dionysius and risk death (350c7-8). To Dion he actually praised the protection he received from Dionysius (350c8-d1) and finally put an end to their cooperation: one should not count on him to do evil (350d3-4).

Dion did not compromise, and so Plato held him responsible for the evil that afflicted the Syracusans (350d5), though he also acknowledged Dionysius's share of responsibility for not having restored Dion's wealth (350d7-e1). Together they caused the calamity (350d5-7). Although Dion wished for the good that every rational human being should desire—a stable constitution and just laws that would minimize death and exile (351c1-6)—in seizing Syracuse he succumbed to injustice (351c7-d1). The *Letter* downplays Dion's great mistake, comparing his ignorance, wickedness and greed to a pilot that does not foresee the violence of a storm (351d1-7).[17] However, it indeed testifies that, when his Athenian companions arrived in Sicily after the liberation, they found Dion in opposition to the Sicilians and ready to become a tyrant (333e6-334a3). Ancient sources less favorable to Dion[18] also report his centralization of power as the reason for his murder at the hands of Callipus. Although the situation was controversial, it is clear that upon reaching power Dion did not undertake the legislative project described in the *Seventh Letter*, which required the participation of respectable Syracusans. Moreover, by refraining from taking a position on the impiety of

---

[17] Platonic sources, like Plutarch, tend to favor Dion and not mention his mistakes. Other more independent ancient sources, such as Nepos, are clear about his autocratic behavior and the motivation of his murder. For contemporary discussions see Westlake, "Dion and Timoleon," 693, and Nails, *The People of Plato*, 135.

[18] This is an important concession to Callipus's own justifications for his actions. For a reconstruction of Callipus's letter to Athens and how it may be the motivation behind the Seventh Letter, see L.J. Sanders, *The Legend of Dion* (Toronto: Edgar Kent, 2008), 96-101.

murder and its motives (334a6-7), the author of the *Letter* claims that his support for Dion was restricted to wise actions (334b4-7). The evidence cannot be denied about Plato's disappointment with Dion, whom he deems responsible for the final failure of all events at Syracuse.

The defense

One possible response to Diogenes's jest at the beginning of this paper may be found in Lewis.[19]. He suggests that Sicily offered an alternative to the Greek dilemma: neither Athenian democracy nor the Spartan oligarchy, but a different kind of monarchy. I would like to conclude by pointing out that the political model advocated by the *Seventh Letter* is none of the above. Plato went to Syracuse in an attempt to put into practice a regime whose best description would be a constitution based on self-control. A strong philosophical party is a condition for seizing power in order to implement this model. Its stability, however, depends on the further involvement of citizens reputed for their self-control. The engagement of these citizens ensures a network of legislative action in a project that aims to transform the city's lifestyle. Therefore, the political model defended by the *Letter* is a participatory government, centered on the force of law, and sustained by a specific lifestyle.

For such a project Plato saw no opportunity in Attica. On his first trip to Sicily, however, he found in Syracuse someone who seemed to him to be a true philosopher devoted to strengthening a philosophical party, Dion. On his second trip, he tried to contribute to the empowerment of this party and consequently of its leader. He tried to do this by persuading the tyrant himself, Dyonisius, to join the party. His mistake was to suppose that he could educate him without his own commitment to self-control. On his third trip, he only intended to save his friends in danger. After all these events, came the biggest disappointment: to realize that the confrontation with power could also change Dion, his best candidate for a true philosopher.

---

[19] Lewis, "Sicily," 120.

Marina Marren[1]
The Historical Background of the *Seventh Letter*: Political Philosophy in Context

Introduction

The elements that make up the *Seventh Letter* are as much philosophical and political as they are historical. Philosophical ideas in the *Seventh Letter* bleed into and engage with such political questions as: What is the best government for a given state? Is it possible to change the mind of tyrants? Should we ever resort to tyranny? Lastly, what is the relationship between philosophy and politics—in theory and in practice? The answers to these questions—and this is my claim—cannot be given based solely on a close reading of the text, but must take into account the contingencies of history. Analysis of the historical background of the *Seventh Letter* (in Section II of this paper) puts pressure on the political prescriptions that the author of the letter issues (Section III). Political theory is subject to both philosophical reflection and historical evaluation. The *Seventh Letter* is a text that invites us to consider how the political history of Athens (circa 430–351 BCE) serves as a basis for the theoretical advice issued to Syracuse and how it would have affected the political life of Sicily, if it were implemented. This exercise in hypotheticals holds value for us, who stand to benefit from the reflective, historically and philosophically armored, foresight as it presents to us the possible landscapes of future political events (Section IV).

Dramatic Date, Historical Context, and Authenticity

The *Seventh Letter*, at the start, indicates a date that sets the political and the historical stage for its composition and, thus, frames the philosophical ideas that can be gleaned from it. We do not have to believe that the author of the *Seventh Letter* is Plato himself in order to believe that the author wants us to know the historical moment at which it is composed. The question of the authenticity of the *Seventh*

---

[1] Marina Marren is an Assistant Professor of Philosophy at the American University in Cairo, Egypt. Marren's research focuses on ancient Greek philosophy and politics, as well as philosophical psychology, ethics, and aesthetics.

Letter remains unresolved. Among the commentators, who address the subject, Caskey cites Morrow and Brandwood in favor and "Levison, Moton, and Winspear" against our taking the *Seventh Letter* as Plato's original.[2] Lloyd and Lewis also take up the matter. Lloyd analyzes the possible relationship between Plato's thinking and its influence on Archytas in order to defend the "unlikelihood of VII being by the same man who wrote XII (addressed to Archytas) or XIII (addressed to Dionysius II)."[3] Lewis, on the other hand, takes the fact that the "rhetorical element [and] …the content of the letter is fully consistent with the teachings of the political dialogues [as a] point that tells in favor of the authenticity of the letter."[4] Whether the author *is* or *is not* Plato, we cannot settle once and for all. However, it is apparent that the author of the *Seventh Letter*, who identifies himself as "Plato" in the salutation, intends us to think that Plato, the philosopher, wrote the *Seventh Letter* and that all references to "Plato" that we find in it, are to the philosopher. Therefore, we have to assume, when we read, "I was nearly forty when I came to Syracuse" (324a), that it is Plato, who was forty in 387 when Dion of Syracuse was eighteen.[5] At the time of composition, Hipparnius (Dion's son), is of the same age as Dion was in 387. Hipparnius III of Syracuse, as Nails deduces, is alive between 373–354 and is eighteen in 355/4.[6] The

---

[2] Consult Caskey on other contemporary as well as ancient authors, who address the question of the authenticity and the possible intended purpose of the *Seventh Letter* in Elizabeth G. Caskey, "Again Plato's Seventh Letter." *Classical Philology*. 69:3 (1974): 220–27, 221. See also, a discussion of authenticity in Burnyeat and Frede, *The Pseudo-Platonic Seventh Letter*, D. Scott, ed. (Oxford, UK: Oxford University Press, 2015).

[3] E. R. G. Lloyd, "Plato and Archytas in the 'Seventh Letter'." *Phronesis*. Vol. 35:2 (1990): 159-74.

[4] V. Bradley Lewis, "The Rhetoric of Philosophical Politics in Plato's 'Seventh Letter'" *Philosophy and Rhetoric* 33:1 (2000): 24.

[5] All translations of the *Seventh Letter* from ancient Greek are my own. I use the 1929 edition of Loeb Classical Library ancient Greek text of the *Seventh Letter* in *Timaeus, Critias, Cleitophon, Menexenus, Epistles* (No. 234). Loeb Classical Library (Cambridge, MA: Harvard University Press).

[6] Debra Nails, *The People of Plato: A Prosopography of Plato and Other Socratics* (Indianapolis, IN: Hackett Publishing Company, 2002).

intended date for the context of the *Seventh Letter* is 355/4 BC, which is the year (354) in which Dion is assassinated.

Everitt cites 355/354 as the year of Athens' defeat in the so-called Social War against its former allies, "Rhodes, Chios, and Byzantium." The reason for this conflict, as Everitt explains, is that the Greek "Thebes turned its attention to central and northern Greece [and] [b]uilt a fleet to rival that of the Athenians and fostered discontent among their allies."[7] Although the Thebans did not fare well in that skirmish, that did not change the fate of Athens for the better. Everitt relates that "in 355 Athens was obliged to agree to a peace. The three island rebels [Rhodes, Cos, and Chios] were allowed to leave the league and the independence of Byzantium was recognized. The dismembered confederation struggled on, but the renewed dream of empire was over."[8]

Shortly thereafter, in 351, Demosthenes speaks to the Athenians about a new power rising in Macedon. The opening of the *Seventh Letter* (324b–326a), then, marks the end of the historical aftermath of the political decisions and choices that the Athenians made in the wake of the Peloponnesian War. One of the possible reasons why the author of the *Seventh Letter* recites the political turmoil that followed the overthrow of the former constitution of Athens—a "political arrangement, which they [Athenians] came to despise" (324c)—is to issue a warning. The author of the letter witnessed the ills that followed the establishment of the tyrannically minded oligarchs in Athens (324c–d). The author warns the Syracusan friends of Dion, who are biding their time in Leontini while plotting to overthrow Dionysius II, against taking some such actions as may result in the same anarchical undoing of their own *polis*.

Tyranny of Athens as Background for Political Advice

This point about the *Seventh Letter* being a cautionary tale issued to the friends of Dion is pursued by Lewis. Lloyd sees in the *Seventh*

---

[7] Anthony Everitt, *Rise of Athens: The Story of the World's Greatest Civilization* (New York, NY: Random House, 2016), 415.
[8] Ibid. 420.

Letter a political and philosophical apologetics dressed up as a story about the education of Dionysius II. The[9] view that the *Letter* is an apology for the author's failure to change the minds of Syracusan tyrants is consistent with Edelstein.[10] However, Lewis in "The *Seventh Letter* and the Unity of Plato's Political Philosophy," which is his other article on the topic, argues that the author of the *Seventh Letter* offers for our consideration not an apology for his inadequacy to face up to and change the tyrant's mind, but an account of how the "enemy of tyrants … may … become one himself" (233).[11] If we take Lewis's and Lloyd's arguments in tandem and observe that both agree on the philosophical and political importance of the letter, but that Lloyd interprets it as an analysis of tyranny rather than a record of excuses for kowtowing to a tyrant, then we can interpret the *Seventh Letter* as containing philosophically pertinent ideas about tyrannical power—how it comes to be and how to guard against its coming into being. Seen as a treatise on tyranny and its relationship to philosophy, the *Seventh Letter* is as much a reflection on why tyranny (and the violence that it stirs up among the citizens) led to the fall of Athens, as it is a caution against violent actions aimed at deposing a tyrant issued to Syracusans. The criticism of Athens that the author of the *Seventh Letter* presents is especially poignant to the minds of ancient Athenians in the 4th. C. BCE.

During the heyday of its imperial glory, in 446–445, Athens, a city that dominates its neighbors in the Delian league, takes over Skyros and Euboea and exacts strict control over its annexed territories.[12] Athenians, although recovering from the great plague

---

[9] Lloyd, *Plato and Archytas*, 161.

[10] Ludwig Edelstein, *Plato's Seventh Letter* (Leiden: E. J. Brill Publishing, 1966).

[11] V. Bradley Lewis, "The *Seventh Letter* and the Unity of Plato's Political Philosophy." *The Southern Journal of Philosophy* 38 (2000): 233.

[12] After Cimones, the advocate for peace with Sparta, dies in 450 BCE, the land allotments are made and Athenian cleruchies are "set up on Carystus, Naxos, Andros, Lemnos, Imbros, and in the Chersonese" Donald Kagan, "The Athenian Empire. Lecture 13, The Delian League." *Introduction to Ancient Greek History*. Open Yale Courses, 2016), 7. (http://oyc.yale.edu/sites/default/files/08athenianempire 3.pdf. Accessed 11/3/2017. To Kagan, the colonies are

(430–426),[13] continue to secure their territorial dominion and terrorize Mytilene, which seeks to throw off their yoke with the help of the Spartans. Thucydides records Cleon as the man who rallies to cleanse Mytilene of all of its men by a decree from Athens; a polis, which to Cleon's mind is a tyranny and which should embrace its tyrannical power. The Athenian assembly backpedals from this cruel plan, but only to agree with Cleon's second proposition, which is to eliminate all of the ringleaders who instigated the revolt and allied with Sparta. Why would Athenians follow any advice from a man who thinks that a *polis* is a tyranny and that it should act accordingly? Why would Athenians agree with no less dangerous an agitator than Alcibiades, who in 415 appeals to the avaricious as well as to the glory and entertainment-seeking (if we are to believe Thucydides) members of the polis in order to advance against Syracuse?[14] What

---

extended to Imbros, Chalcis, and Eretria after 447 BCE Pericles's expedition to Thracian Chersonese (page 8). In 446 – 445 BCE, an "Athenian colony Oreos [is] founded on site of Euboean Hestiaea, after the expulsion of the Hestiaeans" (Ibid.). In 440 BCE, following democratization of Samos and the Samians oligarchs' attempts at overthrowing democracy, Pericles heads a punitive mission to Samos. He enlists Sophocles as a general (Ibid.). In 428 BCE Cleon attempts to persuade the Athenians that the punishment administered to Lesbos for the attempt to revolt should amount to an execution of all of the Mytilenian men and the consequent enslavement of the rest of the citizens. In the aftermath, only the leaders of the revolt are executed.

[13] The plague was devastating and all the more so because it undermined the strength of Athens at the outset of the second state of the Peloponnesian war. Thucydides describes the iniquities (starting with the mention of the forbidden dwelling in the sacred temples and ending with the casting aside of honor and regard for laws divine and human) that surfaced during the plague, which began in Egypt, settled in Piraeus, and hit Athens hardest in 430 (II.53, page 121). Consult Thucydides, *The History of the Peloponnesian War. The Landmark Thucydides: A Comprehensive Guide to the Peloponnesian War*, ed. B. R. Strassler (New York, NY: Touchstone Publishing, 1998).

[14] Thucydides tells us about people's motivations. He says that the old sought to subdue the rebels, those in their prime wanted to sail for the sake of seeing spectacles and sights (ἡλικία τῆς τε ἀπούσης πόθῳ ὄψεως καὶ θεωρίας), and that many of the poorer folk thought that the victory would bring unlimited (ἀίδιον) recourses.

passion stirs and strengthens as the Athenians side with the violent demands of warmongering leaders of their state?

The aftermath of the Sicilian expedition, as the Athenians and the Syracusans well know, is devastating to Athens. Plato, who composes *Timaeus*, frames the opening scene of that dialogue by presenting for us a key figure who brings together Sicilian cities and Carthage as a counter force to the expansion of Athenian interests.[15] The man is Hermocrates. This character is parsimonious with words. At a later time, at a time that falls outside of the possible dramatic dates of the *Timaeus*, Hermocrates advises the Spartans while they plan their initial successful resistance to the Athenian aggression in Syracuse.[16] Hermocrates's character is a reminder to us and to the dialogical interlocutors of the expansionist actions of Athens. The city, at the time that the conversations in the *Timaeus* take place,[17] is at peace. This peace (of Nicias) will be shortly broken. Athens will begin preparing for the second and (for it) disastrous stage of the Peloponnesian War. No advice or warning issues from Hermocrates. Yet, his very presence invokes the painful truth that history remembers—that aggression against and subjugation of its neighbors grants only an impermanent supremacy to Athens, while implanting in it what Thucydides describes as a fantastic passion.[18]

---

[15] Plato, *Timaeus*m, trans. P. Kalkavage (Newburyport, MA: Focus Publishing, 2001).

[16] Everitt, *Rise of Athens,* 331, places the Athenian invasion of Melos in 415; the "same year as Agathon's symposium." Everitt portrays the aftermath of Melian refusal to join Athenian Empire as a massacre in which "[a]ll adult males were put to death and the women and children sold into slavery" (332). According to Everitt, "Alcibiades actively approved of the expedition and its cruel conclusion" (Ibid.).

[17] Nails, *People of Plato,* places the "earliest possible dramatic date for the dialogue [in] ... 429" (107). Alfred E. Taylor writes that "the *Republic* no less than the *Timaeus*, presupposes a date no later than about the time of the peace of Nicias (421 B. C.)" *A Commentary on Plato's Timaeus*. Oxford, UK: Oxford University Press, 1982), 16.

[18] The story of the mythical Atlantis and its aggressive militaristic expansion (*Timaeus*, 24d–25d), further, indicates that Plato could have been composing a cautionary tale meant to give pause to belligerent Athenians. See Kathryn A.

Thucydides writes about the proposed Sicilian expedition that "All alike fell in love [ἔρως] with the sailing campaign."[19] This *erōs*, which incites and fuels not the justice-seeking, but the warmongering *thumos*; this passion that leaves the Athenian *polis* all but undone, and which Socrates, in the *Republic*, calls "a great winged drone," (572e) is tyranny. The author of the *Seventh Letter* draws on historical events because they set the content of the letter against a background that qualifies both the Syracusan addressees as well as we, now, might understand its meaning. Passages that describe violence against the non-Greeks, for instance (ἀπὸ τῶν βαρβάρων ποιεῖν, τοὺς μὲν ἐκβάλλων, τοὺς , 336a), are hardly unambiguous in the Syracusans' eyes. The memory of 413, which marked the expulsion not of the barbarian, but of the Athenian attempts at subjugating Syracuse, is only one generation removed from those whom the author of the *Seventh Letter* addresses. At any rate, the power struggle in Syracuse revolves around one ruling family (Dionysius I, his son Dionysius II, and Dion, who is an uncle to Dionysius II) and is confined to Syracusan natives. Thus, not the warmongering barbarians, desirous of territorial expansion (such as Persians, for example), but other Greeks would be the target of expulsion and subjugation, should the Syracusan friends of Dion do to Sicily the sorts of things that the author of the *Seventh Letter* says Dion would have done, if he held power. However, the author describes, at length, the troubles that the expansionist mindset brings to Athens. What does it mean that, avowedly, the author of the *Seventh Letter* is against tyrannical expansionist aggression, but that, nonetheless, in several passages (331d–332c, 335e–336b) seems to prescribe actions and ideas that would end up installing tyranny?

The historical context of the *Seventh Letter* helps us make sense of this seeming contradiction and it also bolsters the philosophical conclusions we can draw. We cannot take all of the prescriptive passages in the *Letter* univocally when we observe that history

---

Morgan, "Designer History: Plato's Atlantis Story and Fourth-Century Ideology" *The Journal of Hellenic Studies* 118 (1998): 101–18.

[19] VI.24.3, 375.

contradicts ideas and advice that its author issues. Take the remarks about political friendships, for example (331d–332c). We read that successful rulers control the overtaken territories on the basis of friendships that they have with the summarily appointed loyalist or local leaders (331d–332c). That sounds good, but should the Syracusan friends of Dion or we ourselves follow this political schema? If the examples that the author of the letter cites (1.) Darius I, who seeks to conquer Greece or (2.) those Athenians, who fought the Persians off, but who sought, also, to yoke the Greek peoples under the rule of Athens) do not give us pause, then we may consider a historical example, which involves both Athens and Syracuse.

To establish territorial security on the basis of political friendships is exactly what an Athenian, who rallies *against* Syracuse, proposes when he seeks to undermine the power of Syracuse in Sicily in 415–414. Euphemus complains that "for tyrants and imperial cities nothing is unreasonable if expedient ... friendship or enmity is everywhere a matter of time or circumstance."[20] Euphemus, practically says the same thing that the author of the *Seventh Letter* says about the strength of friendship and the whimsical nature and weakness of tyranny. The difference is that in the *Seventh Letter*, Syracusans are recommended to make friendships, which a tyrant, Dionysius II, is unable to make, whereas Euphemus reassures that "in Sicily, our [Athenian] interest is not to weaken our friends, but by means of their strength to cripple our enemies,"[21] namely, Syracuse. The Syracusan *polis* needs to be undermined, if Athens is to prevent it from gaining hegemony in Sicily.

Euphemus speaks at the time when Athens is about to step onto the path, which leads to its certain destruction. The author of the *Seventh Letter* encapsulates the resultant dissipation of the Athenian polis in the "destruction of [its] written laws and [its] customs" (τῶν νόμων γράμματα καὶ ἔθη διεφθείρετο, 325de). In that city, we read, "such as it was, without friendly men and trustworthy companions, it was impossible to do anything" (οὔτε γὰρ ἄνευ φίλων ἀνδρῶν καὶ

---

[20] Thucydides, VI.85, 408.
[21] Ibid.

ἑταίρων πιστῶν οἷόν τ᾽εἶναι πράττειν, 325d). However, as the author of the *Seventh Letter* explains, the use that the Syracusans might have for the friends that they will make necessitates the conclusion which Euphemus points out some seventy years earlier, but about which the author of the *Seventh Letter* is silent, namely, that such friendships as the author of the *Seventh Letter* recommends will be used not only in order to avoid any harm from, but also to undermine, those who are perceived as enemies of the state.[22] Historical detail suggests that if we adopt this notion of friendship and use it to secure power and expedite government of a state, then we end up not with the "rule of laws" (ὑπὸ νόμοις, 334c), but with the unjust and "irreverent actions" (ἀνοσίων...ἔργων, 325a) that undermine the *polis* and do away with those citizens who oppose the atrocities (325a). In other words, we end up with the opposite state of affairs from the one that the author forecasts for the friends of Dion. If we do not take historical context into consideration and assume that the author means for us to follow this advice about political friendship, we end up with tyranny.[23]

---

[22] Dion, at the end of his life, vexes with anger and grief as he realizes that "it is preferable to die many times and to allow those wishing to kill him [Dion] to succeed, if it were necessary for him, now, to spend his life guarding not only against the ones he hates [against enemies], but also against his friends" (Plutarch, *Life of Dion*, 56.2), author's translation from Plutarch, *Lives, VII: Dion and Brutus. Timoleon and Aemilius Paulus* (Loeb Classical Library. Cambridge, MA: Harvard University Press, 1918).

[23] The analysis of friendship I present puts into question the passages in the *Seventh Letter* (331d – 332c), *Republic* (331d – 332b, 375b, 576a), and *Laws* (695d), where friendship is recommended as a basis for coherent character of a ruler and as a model for a well-run city. However, if we trace the idea of friendship, in the *Republic*, for example, back to Bk. I, we notice that it is problematized at the outset by being opposed to enmity as well as to the status of friendship under certain conditions that prohibit us from keeping a promise to a friend (331e). The model of the guardian-protected *polis* draws on the division between friends and enemies, as if this division is unequivocal and easy to establish. It is up to us to keep in mind that the question of friendship, as presented in Bk. I, is never resolved. Thus, friendship, as a means of securing political influence or as a determining factor in who to protect and who to wage war against, remains problematic. I choose not to dissolve this problematic character of

Philosophically this means several things. One conclusion we may draw is that tyrannical actions are simply necessary. If the situation dictates, we ought to resort to tyranny. However, this conclusion is inconsistent with the opening of the *Seventh Letter*, where the author questions the rationale of thinking that an exceptional situation justifies tyrannical acts (325a–e). Neither can we conclude that tyranny should be available as means of political activity to Syracusans because their circumstances are wildly different from those of the Athenians. The correspondences that we established between the historical events that set into motion the tyranny of Athens, that perpetuated it, and that led to the Athenians' demise—the events that are alive in the memory of Dion's friends in Leontini—serve to underscore the possibility that Syracuse and Sicily will not end up well, if they adopt the sorts of measures against the rule of tyranny that Athens herself did. In fact, it took another ten years, give or take, until a Corinthian general, Timoleon, laid civil strife to rest in Syracuse.[24]

Purgation of Violent Passions through Philosophical Reflection

There is one other way to think about the effect that the *Seventh Letter* might have on its addressees, whether in 355 BCE or now. I adopt the view that neither such actions and ideas as may lead to tyranny, nor tyrannical actions, nor tyrannical government, are desirable. Ultimately, tyranny leads to a dissolution of the written laws and morals in the city. It thus undermines the very *politeia* or the spirit that holds the community together. Following this view, I propose that the *Seventh Letter* does not invite any such response as

---

friendship, but to see how the friend/enemy distinction plays itself out in the historical imagination of the ancient Greeks.

[24] Although the *politeia* that Timoleon establishes in Syracuse is a mixture of oligarchy, democracy, and monarchy and so it is a mixed regime, some authors (e.g., Sordi 1961) speculate that Timoleon follows closely the advice of the *Seventh Letter* and that Timoleon, moreover, is an admirer of Plato. See Marta Sordi, *Timoleonte, Sikelika* (Palermo: Flaccovio, 1961). Talbert argues against such views. See J. A. R. Talbert, *Timoleon and the Revival of Greek Sicily: 344–317 B. C.* (Cambridge, UK: Cambridge University Press, 1974).

The Historical Background of the Seventh Letter

would solicit or lead to *tyrannical* actions. However, this does not mean that the *Letter* does not solicit *any* action. The action for which it calls, I claim, is not any deed that seeks to alter a government (e.g., depose a tyrant) or change a constitution (e.g., establish a set of new laws) of a city. The *Seventh Letter* does not seek to change a *politeia* or the soul of the polis directly;[25] instead, it can be read as an invitation to work on the constitution of one's own soul.

Lewis notices that the author (whom Lewis takes to be Plato) at the outset "confesses to having nurtured political ambitions as a young man, these ambitions had already been purged by the time of his involvement in Syracuse" (The *Seventh Letter*, 233). The author of the *Seventh Letter* describes Plato as someone who was privy to the tumultuous events that led to the demise of Athens. Plato witnessed and suffered or at least lived through these events. However, we read that there is a distance Plato is afforded from the political machinations of his time. His involvement in Athenian troubles is not direct, but rather emotional and, also, reflective. It appears that the *Seventh Letter* seeks to enact in the Syracusan friends of Dion, to whom it is addressed directly, as well as in us, its indirect addressees, a sort of *pathei mathos*.[26] We can, if we reflect on how the historical context of the letter shapes its political and didactic content, learn by undergoing. However, such an experience entails that we feel the passions of someone who observes tyranny, but neither chooses to

---

[25] S. Benardete observes that it makes sense for "Aristotle [to] say that the *politeia* is the soul of the city." Transcription of the Spring term lectures on Aristotle's *De Anima* (Chicago, IL: University of Chicago, 1993).

[26] I have it mind that we should put together Aeschylus's poetic phrase about human experience of learning through suffering (*Agamemnon* 177) with Aristotle's analysis of drama and, specifically, of tragedy. Aristotle, in the *Poetics*, would have us understand that when we are deeply saddened or very frightened by the spectacle of tragic drama, our emotions undergo a sort of purgation (1449b21–29). Aristotle, *On Poetics*, trans. S. Benardete and M. Davis, (South Bend, IN: St. Augustine Press, 2002). Davis in his commentary on the *Poetics*, offers an insightful discussion of the relationship between the passions of the tragic characters and the audience's impassioned response. See Michael Davis, *The Poetry of Philosophy: On Aristotle's Poetics* (South Bend, IN: St. Augustine's Press, 1999). He also gives a helpful account of Aristotle's remarks on purification of fear and pity (38–39).

participate in it, nor in the political actions that lead to its installment. Note that this is not the same as choosing to abstain from opposing tyranny. The passions that the Syracusans felt or that we may experience when we read the *Seventh Letter* do not all have to be ferocious or negative. The sentiments that the letter arouses can even be hopeful (e.g., promises of a better life for Syracuse at 327d–328a, 336ab), if not idealistic (appeal to victorious new rulers that would build up the city based on the ideals of the glorious past at 337b–d). Once the readers experience these passions of vengeance, comradery, patriotism, and hopeful idealism, the point is not to act on them, but to purge them.

The political provocations and didactic tenor of the letter excite our passions. The historical context puts into question some of its straightforward political prescriptions and, thus, serves as a deterrent from any immediate action to which the excited passions may call. The pause that the readers take, and the distance from immediate action that they gain, make room for philosophical reflection. In this reflective attitude the readers are, finally, able to examine and to purge the idealistic sentiments, the tyrannical zealotry, and the excessive inclinations of the soul; whether these be patriotic altruism or mercenary avarice. It might sound somewhat odd to us today that the *Seventh Letter* can provoke tyrannical sentiments in some of its readers, but Syracusans of the past, who sought to avenge Dion and to depose Dionysius II, were all too eager to repeat the mistakes of which the author accuses the assassins of Dion (335c–e). Moreover, it is my position that the *Seventh Letter*, above all, intends to rid the reader of convictions and desires that might foment or culminate in violent tyranny. I propose that this purgation of our passions is not so much for the sake of learning about what tyranny is via a direct encounter with it, as much as it is for the sake of avoiding first-hand acquaintance with tyranny in the first place.[27] My view applies both to the immediate addressees of the

---

[27] Wians takes a position that is less radical and claims that human knowledge of politics must be understood in terms of our experiential acquaintance with the

letter and to any of its other readers. As far as the former are concerned, the Syracusan friends of Dion do not need to be familiarized with tyranny. They have experienced it. As to the latter, I claim that it is preferable to become acquainted with tyranny by proxy, i.e., through historical and fictional means, as well as by imagining its effects upon oneself or one's political environment, rather than by participating in it directly.

The experience of purification of passions which I here describe may not be available to all of the readers of the letter. It is, as Lewis says, "naïve" to hope to turn a "ruling tyrant," who is wary of self-examination and reflection, into a philosopher,[28] whether through education (as with the historical Dionysius I and II) or on the basis of one letter (as with those tyrannically-minded individuals, who may read and dismiss any educational value in the *Seventh Letter* in our time). However, it is also naïve to simply agree with the author of the *Seventh Letter* that, on account of it being a written document, the letter does not contain any really serious thoughts (344c). We see that the letter has very important advice to give. Although this advice holds universally and across the expanses of time, we only arrive at it through a philosophical study of the historical contingencies as these relate to politics. The recommendation, in shorthand, is this: It is advisable to suffer in imagination, but not to follow up in action those passions that might lead to ideas, choices, and deeds which install, presage, or perpetuate tyranny. The whole gravity of this proposition is inaccessible unless we take note of the fact that our attentiveness to the historical setting of the letter changes the meaning of a number of its prescriptive passages that deal with political rule. The recommendation, which says "tyranny is unadvisable" is simplistic. This is not what the *Seventh Letter* is about.

---

things about which we seek to know. However, as Wians knows, such experientially-bound knowledge only attains to theoretical rigor upon reflection and it presupposes, if not necessitates, the possibility of very real, and not solely imaginative (as I suggest), suffering. See W. Wians, "The Agamemnon and Human Knowledge." *Logos and Muthos: Philosophical Essays in Greek Literature* (New York, NY: SUNY Press, 2009).

[28] Lewis, "The *Seventh Letter*," 242.

Marina Marren

Instead, as I understand it, the letter recommends that we identify and deflate the sorts of sentiments and convictions that prevent us from examining political ideals such as patriotism or absolute power of freedom, for example; ideals that orient our life and that appear desirable, but that turn out to be anything but benign in our historical time.

Marion Theresa Schneider[1]
Success Against All Odds, Failure Against All Logic:
Plutarch on Dion, Timoleon, and the Liberation of Sicily

When looking at the beautiful scenery of Syracuse today, one can hardly believe that there once was a time when it was regarded as almost synonymous with enslavement and tyranny; yet, there really *was* a time when people hardly believed that Sicily *could* be free. Take, for example, Plutarch's account of the two attempts at freeing Sicily from tyranny made by Dion of Syracuse in 357 BCE and Timoleon of Corinth in 345/4 BCE: In his *Life of Dion*, the Platonic philosopher and biographer Plutarch (c. 45–c. 125 CE) paints a brilliant picture of the scene when in 355 BCE, Apollocrates, eldest son of Dionysius II, and at this point commander of the tyrant's citadel on the island of Ortygia, finally had to surrender the citadel to the people of Syracuse and leave the city, accompanied by the royal family. The picture Plutarch paints of the Syracusans' reaction to this event is full of vivid imagination, joy – and wonder (Plut. *Dion* 50, 3-4):

> …and no one who was then in Syracuse missed that sight, nay, they called upon the absent ones also, pitying them because they could not behold this day and the rising of the sun upon a free Syracuse. For since, among the illustrations men give of the mutations of fortune, the expulsion of Dionysius is still to this day the strongest and plainest, what joy must we suppose those men themselves then felt, and how great a pride, who, with the fewest resources (ἐλαχίσταις ἀφορμαῖς), overthrew the greatest tyranny that ever was (τὴν μεγίστην τῶν πώποτε τυραννίδων)![2]

---

[1] Marion Theresa Schneider is research assistant at the Institut für Klassische Philologie, Julius-Maximilians-Universität, Würzburg. She is working on a commentary on Plutarch's *Life of Dion* and would like to express her thanks to Heather Reid, in particular for revising this article and including it in this volume, but also in general for her inspiring educational enthusiasm.

[2] Plut. *Dion* 50, 3-4: All translations from the *Lives of Dion* and *Timoleon* from Plutarch, *Lives, Vol. VI*, trans. by Bernadotte Perrin (Cambridge, MA: Harvard University Press, 1918).

It is not only in the *Life of Dion* that Plutarch lays great stress on the paradox between the rather hopeless starting-points of Dion's enterprise of freeing Sicily and its unbelievable success (however short it may have been); he also does so in his biography of Dion's more successful 'successor', Timoleon. Here (*Timol.* 1, 4) we are told with equal astonishment about the strange facts concerning the temporary liberation of Sicily from the tyranny achieved by Dion, and about its temporary re-enslavement in 346 BCE (after Dion had been murdered): The tyrant, Dionysius II, "had been unaccountably (παραλόγως) deprived by a small force of the greatest tyranny that ever was, and now more unaccountably still (παραλογώτερον) he had become, from a lowly exile, master of those who drove him forth"(*Timol.* 1, 4). Not much later (16, 1), the fortune of Dionysius is reversed again, and this time ultimately, due to the success of Timoleon. As Plutarch notes: "But though the misfortune of Dionysius seemed extraordinary (παραλόγου), none the less did the good fortune of Timoleon have something marvelous (θαυμαστόν) about it" (16, 1-3).

Two questions may arise when looking at these statements of astonishment: First, one may wonder what truth there was to this 'paradoxical' nature of the liberation of Sicily as perceived by Plutarch. Was he the only one to regard the liberation of Sicily as an unexpected, inexplicable event, or was this notion of astonishment at Dion's, and later Timoleon's, achievements against all expectations common to other historians as well, even contemporaries, and as such almost amounting to a fact? Secondly, whether fact or fiction, may there have been a special end to whose purpose Plutarch employed or stressed the theme of 'inexplicability' in telling the story of Dion and Timoleon at Syracuse? It was, after all, also the story of the failed historical attempt to put into practice the theoretical political ideals of his philosophical teacher, Plato, at Syracuse, and the more successful story of the unphilosophical general Timoleon.

In order to answer these questions, a comparison will be needed with other reports on Dion's enterprise in Sicily and with the views held by their authors (e. g. Diodorus Siculus or Nepos) as well as between Plutarch's contrasting *Lives* of Dion and Timoleon. Both

Success Against All Odds, Failure Against All Logic

comparisons, I argue, can lead us to a deeper understanding of Plutarch's perception not only with regard to the 'inexplicable' liberation of Sicily launched by the teachings of Plato, but also the 'inexplicable' failure of Dion and the teachings of Plato at Syracuse.

The 'inexplicable' liberation of Sicily - facts or fiction?

Of course, literature, especially in antiquity, is full of 'paradoxical' stories like those of Dion and Timoleon as told by Plutarch. We might think of the whole genre of Paradoxography or Thaumasia-literature.[3] This popularity of paradoxical stories might be due either to a literary *topos* or to an anthropological constant in human experience (which both could be termed "David against Goliath"). In the case of the liberation of Sicily, the notion of a success that no logical calculation would have predicted actually seems to have been so common to historians that we may with good reason assume that there must have been some historical truth to it. Compare the way in which Diodorus Siculus (1st century BCE) phrases his view on Dion's victory over Dionysius II in 357 BCE in his universal history, the *Bibliotheke* (16, 9, 1-3):

> Dion, son of Hipparinus, sailed to Sicily intending to overthrow the tyranny of Dionysius, and with slenderer resources than those of any conqueror before his time (ἐλαχίσταις δὲ τῶν πρὸ αὐτοῦ πάντων χρησάμενος ἀφορμαῖς) he succeeded contrary to all expectation (ἀνελπίστως) in overthrowing the greatest realm in all Europe (μεγίστην δυναστείαν τῶν κατὰ τὴν Εὐρώπην). Who, indeed, would have believed that, putting ashore with two merchantmen, he could actually have overcome the despot who had at his disposal four hundred ships of war, infantry numbering nearly one hundred thousand, ten thousand horses, and as great a store of arms, food, and money as one in all probability possessed who had to maintain lavishly the aforesaid forces; and, apart from all we have mentioned, had a city which was the largest of the cities of Hellas, and harbours

---

[3] See Otta Wenskus and Lorraine Daston, "Paradoxographoi," in *Der neue Pauly*, vol. 9, ed. H. Cancik et al. (Stuttgart: Metzler, 2000), cols. 309–14.

and docks and fortified citadels that were impregnable, and, besides, a great number of powerful allies? The cause for Dion's successes was, above all others, his own nobility of spirit (ἡ ἰδία λαμπρότης τῆς ψυχῆς), his courage (ἀνδρεία) and the willing support of those who were to be liberated (ἡ τῶν ἐλευθεροῦσθαι μελλόντων εὔνοια), but still more important than all these were the pusillanimity of the tyrant and his subjects' hatred of him (ἥ τε ἀνανδρία τοῦ τυράννου καὶ τὸ τῶν ἀρχομένων πρὸς αὐτὸν μῖσος); for when all these characteristics merged at a single critical moment (πάντα γὰρ ταῦτα πρὸς ἕνα καιρὸν συνδραμόντα), they unexpectedly (παραδόξως) brought to a successful close deeds which were considered impossible (τὰς ἀπιστουμένας πράξεις πρὸς τέλος ἤγαγεν).[4]

We note the striking similarities between Plutarch and Diodorus concerning the focus on the paradoxical side of the events leading to the liberation of Sicily; admittedly both authors generally shared a striking fascination with paradoxical events,[5] but while this fascination may explain some of the interest they took in the stories of Dion and Timoleon first-hand, it does not tell us much about the historical truth behind them. Of course, since the similarities between Plutarch and Diodorus are even such that they use the same phrases (τὴν μεγίστην... τυραννίδων... ἐλαχίσταις ἀφορμαῖς/ἐλαχίσταις ἀφορμαῖς...μεγίστην δυναστεία), the notion of paradoxical success might be due to a common source both authors shared at this point of the story. This common source may have been Ephorus, probably

---

[4] Diod. Sic. 16. 9.1-3. Diodorus Siculus, *Diodorus of Sicily in Twelve Volumes*, trans. C. H. Oldfather. Vol. 4-8. (Cambridge, Mass.: Harvard University Press; London: William Heinemann, Ltd. 1989). Cf. also 16, 11, 1-2. For Diodorus's contemplations on the fickleness of fortune when describing the great changes in the fortune of Dionysius II, cf. as well 16.70.1-3.

[5] Παράδοξος is certainly one of Diodorus's favourite terms, cf. Rudolf Neubert, *Spuren selbständiger Thätigkeit bei Diodor* (Bautzen: Monse, 1890), 10; 22–23. For Plutarch, cf. e.g. *De def. or.* 418c; *Rom.* 8,8f.; *Galba* 19, 5; *Sertorius* 19, 8; *Cato Min.* 11, 3, etc.

Diodorus's main source for the passages on Dion and at least one of the major sources used by Plutarch;[6] since Ephorus in turn may have been influenced by the report of Dion's comrade, Timonides of Leucas,[7] which was widely used by Plutarch for the middle section of his biography, there may also have been a more indirect link between the versions of Diodorus and Plutarch. Yet, generally Plutarch and Diodorus are considered as representing two different, and often opposite, strands of tradition on the history of Dion.[8]

Common source or not, however, there is still one major difference between both authors that cannot be explained away so easily, namely the way they actually use the shared information on the paradoxical nature of the liberation of Sicily: Diodorus, in contrast to Plutarch, at once adds a variety of logical explanations for the strange facts related (Dion's nobility of spirit and courage, the willing support of the tyrant's subjects, the tyrant's cowardice and the hatred he inspired in his people); in his eyes, a series of plausible events and sentiments coming together at the right point in time made the impossible happen. In Plutarch, the statements of inexplicable success and failure are not followed by any such clear explanation on the author's side; rather, they feature as a kind of concluding comment on the strangeness of these events.

Almost the same is the case when we compare Plutarch's account of Dion's enterprise with that of Cornelius Nepos (1st century BCE) in his book on *Great generals of foreign nations* (*Excellentium Imperatorum Vitae*). Nepos's short report on the liberation of Sicily through Dion features two numerical facts (10,000 horsemen, 100,000 on foot) that must derive from a common source with Diodorus (maybe, again, Ephorus, since Nepos's main source, Timaios, is usually held to be responsible for the many striking differences

---

[6] For Ephorus in Diodorus, see Christian August Volquardsen, *Untersuchungen über die Quellen der griechischen und sicilischen Geschichten bei Diodor, Buch XI bis XVI* (Kiel: Schwers'sche Buchhandlung, 1868), 85; Müller, *De fontibus*, 40–47; Lionel Jehuda Sanders, *The legend of Dion* (Toronto: Edgar Kent, 2008), 153 n. 327.

[7] Cf. Müller, *De fontibus*, 43.

[8] Cf. Sanders, *Legend of Dion*, 153–54.

between him and Diodorus;[9] but since there are scholars who argue that Nepos's biography wholly relied on one single source, namely Timaios,[10] the similar numbers may as well derive from another tradition). Far more importantly, though, it also includes two further formulations that again stress the general perception of Dion's paradoxical success (*Dion* 5,3):

> Nevertheless Dion, relying less upon his own resources than on hatred of the tyrant (*fretus non tam suis copiis quam odio tyranny*), although he had but two transports, sallied forth with the greatest courage to attack a dynasty of fifty years' duration, defended by five hundred war ships, ten thousand horsemen and a hundred thousand on foot. And he so easily (*adeo facile*) overthrew his opponents – a success which filled all nations with amazement (*quod omnibus gentibus admirabile est uisum*) – that two days after landing in Sicily he entered Syracuse; which goes to show that no rule is secure which is not founded upon the devotion of its subjects.[11]

Nepos, we see, adds more and more evidence to a common thread running through ancient historiography, i.e. the tendency of portraying the liberation of Sicily as something perceived already by its contemporaries as a paradoxical event. But Nepos, like Diodorus and unlike Plutarch, does not simply identify with the amazement of Dion's contemporaries. He at once gives his own logical explanation for the events, based on his own political convictions: as a lover of freedom, *libertas*, and a hater of tyrants; to him, no tyranny, however strong, can be safe from being overthrown if the tyrant cannot make his subjects love him and consent to his rule.

At this point, having seen already some of the numbers given by Diodorus and Nepos to visualize the factual discrepancy between the mighty army of the tyrant of Syracuse and Dion's small band of

---

[9] Cf. Müller, *De fontibus*, 40–47; Morrow, *Platonic Epistles*, 34.
[10] Cf. Müller, *De fontibus*, 9–10.
[11] Nepos, Dion 5, 3. *Cornelius Nepos, On Great Generals. On Historians*, trans. by J. C. Rolfe (Cambridge, MA: Harvard University Press, 1929). On Timoleon cf. Timol. 2, 1: Timoleon missus incredibili felicitate Dionysium tota Sicilia depulit.

desperadoes setting out to overthrow him and granted with such inexplicable success, we might – with all due caution – want to ascertain some of the truth behind their numbers and behind the theme of their unexpected success.

Of course, there can be no doubt that the tyrant Dionysius, with his army and his fortifications, was indeed powerful – whether the numbers of his men, listed by both Diodorus and Nepos as accruing to 10,000 horsemen, 100,000 foot soldiers, and between 400 and 500 ships, be exact or not. But there has been some doubt concerning the numbers of Dion's men as given by Plutarch and Diodorus Siculus. Plutarch lists 800 Greek mercenaries crossing the Adriatic onboard about five ships (cf. Plut. *Dion* 22, 8). They are joined by about 5,000 Sicilians (Plut. *Dion* 27, 5), accruing to a total of only 5,800 men fighting against the army of Dionysius – a small band indeed, one might say. Diodorus however paints a somewhat different picture: In his version, Dion's 1,000/3,000 Greek mercenaries (Diod. Sic. 16.9.5-6; 16.17.3 – the numbers vary) are joined by no less than 20,000 Sicilians (Diod. Sic. 16.9.5-6); for the battle of Syracuse we even read of a total of 50,000 men on Dion's side (Diod. Sic. 16.10.5 – however this calculation may have come about): a bit more of an *army* of liberators and ten times as many as related by Plutarch.

So what is to be made of all these numbers? Very little but the conclusion that there must have been more than one tradition on the liberation of Sicily,[12] with all traditions agreeing on the unpredictable nature of Dion's success, while disagreeing somewhat on its extent. Concerning Diodorus and Plutarch, the contradictory numbers have been blamed on their somewhat biased sources, Plutarch's number of 5,800 men being received from Dion's fellow-combatant, Timonides, and being meant to glorify Dion's success, Diodorus's 50,000 being a typical exaggeration as so many found in Ephorus.[13]

---

[12] On the traditions on Dion, see Sanders, *Legend of Dion*.

[13] Cf. Müller, *De fontibus*, 46; J. Harward, *The Platonic Epistles* (Cambridge, MA: Harvard University Press, 1932), 30; Sanders, *Legend of Dion*, 49. On typical numbers in ancient historiography in general, see Detlev Fehling, *Die Quellenangaben bei Herodot. Studien zur Erzählkunst Herodots* (Berlin: de Gruyter, 1971), 159 and 163.

So far then, it has already become rather unlikely that the general agreement on the paradoxical nature of Dion's success against Dionysius was simply due to the character of one single early source that influenced all our other evidence, directly or indirectly. Yet, we might want to strengthen this argument by looking into one last piece of evidence, this time more or less contemporary to the events in question: In his *Adversus Leptinem* the rhetorician Demosthenes refers to the events concerning Dion's expedition to Sicily only one or two years afterwards[14] in a manner very similar to Diodorus, Nepos, and Plutarch (Demosthenes 20, 162):

> Nor again could the present Dionysius ever have expected (οὐδέ γ' ὁ νῦν ὢν Διονύσιος ἤλπισεν ἄν ποτ' ἴσως) that Dion would come against him in a cargo-boat with a handful of soldiers and expel the master of so many warships and mercenaries and cities. But, methinks, the future is hidden from all men, and great events hang on small chances (μικροὶ καιροὶ μεγάλων πραγμάτων αἴτιοι γίγνονται). Therefore we must be modest in the day of prosperity, and must show that we are not blind to the future.[15]

Here, Demosthenes is not really concerned with the actual liberation of Sicily nor is he favoring any of the participants: he merely uses the unexpected downfall of Dionysius as an example supporting his own argument of how little men (and namely, his opponent in this case, the legislator Leptines) can predict the future.[16] Even if the Athenians' only source on Dion's victory may have been the letters Timonides sent to Plato's disciple Speusippus, the example of Dionysius and Dion would certainly not have had any plausibility

---

[14] Demosthenes's *Adversus Leptinem* is dated by Dionysios of Halikarnassos to the archonship of Kallistratos, that is to the second year of the 106th Olympiad = 355/4 BC; for a discussion of this date, see Christos Kremmydas, *Commentary on Demosthenes* Against Leptines. *With Introduction, Text, and Translation* (Oxford, New York: Oxford University Press, 2012), 33–34.

[15] Demosth. 20, 162. *Demosthenes*, trans. by C. A. Vince, M. A. and J. H. Vince, M.A. (Cambridge, MA: Harvard University Press; London: William Heinemann Ltd., 1926).

[16] For more detailed discussion, see Kremmydas, *Adversus Leptinem*, 162f.

Success Against All Odds, Failure Against All Logic

for Demosthenes's audience, if there had been any dispute about the unexpectedness of Dion's success beforehand: If there had been more than a few smaller ships leaving from Greece with more than one thousand mercenaries and joined by more than a few thousand Sicilians, in short, if the victory over Dionysius had not come against all expectation (παρὰ δόξαν), the audience of Demosthenes, being fully aware of the events and their outcome (since it had happened only one or two years earlier), would not have been convinced by his exaggeration.[17] Therefore, the whole use of the example within Demosthenes's argumentation before his audience of contemporary Greeks rests on the factual character of Dion's 'unexpected' success.

Explaining the 'inexplicable' – Plutarch's interpretation

So we have seen that all of the more important sources on Dion's enterprise in Syracuse refer to the liberation of Sicily as a kind of inexplicable, paradoxical event. We have also seen, though, that Diodorus as well as Nepos at once added what rational explanations they could find for the inexplicable to have come to pass the way it did: For Diodorus Siculus, the Sicilian patriot who revels in highlighting deeds and achievements brought about by his countrymen,[18] it had been the natural prowess and nobility of the Syracusan prince Dion and the courageous people of Syracuse and Sicily that, combined at the critical moment, had made the impossible possible. For Nepos, the Roman Republican and hater of tyrants, who ponders on what keeps powerful military leaders from becoming a risk to *libertas* and on what gives some people the strength to defeat a tyrant,[19] it is the intrinsic weakness of every tyranny – the inability to win the support of its people – that inevitably led to the end of the tyranny of Dionysius. In Demosthenes, the liberation of Sicily becomes only one in a row of similar examples in his line of argument, which states that there are events that cannot be predicted

---

[17] Cf. Harward, *Platonic Epistles*, 31.
[18] Cf. e.g. Neubert, *Spuren selbständiger Tätigkeit*, 9.
[19] Cf. A. C. Dionisotti, "Nepos and the generals," *Journal of Roman Studies* 78 (1988): 35–49; on contemporary history influencing Nepos's perception and depiction of the past, see also Sanders, *Legend of Dion*, 156–163.

and therefore should be a warning to people prone to hubris like his opponent, Leptines. Each of these authors commenting on the liberation of Sicily uses the simple, general perception of a seemingly inexplicable event to support their own argument and conviction.

So what about Plutarch: does he, too, offer some clear logical explanation for the paradoxical events he observes? The case is not as clear in Plutarch as it is in Diodorus, Nepos, or Demosthenes: There is no explanation directly following Plutarch's observations on the paradoxical liberation and re-enslavement of Sicily. Rather these observations stand for themselves, more like a concluding comment than a question aiming at an answer. In order to find reasons that could explain the inexplicable nature of the liberation of Sicily in the eyes of Plutarch, or to discover more about his purpose when he employs this trope in his story of Dion, one should best take a closer look at his *Life of Dion* and his *Life of Timoleon* together.

a) Dion's rise against all odds

Even though Plutarch is less explicit on his explanations for the extraordinary liberation of Sicily than Nepos or Diodorus, there is, of course, a line of more or less *implicit* logical reasons for Dion's success that can be extracted from his narration in the course of the *Life*. Like Nepos and Diodorus for example, Plutarch refers to the people's hatred of Dionysius as an important element clearing the way for Dion's glorious entry into Syracuse (*Comp. Dionis et Bruti* 4, 1-2): "For Dionysius must have been despised by every one of his associates, devoted as he was to wine, dice, and women... Therefore Dion had only to be seen in Sicily, and many thousands joined him in attacking Dionysius (διὸ τῷ μὲν ὀφθέντι μόνον ἐν Σικελίᾳ μυριάδες οὐκ ὀλίγαι συνέστησαν ἐπὶ Διονύσιον)."[20]

This critical observation, though, is only made in comparison with the parallel life of Brutus at the end of both *Lives* (where it marks an important difference between both men). It is not really one that is stressed by Plutarch in the *Life of Dion* itself more than usual in a

---

[20] *Comp. Dionis et Bruti* 4, 1-2.

story about overthrowing a tyrant.[21] In the actual narrative, the 'myriads' of men joining the expedition (a rhetorical exaggeration, obviously) had melted down to a few thousand.

But besides the people's hatred of Dionysius as a natural stimulus for joining Dion's 'march of the Thousand'[22] towards Syracuse, there are also some references to a positive kind of yearning for being saved from tyranny through philosophy which Plutarch perceives in Sicily (*Dion* 19, 1-2): "His [i.e. Plato's] arrival filled Dionysius with great joy, and the Sicilians [Sicily] again with great hope; they all prayed and laboured zealously that Plato might triumph over Philistus, and philosophy over tyranny (Σικελίαν, συνευχομένην καὶ συμφιλοτιμουμένην, Πλάτωνα μὲν Φιλίστου περιγενέσθαι, φιλοσοφίαν δὲ τυραννίδος)" (*Dion* 19, 1-2).

Love of wisdom as an impetus for the Sicilians to turn their eyes towards Plato and Dion – wouldn't that be an excellent explanation for the liberation of Sicily from the perspective of a Platonic philosopher like Plutarch? On closer inspection, though, observations like this are, unlike those of Diodorus before, not stated by Plutarch as facts that already have come to pass; rather, they are hopeful illusions that often do not even reflect his own opinions on the people of Sicily, but those of his sources and/or agents in the story (e.g. Timonides or Speusippus) who follow a clear aim: Their portrait of the people of Syracuse as longing for Plato's philosophy and Dion's military aid was meant to convince either Plato and Dion of the necessity to return to Syracuse or to demonstrate to their other readers how right Plato and Dion were in actually doing so. See for example Speusippus's entreaty shortly before Dion's actual return to Sicily and the way it anticipates the trope of the small resources overpowering a tyranny (*Dion* 22, 1-3):

> From this time on Dion turned his thoughts to war. With this Plato himself would have nothing to do, out of respect for his tie

---

[21] Hartmut Erbse, "Die Bedeutung der Synkrisis in den Parallelbiographien Plutarchs," *Hermes* 84 (1956): 414ff. argues, though, that there is no point of comparison that is not dealt with in the narrative *Dion* and *Brutus*.

[22] Harward, *Platonic Epistles*, 32.

of hospitality with Dionysius, and because of his age. But Speusippus and the rest of his companions co-operated with Dion and besought him to free Sicily, which stretched out her arms to him and eagerly awaited his coming (Σικελίαν, χεῖρας ὀρέγουσαν αὐτῷ καὶ προθύμως ὑποδεχομένην)... For all now spoke in the same strain, begging and exhorting Dion to come without ships, men-at-arms, or horses; he was simply to come himself in a small boat, and lend the Sicilians his person and his name against Dionysius (παρὰ πάντων λόγος, δεομένων καὶ παρακελευομένων ἐλθεῖν Δίωνα μὴ ναῦς ἔχοντα μηδ' ὁπλίτας μηδ' ἵππους, ἀλλ' αὐτὸν εἰς ὑπηρετικὸν ἐμβάντα χρῆσαι τὸ σῶμα καὶ τοὔνομα Σικελιώταις ἐπὶ τὸν Διονύσιον).

Could these hopes and expectations which the Sicilians allegedly set on Dion, his person and his name, be an explanation for his inexplicable success? Not in the eyes of Plutarch, I argue. The opinion Plutarch had of the people of Syracuse/Sicily seems to have differed very much from that professed by some protagonists in the *Life*. Of course, Plutarch observes, the people of Sicily were longing for liberty, and this emotional element of longing made up for some deficiencies in their numbers or weapons (cf. 27, 5). Of course, he observes, the Syracusans wanted to be saved from tyranny and, accordingly, received Dion and his men with a welcoming worthy of gods when they proved to be successful (cf. 24, 5-10; 28, 4; 29, 2; 46, 1-2). But in between these moments of triumph and success, when times were getting harder and actual choices had to be made, the Syracusans again and again proved to be a fickle, unwise, and egoistic people – philosophy did not rank that high among them when it came to decision making (see especially chapter 32 onward).

If there was any human contribution to Dion's military success in Sicily on the part of other parties worth mentioning, in the eyes of Plutarch it was surely not that of the Sicilians, but the prowess, the experience, and the spirit of the Greek mercenaries that could make up for any lack in numbers (cf. 22, 8). Again and again, they play the crucial roles among Dion's men, more than once saving the day for the rest of them. And again and again, the expectations of the enemy (the Syracusans themselves, respectively) to find the smaller force of Dion easy prey are confounded because of just these characteristics (e.g. 30, 10-11; 38, 6). Afterwards, of course, their number is exaggerated by the responsible commanders who are overtaken by this small force without too much of a fight of resistance (e.g. Timocrates in 28, 2).

Yet, none of these rational explanations implicitly given by Plutarch in the course of events suffices to explain the paradoxical success of Dion as observed in the passages above. Rather, Plutarch from the beginning of the *Life of Dion* explicitly stresses a different, irrational element that in his eyes seems to have been at the core of the whole liberation of Sicily: the support Dion and Plato received from some divine power that wanted to use both the prince and the philosopher for laying the foundation of a free Sicily. It was "by some divine good fortune (θείᾳ τινὶ τύχῃ)," Plutarch observes, that "Plato came to Sicily. This was not of man's devising, but some heavenly power, as it would seem (κατ' οὐδένα λογισμὸν ἀνθρώπινον· ἀλλὰ δαίμων τις ὡς ἔοικε), laying far in advance of the time a foundation for the liberty of Syracuse, and devising a subversion of tyranny, brought Plato from Italy to Syracuse and made Dion his disciple"(*Dion* 4, 3-4). Plutarch here is taking up the argumentation, even the wording of Plato's *Seventh Letter*,[23] but the meaning of words and, consequently, the meaning of the whole passage reflecting the intention of the writer has changed since the *Seventh Letter* was written: When Plato points to *tychē*'s role in his coming to Sicily, he is speaking of blind fortune, a more or less irrational power that he cannot control at all (at the end of the letter, it is plainly characterized as τύχη τις ἀνθρώπων κρείττων, 737d). It is this blind fortune that consequently can be made responsible for all the mishaps to follow, without passing any judgement on Plato's own intentions or actions regarding Syracuse.[24] *Tychē* still has a similar meaning in the philosophical writings of Plutarch, but in his *Lives* the term has become something different: here *tychē* (as expressed in the epithet

---

[23] Plat. *Ep.* VII, 326e.
[24] Cf. Arnd Zimmermann, *Tychē bei Platon* (PhD. Diss., Bonn, 1968), 91–97.

theios above) denotes a godlike, divine power that is not blind, but steers the world intentionally, although men cannot know these intentions. Plutarch uses *tychē* in his *Lives* as almost a synonym for providence (πρόνοια).[25] Accordingly, *tychē*'s influence on the events in Sicily does not so much diminish Plato's or Dion's responsibility for its liberation, but rather lends them authority. It elevates their intentions, their actions, and their outcome. The fact that Plato and Dion were right in taking action in Syracuse is proven by the success bestowed upon them by divine powers. Again and again, these forces interfere on their behalf causing the most extraordinary, inexplicable events to happen so the impossible liberation of Sicily can take place. For example, when Dion finally reaches Sicily, he learns from the Carthaginian commander Synalos that Dionysius has by chance just sailed to Italy with eighty ships (26, 1): "But what most of all encouraged them was the accidental (τὸ συμβεβηκὸς αὐτομάτως) absence of Dionysius from Syracuse; for it chanced (ἐτύγχανεν) that he had recently sailed with eighty ships to Italy." The tyrant learns of Dion's expedition later still, due to an even stranger accident (τύχη τις παράλογος) befalling the messenger sent to him by the then commander of Syracuse, Timocrates: a wolf steals the wallet containing the report for Dionysius, and the messenger, out of fear of Dionysius's reaction, runs away rather than telling the tyrant about his mishap (26, 7-27, 1). In addition, a row of prodigious *omina* accompanies Dion's march towards Syracuse and his entry into the city. Plutarch's observation that there was something extraordinary, unaccountable about Dion's success in Sicily does fit very well with these reported stories, which do not feature in Diodorus or Nepos.

---

[25] On the different meanings of *tychē* in Plutarch, see Simon Swain, "Plutarch: Chance, Providence, and History," *The American Journal of Philology* 110 (1989): 272–302. It has been argued that the concept of a Roman goddess *Fortuna/Felicitas* played some part in Plutarch's conception of fortune, cf. Sven-Tage Theodorsson, "Timoleon, the fortunate general," in *The statesman in Plutarch's works. Proceedings of the Sixth International Conference of the International Plutarch Society, Nijmegen/Castle Hernen, May 1-5, 2002. 2, The statesman in Plutarch's Greek and Roman lives*, ed. Lukas De Blois et al. (Leiden: Brill, 2005), 221.

Yet, of course, Plutarch's narration cannot end here: At the peak of his success, as it were, Dion's fortune seems to undergo a serious change. This change of fortune is put in one very expressive scene by Plutarch: The hour of Dion's greatest triumph over tyranny, when he addresses the people of Syracuse to proclaim their freedom standing on the monumental sun-dial built by the tyrants, is overshadowed by the very ambiguous interpretation of the soothsayers who interpret the circumstances of this address as both a good omen for Syracuse and a bad omen for the personal career of Dion (29, 5): "To the soothsayers … it seemed a most happy omen, that Dion, when he harangued the people, had put under his feet the ambitious monument of the tyrant; but because it was a sun-dial upon which he stood when he was elected general, they feared that his enterprise might undergo some speedy change of fortune (μὴ τροπήν τινα τῆς τύχης αἱ πράξεις ταχεῖαν λάβωσιν)."

b) Dion's fall against all logic

There seems to be a clear cut in Dion's fortune: while providence together with the people of Syracuse seems to have supported his endeavor of freeing Sicily from tyranny, the gods obviously abandoned his cause as soon as it has been achieved. Dion's further endeavors to install a Platonic government in Syracuse are neither supported by the people nor by the gods. Does Plutarch give us any hints as to why Dion stopped being successful?

Although one might call the whole *Life of Dion* a careful analysis of just that same question, Plutarch again does not provide us with an easy answer, perhaps because he himself could only guess what actually went wrong. There are, however, two character traits of Dion that in the eyes of Plutarch may have accounted for much of his failure as a politician:

On the one hand, there is Dion's unfortunate character trait of αὐθάδεια, his lack of amiability and his austere, philosophical mindset that indeed could be blamed for his lacking popularity among ordinary, non-philosophical men. Plutarch pointed to this character trait twice earlier in the life, and it begins to show again after the liberation of Sicily (*Dion* 52, 5-6):

> Nevertheless, he made it a point not to remit or relax at all the gravity of his manners or his haughtiness in dealing with the people (τοῦ μέντοι περὶ τὰς ὁμιλίας ὄγκου καὶ τοῦ πρὸς τὸν δῆμον ἀτενοῦς), although his situation called for a gracious demeanor (χάριτος), and although Plato, as I have said, wrote and warned him that self-will (αὐθάδεια) was 'a companion of solitude.' But he seems to have been of a temper naturally averse to graciousness, and, besides, he was ambitious to curb the Syracusans, who were given to excessive license and luxury.

While before any critical reference to Dion's αὐθάδεια had been made from the perspective of agents in the story (Plato or people at the court of Dionysius II), it is in this passage that we get closest to an explicit critical statement on Dion from Plutarch himself. But mark that it is not Dion's nature that is criticized by the author, but his refusal to work on it and improve it – pointing out that his teacher, Plato, had not been mistaken about Dion's whole true nature, only about one single character trait that may have proved tragic in a politician, but does not detract so much from their philosophical ideals.

On the other hand, Dion more than once displays an unfortunate kind of political and personal naivety that makes him easy prey for demagogues (like Heracleides and his supporters) and false friends (like Callippus). In comparison with Brutus's choice of friends or the good influence that he had on them, Dion's unwise choices may account for his final failure (*Comp. Dionis et Bruti* 4, 7-8): "But Dion either chose unwisely and entrusted himself to bad men, or else treated the men of his choice so as to turn them from good to bad, neither of which are mistakes a prudent man ought to make. And in fact Plato censures him for choosing such friends as proved his ruin (τοιούτους ἑλομένῳ φίλους ὑφ' ὧν ἀπώλετο)."[26]

Yet again, the judgement Plutarch passes on Dion in this comparison differs considerably from the picture he paints of him in the *Life*. And again, the critical assessment of Dion is not expressed as the author's opinion itself, but as the reported opinion of his

---

[26] *Comp. Dionis et Bruti* 4, 7-8.

teacher, Plato, very likely meant to distance himself from Dion's failure and its possible reasons. For one might ask as well: how could someone trained and educated by Plato, his favorite disciple even, living according to Plato's principles and trying to install them in a whole state be so unwise as to die from having chosen "false companions"?

One might want to ask even more in comparison to the success achieved in Sicily some time later by someone who had nothing to do with Plato at all. And indeed, Plutarch himself seems to be puzzled at the fact that Dion, though trying to endow Sicily with the benefits of philosophy and to act himself according to the ideals instilled in him by Plato, turned out to be unfortunate in his efforts, while his successor, Timoleon of Corinth, the honest general without the slightest philosophical aspirations,[27] succeeded in liberating Sicily from tyranny and re-establishing democracy and economic welfare in Sicily. Was it the mere will of the gods, of blind fortune, or of an evil demon that Dion should not be successful, thus making impossible any judgement of his actions or ideals? Or does the comparison with Timoleon's no more logical success indicate that, in the eyes of Plutarch, there never was a real hope for Sicily to be saved by the philosophy of Plato; Plutarch's story of a series of "unaccountable" events being the gentle way of telling us so?

c) Timoleon's rise against all logic

When Timoleon is summoned by the Syracusans for help, some time after Dion's death, his factual situation is not much different from that encountered by Dion on his march towards Syracuse: the number of 1,000 Corinthians against the "great numbers of Carthaginian triremes" which Hicetas, the current tyrant, had sent for, is certainly not in favour of Timoleon's enterprise. When they engage in battle for the first time, it is less than twelve hundred men on Timoleon's side (οἱ σύμπαντες ἦσαν οὐ πλείους χιλίων διακοσίων) against five thousand on Hicetas's side (*Timol.* 12, 4-5). Later on, when the Carthaginian general Mago arrives, the number

---

[27] Theodorsson, "Timoleon," 224ff, argues convincingly against the idea that Timoleon's program for post-tyrannical Sicily was influenced by Plato.

of his ships is specified as a total of 150 containing an infantry of 60,000 men. In addition to this factual deficiency, there is not much enthusiasm left among the people of Syracuse that could make up for their lack in numbers as it might have done in Dion's case: the continuing series of "liberators" of Sicily getting killed by other "liberators" or professed "liberators" turning into tyrants seems to have left them totally disillusioned as to the motives of anyone professing to come to the rescue of Syracuse – not to speak of the desperate state of their city at the very moment (*Timol.* 11, 5-12,1):

> But Hicetas was afraid when he learned that Timoleon had crossed the strait, and sent for great numbers of the Carthaginian triremes. And now it was that the Syracusans altogether despaired of their deliverance, seeing their harbour in the power of the Carthaginians, their city in the hands of Hicetas and their citadel in the possession of Dionysius; while Timoleon had but a hold as it were on the fringe of Sicily in the little city of Tauromenium, with a feeble hope and a small force to support him (ἐπ' ἐλπίδος ἀσθενοῦς καὶ βραχείας δυνάμεως); for apart from a thousand soldiers and provisions barely sufficient for them, he had nothing.

> Nor did the cities feel confidence in him, over full of ills as they were and embittered against all leaders of armies, particularly by reason of the perfidy of Callippus and Pharax, one of whom was an Athenian, and the other a Lacedaemonian; but both of them, while declaring that they came to secure the freedom of Sicily and wished to overthrow its tyrants, made the calamities of Sicily under her tyrants seem as gold in comparison, and brought her people to think those more to be envied who had perished in slavery than those who had lived to see her independence.

> Expecting, therefore, that the Corinthian leader would be no whit better than those who had preceded him, but that the same sophistries and lures were come to them again, and that with fair hopes and kind promises they were to be made docile enough to receive a new master in place of an old one, they all suspected

Success Against All Odds, Failure Against All Logic

and repulsed the appeals of the Corinthians except the people of Adranum.

Timoleon counters the enemy's strength with his tactics (e.g. by overpowering them while still preparing their military camp or secretly supplying the besieged citadel with food from Catana, cf. *Timol.* 12, 3-9; 18, 1). But the fact that Dionysius surrenders to Timoleon after the very first battle out of spite for Hicetas is certainly not due to any of Timoleon's tactics, but considered an unexpectedly lucky event (τὴν ἀνέλπιστον εὐτυχίαν) that even surprises the general himself (*Timol.* 13, 3). Plutarch, who ponders much on the change of fortune in the life of Dionysius II (cf. chapters 13 to 15), very often stresses the paradoxical nature of both the misfortune of Timoleon's enemies and of Timoleon's own luck (cf. 16, 1; 16, 10-12;). At times, he even seems to attribute Timoleon's success more to his luck than to his valor, especially in the case of the inexplicable defeat of the Carthaginians without so much as a battle. The question whether it was τύχη or ἀρετή that led Timoleon to his success is put like a theme at the beginning of the episode (19, 1): "In these successes, then, foresight and valor might still dispute the claims of Fortune; but that which followed them would seem to have been wholly due to good fortune (παντάπασιν ἔοικε συμβῆναι κατ' εὐτυχίαν)..." Timoleon himself seems to answer the question in favor of his own good fortune that outweighs his military deficiencies (cf. 20, 1: "...relying on the good fortune and success that attended his efforts rather than the strength of his army (οἷς εὐτύχει καὶ κατώρθου μᾶλλον ἢ τῇ δυνάμει πεποιθώς); for his followers were not more than four thousand in number"). But the true relationship between the personal valor of a general, the factual numbers of his army, and the part that fortune plays in any military event, is perhaps best phrased from the perspective of the Carthaginian general Mago, who in the end leaves Sicily for no real reason at all, but only out of fear of Timoleon's good luck and suspicion of his allies. Hicetas's hint at the numbers of both armies that seem so favorable to them is reversed by Mago (20, 11):

…when Hicetas begged him to remain and tried to show him how much superior they were to their enemies, he thought rather that they were more inferior to Timoleon in bravery and good fortune (ἀρετῇ καὶ τύχῃ) than they surpassed him in the number of their forces (πλήθει δυνάμεως), and weighing anchor at once, sailed off to Libya, thus letting Sicily slip out of his hands disgracefully and for no reason that man could suggest (κατ' οὐδένα λογισμὸν ἀνθρώπινον).

In the eyes of Plutarch, logic (at least from the human perspective, κατ' οὐδένα λογισμὸν ἀνθρώπινον, the same term that is used in *Dion* 4, 3) cannot account for why Timoleon was successful in liberating Sicily from all its tyrants – Dionysius II, the Carthaginians, and Hicetas – but he perceives a kind of divine quality in the good luck that accompanies all his enterprises (military, diplomatic, and political): a divine presence watching over his actions and leading him to success. It is this higher force, τύχη, that can make up for any lack in numbers and, consequently, serve as an "explanation" for the most inexplicable event. While the facts of Timoleon's extraordinary success in Sicily are, to a large extent, confirmed by Diodorus Siculus as well as by archaeological evidence, this interpretation of it given by Plutarch is singular.[28] In Plutarch, Timoleon himself in his humble way experiences his success as the gift of a higher power: in this divine power's greater plan of liberating Sicily the role of the liberator is granted to him. For that grace Timoleon is thankful and worships his protective deity in return. One may well ask, as Plutarch does at the beginning of the syzygy of *Timoleon* and *Aemilius Paullus* and as many interpreters of both lives have done since, if this divine support does not take away all the credit from Timoleon's achievements. Yet, in the eyes of the equally religious, but more philosophical Plutarch, Timoleon could never have had such divine support if he had not deserved it by his extraordinary virtue. It is the two components coming together, virtue and good fortune joining into a kind of fortunate virtue, that account for Timoleon's success (*Timol.* 36, 4-7):

---

[28] cf. Theodorsson, "Timoleon," 218–19.

Success Against All Odds, Failure Against All Logic

> ...if we compare the generalship of Epaminondas and Agesilaüs, which in both cases was full of toil and bitter struggles, with that of Timoleon, which was exercised with much ease as well as glory, it appears to men of just and careful reasoning a product, not of fortune, but of fortunate valour (ἀρετῆς εὐτυχούσης).

> And yet all his successes were ascribed by him to fortune; for in his letters to his friends at home and in his public addresses to the Syracusans he often said he was thankful to God, who, desiring to save Sicily, gave him the name and title of its saviour (βουλόμενος σῶσαι Σικελίαν ἐπεγράψατο τὴν αὐτοῦ προσηγορίαν). Moreover, in his house he built a shrine for sacrifice to *Automatia*, or Chance, and the house itself he consecrated to man's sacred genius.

What does this conclusion regarding Timoleon's "fortunate virtue" in liberating and re-establishing Sicily tell us about the view Plutarch held on Dion's failure to achieve the same ends? In my opinion, it does no less than lend a new meaning to the introductory sentences of Plutarch's *Life of Dion*, namely *Dion* 1, 3, where it says that

> ...we need not wonder that, in the performance of actions that were often kindred and alike, they [i.e. Dion and Brutus] bore witness to the doctrine of their teacher in virtue [i.e. Plato], that wisdom (φρονήσει) and justice (δικαιοσύνη) must be united with power (δύναμιν) and good fortune (τύχην) if public careers are to take on beauty (κάλλος) as well as grandeur (μέγεθος).

Usually this sentence is held to be one more of those renderings of Plato's statement of the philosopher-kings, but re-read with Plutarch's *Life of Timoleon* in mind and with an outlook on the end of Dion it becomes more than just a list of criteria constituting a philosopher-king: they are criteria which, if lacking, might make a possible philosopher-king fail. Especially one criterion has stolen into the list – or at least gained weight – that did not play too much of a role in Plato, but can explain in a very subtle way why Dion – and with him Plato – failed where Timoleon was successful: it is unpredictable, unavailable τύχη – we might conclude – without which there is no good outcome for any project *however virtuous* it may be.[29] Since human reasoning does not have any influence on this last, unpredictable component of τύχη, no one can be blamed for it either. If there is no logic by which we can explain success, there is also no logic by which to explain failure. By pointing to the inexplicable in the story of the liberation of Sicily and in the failure of Dion, Plutarch can avoid passing a judgement on Dion's and Plato's undertakings in Syracuse. Otherwise, his judgement might not have turned out to be as favorable as he, being a Platonic philosopher himself, would have wished it to be.

---

[29] Plutarch, no doubt regarded Dion as a virtuous man: At the beginning of the *syzygy* he even wonders if the story of Dion and Brutus might not be an argument for the existence of evil *daimones* whose intention is to bring down virtuous men, not by any *logic* of crime and punishment, but out of their own *irrational* envy of virtue and goodness (cf. *Dion* 2, 5-6; compare Plat. *Ep.* VII, 336b).

Philosophical Concepts

Robert Metcalf[1]
Plato's Discovery in Sicily:
Philosophy and Life-Structuring Practices in the *Seventh Letter*

If Plato's *Seventh Letter* is authentic (a matter of ongoing scholarly debate), it offers us a fascinating view into the philosopher's thinking before and after his voyages to Sicily.[2] Most famously, the *Letter* recounts his own disillusionment with politics in Athens before setting forth for Sicily (325c-d) and his hopes for having some meaningful impact on political life if he should convince Dionysius II of his ideas on these matters—an attempt, as he describes it, "to realize our theories concerning laws and government [τὰ διανοηθέντα περὶ νόμων τε καὶ πολιτείας ἀποτελεῖν ἐγχειρήσοι]" (328b).[3] Those hopes were thoroughly disappointed in

---

[1] Robert Metcalf is Associate Professor of Philosophy at the University of Colorado Denver. He is Co-Translator of *Martin Heidegger's Basic Concepts of Aristotelian Philosophy* (Indiana University Press, 2009), and author of *Philosophy as Agôn* (Northwestern University Press, 2018).

[2] It makes sense that the authenticity of Plato's *Seventh Letter* remains a matter of debate, given that the text is first mentioned in antiquity in Cicero's *Tusculan Disputations* (V.35). For skepticism about the its authenticity, see, for example, Ludwig Edelstein, *Plato's Seventh Letter* (Leiden: E. J. Brill, 1966), 24. For a view contrary to Edelstein's, see Glenn Morrow, *Plato's Epistles* (Indianapolis: Bobbs-Merrill, 1963), 57: "As a whole the Seventh Epistle produces as unified an impression upon the reader as does almost any of the later dialogues; and the very inadequacy of its form to the wealth of the material it contains is, if anything, a trait that suggests the hand of Plato in his old age."

[3] Admittedly, the *Seventh Letter* sounds a distinct echo of the *Republic* when Plato writes that it is only by philosophy that "one is enabled to discern all forms of justice both political and individual—wherefore the classes of mankind will have no cessation from evils [κακῶν οὖν οὐ λήξειν τὰ ἀνθρώπινα γένη] until either the class of those who are right and true philosophers attains political supremacy [πρὶν ἂν ἢ τὸ τῶν φιλοσοφούντων ὀρθῶς γε καὶ ἀληθῶς γένος εἰς ἀρχὰς ἔλθῃ τὰς πολιτικάς], or else the class of those who hold power in the *poleis* becomes, by some divine dispensation, really philosophical [ἢ τὸ τῶν δυναστευόντων ἐν ταῖς πόλεσιν ἔκ τινος μοίρας θείας ὄντως φιλοσοφήσῃ]" (326a-b). But as to the idea that the aim of Plato's trip was "translating into practice the ideas about how a state should be run which he worked out in his dialogues, and especially in the *Republic*," see Moses Finley, *Aspects of Antiquity:*

Sicily, and no doubt the bitterness of the experience colored his observations of the place. What is most philosophically significant, however, is what Plato discovered during his time in Sicily: namely, that an appreciation of philosophy as a life-structuring practice [*epitēdeuma*]—and, indeed, one that is radically incompatible with the practices that he found to be prevalent in Syracuse—goes hand in hand with the critique of writing famously articulated in the *Seventh Letter* (especially 341c-344d) as well as in the *Phaedrus* 275b,ff and the *Statesman* 294a-299e.[4]

The core idea here, implicit throughout Plato's writings but presented most explicitly in the *Seventh Letter*, is that philosophy is not the sort of thing that one can take up aside from or untouched by one's other practices, as if it were comparable to going once to the gym or taking up flute-playing on a whim (cf. *Republic* 561c-d). Rather, unless one takes up philosophy in the sustained and committed way required of it as an *epitēdeuma*, one will not understand the claims made within philosophical discourse. And yet, the 'fixed' character of writing (or at least treatise-writing) is shown by Plato to be anathema to the integrity of philosophy as an *epitēdeuma* allowing for, and requiring, change over time. In what follows I shall focus on the connections drawn in the *Seventh Letter* between Plato's understanding of "life-structuring practices," *epitēdeumata*, and the critique of a certain kind of writing as the proper medium for philosophy.

Epitēdeumata in the *Republic*

But to begin, we should note that life-structuring practices [*epitēdeumata*] are thematized extensively in Plato's writings, and

---

Discoveries and Contoversies (New York: Viking, 1968): "It is hard to imagine a more improbable arena in which to try out Plato's radical political theories" (76); and, "nothing in either [the *Seventh Letter* or *Eighth Letter*] warrants the view that Plato proposed to convert Dionysius II into a philosopher-king and thus realize on earth the ideal state of his *Republic*" (80). See also S. Monoson, *Plato's Democratic Entanglements* (Princeton University Press, 2000), 150.

[4] The latter two texts I have analyzed at greater length in my essay, "Syngrammatology in Plato's *Statesman*," in *Plato's 'Statesman': Dialectic, Myth and Politics*, edited by John Sallis, Albany, NY: SUNY Press, 2017, 197-221.

particularly in the *Republic*, where we find a sustained account of life-structuring practices that is most illuminating for reading the *Seventh Letter*. The question posed in Book II of the *Republic*, and then in play until the end of the work, is whether justice is "to be practiced [*epitēdeuteon*]" for its own sake or for some other benefit (358a, 358c, 359b, 360e, 362a). As he then goes about crafting a response to this question, Socrates theorizes guardians who are 'naturally suited' to their life-structuring practice (374e)—an *epitēdeuma* incompatible with that of 'imitation' (394e-395d), as well as other things. Later, in Book IV, Socrates will lay down the rule that "each person must practice the one pursuit … for which he is naturally best suited" [ἐν δέοι ἐπιτηδεύειν τῶν περὶ τὴν πόλιν, εἰς ὃ αὐτοῦ ἡ φύσις ἐπιτηδειοτάτη πεφυκυῖα εἴη]" (433a), the philosophical/political importance of which is presented in a memorable passage:

> Every other citizen, too, must be assigned to what naturally suits him, with one person assigned to one job [καὶ τοὺς ἄλλους πολίτας, πρὸς ὅ τις πέφυκεν, πρὸς τοῦτο ἕνα πρὸς ἓν ἕκαστον ἔργον δεῖ κομίζειν], so that, practicing his own pursuit [ὅπως ἂν ἓν τὸ αὑτοῦ ἐπιτηδεύων], each one of them will become one not many, and the entire polis thereby naturally grow to be one, not many [ἕκαστος μὴ πολλοὶ ἀλλ᾽ εἷς γίγνηται, καὶ οὕτω δὴ σύμπασα ἡ πόλις μία φύηται ἀλλὰ μὴ πολλαί]. (423d)

Yet, famously, the idea of what is 'naturally suited' to a person is problematized by Socrates in the *Republic*, most dramatically in his discussion of women and guardianship in Book V. While women traditionally had been confined to the traditional practices of weaving, cooking, etc. (455c), Socrates argues that

> there is no practice [ἐπιτήδευμα] relevant to the management of the *polis* that belongs to a woman because she is a woman, or to a man because he is a man; but the various natural capacities are distributed in a similar way between both creatures, and women can share by nature in every practice [ἐπιτήδευμα]. (455d)

Accordingly, since what is at issue are not every kind of difference or sameness in natures, but only what pertains to practices [πρὸς αὐτὰ τείνον τὰ ἐπιτηδεύματα]" (455c-d), and since men and women differ only sexually (454d-e), Socrates concludes that "we shall believe that guardians and their women must have the same practices [δεῖν τὰ αὐτὰ ἐπιτηδεύειν]" (456b)—repeated later when he says that they "must practice all things in common" [δεῖ κοινῇ πάντα ἐπιτηδεύειν] (457b-c).

The underlying conceptualization of *epitēdeumata* has it that they are practices shaping one's life, and often at a pre-theoretical level—as is indicated for example, when Socrates remarks that the lawgivers for *Kallipolis* will not need to legislate everything, since some things will follow of themselves from the life-structuring practices in place [τὰ δὲ ὅτι αὐτόματα ἔπεισιν ἐκ τῶν ἔμπροσθεν ἐπιτηδευμάτων] (427a).[5] In later Books of the *Republic*, the fundamental significance of *epitēdeumata* is shown to have significant implications for Socrates's discourse as to the relation between philosophy and the *polis*. In fact, his bold claim that those who are philosophical by nature should exercise political power will seem crazy to *hoi polloi*, since they "think that those who engage in philosophy long-term become utterly useless to society on account of the practice [ὑπὸ τοῦ ἐπιτηδεύματος]" (487a-d). For this reason, Socrates says that they must show *hoi polloi* what they mean by 'philosophers' and define their nature and show that the philosophical practice [ἐπιτήδευμα] that they have in mind is, in fact, the opposite of what it now is (497e, 499e-500a). At the same time, however, Socrates recognizes that the *epitēdeumata* now structuring the *polis* will be an obstacle to those with the right nature pursuing the philosophical practice. Referring to this predicament as "Diomedean compulsion," Socrates asks how a

---

[5] On the 'pre-theoretical' operation of *epitēdeumata*, see also Socrates's claim that the real threat to a well-structured *polis* is that lawlessness [*paranomia*] will flow over *pros ta ēthē kai ta epitēdeumata*, "toward character traits and life-structuring practices"—and ultimately then "overthrow everything public and private" (424d-e). Similarly, in the *Seventh Letter*, we find Plato writing of "the true conviction [δόξαν...τὴν ἀληθῆ] that no *polis* nor any individual man can ever become happy unless he passes his life devoted to justice with wisdom, whether it be that he possesses these virtues within himself or as the result of being reared and trained righteously under pious/holy rulers in their ways" (335d-e).

young man with a philosophical nature can survive the rhetorico-political situations of the present, where there will be extreme pressure to "call the same things fair or foul as these people, practice what they practice, and become like them? [φήσειν τε τὰ αὐτὰ τούτοις καλὰ καὶ αἰσχρὰ εἶναι, καὶ ἐπιτηδεύσειν ἅπερ ἂν οὗτοι, καὶ ἔσεσθαι τοιοῦτον;]" (492c; see also 492d-493d). We shall return to the political problem of philosophy understood as an *epitēdeuma* in what follows.

Epitēdeumata in the *Seventh Letter*

In any case, on the basis of these reflections upon life-structuring practices from the *Republic*, we can appreciate the issue addressed early in the *Seventh Letter*, when Plato writes about what he found in Sicily when he first traveled there:

> [A]t the time of my first arrival…I was in no wise pleased at all with the "happy life" as it is they call it there, replete as it is with Italian and Syracusan banquetings; for thus one's existence is spent in gorging food twice a day and never sleeping alone at night, and all the practices which accompany this mode of living [καὶ ὅσα τούτῳ ἐπιτηδεύματα συνέπεται τῷ βίῳ]. For not a single man of all who live beneath the heavens could ever become wise [φρόνιμος] if these were his practices from his youth [ἐκ νέου ἐπιτηδεύων], since none will be found to possess a nature so admirably compounded; nor would he ever be likely to become temperate, and the same may truly be said of all other forms of virtue. And no *polis* would remain stable under laws of any kind, if its citizens, while supposing that they ought to spend/consume everything to excess, yet believed that they ought to cease from all exertion except partying and drinking and serious pursuit of sexual escapades [καὶ ἀφροδισίων σπουδὰς διαπονουμένας]. Of necessity these *poleis* never cease changing [μεταβαλλούσας] into tyrannies, oligarchies, and democracies, and the men who hold power in them cannot

endure so much as the mention of the name of a just government with equal laws. (326b-d).[6]

While Moses Finley calls "outright nonsense" the complaint voiced in the *Seventh Letter*, to the effect that "that the people indulged in too much eating and too much sex,"[7] the more basic point—namely, that the life-structuring practices that define a *polis* may be inhospitable to, or possibly even altogether incompatible with, becoming wise [φρόνιμος] or temperate [σώφρων]—clearly echoes the other texts of Plato that we have considered. Furthermore, we should note that the inhospitability of Sicilian practices to Plato's political-philosophical project is made evident a bit later in the *Seventh Letter*, when Plato writes that people living according to these life-structuring practices will not heed "the ancient and holy doctrines which declare to us that the soul is immortal and that it has judges and pays the greatest penalties," for

> to these doctrines the man who is fond of riches but poor in soul listens not, or if he listens he laughs at them (as he thinks) to scorn, while he shamelessly plunders from all quarters everything which he thinks likely to provide himself, like a beast, with food or drink or the satiating himself with the slavish and graceless pleasure which is miscalled by the name of the Goddess of Love (334e-335a).

---

[6] Right after the last sentence of this passage, Plato writes: "Holding these views, then, as well as those previously formed [ταῦτα δὴ πρὸς τοῖς πρόσθε διανοούμενος], I travelled through to Syracuse" (326d), so that the passage as a whole is framed by remarks on what conception he had [τὴν διάνοιαν ἔχων], what he was thinking [διανοούμενος] as he traveled to Syracuse. Note, too, that the verb Plato uses in connection with the polis 'remaining stable [*eremein*]' is used in the *Gorgias* for the *logos* that remains stable while others have been refuted (527b).

[7] See Finley, op cit., 79. The full quotation is as follows: "Finally, the letters contain some outright nonsense, of which two examples: On his first visit to Syracuse, the private visit, the letter states that Plato found conditions there unsatisfactory and disagreeable. Because of the tyranny of the elder Dionysius, no doubt? But there is not a word about that. The actual complaint is merely that the people indulged in too much eating and too much sex," 79.

Plato's Discovery in Sicily

Plato's reaction to the Sicilian life-structuring practices is extreme, to be sure, but it is arguably of a piece with the *Republic*'s portrait of most people, 'always occupied with feasts and the like,' being "always looking downward like cattle and, with their heads bent over the earth or the dinner table, they feed, gorge themselves, and copulate [ἀλλὰ βοσκημάτων δίκην κάτω ἀεὶ βλέποντες καὶ κεκυφότες εἰς γῆν καὶ εἰς τραπέζας βόσκονται χορταζόμενοι καὶ ὀχεύοντες]" (586a). Accordingly, when Socrates 'purges' *kallipolis* of the luxuries desired at least initially by Glaucon and Adeimantus, including prostitutes and pastries (cf. 373a, 404d), Socrates includes Syracusan cuisine and "complex Sicilian delicacies" among the prohibited luxuries for the sake of safeguarding the guardians' healthy and virtuous way of life (404d). Nonetheless, the *epitēdeumata* contrary to those of the philosopher remain an ongoing concern in the *Republic*. For example, in *Republic* Book VII, in a discussion of the *dogmata* that we hold from childhood about what things are just and fine (538c), Socrates says that there are life-structuring practices committed to moral virtue, heeding the traditional *dogmata*, but, opposed to these there are also "other practices... which possess pleasures that flatter our soul and attract it to themselves, but which do not persuade people who are at all moderate—who continue to honor and obey the convictions of their fathers [καὶ ἄλλα ἐναντία τούτων ἐπιτηδεύματα ἡδονὰς ἔχοντα, ἃ κολακεύει μὲν ἡμῶν τὴν ψυχὴν καὶ ἕλκει ἐφ᾽ αὑτά, πείθει δ᾽ οὒ τοὺς καὶ ὁπηοῦν μετρίους· ἀλλ᾽ ἐκεῖνα τιμῶσι τὰ πάτρια καὶ ἐκείνοις πειθαρχοῦσιν]" (538d).[8] Here we have a reiteration of the claim implicit in Socrates's question: "Is it not the case that fine practices lead to the possession of virtue, shameful ones to vice [ἆρ᾽ οὖν οὐ καὶ τὰ μὲν καλὰ ἐπιτηδεύματα εἰς ἀρετῆς κτῆσιν φέρει, τὰ δ᾽ αἰσχρὰ εἰς κακίας;]?" (444e-445a). The very concept of a life-structuring practice at issue here entails the idea that being virtuous, and remaining virtuous in the face of temptation,

---

[8] Numerous times in the *Republic* Socrates speaks of such starkly contrasted *epitēdeumata* as being the "opposites" of one another—for example, at 489c-d, he says: "It is not easy for the best practice to be highly honored by those whose practices are its very opposites [οὐ ῥᾴδιον εὐδοκιμεῖν τὸ βέλτιστον ἐπιτήδευμα ὑπὸ τῶν τἀναντία ἐπιτηδευόντων]."

requires steadfast habituation and moral training—see, for example, Socrates's claim that virtues of the soul besides 'wisdom' [*phronēsai*] are acquired "by habit and by practice [ἐμποιεῖσθαι ἔθεσι καὶ ἀσκήσεσιν]" (518e).

But it's not just that specific *epitēdeumata* divide the philosopher from the satisfied hedonist. Plato diagnoses the profound difference between a true philosopher and the skin-deep 'intellectual' in terms of the fundamental importance of life-structuring practices, as we see in the following passage from the *Seventh Letter*:

> For on hearing this—if the pupil be truly philosophic, in sympathy with the subject and worthy of it, because divinely gifted [ἐὰν μὲν ὄντως ᾖ φιλόσοφος οἰκεῖός τε καὶ ἄξιος τοῦ πράγματος θεῖος ὤν]—he believes that he has been shown a wondrous path [ὁδόν... θαυμαστὴν] and that he must brace himself at once to follow it, and that life will not be worth living if he does otherwise [καὶ οὐ βιωτὸν ἄλλως ποιοῦντι]. After this he braces both himself and him who is guiding him on the path, nor does he desist until either he has reached the goal of all his studies, or else has gained such power as to be capable of directing his own steps without the aid of the instructor. It is thus and in this frame of mind that such a student lives, occupied indeed in whatever occupations he may find himself, but always beyond all else cleaving fast to philosophy and to that mode of daily life which will best make him apt to learn and of retentive mind and able to reason within himself soberly; but the mode of life which is opposite to this he continually abhors [ταύτῃ καὶ κατὰ ταῦτα διανοηθεὶς ὁ τοιοῦτος ζῇ, πράττων μὲν ἐν αἴστισιν ἂν ᾖ πράξεσιν, παρὰ πάντα δὲ ἀεὶ φιλοσοφίας ἐχόμενος καὶ τροφῆς τῆς καθ᾽ ἡμέραν ἥτις ἂν αὐτὸν μάλιστα εὐμαθῆ τε καὶ μνήμονα καὶ λογίζεσθαι δυνατὸν ἐν αὑτῷ νήφοντα ἀπεργάζηται· τὴν δὲ ἐναντίαν ταύτῃ μισῶν διατελεῖ]. Those, on the other hand, who are in reality not philosophic, but superficially tinged by opinions—like men whose bodies are sunburned—when they see how many studies are required and how great the labor, and how the orderly mode

of daily life is that which befits the subject, they deem it difficult or impossible for themselves, and thus become in fact incapable of practicing it [ἐπιτηδεύειν δυνατοὶ γίγνονται]. (340c-e).

Before this passage, the word *'ponos'* — "labor" or "exertion" — was used in the *Seventh Letter* only ironically for the 'effort' devoted to sexual escapades. Here the word is used for the labor that must be expended in order to pursue philosophy as an *epitēdeuma*. Now, of course, philosophy is portrayed as an *epitēdeuma* involving considerable effort throughout Plato's writings — most memorably in the *Apology*, where Socrates presents his practice of philosophy as a rather consuming 'occupation' [ἀσχολία] (23b), requiring that he neglect his private interests to some extent in order to attend to something beyond himself (31b), and even as a matter of "labors undertaken to prove the Delphic oracle irrefutable [πόνους τινὰς πονοῦντος ἵνα μοι καὶ ἀνέλεγκτος ἡ μαντεία γένοιτο]" (22a).[9] While Socrates may be indulging in some rhetorical overstatement before the jury, it is nonetheless the case that philosophy is an onerous life-structuring practice, involving a great deal of effort, *ponos*. Philosophy is demanding just in itself, given the energy and commitment required to push through the difficulties involved in its subject matter; but, *in addition,* if it is opposed by the life-structuring practices of the *polis* where it takes shape, then it is easy to imagine what Socrates calls, in the *Republic*, "the sort of destruction and corruption that the nature best suited for the best practice undergoes [οὗτος δή…ὄλεθρός τε καὶ διαφθορὰ τοσαύτη τε καὶ τοιαύτη τῆς βελτίστης φύσεως εἰς τὸ ἄριστον ἐπιτήδευμα]" (495b). In light of the obstacles facing philosophy as an *epitēdeuma*, we can understand the question that Socrates asks in the *Republic*: "[D]o you see any way to preserve a philosophic nature and ensure that it will continue to practice philosophy and reach the end? [ἐκ δὴ τούτων τίνα ὁρᾷς

---

[9] To be sure, there is more than a tinge of irony in Socrates's account of his philosophical activity as one of "service to the god" (30a). See my discussion of this issue in "The Philosophical Rhetoric of Socrates's Mission," *Philosophy and Rhetoric*, 37 (2004), 143-66.

σωτηρίαν φιλοσόφῳ φύσει, ὥστ᾽ ἐν τῷ ἐπιτηδεύματι μείνασαν πρὸς τέλος ἐλθεῖν;]" (494a, cf. also 495a).[10]

The Critique of Syngrammatic Writing

Now, it is right on the heels of this extended meditation on *epitēdeumata* in the *Seventh Letter* that we find those famous passages formulating a critique of (syngrammatic) writing. Most famous, no doubt, is the key passage at 341c-e, where Plato writes:

> Concerning all these writers, or prospective writers, who claim to know the subjects which I seriously study, whether as hearers of mine or of other teachers, or from their own discoveries; it is impossible, in my judgment at least, that these men should understand anything about this subject. There does not exist, nor will there ever exist, any treatise of mine dealing therewith [οὔκουν ἐμόν γε περὶ αὐτῶν ἔστιν σύγγραμμα οὐδὲ μήποτε γένηται]—for it does not at all admit of verbal expression like other studies [ῥητὸν γὰρ οὐδαμῶς ἐστιν ὡς ἄλλα μαθήματα]. Rather, as a result of prolonged intellectual engagement with the matter itself and living together with it [ἀλλ᾽ ἐκ πολλῆς συνουσίας γιγνομένης περὶ τὸ πρᾶγμα αὐτὸ καὶ τοῦ συζῆν], it is brought to birth in the soul on a sudden, as light that is kindled by a leaping spark, and thereafter it nourishes itself [ἐξαίφνης οἷον ἀπὸ πυρὸς πηδήσαντος ἐξαφθὲν φῶς, ἐν τῇ ψυχῇ γενόμενον αὐτὸ ἑαυτὸ ἤδη τρέφει]. (341c-e)

---

[10] Shortly thereafter in the *Republic*, Socrates goes so far as to relate the difference between philosophical and unphilosophical *epitēdeumata* to the difference between the divine and the human: "There is not one *polis* today with a constitution worthy of the philosophical nature… But if [a philosophical nature] were to find the best constitution, as it is itself the best, it would be clear that it is really divine and that other natures and practices are merely human [εἰ δὲ λήψεται τὴν ἀρίστην πολιτείαν, ὥσπερ καὶ αὐτὸ ἄριστόν ἐστιν, τότε δηλώσει ὅτι τοῦτο μὲν τῷ ὄντι θεῖον ἦν, τὰ δὲ ἄλλα ἀνθρώπινα, τά τε τῶν φύσεων καὶ τῶν ἐπιτηδευμάτων]" (497b).

While it is not clear what exactly Plato means by the "being-together" [*sunousia*] and "living-together" [*suzēn*] mentioned in this passage,[11] what is clear, in any case, is that the matters about which some unnamed others claim to have represented Plato's views "do not admit of verbal expression like other studies." Notice that Plato is not merely denying a *written* formulation, but any verbal formulation like that in other studies. He repeats this denial when he says, first, that the best statement of such things would be his own, but second, he says "And if I had thought that these subjects ought to be fully stated in writing or in speech to the public [εἰ δέ μοι ἐφαίνετο γραπτέα θ᾽ ἱκανῶς εἶναι πρὸς τοὺς πολλοὺς καὶ ῥητά], what nobler action could I have performed in my life than that of writing what is of great benefit to mankind and bringing forth to the light for all men the nature of reality?" (341d-e). In connection with this claim, we should remember that what is problematic about writing here is shown elsewhere in Plato's texts to apply to spoken discourse as well: in the *Protagoras*, for example, Socrates says of public speakers, "[S]uppose you put a question to one of them—they are just like books [ὥσπερ βιβλία], incapable of either answering you or putting a question of their own"—at which point he likens these orators to "brazen vessels [that] ring a long time after they have been struck and prolong the note unless you put your hand on them" (328e-329b).[12]

---

[11] Drew Hyland, *Plato and the Question of Beauty* (Bloomington & Indianapolis: Indiana University Press, 2008) notes this under-determination in his discussion of the *Letter*: "The *sunousias* and *suzen* suggest so strongly the quality of doing something 'together' that many translators simply render this as something like 'after long-continued intercourse between teacher and pupil, in joint pursuit of the subject.' This is certainly plausible and perhaps the most plausible reading... though it must be said that the grammar does not strictly demand that the togetherness be of two people rather than the togetherness of the individual and the matter for thought" (104). See also the argument in Monoson, op cit., that Plato held to the Socratic belief in *sunousia* [conversation] as the basis of higher education—"that is, he not only insisted on discussion as a method but also carefully cultivated an open intellectual environment" (139).

[12] As Desjardins puts it, "the very same criticism that in *Phaedrus* is brought to bear on the *written* word is in the *Protagoras*, *Theaetetus* and *Sophist* brought to bear against the spoken word, and, moreover, in terms that seem deliberately

Thus, whereas some of Plato's contemporaries—e.g., Gorgias, in his "Funeral Oration," and Alcidamas, in *On the Sophists*—contrasted the fluidity and responsiveness of spoken discourse with the rigid inflexibility of writing, Plato's texts target the typical discourse of orators with the very same criticism leveled against writing, here in the *Seventh Letter* as well as in the *Statesman* and *Phaedrus*.[13]

It is shortly after this that the complicated discussion of the 'four' commences, a discussion that clearly is meant to further explain and justify the critique of writing, since the discussion of the four makes clear what Plato calls "the weakness inherent in *logoi* [τὸ τῶν λόγων ἀσθενές]," on account of which, he writes "no man of intelligence will ever venture to commit to it the concepts of his reason, especially when it is unalterable—as is the case with what is formulated in writing [καὶ ταῦτα εἰς ἀμετακίνητον, ὃ δὴ πάσχει τὰ γεγραμμένα τύποις]" (342e-343a). He then concludes as follows:

> And this is the reason why every serious man in dealing with really serious subjects carefully avoids writing, lest thereby he may possibly cast them as a prey to the envy and stupidity of the public [διὸ δὴ πᾶς ἀνὴρ σπουδαῖος τῶν ὄντων σπουδαίων πέρι πολλοῦ δεῖ μὴ γράψας ποτὲ ἐν ἀνθρώποις εἰς φθόνον καὶ ἀπορίαν καταβαλεῖ]. In one word, then, our conclusion must be that whenever one sees a man's written compositions [συγγράμματα γεγραμμένα]—whether they be the laws of a legislator or anything else in any other form—these are not his most serious works, if it so be that the writer himself is serious

---

designed to echo each other"—see Rosemary Desjardins, "Why Dialogues? Plato's Serious Play," in *Platonic Writings/Platonic Readings*, edited by Charles L. Griswold (University Park, PA: The Pennsylvania State University Press, 2002), 111.

[13] Notice that a careful comparison of Plato and Alcidamas challenges Derrida's stance: "Plato is following certain rhetors and sophists before him who, as a contrast to the cadaverous rigidity of writing, had held up the living spoken word, which infallibly conforms to the necessities of the situation at hand... feigning to bend and adapt at the moment that it is actually achieving maximum persuasiveness and control"—see Jacques Derrida, "Plato's Pharmacy," in *Dissemination*, translated by Barbara Johnson (Chicago: University of Chicago Press, 1981), 79.

[ὡς οὐκ ἦν τούτῳ ταῦτα σπουδαιότατα, εἴπερ ἔστ᾽ αὐτὸς σπουδαῖος]: rather those works abide in the fairest region he possesses [κεῖται δέ που ἐν χώρᾳ τῇ καλλίστῃ τῶν τούτου]. If, however, these really are his serious efforts, and put into writing, it is not the gods but mortal men who 'Then of a truth themselves have utterly ruined his senses.' (344c-d)

Arguably, the most important word used by Plato in these latter passages is *syngramma*—for here in the *Seventh Letter* he denies that there is any *syngramma* of his philosophical thinking, as he also does in the *Second Letter*, when he writes: "there is no *syngramma* of Plato's, nor will there be [οὐδ᾽ ἔστιν σύγγραμμα Πλάτωνος οὐδὲν οὐδ᾽ ἔσται], but those so called are of a Socrates become young and beautiful [τὰ δὲ νῦν λεγόμενα Σωκράτους ἐστὶν καλοῦ καὶ νέου γεγονότος]" (314c). But what exactly is a *syngramma*? Most generally, *syngramma* is used in Plato's texts to refer to a treatise that can be scrutinized (cf. *Gorgias* 462b-c; *Theaetetus* 166c-d), which is to say, a 'completed,' and therefore unrevisable, form of writing.[14] Fittingly, then, the passages from the *Seventh Letter* above offer us the following reason for why there can be no *syngramma* of his philosophical thinking: namely, that philosophy cannot properly be transposed "into something unalterable [εἰς ἀμετακίνητον]—as is the case with what is formulated in writing [ὃ δὴ πάσχει τὰ γεγραμμένα τύποις]" (342e-343a). To appreciate this key aspect of Plato's critique of syngrammatic writing, we should compare the *Seventh Letter*'s handling of the issue with what we find in the *Statesman* and the *Phaedrus*.

In the *Statesman*, the Stranger introduces the problematization of *syngrammata* when he asks whether things should be practiced "in conformity with writings and not in conformity with *technē* [κατὰ

---

[14] The word is used precisely in this way in Herodotus's *Histories* (cf. I.47.1-48.2); in later antiquity, Galen uses the distinction between *syngrammata* and *hypomnēmata* to contrast Hippocrates's written treatises as opposed to his own clinical notes (16.532, 543), or his commentaries on Hippocrates's treatises (16.811).

συγγϱάμματα… καὶ μὴ κατὰ τέχνην].”[15] As the greater context of the *Statesman* makes clear, the *syngramma* as a form of writing has its use in limiting the range of meaning—e.g., the meaning of the laws which are to be binding upon rulers, so that the rulers can be held accountable in relation to them.[16] Indeed, the Stranger's thought-experiment at *Statesman* 295a-d relates the situation of a lawgiver to a scenario in which a physician or gymnastic trainer is going away and will be absent for a while from those in his care [ἀποδημεῖν καὶ ἀπέσεσθαι τῶν θεϱαπευομένων συχνόν]. In such a scenario, the one with *epistēmē* might write down instructions as 'reminders [ὑπομνήματα]' of the practice that they had hitherto been involved in (295b-c). But suppose he returned sooner than expected and wanted to revise his written instructions [τὰ γϱάμματα] for the sake of some improvement of care. Would it not be absurd, the Stranger asks, to "persist in the opinion that no one must transgress the old laws, neither he himself by enacting new ones nor his patient by venturing to do anything contrary to the written rules, under the conviction that these laws were medicinal and healthy and anything else was unhealthy and unscientific?" (295d)

---

[15] Note that the Stranger specifies by way of examples what a syngrammatic oversight of the *technai* implies: "[O]r should we in turn observe some kind of feeding of horses occurring in conformity with *syngrammata* or the entire grooming of herds, or divination or whatever entire part serving has comprehended, or draughts-playing or all of arithmetic, or whether it's bare or plane or involved in three dimensions or speeds…" (299d-e). At one point the Stranger even brings in some entomology to explain why laws such as *syngrammata* are indispensable: "since there is no king that comes to be in our *poleis*," he explains, "who's of the sort that naturally arises like the ruler of bees in the hives—one who's right from the start exceptional in his body and his soul—we must, it seems, once we've come together, write up *syngrammata* [δεῖ δὴ συνελθόντας συγγϱάμματα γϱάφειν]" (301d-e).

[16] Indeed, the subsequent line of argument in the *Statesman* presupposes this understanding of *syngrammata* in terms of constraint: the consideration raised by the Stranger as to why failing to adhere to the laws would be even a greater evil than prohibiting *zētein* is the prospect of someone disregarding the writings and acting contrary to them out of graft or favoritism [μηδὲν φϱοντίζων τῶν γϱαμμάτων ἢ κέϱδους ἕνεκέν τινος ἢ χάϱιτος ἰδίας παϱὰ ταῦτ᾽ ἐπιχειϱοῖ δϱᾶν ἕτεϱα] (300a).

Plato's Discovery in Sicily

Thus, the thought-experiment shifts from a situation where the immediate presence of the trainer/physician to the one cared for obviates the need for writing, to a situation of absence requiring the mediation of writing, but in such a way as to preclude any revision or innovation. Writing is something that the true statesman resorts to only as an expedient in the time of his absence; and once the absence is overcome by his return, the writings become an impediment to his *orthē archē*.

Soul-writing in *Phaedrus*

The inflexibility of writing, or at least syngrammatic writing, is underscored in the *Phaedrus*'s account of writing as "continuing to signify just that very same thing forever [ἕν τι σημαίνει μόνον ταὐτὸν ἀεί]" even when it is questioned (275d). Written discourse, Socrates explains, reaches indiscriminately those with understanding and those without it, for it cannot select its readership, and if it is attacked unfairly, Socrates says, "it always needs its father's support—alone, it can neither defend itself nor come to its own support" (275e). But by contrast with this inflexible and indiscriminate form of writing, Socrates then imagines "another kind of speech, or word... The word which is written with knowledge in the soul of the learner [ὃς μετ' ἐπιστήμης γράφεται ἐν τῇ τοῦ μανθάνοντος ψυχῇ], which is able to defend itself and knows to whom it should speak, and before whom to be silent [δυνατὸς μὲν ἀμῦναι ἑαυτῷ, ἐπιστήμων δὲ λέγειν τε καὶ σιγᾶν πρὸς οὓς δεῖ]" (276a).[17] Socrates then describes this alternative form of writing in the following terms:

> when one makes use of the art of dialectic and plants and sows in a fitting soul words with knowledge which are able to help themselves and him who planted them, which are not fruitless, but yield seed from which there spring up in other characters other words capable of continuing the process for ever, and

---

[17] Notice that, at this point, Phaedrus responds: "You mean the living and breathing word of him who knows, of which the written word may justly be called the image/ghost [τὸν τοῦ εἰδότος λόγον λέγεις ζῶντα καὶ ἔμψυχον, οὗ ὁ γεγραμμένος εἴδωλον ἄν τι λέγοιτο δικαίως]" (*Phaedrus* 276a).

> which make their possessor happy, to the farthest possible limit of human happiness [ὅταν τις τῇ διαλεκτικῇ τέχνῃ χρώμενος, λαβὼν ψυχὴν προσήκουσαν, φυτεύῃ τε καὶ σπείρῃ μετ' ἐπιστήμης λόγους, οἳ ἑαυτοῖς τῷ τε φυτεύσαντι βοηθεῖν ἱκανοὶ καὶ οὐχὶ ἄκαρποι ἀλλὰ ἔχοντες σπέρμα, ὅθεν ἄλλοι ἐν ἄλλοις ἤθεσι φυόμενοι τοῦτ' ἀεὶ ἀθάνατον παρέχειν ἱκανοί, καὶ τὸν ἔχοντα εὐδαιμονεῖν ποιοῦντες εἰς ὅσον ἀνθρώπῳ δυνατὸν μάλιστα]. (276e-277a)

The soul-writing hypothesized here is not one constrained to only ever signify the same thing, but is instead a form of writing that accomplishes—to borrow a line from Nietzsche—*something pregnant with a future*: casting seed from which there spring up in other characters other words capable of continuing the process undyingly [ὅθεν ἄλλοι ἐν ἄλλοις ἤθεσι φυόμενοι τοῦτ' ἀεὶ ἀθάνατον παρέχειν ἱκανοί].[18] This alternative form of writing, as formulated by Socrates in the *Phaedrus*, has much to recommend it philosophically—not least of all the prospect of helping us make sense of Plato's own dialogue-form of writing as something quite different from syngrammatic writing.[19] Indeed, the wide gulf

---

[18] Accordingly, "soul-writing" points toward a distinctive philosophical practice of educating others—and quite at odds with the sort of learning denigrated in the *Seventh Letter* under the description "crammed with borrowed doctrines [τοῖς τῶν παρακουσμάτων μεστοῖς]" (340b). See my discussion of the teaching of philosophy as understood in terms of Plato's concept of *epitēdeumata* in Robert Metcalf, "Living with the Matter Itself: The Practice of Philosophy Reexamined," *Philosophy in the Contemporary World* 21 (2014): 41-53. The line from Nietzsche is taken from the Second Essay of *On the Genealogy of Morals*, section 16.

[19] At the very least, Plato's dialogues are radically unlike syngrammatic writings in that they preserve authorial silence about the matters discussed. Aryeh Kosman captures this well when he quotes the *Second Letter*'s assertion that there is no *syngramma* of Plato, but writings of a Socrates 'refurbished and made young' (314c), and then comments "This surely makes it seem that Plato has crafted the dialogues with authorial silence and the resultant mimesis very much in mind"—see Kosman, "Silence and Imitation in the Platonic Dialogues," in *Methods of Interpreting Plato and His Dialogues: Oxford Studies in Ancient Philosophy—Supplementary Volume*, eds. James C. Klagge and Nicholas

Plato's Discovery in Sicily

between syngrammatic writing and Plato's writing of dialogues is captured well by David Halperin when he writes, commenting on these passages from the *Phaedrus*:

> [K]nowledge must not be conceived as something that that can be captured by a written formula. Rather, it is a dynamic, self-regenerating possession of a living soul, dependent on melete; it is a continuing capacity to understand, and so it cannot be reduced to a set of mere propositions: it cannot be fixed in any static form.[20]

Though Halperin does not connect this idea with Plato's concept of *epitēdeuma*, it should be clear that the understanding of philosophy as an *epitēdeuma* is the most promising route to make sense of the 'knowledge' that he has in mind, as well as the sense of 'knowledge' that Michael Frede locates in Plato's thinking: "Knowledge," he writes, "involves that the rest of one's beliefs, and hence, at least in some cases, one's whole life, be in line with one's argument… In this way knowledge, or at least a certain kind of knowledge Plato is

---

D. Smith (Oxford: Clarendon Press, 1992), 83. Later in the same essay Kosman writes: "We shall not be able to read directly out of the dialogues anything that counts *eo ipso* as a theory of Plato; we shall be unable simply to extract a passage and imagine that straight away we have Plato's theory of this or of that" (85). Likewise, Michael Frede writes: "Plato writes in such a way that it is not clear from the very form of his writing whether he endorses an argument or not… [T]he form of a Platonic dialogue is such that the mere fact that an argument is advanced in the dialogue does not yet mean that it is endorsed by Plato" — see Frede, "Plato's Arguments and the Dialogue Form," in *Methods of Interpreting Plato and His Dialogues: Oxford Studies in Ancient Philosophy — Supplementary Volume*, eds. James C. Klagge and Nicholas D. Smith (Oxford: Clarendon Press, 1992), 203. See also Kathryn Morgan, *Myth and Philosophy from the Presocratics to Plato* (Cambridge: Cambridge University Press, 2000), which argues that "[w]e have the evidence of the *Phaedrus* and the *Seventh Letter* that literary dialogues, and possibly language in general, cannot reproduce philosophical insight, although they may play (seriously) at doing so" (287).

[20] David M. Halperin, "Plato and the Erotics of Narrativity," in *Methods of Interpreting Plato and His Dialogues: Oxford Studies in Ancient Philosophy — Supplementary Volume*, eds. James C. Klagge and Nicholas D. Smith (Oxford: Clarendon Press, 1992), 104.

particularly interested in, is a highly personal kind of achievement... tied to one's own experience, way of life, interests, status, and the like."[21] To capture this insight in Plato's own words, we would want to reiterate that philosophy, at least as presented in Plato's texts, is not a set of doctrines that one might set down in syngrammatic form, but is rather a life-long, life-structuring practice, to which writing and teaching relate somewhat obliquely.[22] Presumably, one might inspire others, too, to take up philosophy through the soul-writing imagined in the *Phaedrus*, or through the writing of dialogues like Plato's—if this is something different from the 'soul-writing' that Socrates has in mind. But at the very least we can see why the *Seventh Letter* connects the attention to *epitēdeumata*—both the problematic *epitēdeumata* that Plato observed in Sicily, as well as the *epitēdeuma* that philosophy itself represents—and the critique of syngrammatic writing.

While writing is approached from different directions and dramatic contexts in the *Seventh Letter*, *Phaedrus* and *Statesman*, we can nonetheless discern a shared problematization of writing underlying these texts: namely, all three texts contrast the inalterability of writing over against a living, dynamic practice that requires an ability to articulate things differently than before. What is distinctive about the *Seventh Letter* in this regard is that Plato here makes more explicit the character of philosophy itself as an ongoing, dynamic, life-structuring practice, while denying that there is any

---

[21] Frede, op cit., 216.

[22] D. Hyland, *Plato and the Question of Beauty* (Bloomington: Indiana University Press, 2008), 134 writes: "Surely if philosophy, if Plato's philosophy, were a set of doctrines—what we have come to call in our day 'philosophical positions'— then it could be put into words just as mathematical, historical, or literary theories can be put into words... At the very least then, the first implication of this remarkable statement in the *Seventh Letter* is that Plato emphatically did *not* think of his philosophy as that set of formulated doctrines we call 'Platonism'" (104). He then writes later: "To speak properly then—and in a sense which we should call 'Platonic'—one should not speak, strictly, of 'philosophy,' nor of 'my philosophy,' much less of 'Plato's philosophy.' One should speak rather of 'philosophical existence.'"

syngramma of "Plato's philosophy." Thus, the fact that the critique of writing and the understanding of philosophy as a life-structuring practice are joined here in the *Seventh Letter* is what justifies us in calling it Plato's "discovery in Sicily."[23]

---

[23] An earlier and shorter version of this essay was presented at the *Fonte Aretusa* conference held in Siracusa, May 2015. I am indebted to the conference organizer, Heather Reid, and to my co-panelists at the conference, for their insightful comments on that earlier version.

Filippo Forcignanò[1]
What is a philosophical πεῖρα?
Some reflections on Plato's *Seventh Letter* 340b-341b

The aim of this chapter is to discuss lines 340b-341b of Plato's *Seventh Letter*, which describe the meeting between the philosopher and Dionysius II at the time of his last trip to Syracuse. Plato had good reasons to embark on this journey and to test Dionysius II's love of philosophy: several people worthy of esteem (Dion, Archytas, others from Tarentum, some Athenians) had attested to the fact that the young tyrant was sincerely passionate about philosophy. Plato himself was confident of the possibility that "a young man of native intelligence who has accidentally heard some talk of lofty matters should conceive a desire to live a better life" (see *Seventh Letter*, 339d-e). At any rate, by the time of his last trip Plato was sufficiently used to life's challenges to know that it is always good to test people's reputation and attitudes. Putting Dionysius II to the test was therefore an absolute priority. In this essay, I argue that (i) the πεῖρα had no theoretical content, but it was a test of Dionysius II's skills, attitude, and way of life; (ii) Dionysius II's book was in itself an indication of his ignorance and inadequacy as a philosopher; (iii) the *Protagoras* offers an interesting and similar use of the verb πειράζω.

The word πεῖρα, according to the *Lexique de Platon* by E. De Places, has two main meanings: *test* and *proof*. In the first meaning, it is used to say "give proof of one's own quality" (*Laches* 189b5: ἔδωκας σαυτοῦ πεῖραν ἀρετῆς ἣν χρὴ διδόναι μέλλοντα δικαίως δώσειν, "you have given the proof of your value that one who wants to do things the right way must give"). But the word πεῖρα also means "to test someone," or "to test one's qualities." It is used this way at *Euthydemus* 275b5, for instance, where Socrates asks his interlocutors to "test Clinias and to discuss with him" (λάβετον πεῖραν τοῦ μειρακίου καὶ διαλέχθητον ἐναντίον ἡμῶν). In this sense, the verb πειρᾶσθαι is similar to βασανίζειν, in the way it is used in *Laches* 187e6 ff.: being tested by Socrates (ὑπὸ Σωκράτους

---
[1] Filippo Forcignanò teaches History of Ancient Philosophy at the State University of Milan (Italy).

βασανίζεσθαι) implies to account for one's present and past lifestyle. The philosophical πεῖρα is always also an examination of one's life, not only of one's opinions. But it is also possible to use the word to mean "to test something." For instance, in *Charmides* 171a3 we read that the σώφρων knows that the doctor has some science, but it is necessary to test what sort it is, because each science is defined as not just a science, but a science of some thing.

Upon his arrival in Syracuse, Plato met Dionysius II precisely in order to verify the young man's passion for philosophy (340a):

> When I arrived, I thought my first task was to prove (ἔλεγχον δεῖν λαβεῖν) whether Dionysius was really on fire with philosophy (ἐξημμένος ὑπὸ φιλοσοφίας), or whether the many reports that came to Athens were false. Now there is a certain way of putting this to a test (ἔστιν δή τις τρόπος τοῦ περὶ τὰ τοιαῦτα πεῖραν λαμβάνειν), a dignified way and quite appropriate to tyrants, especially to those whose heads are full of philosophical commonplaces (and I saw at once, upon my arrival, that this was especially true of Dionysius) [transl. Morrow].

In this context ἔλεγχος has the same meaning as πεῖρα: test. The verb πειράζω with the personal accusative means "to *try, tempt* a person, *put* him *to a test*" (LSJ). In this sense, a πεῖρα is a sort of exam that someone gives to another to verify their skills and attitudes. For instance, when a person asks to join a sports team, the coach routinely asks them to display their abilities, skills, and techniques, in order to evaluate their future contribution to the team, their appropriate role in it and, more radically, whether they should join the team at all. Analogously, when a person asks for admission to a selective school, for instance a famous piano school, it is normal for the teacher to test the prospective pupil: do they have the right motivation? The right skills? Do they understand the tasks required by the school? Do they really have a sincere passion for the discipline? There are many tests and many situations in which it makes sense to be tested in this way. We learn from Plato's dialogues and the *Seventh Letter* that there is also a Platonic philosophical test.

What is a philosophical πεῖρα?

The passages quoted above clarify that the test which Plato has in mind is a well-established test, not an impromptu one. It is a sort of customary evaluation that a philosopher should resort to when meeting a prospective new pupil. Before going into the details of the πεῖρα to which Plato subjected Dionysius II, we have to ask whether there are any similar situations to be found in the Platonic dialogues. We find a similar context and an analogous use of the verb πειράζω at the beginning of the *Protagoras*. Let me summarize the context. Hippocrates, son of Apollodorus, shows up at Socrates's home one night, shouting with joy: "Protagoras is in the city!" Socrates tries to downplay the matter: "What do you care? Protagoras hasn't done you a wrong, has he?" [transl. Allen]. Hippocrates answers: "Heavens no, Socrates. Except maybe that only he is wise (γε μόνος ἐστὶ σοφός) and doesn't make me so." Socrates replies that it's just a fact of money and persuasion: "If you give him money and persuade him he'll make you wise too" (310d). Of course, Socrates knows very well that this is false (being wise is not the result of having passively followed some lessons), but he teases Hippocrates, who does not understand his interlocutor's irony and indeed asks Socrates to intercede for him with Protagoras. Since the hour is very early, Socrates proposes to while the time away by chatting and taking a stroll in the courtyard. The way Socrates presents this conversation is of the utmost interest for the purpose of this paper:

καὶ ἐγὼ ἀποπειρώμενος τοῦ Ἱπποκράτους τῆς ὁρμῆς διεσκόπουν αὐτὸν καὶ ἠρώτον
and I examined Hippocrates, questioning him to test his mettle.

The verb ἀποπειράομαι is rather infrequent in Plato: it occurs just eight times in the dialogues, three of which are in the *Protagoras*. In no other passage is it used in relation to a potential pupil in order to test his intentions and skills. It is true that Hippocrates wants to be a pupil of Protagoras, and not Socrates, but this does not change the type of question Socrates submits to him. The most important thing to note is that this verb anticipates two very important occurrences of πεῖραν λαμβάνειν in a passage on the difference between the exegesis of poetry and philosophical discussions, 347c-348a:

Actually, I think discussing poetry is much like attending the drinking parties of worthless and vulgar people. They're unable to associate with each other through their own voice and words, due to their lack of education, so they run up the price of flute girls and spend a great deal for the alien voice of the flute, and associate with each other through such voices as that. But where the drinkers are gentlemen and properly educated, you'll see neither flute girls nor dancing nor harp girls; they're capable of associating with each other in their own voices without this childish nonsense, speaking and listening decorously each in his turn even when they've drunk a great deal of wine. So too a meeting like this, it if consists of men of the sort most of us claim to be, has no need of an alien voice, nor of poets who cannot be questioned about what they mean. The Many adduce them in argument, some claiming the poet means this, others that, arguing about something they cannot test. But those met in familiar intercourse among themselves dismiss this sort of meeting, and test each other by receiving and rendering accounts in discussions of their own (ἐν τοῖς ἑαυτῶν λόγοις πεῖραν ἀλλήλων λαμβάνοντες καὶ διδόντες). I think you and I should rather imitate people like that. We should set aside the poets and fashion accounts with one another, putting the truth and ourselves to test (δι' ἡμῶν αὐτῶν πρὸς ἀλλήλους τοὺς λόγους ποιεῖσθαι, τῆς ἀληθείας καὶ ἡμῶν αὐτῶν πεῖραν λαμβάνοντας).

Not everyone can philosophize. We can't talk philosophy at every social gathering. Philosophy implies testing each other to verify aptitude for participating in such discussions. The πεῖρα has, so to speak, a double value: firstly, it tests the attitude of those who intend to practice philosophy; secondly, it verifies the content of what they say. The *Seventh Letter* describes the Syracusans' way of life in a way that is reminiscent of the bad *synousiai* of *Protagoras* (326b6 ff.):

When I got there and saw the proverbial happy life of Sicilian and Italian tables, with men gorging themselves twice every day and never sleeping alone at night and practicing all the other habits that go with these debaucheries, I was completely disgusted. For no man under heaven who has followed such practises from his youth could keep his head; so strange a temper is against nature. Nor would he ever learn self-control nor, indeed, acquire any other part of virtue. Nor can any city be at peace [...]

Parties, a lot of wine, the inversion of day and night: this is what the Sicilians call a "happy life." There are, of course, quite a few differences between Sicilian feasts and Athenian *symposia*, and between the political situation in Greece (and Athens in particular) and that in Syracuse. But in both cases Plato links a dissolute lifestyle with the decline of the city. Plato does not mention poetry in the *Seventh Letter*, but we know that many important poets were invited to Syracuse by Dionysius I, as well as his son. Dionysius II, the scion of the most powerful family in Syracuse, stood, in Plato's mind, as the embodiment of a non-philosophical city, exactly the opposite of the *kallipolis*.

As is well known, the δυναστεία of Dionysius II is described in many sources – by historians as well as Peripatetic philosophers – as being characterised by constant drunkenness.[2] Plutarch quotes[3] Aristotle's claim that once Dionysius II was drunk for ninety days in a row.[4] Aristotle even defends the idea that Dion acted against the tyrant because he was moved by the Syracusans' hatred of him; indeed, they hated him because he was always drunk.[5] This information should not be taken literally: the drunkenness of the tyrant is a *topos* in Greek literature. Plato never mentions this aspect in the *Letter*, but it is well known that he is particularly lenient towards Dionysius II and his vices.

---

[2] See [Arist.] *Probl.* XXVIII, 949a, 25-28; Theofr. F 548 Fortenbaugh; see also Athen., X, 435d-436b, Theopomp. *FGrHist* 115 FF 185-88.

[3] *Dio*, 7, 7.

[4] F 588 Rose = F 605, 2 Gigon.

[5] *Pol.* V, 1312a, 4-6.

Filippo Forcignanò

What did Plato and Dionysius II say during the πεῖρα?

It is very difficult to answer this question. The *Letter* doesn't give us this information *apertis verbis*. But Plato provides some clues:

1. 341b8-9: "You must present to such a man the whole of the philosophic undertaking, describing what its nature is, and how many difficulties must be surmounted, and how much labor is involved" (δεικνύναι δὴ δεῖ τοῖς τοιούτοις ὅτι ἔστι πᾶν τὸ πρᾶγμα οἷόν τε καὶ δι' ὅσων πραγμάτων καὶ ὅσον πόνον ἔχει).

2. 341c2-4: "...marvellous journey which he must at once undertake with all his strength, or life is not worth living" (ὁδόν τε ἡγεῖται θαυμαστὴν ἀκηκοέναι συντατέον τε εἶναι νῦν καὶ οὐ βιωτὸν ἄλλως ποιοῦντι);

3. d5-6: "while for the opposite kind of life he has a confirmed disgust" (τὴν δὲ ἐναντίαν ταύτῃ μισῶν διατελεῖ);

4. 341a8-b1: "I did not explain all of my philosophy to him" (πάντα μὲν οὖν οὔτ' ἐγὼ διεξῆλθον).

Philosophy is a long, difficult, discouraging journey, but it is the best journey one can make. If you live philosophically, you will hate the opposite kind of life. Plato surely taught these things to Dionysius II, but he did not explain all of his philosophy during the first – and last! – conversation. Was the πεῖρα something like "an introductory lesson in Platonic philosophy"? I don't think so. It was just an *aperitivo* to his philosophy, as people say in Italy.

On a more serious note, Plato did not explain to Dionysius II the content of his philosophy, except for a few vague hints. But he clearly explained that philosophy is a serious and strenuous task; a task that concerns one's way of life and happiness, which is why a true philosopher must be ready to change her or his life. For this reason, I disagree with those[6] who think that the πεῖρα consisted in the

---

[6] See G. Pasquali, *Le lettere di Platone* (Pisa, 1938), 75 ff.; H. Gundert, "Zum philosophischen Exkurs im 7. Brief," in *Idee und Zahl. Studien zur platonischen*

What is a philosophical πεῖρα?

philosophical *excursus*. As Paulo Butti de Lima has written, πεῖρα and *excursus* serve different purposes.[7] The purpose of the πεῖρα was precisely an ἔλεγχος, and not the explanation of any philosophical doctrine or corpus of doctrines. In Plato's words, the function of the πεῖρα is to test people and unmask those "who are pampered and unable to work hard" τοὺς τρυφῶντάς τε καὶ ἀδυνάτους διαπονεῖν (341a).[8] This expression is a clear reference to 326b-d, where Plato describes the "happy life" of the Syracusans as a non-stop party. And this proves that the link between the bad *symposia* of the *Protagoras* and the *Letter* is not pie in the sky, as it may seem at first sight.

An aspiring philosopher must possess certain physical, mental and attitudinal skills. This is made clear by the selection of rulers in the *Republic*. Testing them is a fundamental moment of the selection. For instance, it is urgent to test who will be the best defender of his own decision to do what is best for the city in every situation (III 413c5-7). This test is both physical and mental: καὶ πόνους γε αὖ καὶ ἀλγηδόνας καὶ ἀγῶνας αὐτοῖς θετέον ("we must expose them to labors, pains, and agonies"). The analogy between the physical test of the *Republic* and the philosophical πεῖρα is possible because the *gymnastikē* of the *Republic* is not just physical training.[9] Both philosophical and physical training contribute to forming a man who lives in a correct way. In addition, both tests involve labors and pains. Being able to bear πόνος is a fundamental philosophical skill. In a very significant passage of Book VII, we read that

> [the person we are looking for] must have penetration into their studies and ease of learning. For souls become discouraged in the difficulties of study more than in those of physical exercises,

---

Philosophie, hrgs. von H.-G. Gadamer and W. Schadewaldt (Heidelberg 1968), 103 ff.; H. Krämer, *Arete bei Platon und Aristoteles: zum Wesen und zur Geschichte der platonischen Ontologie* (Amsterdam, 1959), 404-408.

[7] P. Butti de Lima, *Platone: L'utopia del potere (La* Settima lettera*)*, (Venezia, 2015), 163.

[8] Radding translation from this volume. See M. Tulli, *Dialettica e scrittura nella VII Lettera di Platone* (Pisa, 1989), 14.

[9] See H. Reid, "Sport and Moral Education in Plato's *Republic*, *Journal of the Philosophy of Sport*,34:1 (2007): 160-75.

since the labor [of study], indeed, is more peculiar to them and not shared with the body. [...]

And, sure, a person who has a good memory, persistence, and in general who is a labor-lover is to be looked for. Or in what way do you suppose one will be willing to bear at the same time the labors of the body and to complete such hard study and practice?"[10]

Because the tests are so important, it is crucial to try to understand what Plato and Dionysius II told each other during their encounter. Indeed, to quote Tulli, "non v'è dubbio che il colloquio tra Dionigi e Platone si risolse nella πεῖρα."[11] Plato did not say anything else, but Dionysius II felt authorized to write a book on Platonic philosophy.[12] It is hard to believe that Plato explained to Dionysius II that it's impossible to write down the core of his philosophy. Therefore, Dionysius did not violate this prohibition. Nothing in the text authorizes us to assume the contrary. The link between Dionysius II's book and Plato's criticism of writing philosophy is an *escamotage* by which Plato introduces this new topic. But Dionysius didn't write a book on philosophy in order to transgress Plato's orders. Dionysius wrote a book on Platonic philosophy because he felt that Plato's belief that philosophy implies πόνος and steadfastness was absurd. Son of a tyrant and a tyrant himself,

---

[10] 535b5-c3: Δριμύτητα, ὦ μακάριε, ἔφην, δεῖ αὐτοῖς πρὸς τὰ μαθήματα ὑπάρχειν, καὶ μὴ χαλεπῶς μανθάνειν. πολὺ γάρ τοι μᾶλλον ἀποδειλιῶσι ψυχαὶ ἐν ἰσχυροῖς μαθήμασιν ἢ ἐν γυμνασίοις· οἰκειότερος γὰρ αὐταῖς ὁ πόνος, ἴδιος ἀλλ' οὐ κοινὸς ὢν μετὰ τοῦ σώματος.
Ἀληθῆ, ἔφη.
Καὶ μνήμονα δὴ καὶ ἄρρατον καὶ πάντῃ φιλόπονον ζητητέον. ἢ τίνι τρόπῳ οἴει τά τε τοῦ σώματος ἐθελήσειν τινὰ διαπονεῖν καὶ τοσαύτην μάθησίν τε καὶ μελέτην ἐπιτελεῖν;

[11] *Ivi*, 12.

[12] I write "Platonic" because the following protest of Plato's ("I heard that he wrote a book *on the things he had heard*, presenting it as his own work, different from the things he had heard") makes sense if and only if Dionysius's book was a *pamphlet* on Platonic philosophy, or somehow dependent on Plato's teachings (in Dionysius's intentions).

What is a philosophical πεῖρα?

Dionysius was used to having everything right away. From his point of view, it was intolerable that a hobby (since that is precisely what philosophy amounted to for him) might require a lot of patience, considerable effort, and a moderate lifestyle[13].

Dionysius was sure to know and to possess in adequate manner many of the *most important things* since he had heard them from others[14]. This passage should not be overinterpreted, as the trailblazers of the ἄγραφα δόγματα (Unwritten Doctrines) usually do. The word μέγιστα does not recall the μέγιστον μάθημα of the *Republic* (504e-505b) and does not allude to the "Theory of Principles" that Aristotle attributes to Plato in the *Metaphysics*.[15] Similarly, it makes no sense to explain this passage in relation to Plato's alleged public speaking on the Good, as reported by Aristossenus.[16] Morrow's translation has the merit of avoiding misunderstanding on this matter: "for he claimed to have already a sufficient knowledge of many of the most important points from his casual conversations with others." With the arrogance typical of powerful men, Dionysius thought he could do whatever he wanted; since at that moment he wanted to be a philosopher, he wrote a book of philosophy. Any other esoteric explanation of this fact is over the top.

How do people normally react to the πεῖρα?

As I have said, the πεῖρα has the purpose of distinguishing good and bad pupils. People's reaction to the πεῖρα is therefore essential in order to select or turn down potential pupils. The *Letter*

---

[13] On the frugal eating habits at the Academy, see Helian. *Var. Hist.* 2, 18 and R.S. Bluck, *Plato's Life and Thought* (London, Routledge & Paul, 1949), 81-82.
[14] 341b2-3: πολλὰ καὶ μέγιστα εἰδέναι τε καὶ ἱκανῶς ἔχειν διὰ τὰς ὑπὸ τῶν ἄλλων παρακοάς.
[15] See Krämer, *Arete*, 141; Id., *Platone e i fondamenti della metafisica. Saggio sulla teoria dei principi e sulle dottrine non scritte di Platone, con una raccolta dei documenti fondamentali in edizione bilingue e bibliografia*, Milano 1982, 105 n. 82; T.A. Szlezák, *Platon und die Schriftlichkeit der Philosophie. Interpretationen zun den frühen und mittleren Dialogen* (Berlin-New York, 1985), 399 ff.; Gundert, *Exkurs*, 90.
[16] See Krämer, *Arete*, 404 ff; Gaiser, *Platons*, 6 f. and 452 nt. 7; *contra* H. Cherniss, *The Riddle of the Early Academy* (Berkeley-Los Angeles, 1945), 1 ff.

distinguishes two kinds of reaction. A perspicuous discussion of this topic is provided by Tulli, who speaks about three (and not two) kinds of reaction[17]. On his interpretation, my ii. and iia are different reactions:

> i. If the listener is a real philosopher and is worthy of doing philosophy because of his divine nature (ἐὰν μὲν ὄντως ᾖ φιλόσοφος οἰκεῖός τε καὶ ἄξιος τοῦ πράγματος θεῖος ὤν: 340c1-4), he will think that the philosophical journey is terrific and the only possible way of life;

> ii. Those who are not really philosophers (οἱ δὲ ὄντως μὲν μὴ φιλόσοφοι), but have only a veneer of δόξαι, "when they see the full extent of the learning and labor required, and perceive that they must strictly regulate their daily lives if their quest is to be successful, conclude that the task is too difficult for their powers"

> iia. Some of them persuade themselves that they have been sufficiently instructed in the whole topic and no longer require further effort (ἔνιοι δὲ αὐτῶν πείθουσιν αὐτοὺς ὡς ἱκανῶς ἀκηκοότες εἰσὶ τὸ ὅλον καὶ οὐδὲν ἔτι δέονταί τινων πραγμάτων). This is the case of Dionysius.

These reactions shed further light on the content of the πεῖρα. What I mean is that no one reacts to it by denying some thesis or showing himself perplexed by some aspects of the content. People react to the πεῖρα either by concluding that the long, complex and demanding work of doing philosophy is a game worth playing, or by refusing to face such a struggle, either out of laziness or out of arrogance. The first thing that Plato teaches to his potential pupils is that philosophy is the only way to attain a happy life, but it is a bone-crushing and often discouraging labour. "Are you able to bear it? Are you ready to make some sacrifices? Are you ready to change your life?" The πεῖρα does not go beyond these questions. But it is enough to discourage those unfit for the task.

---

[17] See Tulli, *Dialettica*, 12 ff.

What is a philosophical πεῖρα?

The contents of the book

I wish to briefly get back to Dionysius's II book. Someone could stress the fact that Dionysius reacted to the πεῖρα by writing a book, denying what I have said about the purpose of his writing. Indeed, a book (any book) has some contents. It is of course possible that Plato and Dionysius discussed some philosophical content, but Plato's judgment of this book denies that the problem was its content. In this case, Morrow's translation is misleading: "Later, I hear, he wrote a book about what he had heard, putting it forward as an outline of his own philosophy, and not as a *doctrine* he had gotten from me." The Greek says something different: οὐδὲν τῶν αὐτῶν ὧν ἀκούοι (341b5). This clearly recalls the previous περὶ ὧν τότε ἤκουσε (b4). What the text says is that "Later, I heard that he wrote a book on the things he had heard, presenting it as his own work, different from the things he had heard." Plato does not know anything about this book: there is no other way to translate οἶδα δὲ οὐδὲν τούτων. Morrow's proposal (i.e. "whether this is true or not I do not know") is again rather misleading. Plato has absolutely no idea of the content of Dionysius II' book (or at least that is what he wants the reader to think). But for the mere fact that the tyrant wrote it and did so before having adequately studied, he definitely made a mistake.

Plato now introduces his criticism of writing philosophy. Even in this case, however, I would like to dispel the idea that the real problem is merely the fact that Dionysius II wrote a book. If he had said the same things orally, nothing would have changed. The text itself clearly states this:

> I do know that others have written on these same things,[18] but I don't know them and they do not even know themselves. And this much at least I can affirm with confidence about anyone who has written or proposes to write on these things,[19] pretending to a mastery of the problems with which I am occupied: it matters

---

[18] Morrow translates "on this subject" because he is thinking of a specific topic, such as the Good, but this is misleading.

[19] Again, Morrow translates "on this matter."

not whether he claims to have learned what he knows from me or some one else or to have discovered it for himself. It is not possible, at least in my opinion, that they understood something of the enquiry.[20] There is no book of mine that expounds these things, nor will there ever be one; for this knowledge is not a matter that can be transmitted[21] like other branches of knowledge. [...] And this too I know: if these matters are to be expounded at all *in writings or in oral discourses*, it is better that they should come from me. Certainly I am harmed more than anyone else if these things are misrepresented in a book.[22] If I thought they ought to be spread abroad *in writings or in oral discourses*, what nobler service could I render mankind during my life than to write a book on them? (341b6-e1).

I have heavily modified Morrow's translation. Indeed, it insists that Dionysius II wrote about something *specific*. This is also the position of many of those who defend the Unwritten Doctrines theory. But nothing in the text authorizes such a reading. Plato writes that he knows nothing about Dionysius II's book and that he does not even know the others who wrote about his philosophy. He ignores what they actually wrote. But the mere fact that they wrote his teachings down suggests that they have all gone astray.[23]

However, a connection between written and oral speeches is drawn twice in just a few lines: γραφέντα ἢ λεχθέντα (in writing and in oral discourses) and γραπτέα θ' ἱκανῶς εἶναι πρὸς τοὺς πολλοὺς καὶ ῥητά (if they ought to be spread abroad in writings and in oral discourses). The two participles of γράφω and λέγω, as well as γραπτέα and ῥητά, explain that the real problem is not that Dionysius II and other anonymous authors wrote books, but that

---

[20] For "of the enquiry" see Tulli, *Dialettica*, 51.
[21] Morrow adds "in writing," but this is not in the text.
[22] Morrow omits this, but γεγραμμένα has no other meaning.
[23] See 341b8-c1: τοσόνδε γε μὴν περὶ πάντων ἔχω φράζειν τῶν γεγραφότων καὶ γραψόντων, ὅσοι φασὶν εἰδέναι περὶ ὧν ἐγὼ σπουδάζω κτλ, "this is the only thing I have to say about who wrote and about who will write *saying to know what I care about*...." It is clear that Dionysius II and those anonymous writers wrote books on *Plato's* philosophy, not on philosophy in general.

they thought it was possible to express the core of Plato's philosophy once and for all in a systematic dissertation. They assumed it was possible to treat philosophy as the other branches of knowledge. In this respect, there is no difference between writing and speaking about philosophy. Philosophy is not a corpus of doctrines that someone can communicate through lectures; rather, "it requires long-continued intercourse between pupil and teacher in joint pursuit of the object they are seeking to apprehend; and then suddenly, just as light flashes forth when a fire is kindled, this knowledge is born in the soul and henceforth nourishes itself."

Which kind of knowledge is promoted by the *Seventh Letter*?

In a recently published book, Myles Burnyeat stated that the author of the *Seventh Letter* (who is not Plato) is "philosophically incompetent." It follows that the letter "is not a trustworthy source of information either about Plato's philosophical development or about his biography. It sheds no light on the Academy or on Sicilian history."[24] It is not at all clear to me why the author's philosophical incompetence should invalidate his historical credibility (i.e. he could be a contemporary of Plato perfectly informed of the facts, but unfit to philosophize).[25] This is not the place for a detailed refutation of Burnyeat's proposal. What I intend to do in conclusion is to better specify why philosophy is not, according to Plato, similar to the other branches of knowledge.

At 341c5-d2, Plato explains that knowledge appears like a spark after a long communion with the thing itself, περὶ τὸ πρᾶγμα αὐτό. Philosophy, in other terms, does not proceed by accumulation, step by step, but through a long and laborious dialectical exercise that produces – assuming it produces something – a sudden

---

[24] M. Burnyeat- M. Frede, *The Pseudo-Platonic* Seventh Letter, ed. D. Scott (Oxford: Oxford University Press, 2015), 122.

[25] The *Seventh Letter* does not contain any clear anachronism, does not contradict any other source, and it is rather trustworthy on the facts concerning Dionysius II's life. See F. Muccioli, *Dionisio II: storia e tradizione letteraria*, (Bologna, 1999), *passim*.

comprehension. This is the reason why the πεῖρα is fundamental: the teacher must verify that the pupil can bear this long preliminary work. There is a true discourse (λόγος ἀληθής) that condemns anyone who dares to write what cannot be written (341a3-6). This λόγος states that there are three gnoseological instruments with which we have to try to approach knowledge of the thing itself: name (ὄνομα), discourse (λόγος),[26] and image (εἴδωλον). The fourth thing involved in the process of knowing the "fifth" is a set of three kinds of knowledge: ἐπιστήμη (science), νοῦς (intellection) and ἀληθής δόξα (true opinion).[27] We must pass through the four elements to reach the fifth (i.e. the thing itself), but "these elements tend to show as much the quality of each object as its essence, because of the weakness of the discourses." Anyone who wants to fully (τελέως) grasp the fifth must somehow (ἁμῶς γέ πως) get the first four (342e3-5). Nevertheless, they remain irremediably obscure. The reason is explained in a more technical way at 343b6 ff: "being two terms, the essence and the quality (τοῦ τε ὄντος καὶ τοῦ ποιοῦ τινος), while the soul tries to know not the quality, but the essence, each of the four offers the soul, in words and deeds, that which is not sought." In other words, the soul wants to know the τι in itself, the nature of the thing, its essence, but our gnoseological tools mix it with the ποιόν τι (the quality). Whoever dares to say the thing itself is therefore easily refuted.

How to get out of this situation? How to try to reach the fifth? At 343e-344c1, Plato explains that

> only being guided through them [i.e. the first four], going back and back, produces with effort, in he who has a good nature, the knowledge of what has good nature [...] If each of these elements – names, discourses, visual images, and perceptions – is rubbed with others, with great effort, in benevolent confutations and in discussions conducted without hostility, then the knowledge

---

[26] In this context – and in Plato in general – λόγος does not mean "definition," but "discourse": see Tulli, *Dialettica*, 27-28.

[27] The fact that science, intellection and true opinion are linked together in a single set is not problematic: see *Resp.* 585b14-c1, *Phil.* 11b4-c1, 60d4-5, *Leg.* 688a-b.

What is a philosophical πεῖρα?

and the intellection around each thing suddenly flashes, with the greatest possible intensity within the limit of human abilities (ἐξέλαμψε φρόνησις περὶ ἕκαστον καὶ νοῦς, συντείνων ὅτι μάλιστ' εἰς δύναμιν ἀνθρωπίνην).

Some scholars think that what Plato means here is that there is a peculiar faculty, i.e. intellection, which is able to overcome the limits of human nature and to grab the thing itself in its purity. The intellection of the fifth (i.e. the Form) would therefore not be a linguistic form of knowledge. This interpretation can be declined in two ways: (i) a mystic and (ii) a non-propositional (but rational) one. According to (i), the intellection of the fifth is an illogical *unio mystica* with the thing itself; according to (ii), this kind of enlightenment is not irrational (in Julius Stenzel's lexicon, it is a rational *Erleuchtung*[28]), but it is not verbal.

In my opinion, it is easy to reject (i). At 340d1-5, where Plato is speaking of the *philo-sophers*, we read that the good pupil is able to λογίζεσθαι, which is beyond suspicion a rational act. Pasquali has masterfully clarified that at 341c5-d2, where Plato alludes to a knowledge that flashes as a spark, he uses the present tense (ἐκ πολλῆς συνουσίας γιγνομένης περὶ τὰ πρᾶγμα αὐτὸ καὶ τοῦ συζῆν), as if to say that the communion and the living together will continue (unlike a mystical union).[29] There's a fundamental difference between knowing (μαθεῖν) and experiencing something (παθεῖν), as in Aristotle's *De phil.* fr. 15 -- Ross explains: the initiates do not have to know (οὐ μαθεῖν τι δεῖν), but to experience something and to be in a certain disposition (ἀλλὰ παθεῖν καὶ διατεθῆναι). Quoting the fragment, Michael Psellos is more explicit: the initiates do not hear something; their mind passively experiences the enlightenment (αὐτοῦ παθόντος τοῦ νοῦ τὴν ἔλλαμψιν)[30]. Nothing like that is described in the *Seventh Letter*.

---

[28] See J. Stenzel, *Plato der Erzieher*, (Leipzig, 1928), 270-96, quoted from the Italian translation, Bari 1936.
[29] G. Pasquali, *Lettere*, 86.
[30] *Schol. ad Joh. Clim.* 6, 171.

More interesting and philosophically promising is (ii). On this view, defended by Wilhelm Wieland and Francisco Gonzalez (among others), the kind of knowledge of which the *Seventh Letter* speaks is rational, but non-propositional.[31] This means, to use Gonzalez's very perspicuous summary, that "something can be manifest without being describable." Non-propositional knowledge is beyond true-false opposition and admits gradation (i.e. it can be more or less clear). According to the Wieland-Gonzalez interpretation of the *Seventh Letter*, it is true that the *logos* says both the essence and the quality, but it is false that this is the only kind of knowledge: there is a non-logical understanding of the thing in itself. The difference between my view and the non-propositional view is therefore that both consider the *logos* a diaphragm, but I think that there is no hope of overcoming the diaphragm.[32] And this is exactly the reason why the *Seventh Letter* places in the same set *episteme*, *nous* and *true opinion*: the *nous* is higher than *episteme* and true opinion, but it is not able to bridge the distance between us and the "fifth." The "spark" that flares up is not a non-propositional form of knowledge, but the precise moment in which the soul understands what the "rubbing" of our gnoseological tools shows. The best comment on this is Hegel's *Enzyklopädie*, § 66:

> immediate knowing is to be taken as a *fact*. With this, however, the consideration is directed towards the field of *experience*, to a *psychological* phenomenon. - In this respect, it should be noted that it is one of the most common experiences that truths (which one knows very well to be the result of the most intricate and highly mediated considerations) present themselves *immediately* in the consciousness of someone conversant with such

---

[31] See W. Wieland, *Plato und die Formen des Wissens*, (Göttingen, 1982), esp. 224-36; F.J. Gonzalez, *Dialectic and Dialogue. Plato's Practice of Philosophical Inquiry*, (Evanston, Northwestern University Press, 1998), esp. ch. 9.. See also F.J. Gonzales., "Nonpropositional knowledge in Plato," *Apeiron*, 21 (1998): 235-84.

[32] For my general interpretation of the *excursus*, see F. Forcignanò, "La debolezza strutturale del linguaggio nella *Settima Lettera* di Platone," in *Ética e Filosofia Política*, XIX/2 (2016); also "Poder e limite da linguagem na Filosofia Antiga," 153-79.

knowledge. Like everybody else who has been trained in a science, the mathematician immediately has at his fingertips solutions to which a very complicated analysis has led. (transl. Brinkmann-Dahlstrom).

Dialectic is not a preparation for illumination. The distinction between a mediate work and an immediate comprehension is not the distinction between two kinds of knowledge. The long and laborious work of philosophy can also produce nothing, or take a lifetime. And this is the reason why not everyone can philosophize.

Mary R. McHugh[1]
Plato's *Timaeus* and Time

The Earth he devised to be our nurturer, and, because it curls around the axis that stretches throughout the universe, also to be the marker and guardian of day and night. Of the gods that have come to be within the universe, Earth ranks as the foremost, the one with the greatest seniority. To describe the dancing movements of these gods, their juxtapositions and the back-circlings and advances of their circular courses on themselves [...] to tell all this without the visible use of models would be labor spent in vain. (*Timaeus* 40b-d, Zeyl trans.)

The Syracusan Archimedes's planetaria and horological devices are considered to be innovations of the mid- to late-third century BCE, nearly a century after Plato's death in 347 BCE. However, the Roman statesman and orator Cicero (106-43 BCE) makes an explicit connection between Plato's *Timaeus* and Archimedes's invention:

For when Archimedes fastened on a globe the movements of moon, sun and five wandering stars, he, just like Plato's Demiurge who built the world in the *Timaeus*, made one revolution of the sphere control several movements utterly unlike in slowness and speed. Now if in this world of ours phenomena cannot take place without the act of the divine, neither could Archimedes have reproduced the same movements upon a globe without divine genius.[2]

---

[1] Mary R. McHugh is a Professor of Classics at Gustavus Adolphus College, St. Peter, MN, currently serving as Associate Provost. She earned Master's degrees in Classics from both Tufts University and the University of Wisconsin-Madison and her Ph.D. in Classics at UW-Madison. Her study of Plato began in earnest with her undergraduate major in ancient Greek and philosophy at Mt. Holyoke College. She is grateful to Prof. Heather Reid for organizing the Fonte Aretusa conference series, to Prof. Jean De Groot and Prof. Suzanne Obdrzalek, who generously provided feedback on an earlier version of this paper presented at the first Fonte Aretusa conference in 2015, and to the participants in the 2018 pre-conference workshop for their constructive comments.

[2] Cicero, *Tusculan Disputations*, Book I, Section XXV(63).

While Cicero's association of Plato's literary work with Archimedes's device is not causal, the aim of this paper is to trace the intellectual lineage from Plato's suggestion at *Timaeus* 40c to Archimedes's innovation. Cicero provides additional clues, but establishing a credible link between Plato's cosmology and Archimedes's armillary sphere or planetaria – at this time – requires delving deeper into Plato's mathematical thought and its connections to Pythagorean and Tarentine thinkers. We know from Plato's *Seventh Letter* that he was in contact with these scientists and intellectuals.

The oldest literary accounts we have written in ancient Greek offer explanations for how the world works. These "cosmogonies" attempt to order observable phenomena in such a way as to make sense of the workings of the universe. For Homer and Hesiod, cosmogonies are inseparable from theogonies, that is, stories that explain the origins of the gods and their rise to power. Both poets account for the oldest elements of the universe - earth, air, fire, and water, etc. - and each author anthropomorphizes these elements as deities. The *Timaeus* is Plato's cosmology, his account of how the physical universe came into being, and it represents his synthesis of the mytho-poetic traditions of Homer and Hesiod with the first rationalistic accounts of the universe provided by such early Ionian scientists and thinkers as Thales and Heraclitus. The quote from the *Timaeus* above hints at that dual lineage, since Plato divinizes natural phenomena – the planets are referred to as "gods" – and yet, direct observation, measurement, recording, and analyses of these complex celestial phenomena are critically necessary in order to describe them accurately. The latter sounds rather more like scientific inquiry and a move away from superstitious ignorance, rather than religious devotion. Yet reverence for the Demiurge and divine forces in nature permeate this work, likely ensuring its survival through the Middle Ages in Europe – the only of Plato's works available and read in Latin in the Christian West until the Renaissance.[3]

---

[3] Cicero's Latin translation of the Greek text of Plato's *Timaeus* was certainly read by early Church fathers, who quote Cicero extensively. The 4th century CE

Plato's *Timaeus* is one of his later works, likely written after the philosopher's first two trips (c. 387 and 366 BCE) to Syracuse recounted in the *Seventh Letter*. Although the conversation at the very beginning of the *Timaeus* takes place at Athens, its intellectual debt to Sicily is evident as Socrates's partners in conversation include two men from Magna Graecia, Hermocrates of Syracuse and Timaeus, from the Southern Italian city of Locri.[4] The fictional title character is perhaps modeled after Archytas of Tarentum, philosopher, statesman, general, and renowned mathematician, the founder of mathematical mechanics, a discipline in which Archimedes would later excel.[5] Archytas was a friend of Plato, whom Plato had introduced to Dionysius II, "apparently in the hope of persuading the Syracusan tyrant to emulate Archytas's just rule."[6] And in 360 BCE, when Plato fell out of favor with Dionysius II, it was Archytas who arranged for Lamiscus to rescue Plato from Syracuse on a Tarentine ship.[7]

---

philosopher Chalcidius also translated the first half of the *Timaeus* into Latin. These two Latin translations – those by Cicero and Chalcidius - were essential in the transmission of knowledge of the *Timaeus* in the Frankish kingdoms in the Carolingian era (780s – 900 CE). Rosamund McKitterick, "Knowledge of Plato's 'Timaeus' in the Ninth Century," in *From Athens to Chartres, Neoplatonism and Medieval Thought: Studies in honour of Edouard Jeauneau*, ed. Jeauneau, E., & Westra, H. (Studien und texte zur geistesgeschichte des mittelalters, bd. 35), (Leiden: E.J. Brill, 1992), 86-87. I am grateful to former Gustavus Classics alumnus Andrew Smith for his research on the *Timaeus* manuscript tradition to the 9th century CE as part of his 300-level Plato course work in Spring 2016.

[4] Nails writes that "Timaeus – well-born, rich, an astronomer and philosopher elected to high office in Locri (Epizephyrii) – is unknown outside of the dialogues: the historian of the same name who is a source for some of the 4th c. Sicilian material is about a century later." While other prosopographers "emphasize that Cicero says twice that Plato studied with Timaeus of Locri (*De Fini.* and *Rep.*)," according to Nails, "one cannot rule out the possibility, however, that Cicero inferred the association from the dialogues." Debra Nails, *The People of Plato: A Prosopography of Plato and Other Socratics*, (Indianapolis: Hackett Publishing Company, Inc., 2002), 293.

[5] Diogenes Laertius 8.83. M.F. Burnyeat, "Plato on Why Mathematics is Good For the Soul" in *Proceedings of the British Academy* 103 (2000): 16.

[6] Nails, 2002, 44.

[7] Plato's *Seventh Letter*, 350 a-b. Nails, 2002, 45.

In this work, Timaeus delivers extensive speeches on the foundations of the sciences of astronomy, physics, chemistry, and physiology. His conclusion to a lengthy and complicated description of astronomical phenomena and their role in measuring time is at the heart of this paper, as he points out that a physical model is necessary to illustrate and fully understand the quite complicated movements of heavenly bodies (*Timaeus* 40b-d, quoted above). In the Greco-Roman world, such models – orreries, planetaria, and even the Antikythera mechanism - are typically dated to the later, Hellenistic period (323 – 31 BCE).

Cicero, Archimedes, and Plato

Cicero describes two different devices designed by Archimedes, both of which model the movements of the heavens. While one demonstrates his reception and mastery of the legacy of earlier scientists, the other illustrates Archimedes's own ingenuity. In *De Re Publica*, Cicero relates a discussion that took place in 129 BCE. The interlocutor tells a story of the visit of the Roman consul, Gaius Sulpicius Gallus, to the home of Marcus Marcellus, whose grandfather, the Roman general Marcellus, had sacked Syracuse in 212 BCE. (It was this Roman occupation that led to Archimedes's untimely death, murdered by a Roman soldier, despite Marcellus's instructions to his soldiers to find Archimedes and to bring the Syracusan scientist and inventor to Marcellus unharmed.[8]) According to Cicero's account, the general Marcellus had stolen from Syracuse two devices designed by Archimedes, both of which the victorious general had brought back to Rome. Marcellus dedicated the "more beautiful" of the two, a celestial globe, in the Temple of Virtue, where it was kept publicly on display among the spoils of war. The other he kept for himself and took home (and only this singular object, out of all the abundance of plunder looted from the famously wealthy and beautiful city of Syracuse.) The consul Gallus – nearly a century later - asks his host, the grandson of Marcellus, to bring out this device so Gallus and the other guests can admire it. Gallus is quite knowledgeable about Archimedes's work and

---

[8] Cicero, *De finibus* 5.50; Cicero, *In Verrem* 2.4.131; Plutarch, *Marcellus* 19.

Plato's Timaeus and Time

describes the object dedicated in the Temple of Virtue – the other one - as a solid globe, the scientist's model of an earlier invention constructed by Thales of Miletus (c. 624 – c. 546 BCE) and further elaborated with the constellations and stars in the sky by Eudoxus of Cnidus.[9] The consul Gallus, eager to see this famous device now in the hands of a private collector, one not normally on public display, enthuses about the further development and innovation Archimedes brought to this modeling of the heavens and the solar system that his predecessors had earlier described.

> "But this newer kind of globe," he said, "on which were delineated the motions of the sun and moon and of those five stars which are called wanderers [the five visible planets], or, as we might say, rovers, contained more than could be shown on the solid globe, and the invention of Archimedes deserved special admiration because he had thought out a way to represent accurately by a single device for turning the globe those various and divergent movements with their different rates of speed." And when Gallus moved the globe, it was actually true that the moon was always as many revolutions behind the sun on the bronze contrivance as would agree with the number of days it was behind in the sky. Thus the same eclipse of the sun happened on the globe as would actually happen, and the moon came to the point where the shadow of the earth was at the very time when the sun [was]. . . out of the region.[10]

---

[9] Nails describes Eudoxus as a student of Archytas of Tarentum, and possibly also a student of the physician Philistion of Locri Epizephyrii. "Eudoxus was an astronomer and geographer as well as a brilliant mathematician. . . but Eudoxus's most stunning legacy is a geometrical model of the apparent motions of the sun, moon, and planets in homocentric spheres that was able to show retrograde motion and was not overturned before Kepler." And Eudoxus had a school at Cyzicus which is said to have occasionally combined with Plato's Academy. Eudoxus is reported to have been *scholarch* at the Academy in Athens while Plato was away at Sicily in 366 BCE. Nails, *People of Plato*, 147.

[10] Cicero, *De Re Publica*, Book I, Sections 21-22.

Mary R. McHugh

What exactly was this device? Illustrations do help to distinguish among the types of this kind of model, but, for the moment, in the absence of such images, a few definitions will suffice. A "celestial globe" is a sphere on which the stars, constellations, and various astronomical orbits are drawn or incised. It is likely that this is the type of globe that Marcellus dedicated in the Temple of Virtue. An "orrery" is a heliocentric model of the solar system in which the planets move about a stationary sun through a clockwork mechanism. A "planetarium" is a geocentric model of the solar system that shows the positions of the sun, moon, and planets as viewed from the earth at various times. An "armillary sphere" is a skeleton made of graduated metal circles linking the poles and representing the equator, the ecliptic, meridians and parallels. Usually a ball representing the Earth or, later, the Sun is placed in its center. It is used to demonstrate the motion of the stars around the Earth. It is unclear from Cicero's descriptions whether the second mechanism, the one kept by Marcellus as his personal possession, was an orrery, planetarium, or armillary sphere, but it does appear to be a working model along the lines of what Plato describes as essential for understanding the complicated movements of the heavens (*Timaeus* 40c).

Eudoxus, Student of Plato(?), Inventor of Celestial Globe

Cicero credits Thales[11] and Eudoxus, the latter said to be a student of Plato, with the invention of the celestial globe. Gregory argues that "while the astronomy of the *Timaeus* is actually quite crude and poor . . . the astronomy and cosmology of the *Timaeus* was

---

[11] Hahn notes that building the cosmos out of right triangles is a narrative preserved in *Timaeus* 53Cff. "This metaphysical project began with Thales and is taken up by Pythagoras, who is also credited with the 'application of areas' theorem, the construction of all rectilinear figures out of triangles in any angle, and the 'putting together' of the regular solids, later called 'Platonic solids,' that are the molecules, created from right angles out of which all other appearances are constructed." Robert Hahn, *The Metaphysics of the Pythagorean Theorem: Thales, Pythagoras, Engineering, Diagrams, and the Construction of the Cosmos out of Right Triangles*, (Albany: SUNY Press, 2017), xi and 195-212.

of paramount importance to the development of these disciplines in ancient Greece"[12] and he notes how details of the work of Eudoxus and Callippus "show just how immediately fruitful the challenge set by Plato was. They tackle precisely the problems that Plato sets in the *Timaeus* in precisely the way he would like."[13] This description appears to reinforce the impression of Eudoxus as a dutiful student, who took to task Plato's assignment to develop a physical model of the heavens as described in *Timaeus* 40c, and for the successful completion of which Cicero awards credit.

However, Zhmud has argued that "there is no reliable evidence that Eudoxus, Menaechmus, Dinostratus, Theudius, and others, whom many scholars unite into the group of so-called 'Academic mathematicians' ever were [Plato's] pupils or close associates."[14] While it is difficult to determine whether Plato learned from Eudoxus or Eudoxus from Plato,[15] Eudoxan mathematics are evident in the *Timaeus*.[16] The transmission of ideas in antiquity is difficult to trace,

---

[12] Andrew Gregory, *Plato's Philosophy of Science*, (London: Duckworth, 2000), 124-58.

[13] Gregory, 2000, 183.

[14] Leonid Zhmud, "Plato as 'Architect of Science'" in *Phronesis* 43:3 (1998), 211.

[15] Wilbur Knorr investigates the claim of Simplicius (early sixth century CE) in his commentary on Aristotle's *De caelo* that it was specifically Plato who inspired Eudoxus in his astronomical study, citing the second-century CE. Aristotelian teacher and commentator, Sosigenes. Knorr concludes, "It thus appears to be only Sosigenes's opinion that Plato played this role; certainly, Simplicius has not transmitted the identities of any special sources that Sosigenes might here have had, if indeed there were such." Wilber Knorr, "Plato and Eudoxus on the Planetary Motions." *JHA* 21 (1990), 318-20. In the end, he concludes that "there can be no doubt that Eudoxus knew Plato's *Republic*, and most likely also the *Timaeus*, before engaging in his own astronomical studies. But he must also have known the technical research on which Plato's astronomical visions are founded, for instance, the work of 'the very few men who are aware of the periods of the other planets', not just of the Sun, Moon and stars known to the many (*Timaeus* 39c), and the work of those who contrive the 'visual representations' that would facilitate serious investigation of intricate planetary phenomena (40c)." Knorr, "Plato and Eudoxus," 323-24.

[16] The Eudoxan mathematics De Groot sees in the *Timaeus* is the scheme of circles of Same and Different. From a cosmic point of view, the Different is the turning in the opposite direction that Eudoxus introduced of the circles of the ecliptic

especially in a far-flung world such as Western Greece, where scholars such as Plato traveled at will from Athens to Syracuse and elsewhere, much in the manner of earlier itinerant philosophers. Discussions were not confined to the Academy *per se*, nor were all conversations documented in ancient sources. Nor are many ancient sources extant. Nevertheless, this bit of Eudoxan mathematics in the *Timaeus* is evidence that there was an intellectual exchange. The text of the *Timaeus* itself no doubt sparked discussion and innovation over the course of space and time. Indeed, the millennia over which it was read in Greek and Latin, together with the works of astronomers, mathematicians, and engineers, yielded time-measuring devices – astronomical clocks and lunar and solar calendars still used today by major world religions. If one thinks about it in metaphysical terms, although time has preceded us and will continue long after our mortal lives are past, humankind has instituted time by means of making a model of the "timemakers" of our world, the heavens.

"Armillary Sphere" in the *Timaeus*

We know that the philosophy of mathematics at Ptolemaic Alexandria was Platonistic, given Hipparchus's reliable testimony about Eratosthenes.[17] They would have taken seriously the model that Plato describes. Generally, scholars make a connection between the armillary sphere ascribed to Eratosthenes in the 3rd century and the *Timaeus*. The mythic account of the Demiurge constructing the Circles of Same and Different and the planetary circles (36 b-d)

---

and of the planets (at least we do not know of an earlier astronomer who actually suggests that planets move west to east on their own circles at the same time they participate in the east to west movement of the whole sphere of fixed stars). Plato's speaking of Same and Different as bands with divisions solidifies their cosmic significance. When he speaks of divisions filling up at the space on the bands, proportions leaving over a fraction with a tiny ratio, this suggests the "method of exhaustion" introduced by Eudoxus and used so extensively by Archimedes. These comments from Prof. Jean De Groot, email dated June 14, 2015.

[17] This comment needs more research. I am grateful to Prof. Jean De Groot for this lead.

sounds as though Plato were lending the Demiurge the tools of Hephaestus to forge the heavens, giving it patterns of figures, turning the heavenly bodies on a lathe, and shaping each to its proper form.

According to Cornford, the language describes the construction of a material model of the revolutions of heavenly bodies, an armillary sphere.[18] And, indeed, Cornford assumes that the Academy had such a sphere, and he cites Theon, who quotes *Timaeus* 40c, saying that he (Theon) had himself made a 'sphere' (σφαιροποιία). Plato's *Second Letter*, 312d, mentions a sphere (σφαιρίον) at Syracuse.[19] Cornford speculates that the 'sphere' at the Academy was, like the latter, "a simpler construction than the 'mechanical sphere' of the Syracusan Archimedes, which is said to have reproduced simultaneously all the celestial motions."[20]

Poetry of the Heavens in the *Timaeus*

Plato is one of the Greek philosophers who discuss the problem of time, (a theme raised by earlier thinkers, e.g. Anaximander[21] and Heraclitus). Plato does not define time, but speaks of it in terms of analogies and metaphors, within the context of the entire plan of the universe. The meaning of time can only be understood within this framework, and the significance of time can only be grasped by

---

[18] Francis M. Cornford, *Plato's Cosmology*, (New York: The Humanities Press, Inc., 1952), 74.

[19] Cornford, 1952, 73-75.

[20] Cornford, 1952, 75.

[21] The Anaximander fragment, reproduced by the Neoplatonist Simplicius in his c. 530 CE commentary on Theophrastus's Φυσικῶν δόξαι, thus preserving it, is well known in Western continental philosophy. The Greek text was translated by Nietzche in his 1873 lecture, entitled *Philosophy in the Tragic Age of the Greeks*, published posthumously in 1903. Here is Nietzche's translation: "Whence things have their origin, there they must also pass away according to necessity; for they must pay penalty and be judged for their injustice, according to the ordinance of time." Heidegger's chapter, "The Anaximander Fragment" in his work *Early Greek Thinking* is a fairly well known treatment of the fragment and its reflection on time. David Farrell Krell, "Martin Heidegger: the Anaximander Fragment," *Arion: A Journal of Humanities and the Classics* 1:4 (1973): 576-626. http://www.jstor.org/stable/20163348. I am grateful to Tony Leyh for pointing out this specific example of Presocratic thinkers reflecting on time and being long before Plato.

observing its relationship to other beings in the universe. Time is relative - it is measured through motion.

Plato's approach to time is a cosmological one, he is fully aware of the effectiveness of the use of allegory and metaphor, such as we see in the Western Greek poetic tradition, for making sense of the observable phenomena of the workings of the universe. Its order and harmony, mathematics, musical progression, the fundamental harmony in the universe is most evidently, though only partially, manifested in the motions of the heavenly bodies.

In the terms of such poetic language, the sun, moon, and planets were created to distinguish and guard the numbers of time. Their orbits and their duties assist in the fashioning of time. Thus, we have days, months, and years. Time is the wandering and revolution of heavenly bodies and their measurement with numbers. Time and the universe are inseparable and time came into being with the ordering of the universe.

> For before the heavens came to be, there were no days or nights, no months or years. But now, at the same time as [the Demiurge] framed the heavens, he devised their coming to be. These all are the parts of time, and *was* and *will be* are properly said about the becoming that passes in time, for these two are motions. (*Timaeus* 37e)

Plato as Scientist, Innovator, and Teacher

Plato describes astronomical phenomena at length and their role in measuring time. However, he concludes this section of the work with an important observation - he points out that a physical model is necessary to illustrate and fully understand the quite complicated movements of heavenly bodies.

> The Earth he devised to be our nurturer, and, because it curls around the axis that stretches throughout the universe, also to be the marker and guardian of day and night. Of the gods that have come to be within the universe, Earth ranks as the foremost, the one with the greatest seniority. To describe the dancing movements of these gods, their juxtapositions and the back-circlings (Ptolemaic epicycles) and advances of their circular

courses on themselves . . . to tell all this without the visible use of models²² would be labor spent in vain. (*Timaeus* 40c)

This passage is extraordinary for a number of reasons. First, it raises questions about general notions of Plato's epistemology, according to which the data provided by sense-perception is not reliable. Second, implicit in this statement is the idea that a (presumably accurate) μίμημα (model) of an εἰκών (likeness) could lead us (or as close as we can get) to knowledge of the παράδειγμα, the divine plan (or Broadie's "recipe"²³) for the workings of the universe. We are at three (four?) degrees of separation from what is eternal and yet it is seemingly still accessible to us. This doesn't seem to synch up with our general understanding of Plato's theory of knowledge. What gives? What is happening here?

I'll begin with a caveat. The character Timaeus does caution that his entire cosmology is at best an εἰκὼς μῦθος, a "likely story" that must necessarily lack full consistency and accuracy (cf. 29c-d). His astronomical account is presented as a description of the soul of the cosmos, not of the visible system of the heavens. In Plato's ontology, sensible objects are but changing and imperfect copies of the associated Forms, which are perfect and unchanging.²⁴

Broadie's argument that Plato in the *Timaeus* is truly concerned to explain the cosmos because the Demiurge was truly concerned to create the best possible world is best set forth in her own brilliant explanation:

> On one of these approaches, the cosmos is the subject-matter for the human scientist, and the paradigm is epistemically subordinate. This is because the scientist reconstructs the paradigm as far as possible just in order to have a well-reasoned theory of the cosmos. What makes it reasonable to hope for such

---

[22] For those interested in the original Greek translated as "models," it is not παράδειγμα or εἰκών but μίμημα.

[23] Sarah Broadie, *Nature and Divinity in Plato's* Timaeus (Cambridge: Cambridge University Press, 2014) 62.

[24] Wilbur R. Knorr, "Plato and Eudoxus on the Planetary Motions." *JHA* 21 (1990) 318.

a theory is the framework assumption that the cosmos was made in accordance with the paradigm. Moreover, the paradigm in this act of making (or the maker's use of the paradigm) is also subordinate – to the production of the best possible physical world. This world is the maker's primary objective, just as it is the natural scientist's primary object of study. According to the other approach, the intelligible paradigm is the primary object for the Platonic investigator, and the physical cosmos is useful as conveying it by representation. The evidence is strong that the *Timaeus* cosmology is governed by the first approach, even though there are some conspicuous passages whose language suggests the second.[25]

While Plato takes the first approach in the *Timaeus*, we see Broadie's second approach at work in Plato's *Republic*, when Socrates makes a recommendation about the kind of research astronomers ought to engage in:

> By using problems, then, we shall pursue astronomy, just like geometry, but we shall set aside the things in the sky, if we intend to take hold of astronomy in the true sense and so make useful the natural intelligence in the soul (530b).

This new astronomy is "a purely mathematical study of geometrical solids (spheres) in rotation (528a, e), a sort of abstract kinematics; for only a study of *invisible* being will turn a soul's gaze upwards in the sense that interests Socrates (529b)."[26] Now this sounds closer to the Plato we thought we knew. And yet, as Burnyeat points out, "the astronomy section of the *Republic* stands at the origin of the great tradition of Greek mathematical astronomy which culminated in the cosmological system of Claudius Ptolemy."[27] As Knorr comments,

> This remark bears specifically on the kind of study that will suit the purposes of a general liberal education for the state's elite. But, as Bulmer-Thomas has argued, it also embraces a fully

---

[25] Broadie, 2012, 82-83.
[26] Burnyeat, 2000, 12.
[27] Burnyeat, 2000, 12.

reasonable program for researchers. By 'setting aside' the visible phenomena, one is not to dismiss altogether the empirical facts, but rather to give priority to the discovery of the underlying geometric regularities, 'the actual swiftness and the actual slowness of the motions in the true number and all the true figures" (529d), through which the phenomena can be accounted for.[28]

In the *Republic*, Socrates says that astronomy should be pursued in the same way as geometry. The visible patterns of motion in the heavens should be studied like the diagrams of geometry, as an aid to thinking about purely abstract mathematical problems (529d-530c). But sense perception again intervenes, as Socrates then describes several distinct types of motion, each with its own proper mode of perception.

> "It is probable," I said, "that as the eyes are framed for astronomy, so the ears are framed for harmonic motion, and these two sciences are sisters of one another, as the Pythagoreans say – and we agree, Glaucon, do we not?"
>
> "We do," he said. (*Republic* 530d)

If, then, the observation of astronomical phenomena goes beyond mere perception, including measurement, gathering data on various movements of bodies in the heavens, and recording observations and analyses, representation of this data would necessarily mean creating a model which was similarly movable and changeable but similarly reflecting the realities and inter-workings within the cosmos that its observers documented. Thus, the orreries, armillary spheres, and planetaria were all moving models, capturing the distillation of the measurement of astronomical time which they represented. And, of course, models could get it wrong, just as human observation might prove faulty, never mind hypotheses and theorems. But the plausibility of such an account, a "likely story," at least provides a point of departure, a basis for further investigation and argument.

---

[28] Knorr, 1990, 324.

Mary R. McHugh

Medieval Arabic reception of the *Timaeus* and Hellenistic Science

The story does not end there, for making the theoretical visible, in the form of geared devices, would have a significant effect on horological devices, from Hero of Alexandria's water clocks to the astronomical clocks of the Islamic world and late medieval Europe. In the introduction to his *Pneumatica*, Hero of Alexandria (*fl.* 1st cent. CE) explains that this (pneumatic) technology is fundamental to his earlier treatise on water clocks (*hōroskopeia*).[29] His four-volume work on water clocks has not survived, but its mention is revealing.[30] Much of Hero's extant work can be regarded as a kind of palimpsest, both for some of his other works, since lost, and, more importantly, for the works of several Hellenistic scientists, especially Archimedes, Ctesibius, and Philo of Byzantium. Hero was familiar with the technological achievements of earlier scientists and sought to explain, adapt, and improve upon their innovations, although he may not have always fully understood his sources.[31] Hero's surviving documentation of Hellenistic technology is justly famous, especially for the "marvelous engines" which he describes in two of his works, the *Pneumatica* and the *Automata*. These works may have survived precisely because his inventions were entertaining and his descriptions less taxing for the novice reader than the original works of Hellenistic scientists.[32]

The Arabic reception of Hero's works in 9th-century Baghdad led to further research into his sources (which may still have existed in manuscript at that time). Interestingly enough, all of Plato's works, including the *Timaeus*, were available, read, and studied by Arabic scholars in the original Greek and in some Arabic translations

---

[29] Schmidt, W., ed. 1899-1914, *Heronis Alexandrini opera quae supersunt omnia*, 5 vol., (Leipzig: Teubner, 1899), Vol. I, 2.

[30] A fragment of Hero's treatise on water clocks can be found in Schmidt, ed., *Heronis*, Vol. I, 456.

[31] Lucio Russo, *The Forgotten Revolution: How Science Was Born in 300 BC and Why It Had to Be Reborn.* (Heidelberg and New York: Springer-Verlag, 2004), 141.

[32] Russo, 2004, 137-41.

Plato's Timaeus and Time

(prepared in the 9th and 10th centuries) throughout the Middle Ages.[33] Further, enthusiasm for the *Timaeus* led to a split or twofold Arabic transmission of the text, with separate emphases on its philosophy, *Timaeus on Metaphysics*, and on its preservation of earlier Greek scientific and physiological theories, the *Medical Timaeus*.[34]

In turn, Arabic scholars' application of this theoretical knowledge led to a number of important technological innovations within Abbasid culture. Specifically, the development of the astronomical clock provides an excellent case study for the reception of Hellenistic science in Arabic culture, for Arabic scholars' adaptation and development of that technology within their own specific cultural and religious context, and for the subsequent appropriation of this technology, claimed as one of the "rediscoveries" of classical antiquity in the European Renaissance.

Ctesibius had introduced the first real clocks to Alexandria in the first half of the third century BCE, solving all of the problems inherent in the earlier Egyptian water clepsydra and in this way transforming the clepsydra into a reliable and accurate instrument for measuring time.[35] An anonymous work preserved in Arabic describes and attributes to Archimedes a remarkable design for a water clock which is strikingly similar to the Elephant Clock of the famous 12th-century Islamic engineer Ibn Isma'il al-Jazari.[36] Al-Jazari is best known for his *Book of Knowledge of Ingenious Mechanical Devices*, which describes fifty mechanical devices and gives instructions on how to construct them.[37] Such a work is reminiscent of Hero's

---

[33] Rüdiger Arnzen, "Plato's *Timaeus* in the Arabic Tradition," in Celia, Francesco, et al. *Il Timeo : Esegesi Greche, Arabe, Latine : Relazioni Introduttive Ai Seminari Della 5. "Settimana Di Formazione" Del Centro Interuniversitario "Incontri Di Culture. La Trasmissione Dei Testi Filosofici E Scientifici Dalla Tarda Antichità Al Medioevo Islamico E Cristiano," Pisa, Santa Croce in Fossabanda, 26-30 Aprile 2010.* (Pisa: Plus-Pisa University Press, 2012), 182.

[34] Arnzen, 2012, 188.

[35] Russo, 2004, 102.

[36] Russo, 2004, 102.

[37] Jim Al-Khalili, *The House of Wisdom: How Arabic Science Saved Ancient Knowledge and Gave Us the Renaissance*, (New York: Penguin, 2011), 277-78.

Mary R. McHugh

Automata, and it is likely that familiarity with Hero's work and possibly Hero's source, Philo of Byzantium, led to the development of a guild of automata builders in the Islamic world, which flourished for centuries.[38] Arabic scientists' interest in the Hellenistic technology of automata and geared mechanisms led to the development of the astronomical clock, fully in keeping with their interest in astronomy and astrology, the latter deemed the "mistress of the sciences" in Abbasid culture.[39]

Although not described by Hero in any of his extant works, the astronomical clock has special mechanisms and dials to display astronomical information, such as the relative positions of sun, moon, constellations of the zodiac, and sometimes major planets. It is sensible to assume that such a device existed in Hellenistic technology, thanks to the modern discovery of the Antikythera mechanism, named after the Greek island where the remains of ancient shipwreck dated to the 1st cent. BCE were discovered nearly a century ago. Researchers describe the mechanism as an astronomical calculator with the ability to predict both lunar and solar eclipses, and they confirm that the device has a mechanical display of planetary positions that appears to follow the theories of Hipparchus, who realized that the moon's unusual positions in the sky are caused by its elliptical orbit, a theory demonstrated by the mechanism's complicated planetary alignments.[40]

A similar device, certainly a descendant of the Antikythera mechanism, was described by the Persian scholar al-Biruni around

---

[38] Russo, 2004, 332. For the Arabic tradition of building "marvelous mechanisms," which goes back to the eighth century, see Donald R. Hill, "Mathematics and applied science," in *Religion, learning and science in the 'Abbasid period'*, edited by M.J.L. Young, John D. Latham and Robert J. Serjeant. (Cambridge: Cambridge University Press, 1990), 248-73.

[39] Dimitri Gutas, *Greek Thought, Arabic Culture. The Graeco-Arabic Translation Movement in Baghdad and Early 'Abbāsid Society (2nd-4th/8th-10th centuries)*, (London and New York: Routledge, 1998), 108.

[40] Jarrett A. Lobell, "The Antikythera Mechanism" in *Archaeology*, Vol. 60, No. 2 (March/April 2007), 42-45.

1,000 CE.[41] Two early astronomical clocks, Al-Jazari's Castle Clock (1206) and the Three Kings' Clock at Strasbourg Cathedral (1352-54), demonstrate the Arabic reception and development of this particular Hellenistic technology and its subsequent spread across Europe in the thirteenth century.

Conclusion

Plato's *Timaeus* is a complex work, preserving early Greek scientific theories long since considered obsolete by modern Western astronomy and other disciplines. We set ourselves the task at the beginning of this paper to investigate whether Archimedes's device – mentioned by Cicero – may perhaps have been a response to or inspired by the specific assignment or challenge – if indeed it was one – that Plato poses at *Timaeus* 40c, that is, to create a working model that distills a complex knowledge of the patterns of celestial movements, gained through detailed observation, recording, and analyses of that data over time. This investigation reveals another complex, diachronic interplay, that between individual thinkers over space and time and the communication and transmission of ideas and the sparking of inspiration despite barriers of language, religion, and geographic location. The locus, originally, is small. We began with Plato at Syracuse, a visitor from Athens. But that circle rapidly expands, back in time to earlier poets such as Homer and Hesiod and to earlier thinkers such as Thales of Miletus, Anaximander of Miletus (Thales's pupil), Pythagoras of Samos (Anaximander's student), and Heraclitus of Ephesus to Plato's contemporaries in Sicily such as Archytas of Tarentum and Philistion of Locri Epizephyrii, and their students such Eudoxus of Cnidus and Aristotle, and yet another generation of their students at Cyzicus and at the Academy in Athens. The ripples further enlarge and radiate over time to Hellenistic Alexandria, to Archimedes's Syracuse and Rome, to Cicero, Hero of Alexandria, the early Church fathers, Late Antiquity,

---

[41] Derek J. de Solla Price, "Gears from the Greeks: the Antikythera mechanism – a calendar computer from ca. 80 B.C.," in *Transactions of the American Philological Society* 64, part 7 (1974), 42-43.

to 9th century Baghdad, medieval and Renaissance Europe, and even to the present day. While this description might seem poetic, even romantic, a vision in the vein of the Renaissance artist Raphael's fresco, *The School of Athens*, the traces of evidence are there, preserved in our texts – though with many lacunae - and in the technology of timekeeping devices themselves, documenting the remarkable human collaborations of scientific study and ingenuity over the course of millennia and around the circumference of the globe. Although Plato's science is now obsolete, there is no question that the *Timaeus* was part of an ongoing conversation inspired by Plato's own engagement with his predecessors and contemporaries, producing a text that motivated its readers to test, respond, and innovate in a process that, while it created the text's own obsolescence, also regenerated itself by inspiring new research, science, and technology.

Political Context

Christos C. Evangeliou[1]
Plato and Sicilian Power Politics:
Between Dion and Dionysius II

Plato's First Visit to Syracuse

Whether or not he actually wrote the *Seventh Letter*, it is worthwhile trying to understand Plato's motivations for getting involved in Sicilian politics and to reconstruct – as far as possible – his point of view. At the time of Socrates's tragic death (399 BCE), Plato was twenty-nine years old and deeply disaffected by Athenian politics, both under the Thirty Tyrants and under the Restored Democracy. They had both mistreated Socrates, his beloved teacher of virtue and friend of justice in turbulent Athens. At that critical time in his life, Plato decided to take some time off from his serious philosophical studies and travel to see the larger and richer world of the Greek Colonies and beyond, following in the footsteps of Pythagoras, Thales, Solon, and other distinguished Hellenes.

His travels took the young Plato from Athens to Megara, to Cyrene, to Egypt, to Southern Italy, to Sicily, and to the city of Syracuse where he met Dion (408-354 BCE), a precocious teenager, brother in law to powerful Sicilian Tyrant Dionysius I (who married Dion's sister Aristomache) and later son in law (by marriage to their daughter Arete). Through Dion, Plato was introduced to Dionysius I, but the hardened ruler, unlike the impressionable youth, was not impressed by the philosopher's theories about the supposedly miserable life of tyrants and the happiness of the just man under any circumstances. That first and rather unfortunate confrontation between philosophy and tyranny led to the defeat of the former, with the philosopher ending up for sale in the slave market of Aegina.

---

[1] Christos C. Evangeliou is a native of Greece and Professor Emeritus of Ancient Hellenic Philosophy at Towson University, Maryland, USA. He studied the Classics and Philosophy at the University of Athens, Greece, and at Emory University, where he received his Ph.D. He is author of numerous papers; six volumes of poetry (in Greek and English); and four scholarly books: *Aristotle's Theory of Categories and Porphyry*; *The Genesis of Philosophy*; *Themata Politica: Hellenic and Euro-Atlantic*; and *Hellenic Philosophy: Origin and Character*.

Despite the negative experience of the first encounter between the philosopher and tyrant, at the latter's death about thirty years later, when Plato was in his sixties, he returned to Syracuse for a second time upon the succession to the throne of Dionysius II (the son of Dionysius I, by his third wife, Doris of Locris), who was married to his half-sister Sophrosyne, the sister of Arete, Dion's wife.[2]

Although the motives for his first trip as a young man are obvious, my purpose in this study is to explore the reason Plato was persuaded to go to Sicily for a second and even a third time in his old age, leaving the security and warmth of the Academy to face the challenges of a long trip by boat across the Ionian Sea, and the uncertainties and risks involved in the court struggles and intrigues of Sicilian power politics at that time.

There is evidence that Plato's desire to see his political theories of an ideally virtuous ruler[3] and "political liberty under the limitation of law"[4] put into the test, and his hope to see Dion and Dionysius II reconciled and willing to share political power, led him to make the trips. Once he had failed in these hopes and aspirations, he eventually found the courage to say no to them both, and refused to get involved in the armed struggle between Dion and Dionysius II, which caused so much pain and destruction in Syracuse, Sicily, Magna Graecia, and the entire Western Greek world.

Plato's Second Visit to Syracuse

The *Seventh* and *Eighth Letters* are addressed to the "friends and companions of Dion,"[5] in response to their request that Plato give his

---

[2] Marriage relations in the court of the Sicilian Tyrants at that time are complicated because Dionysius I married two wives, had children by both of them and allowed not only uncles to marry their nieces, but brothers their half-sisters.

[3] That was the ideal presented by Socrates in *Republic* V, but ironically, as a political paradox.

[4] That was the "second best" political ideal presented in the *Statesman* and the *Laws*.

[5] The *Second* and *Seventh Letters* are the most informative and were accepted by most ancient scholars as genuine. We will assume that they, as well as the *Third* and *Eighth Letters*, express Plato's political views and experiences. The fact that

support, in deed and word, to bringing desirable political change to Syracuse after the death of Dion. So in the opening of the *Seventh Letter*, he made it clear that he would help their cause only if their goals were the same as Dion's, who believed, according to Plato, "in liberty for the Syracusans under the guidance of the best system of laws."[6] Then, he added, "The origin of this creed is a tale that young and old may well-hear, and I will try to tell you the story from the beginning for the moment is opportune. Once upon a time in my youth I cherished like many another the hope of entering upon a political career as soon as I came of age" (324a-b).[7]

Plato goes on to describe, in a very moving way, his youthful excitement and then his great disappointment in both regimes, the Thirty Tyrants and the Restored Democracy. The former disappointed him by trying to implicate Socrates in their political crimes and, in so doing, "they in a short time made the former government look in comparison like an age of gold." The latter regime disappointed the young Plato because they brought against Socrates again, "a most sacrilegious charge, which he least of all men deserved. They put him on trial for impiety and the people condemned and put to death the man who had refused to take part in the wicked arrest of their friends" (324d-325c).[8]

Reflecting on these tragic events and on men active in politics, their customs, and the laws of various cities in Greece and abroad, the maturing philosopher reached the conclusion and conviction that, "without exception their system of government is bad ... that accordingly the human race will not see better days until either the

---

    Plutarch refers extensively to the *Seventh Letter* and even quotes from it, indicates that he had no doubt about its authenticity.

[6] By presenting this view of the importance of good and just laws, Plato indicates that in his old ages he moved away from his youthful ideal as expressed in the *Republic*, where virtuous philosophers are to rule with the guidance of their patriotic virtue rather than any written laws.

[7] Besides being a true confession of Plato, this statement is also a true psychological insight into the souls of young and ambitious men at all times and places.

[8] Both Plato's *Apology* and Xenophon's *Memorabilia I* express the same sensibility and surprise on this trial.

stock of those who rightly and genuinely follow philosophy acquire political authority, or else the class who have political control be led by some dispensation of providence to become philosophers" (326a-b).[9]

With such convictions Plato arrived in Italy and Sicily on his first visit and got a taste of the "happy life" in Sicilian style, that is,

> filling oneself up twice a day, never sleeping alone at night, and indulging in all the practices attendant on that way of living. In such an environment no man under heaven, brought up in self-indulgence, could ever grow to be wise.... Neither can a city be free from unrest under laws, be those laws what they may, while its citizens think fit to spend everything on excesses.... It is inevitable that in such cities there should be an unending succession of governments—tyranny, oligarchy, democracy—one after another, while the very name of just and equal government is anathema to those in control. (326c)

With that mindset, Plato traveled to Syracuse not by chance, but as if he was guided by "a higher power," to meet Dion and to find in him a young man uncorrupted and ready to listen to his philosophical ideals regarding the rule of law and the ethical character of the rulers. Here is his confession on this important point for what was to follow in the city of Syracuse:

> In my intercourse at that time with young Dion, as I set before him in theory my ideals for mankind and advised him to make them effective in practice, I seem to have been unaware that I was in a way contriving, all unknown to myself, a future downfall of tyranny. At any rate Dion, who was very quick of apprehension and especially so in regard to my instruction on this occasion, responded to it more keenly and more enthusiastically than any other young man I ever met, and resolved to live for the remainder of his life differently from most of the Greeks in Italy and Sicily, holding virtue dearer than

---

[9] This creed is articulated and elaborated in the *Republic*, 473c-e.

pleasure or than luxury.¹⁰ On that account, the life he led until the death of Dionysius vexed somewhat those who passed their time in accordance with tyrannical wont. (*Seventh Letter*, 327a-b)

Having thus been converted to the philosophical way of life, "under the guidance of right reason," as Plato put it, Dion felt like a neophyte on a mission to discover other young men to join him as kindred spirits in living a sober life dedicated to the service of city. More important, with the succession of Dionysius II to the throne of Syracuse, upon the death of his father, Dion thought that he should try to make his nephew see the beauty of the philosophical life as lived by an absolute ruler.¹¹ Dion confessed that if young Dionysius II "were to become such a one, the result for him and for the rest of the Syracusans would be the attainment of a life beyond all calculation blessed." That it would be the "noblest and best life," worthy to be imitated by all Sicilians, "throughout the land" (*Seventh Letter*, 327c-d).¹²

For this worthy task, Dion needed the help of his mentor and friend Plato, who had returned to Athens about twenty years earlier, founded the Academy and settled happily there, far away from the

---

[10] The "life of virtue," as opposed to life of pleasure, is only for the few and exceptional persons, not for the many.

[11] Plutarch describes the situation thus: "This tyrant's son, as I have said, Dion saw to be dwarfed and deformed in character from his lack of education, and therefore exhorted him to apply himself to study, and to use every entreaty with the first of philosophers to come to Sicily, and, when he came, to become his disciple, in order that his character might be regulated by the principles of virtue, and that he might be conformed to that divinest and most beautiful model of all being, in obedience to whose direction the universe issues from disorder into order; in this way he would procure great happiness for himself, and great happiness for his people, and that obedience which they now rendered dejectedly and under the compulsion of his authority, this his moderation and justice would base upon good will and a filial spirit, and he would become a king instead of a tyrant." B. Perrin, *Plutarch's Lives, vol. VI*, (Cambridge, Mass., Harvard University Press, 1954), x.2.

[12] Dion's enthusiasm for the philosophical "life of virtue" and his effort to convert Dionysius accordingly motivated sophists such as Philistus to imagine a conspiracy for removing Dionysius from power. See Plutarch, *Dion's Life*, XII-XIII.

seats of power politics in Athens and *Magna Graecia*. Not only did Dion persuade Dionysius II to send for Plato, he wrote personally, urging his friend to take this unique opportunity to put his political theories into practice. If he could be as successful with young Dionysius II as he was with young Dion, then Plato may live to witness the miracle of philosophical wisdom and political power united in one wise man for the benefit of Syracuse, Sicily, and the entire Hellenic world. In these circumstances, Plato faced a real dilemma:

> Such arguments he used and a great many more like them. As for my own decision, on the one hand I feared the outcome in the case of the young men, for young men have sudden impulses and often quite contradictory ones. On the other hand I knew that Dion had naturally a solid character and that he had now reached middle age. Hence as I considered and debated whether I should hearken and go, or what I should do, the view nevertheless prevailed that I ought to go, and that if anyone were ever to attempt to realize my ideals in regard to laws and government, now was the time for the trial. If I were to convince but one man, that in itself would ensure complete success. Such were the considerations that inspired and emboldened me to leave home on this journey. (*Seventh Letter*, 328b-c)

Not wishing to be a traitor to his friends, especially Dion, nor to philosophy and his ideals, Plato decided in his sixties to go to Syracuse a second time, "following reason and justice as closely as is humanly possible." He left behind his philosophical pursuits in democratic Athens, and came "under a tyranny, a form of government seemingly inconsistent with my doctrines and my character."[13] He had fulfilled his duty to "Zeus Xenios," by listening to Dion's persuasive arguments, but now had to face ugly reality in the court of Dionysius II with its cabals, fractions and conspiracies, all centered around the rivalry between the pleasure-loving Tyrant

---

[13] Quotations from the *Seventh Letter*. For Plato, as for Aristotle, tyranny is the worst possible form of government, most lawless and unjust, *Republic* IX, and *Politics* III-IV.

and the virtue-loving Dion. The clash was inevitable and Plato was caught unprepared in its impending storm.

By taking the side of Dion in his rivalry with Dionysius II, Plato did not make his own or his friend's position any easier. Dion was "expelled dishonorably," while Plato was placed in the citadel and watched closely, while a rumor was circulated that "he had been executed by Dionysius." The Tyrant wanted something the Philosopher could not give him honestly. As Plato put it, "he wanted me to commend him more than Dion, to think him rather than Dion a special friend," although he refused to follow the only method of attaining that goal, that is, "by receiving instruction and hearing me discourse on philosophy" (*Seventh Letter*, 330a-b).[14]

Plato found himself in a real predicament. His association with Dionysius II made him aware that this young man did not have the drive, the virtues, the potential, and the character of Dion. He perhaps realized, as Plutarch would report later, that the education of the young Prince had been neglected by his powerful father, due to a paranoid fear that his son might conspire to overthrow him and take over the power he craved. At the death of his father in 367 BCE, nevertheless, the Prince in his late twenties, secluded, uneducated, and unprepared for the hard task of governing, found himself on the throne of a great power, which controlled most of Sicily and much of Southern Italy. He did not have the time or appetite to learn philosophy and geometry from Plato, though he desired his friendship, love and commendation. He wanted to take Dion's place in the philosopher's affection.

Plato certainly wanted to help the young Prince reform himself, his life-style, and ultimately his tyrannical rule, but he was not

---

[14] Dionysius II's youthful impetuosity led him to believe that he had grasped all of Plato's philosophy and could even write it down in a book. Such claims led Plato to try to clarify that the ultimate philosophic truth goes beyond language and logical definitions and classifications, and comes to the serious searcher of the truth as a spark and flash of light. Compare the mystical tone to the *scala amoris* in the *Symposium* and the last division of the Divided line in the book VII of the *Republic*.

prepared to sacrifice the friendship with Dion he had cultivated over thirty years. With Dion exiled in the Peloponnese, Plato was kept as a hostage in the Citadel, and Dionysius was frustrated in his effort to make the philosopher behave like the sophist Philistus, that is, flattering the Tyrant and praising tyranny.[15] So, every one of them was unhappy with the situation and no solution was in sight. It was not what Plato had envisioned when he decided to come to Syracuse. As he put it in the *Second Letter*,[16] addressed to Dionysius II:

> As for you and me and our mutual relations, the situation is as follows. There is no Greek, you may say, who has not heard of us as individuals; moreover our association with one another is generally discussed, and, be not deceived, it will continue to be discussed in time to come, for the number of those who have heard of our intercourse corresponds to its closeness and warmth. Well, what do I mean by this? I will back up a little and explain. It is a natural law that wisdom and great power attract each other. They are always pursuing and seeking after each other and coming together. Furthermore, this is a subject that people always find interesting whether they are themselves discussing it in a private gathering, or are listening to the treatment of it by others in poems... My object in saying all this is to point out the moral that in our case too, discussion of our acts will not forthwith cease with our death. Here then is a matter that demands consideration, for we ought, it appears, to consider as well the time to come, since it is a fact that the most slavish men by a sort of natural law give it no thought, while the best men leave nothing undone to acquire a good reputation with

---

[15] See Plutarch, *ibid.*, XI-XII: "But the enemies of Dion, afraid of the alteration in Dionysius, persuaded him to recall from exile Philistus, a man versed in letters and acquainted with the ways of tyranny, that they might have in him, a counterpoise to Plato and philosophy. For Philistus at the outset had most zealously assisted in establishing the tyranny, and for a long time was commander of the garrison that guarded the citadel."

[16] As opposed to the *Seventh Letter*, the *Second Letter* is widely taken to be *in*authentic. I quote it here, nevertheless, as a plausible demonstration of Plato's attitude toward Dionysius.

posterity. To me this is a proof that the dead have some perception of events here, for the noblest souls know this truth by intuition, while the vilest souls deny it, but the intuitions of the godlike are more valid than those of other men. *(Second Letter*, 310d-311d)

Yielding to Plato's entreaties and the friendly pressure of his Tarentine friends, Dionysius II proposed that Plato return to the Academy under the condition that he come back to Syracuse at the end of the present war with Dion, to help bring about their reconciliation and reassume the study of philosophy. Under those terms Plato departed, but the Tyrant did not plan to keep his part of the agreement, because he invited only Plato to return at first, and left Dion waiting. The question as to why Plato returned to Dionysius II's court under these circumstances is puzzling. Here is how Plato explains it in the *Seventh Letter*, 339b-340a:

> 'If you consent and come now to Sicily, in the first place you will have the privilege of making any arrangement that suits you about Dion and his affairs. I am sure that what suits you will be fair, and I shall agree to it. If you do not come, you will find nothing that affects Dion either personally or otherwise arranging itself to your liking.' These were his [Dionysius's] words; the rest would be long to repeat and not to the point. Letters also kept coming from Archytas and the Tarentines to sing the praise of Dionysius's devotion to philosophy and to inform me that, if I did not come now, it would mean a complete break of the friendly relations that I had been instrumental in creating between them and Dionysius, and those relations were not lacking in political importance…. Besides, I knew anyway without being told that no one need be surprised if a young man on hearing a really great enterprise suggested, quick to grasp the idea, had yielded to the spell of the ideal life. It seemed accordingly my duty to make the experiment so as to arrive at a definite conclusion one way or another…. So I did set out under cover of these arguments, full of fears, as you might expect, and foreboding no very good result.

Christos C. Evangeliou

Plato's Third Visit to Syracuse

Plato's fears were not unfounded. Upon arrival, he decided to test Dionysius II to find out how serious he was about philosophical training and a life of virtue. It quickly became clear to Plato that the Tyrant was neither interested in philosophy, nor willing to invite Dion back to Sicily, as they had agreed. On the contrary, he decided to sell Dion's estate, depriving Dion of that source of income and power, trying to involve Plato in the transaction to the philosopher's disgust. Plato felt duped and trapped again by the machinations of the young Tyrant. He meditated on this melancholically thus:

> Up to this point I had in this way taken the part of philosophy and of my friends, but from then on Dionysius and I lived, I looking out like a bird that wants to fly away, he engaged in devising a way of frightening me off without paying me any of Dion's money. Just the same we called ourselves fiends before all Sicily.... I decided, however, that I had no right to quarrel with Dionysius rather than with myself and with those who had forced me to go the third time to the strait of Scylla that 'once more I might pass through the baleful Charybdis,' and I would say to Dionysius that I could not remain now that Dion was so insultingly treated. (*Seventh Letter*, 345d-e, and 348a)

The break in the relation between Tyrant and Philosopher was now complete. The fact that Plato continued to be on good terms with Heracleides and Theodotes, who were prominent friends of Dion whom Dionysius II suspected of plotting against his rule, did not help the situation. The last words of Dionysius II to Plato, reported by a messenger, were these: "He bade me tell you that you by no means do well always to prefer Dion and Dion's friends to him" (*Seventh Letter*, 349e). Plato soon found himself outside the security of the Citadel and exposed to the wrath of the mercenaries, among whom he was unpopular. It was only through the intervention of Archytas and his Tarentine friends that he managed to escape safely from Syracuse and return to Greece. When he reached Olympia he met Dion, who was understandably furious and called upon Zeus as witness, summoning Plato and his friends to prepare "to take revenge on Dionysius." But by then Plato had had enough of this tragicomedy, which was about to turn into tragedy:

> In reply I bade him invite my friends, if they were willing, 'but as for myself,' said I, 'you and the others practically forced me to become guest at the table and at the hearth of Dionysius and a partaker in sacred rites with him. He very likely thought because of the false reports that many were circulating that I was leagued with you in a plot against him and his government, and yet he scrupled to put me to death. For one thing, then, I am now scarcely of an age to help anyone in making war, and for another you have in me a common friend, in case you ever feel a desire to be friends with each other and want to accomplish some good. As long as you are bent on evil, invite others.' (*Seventh Letter*, 350c-e)

Plato may be right in his ensuing speculation as to how things might have gone better in Sicily. It is possible that things would not have reached the point of no return if Dionysius II had not deprived Dion of his property, including his wife and child, whom the Tyrant gave to another man.[17] It is also possible that the worst might have been avoided if Dionysius II was really interested in reconciliation with Dion and had placed his trust in Plato to restrain Dion's ambition. These are good and probable ways the Sicilian disaster might have been avoided, but they are not the only ones.

One may go further back and blame Dionysius I, the strong man and father of Dionysius II, for the mess after his death. Either he should have prepared his son to succeed him on the throne, or seen to it that an experienced man, like his son-in-law Dion, took power. Another possibility was for Plato, on the occasion of Dion's banishment, to insist upon the reconciliation and cooperation of the two rivals if they wanted his help navigating the tricky waters of

---

[17] See Plutarch, *ibid*, LI: "After Dion had greeted his sister first, and then his little son, Aristomache led Arete to him, and said: 'We were unhappy, Dion, while thou wast in exile; but now that thou art come and art victorious, thou hast taken away our sorrow from all of us, except from this woman alone, whom I was so unfortunate as to see forced to wed another while thou was still alive."

Sicilian politics. Since they both desired his friendship and approval, Plato had a way either to achieve the goal of reconciliation and establish a lawful republic, or to return to the Academy in Athens and save his reputation.

As he asserts towards the end of the *Seventh Letter* (351b), Dion's policy was the same as his own, or "any other decent man's ought to be, in regard to the exercise of power by himself and his friends in his own city, namely, by conferring benefits on the city to acquire for himself the greatest power and the highest honors." The goal of the lawful republic should not be enrich those in power by confiscating the wealth of the few, or to plunder small cities and distribute their wealth to make one's own city bigger and more tyrannical.

On the contrary, the wise and just ruler, as envisioned by Plato here and in his *Laws*,[18] "will aim at a republic and at instituting the best and justest laws without resorting in the least to executions and bloodshed." That was the advice he wanted to give to the friends and companions of Dion, to whom the letter was addressed, after Dion had fallen victim to a conspiracy of men led by Calippus, whom he had trusted, at the moment when he acquired supreme power in Syracuse and was ready to implement the ideal republic. He concludes his letter by reflecting on the ironies and the paradoxes of human history, which led him into Sicilian power politics:

> I went back to the subject of my second visit to Sicily because the necessity of dealing with it seemed forced upon me by the surprising and paradoxical nature of the events. If anyone after this account finds the events less paradoxical and if anyone concludes that there was sufficient justification for what

---

[18] This emphasis on the importance of the law to curb the excesses of servitude and freedom is also found in the *Seventh Letter*, 354d-355c: "That is the way they got their tyrants, for either servitude or freedom, when it goes to extremes, is an utter bane, while either in due measure is altogether a boon. The due measure of servitude is to serve God. The extreme of servitude is to serve man. The god of sober men is law; the god of fools is pleasure. Since the law of nature in regard of these things is as I have stated, I exhort the friends of Dion to publish my words of advice to all the Syracusans as the joint counsel of Dion and myself […]."

happened, then what I have said is fairly and adequately put. (*Seventh Letter*, 352a)

I would like to conclude this paper with a poem which captures in verse and sums up well Plato's adventure into the tricky waters of Sicilian power politics in the fourth century BCE.

Voyage

If you take the long trip to Sicily,
The dangerous journey across the sea,
In the ungrateful hour of old age,
Think carefully of what you might achieve.

It's a very complex situation there,
Dion is intelligent and hard-working,
But he doesn't hold the key to power.
Dionysius is steering the ship as king.

Unsteady and uneducated that one,
He doesn't reap any wisdom from words,
Despite all the sophists flocking 'round him,
Like summer flies 'round the butter churn!

How can your soul's bright eye endure
The vision of such outlandish things,
The sumptuous feasts and nightly banquets,
Foreign to your sober ways and thinking?

The Athenian Demos has wounded you,
It is litigious, suspicious, and funny,
With its many excesses of freedom,
Like a tyrannical foe of tyranny!

From the West you saw a light emerging,
A way to blend Syracuse's power
With accumulated Sicilian wealth,
A Greater Greece once again to flower!

You did a bit of fantastic thinking,
Devised a way to shape a new regime,
Dividing up all the noble duties,
In your mind, it's not a difficult thing.

But turning noble theory into practice
Takes a lot of labor, as you know,
It's difficult to tame the human passions,
When conflicts in their interests start to grow.

If one day we somehow could connect
The scepter of a sovereign leader's might
With the power of wisdom and knowledge,
Perhaps human evil would start to die.

But mankind, difficult and demonic,
Would reveal old Plato's fatal flaw,
Soon even Plotinus's way would be blocked,
In the end, both Greece and Rome would fall.

Well, even if you couldn't save the world,
Of which dear Greece is only one piece,
Like Macedonia's Great Alexander,
"Know thyself" and let your soul be free!

Embark on a Socratic style journey,
Of land and ocean you will have no need.
If you make your mind the captain of your soul,
You may safely bring it home from the sea!

Tony Leyh[1]
Friendship and Politics in the *Seventh Letter*[2]

There is much talk of friendship (φιλία) and its various cognates in the *Seventh Letter*. The letter is addressed to the companions and comrades (οἰκείοις τε καὶ ἑταίροις) of Dion. Plato and Dion counsel Dionysius II to cultivate virtue-based friendships (332d). A distinction between two forms of friendship is given at 333e. The so-called philosophical digression is prefaced with a test aimed to determine whether Dionysius II has the proper *philia* for *sophia* (340b-341a). And finally, there are several friendships depicted in the drama of the letter, including those of Plato and Dion, Plato and Archytas, Plato and Archedemus, as well as Dionysius II and several of the Tarentines.[3] In this paper, I explore these different uses of friendship and explain the way in which for Plato friendship is essential to political success.

Scholars have paid relatively scant attention to the philosophical and political import of friendship in the *Seventh Letter*, preferring instead to debate either the letter's authenticity or the digression.[4] Contrary to this tendency, I argue that friendship plays a crucial role. This is clear first in the political advice offered to Dionysius II, and also indirectly, in the dramatic entanglements of Plato's friendships

---

[1] Tony Leyh is a PhD Candidate in philosophy at Emory University. He can be reached at: tony.leyh@emory.edu.

[2] I'd like to thank Heather Reid, Mark Ralkowski, Marta Jimenez, and the participants in the 2018 Fonte Aretusa Seminar on Plato at Syracuse for helpful comments and suggestions on earlier versions of this paper.

[3] For discussion of the last three relationships, see E.R.G. Lloyd, "Plato and Archytas in the 'Seventh Letter.'" *Phronesis* 35:2 (1990): 159-74, who is especially critical of the philosophical aptitude of Archytas as presented in the letter.

[4] Some commentators have noted that friendship has some prominence in the *Seventh Letter*. As far as I am aware, however, no Anglophone study exists that focuses on the extensive role of friendship in the *Seventh Letter*. See Glenn R. Morrow, *Plato's Epistles: A Translation with Critical Essays and Notes* (New York: The Bobbs-Merrill Company, 1990): 228 n.31; L. De Blois, "Some Notes on Plato's Seventh Epistle." *Mnemosyne* 32 (1979): 268-83; B. Lewis "The Rhetoric of Philosophical Politics in Plato's *Seventh Letter*," *Philosophy & Rhetoric* 33 (2000): 23-28; and B. Lewis "The *Seventh Letter* and the Unity of Plato's Political Philosophy," *The Southern Journal of Philosophy* 38 (2000): 241-43.

(especially with Dion and the Tarentines). The descriptions of Plato's friendships, help to explore in greater depth the complexities and challenges of putting his political advice to Dionysius II into practice.

My argument proceeds in several steps. First, I show that the analysis of two forms of friendship at 333e provides us with the relevant framework of friendship for politics. Second, I argue that Plato advises Dionysius II to cultivate friendships because, on the one hand, such friendships ensure the longevity of his rule, and on the other, they enable him to recognize the goods at which the Syracusan polity ought to aim. Third, I offer a reading of the drama of the *Seventh Letter*, where I suggest that Plato's various friendships involve him in political activities that he otherwise should have avoided. At first sight, these friendships create a tension between how Plato himself behaved in Syracuse and how he advises Dionysius II. I conclude, however, that this tension is resolvable. Plato's behavior intimates rather that any political principles and advice ought to be flexible enough to accord with the nuances of any specific political situation.

Towards an Understanding of Friendship

Although φιλία or closely related terms (e.g. οἰκεῖος, ἑταῖρος, ἀδελφός, σύμφωνος, and συγγεγονότος) appear several times, no clear definition of what proper friendship consists of is ever given throughout the letter. In one sense, this is unsurprising: a substantive meditation on friendship might seem inapt in a letter proposing to counsel Dion's companions about the pressing politics of Syracuse. We can, however, unearth a working understanding of what authentic friendship entails by consideration of some dramatic moments in the letter. More specifically, these passages present a working distinction between two general kinds of friendship, which I'll call 'weak friendships' and 'strong friendships.'

Generally, I understand friendship in all of its forms to involve at minimum a kind of reciprocated, other-regarding concern for the friend's welfare. In the *Seventh Letter*, the origin and strength of this other-regarding concern are the most prominent factors in classifying any friendship as either weak or strong. 'Weak friendship' is the most common type and is described by Plato as a "facile comradeship" (τῆς περιτρεχούσης ἑταιρίας) and a "vulgar friendship" (βαναύσου φιλότητος) (333e1; 334b4).[5] This relationship often arises from shared customs, rituals, and other kinds of initiation (333e). It is 'weak' friendship in the sense that whatever other-regarding concern that exists among friends is likely to evaporate at the first sight of difficulty or temptation. In other words, weak friendship is weak because the other-regarding concern characteristic of that friendship is less likely to endure amidst hardships. One clear example is Dion's friendship with two unnamed Athenians. During his exile from Syracuse, Dion befriended two Athenians, who by virtue of their friendship aided and accompanied Dion in returning to Syracuse (333e-334a). Upon Dion's return, however, these Athenians immediately wavered in their opinion of Dion and eventually sided with the Syracusans who accused Dion of treachery and plotting tyranny. The fact that these unnamed Athenians abandoned Dion upon their arrival shows that even if they once possessed some kind of concern for Dion (we have no reason to believe anything to the contrary), their concern for Dion and Dion's goals quickly dissolved once they realized that association with an alleged conniving tyrant and malfeasant may put their own livelihoods in jeopardy.

Plato offers his relationship with Dion as a case of what I call a 'strong friendship.' Plato says that their friendship arose from a "common liberal education" (ἐλευθέρας παιδείας κοινωνίαν) and was a more stable and reliable kind of friendship (334b-c). Earlier in the letter, Plato also tells us that he detected in Dion an unprecedented aptitude and zeal for learning. Presumably, then, Plato and Dion's shared love of philosophy at least in part comprises the 'common liberal education' that serves as the basis of their friendship. In contrast to weak friendship, Plato suggests that the strength of his bond to Dion (aside from exculpating Athens from the

---

[5] All translations of Plato are from Morrow with some modification. Greek text for Plato's *Letters* is based on Jennifer Moore-Blunt, *Platonis Epistulae* (Leipzig: B.G. Teubner Verlagsgesellschaft, 1985). Greek text for Plato's other writings is based on J. Burnet, *Platonis Opera* 5 vols (Oxford: Clarendon Press, 1900-1907).

embarrassment of the Athenians who betrayed Dion) ensured that Plato would go to extraordinary lengths to help his friend, including enduring several long trips and placing himself directly under the purview of a volatile and impetuous tyrant.[6] The principal aspect of this kind of friendship that contrasts with 'weak friendship' is its durability. Plato easily could have declined Dion's initial offer or refused to return to Syracuse upon experiencing the behavior of Dionysius II. Instead, Plato, out of his friendship to Dion (and his passion for philosophy), chose to return to Syracuse and remained steadfast in his support of Dion, despite the calumnies spreading throughout Syracuse about Dion.

The distinction between weak and strong friendships allows us to see that the most relevant characteristic of friendship for politics is friendship's durability. One reason strong friendships are more valuable is because they preserve the stability of the *polis*. One strategy to cultivate strong friendships is to engender a shared love of philosophy because a genuine, cooperative philosophical relationship tends to remain unperturbed by the kind of capricious desires that often frustrate weaker friendships.

The Political Import of Friendship

This distinction between two forms of friendships gains more weight as we consider the actual advice that Plato and Dion offer to Dionysius II (in T1-T3 below). Plato's point is that friendship is crucial for political success. Not just any kind of friendship, however, suffices for doing the job of politics well. Although weak friendships are able to provide a certain level of stability (especially in comparison with a rule absent friendships), only strong friendships make a true difference in the long-term stability and health of political relations. That is, as we will see at the end of this section, even though there are alternative methods of providing stability,

---

[6] Heather Reid has helpfully called my attention to the friendship of Damon and Phintias as recounted in Iamblichus's *Vita Pythagorae* XXXIII. Their friendship, especially in contrast with the overt jealousy of Dionysius displayed there as well, strikes me as another example of the great endurance of strong friendship.

only strong friendships are able to nurture the right kind of philosophical dispositions that conduce to the good life in the *polis*.

Being a tyrant, Dionysius II is in a particularly vulnerable position: he's liable to be swarmed by sycophants and toadies who, instead of looking out for what's best for him and his goals, will placate his baser desires and distract him from ruling well. Whoever wishes to reform a political society, including a Syracusan tyranny, ought to observe the import of this distinction among types of friendship because a ruler's cultivation of one type in lieu of another may make the difference between a polity that aims at its citizens' welfare and one that aims at satisfying the indiscriminate and whimsical desires of its leader.

Indeed, at 331d5ff (T1-T3) Plato suggests that whether Dionysius II develops meaningful friendships both with himself and with others is of decisive importance. First, he indicates that fostering these kinds of strong friendships is instrumental to maintain political stability and avoiding political turmoil (cf. 332e-333a):[7]

> **(T1)** I would advise you all [the comrades of Dion] then in this way, as Dion and I advised Dionysius. First, we advised that he live each day so as to habituate himself to be as empowered as possible and so as to acquire both trustworthy friends and companions. In acting this way, he would avoid the very things his father suffered: when he captured many great cities in Sicily that had been pillaged by barbarians, he was not able to resettle the cities with loyal governments because he lacked trustworthy companions. (331d5-332a1)

The case of Dionysius I, Dionysius II's father and predecessor, illustrates the instrumental reason. No matter how deft and powerful a ruler, the lack of faithful companions in whom you can confide and entrust the management of your empire always portends political turmoil. A similar claim is made in the following lines:

---

[7] De Blois and Lewis "The Rhetoric," 29 both recognize this instrumental line of thought.

(T2) Even though Dionysius I brought together all of Sicily into one city (knowing he could trust no one), he barely kept it all together. For he was poor in trustworthy friends, whose presence or absence is the greater sign of one's virtue or vice. (332c3-6)

So, if Dionysius II fails to find reliable companions, then his time as a ruler will be short-lived simply because the logistics of ruling exceeds the capabilities of any one person. Consider one more passage:

(T3) Dion and I thus advised the following things to Dionysius II, since on account of his father it happened that he was both uneducated and not used to appropriate relationships. First of all, we instructed him to desire to acquire from among his relatives and peers other friends and companions in virtue, but especially to become a friend to himself, since in this regard he was amazingly in need. (332c8-d6)

This last passage (T3) emphasizes that Dionysius II must cultivate not just any kind of friendship, but must find "companions in virtue" (συμφώνους πρὸς ἀρετὴν). The friendships appropriate to Dionysius II, while politically useful, are fundamentally philosophical (as is evident in T3). Why, we might wonder, is a philosophical friendship necessary for a ruler? It certainly cannot be because only philosophical friends are loyal. Cruelty, bribery, fear and other nearly innumerable methods can also be used to generate a reliable enough loyalty independent of friendship. Machiavelli expounds and evaluates this second method in *Il Principe*:

(T4) From this, a dispute arises about whether it is better [for a prince] to be loved than feared or vice versa. The proper response is that one would want to be the one and the other; but because it is difficult to hold them together, it is much more reliable to be feared than loved (*è molto più sicuro essere temuto che amato*).[8] (*Il Principe* XVII)

---

[8] All translations of the Italian are mine and from Niccolò Machiavelli, *Il Principe*, eds. Mario Martelli and Nicoletta Martelli (Roma: Salerno Editrice, 2006).

An effective prince, Machiavelli notes, has a variety of stratagems at his disposal, only one of which is the cultivation of loving relationships (including friendships) with other citizens. The main concern about friendship for Machiavelli is that being a beloved ruler carries with it a litany of other potential problems, since friendships can quickly dissipate and we are more prone to betray those we love than those we fear, presumably because we expect loved ones to forgive us eventually (cf. *Il Principe* XVII). As such, Machiavelli is reticent to endorse friendship as even a tenable means of fostering political constancy and loyalty, let alone a primary one, as the *Seventh Letter* does.

The main reason this Machiavellian line is inapplicable to the *Seventh Letter* is due to what Plato tells us repeatedly, though somewhat obliquely, throughout the text: philosophical friendships are essential because they are a necessary and constitutive feature of realizing the ruler's ultimate aim, the promotion of the citizens' welfare and happiness (viz. 326a-b; 327c-d; 332d-e; 335d-e and 351c-d). The (enthymematic) argument for why philosophy is necessary to achieve this task runs roughly along the following lines:

(1) To govern a polity well, one must promote the citizenry's happiness.
(2) To promote the citizenry's happiness, one must understand what's good for the citizenry generally.
(3) To understand what's good for the citizenry, one must understand what a human being is and what's conducive to human flourishing.
(4) The attempt to know what a human being is and what encourages its flourishing is an essentially philosophical endeavor.
(5) Thus, to be a good ruler one must in some sense be a philosopher.

This argument thus developed only shows, however, that Dionysius II ought to practice philosophy ardently and seriously. It does not yet show how friendship enters into it. My view is that friendship is essential because it is necessary for practicing philosophy properly. In the *Seventh Letter*, Plato describes philosophy as fundamentally interpersonal and dialogic. Concretely, philosophy requires dialogue and discussion with others interested in philosophical topics who can encourage, challenge and develop our beliefs and insights. We find this thought captured in the perhaps most famous line of the letter:

> **(T5)** For this [philosophical] knowledge cannot be put into words like other sciences; but after *long-continued intercourse between teacher and pupil, in joint pursuit of the subject*, suddenly, like light flashing forth when a fire is kindled, it is born in the soul and straightaway nourishes itself.[9] (341c-d, my emphasis; cf. 330a-b)

There are two lessons we can draw from this. First, philosophy cannot be an isolationist endeavor. When Plato and Dion recommend that Dionysius II practice philosophy, they intend for him to express his beliefs seriously, be receptive to criticism of those ideas from adroit interlocutors, and attempt to live his life according to those beliefs forged through philosophy. The recommendation to Dionysius II to practice philosophy is necessarily a recommendation to work cooperatively with others in thinking carefully and critically about what's real, true, and good. Only by doing the latter can he come to recognize the best and proper way to rule the Syracusan polity.

The second lesson is that philosophy, when practiced well, nurtures a kind of friendship with one's interlocutors. Anyone engaged in the sincere practice of philosophy—especially when philosophy is understood as inherently dialogic and interpersonal—develops care for his or her interlocutors. This care arises in part from

---

[9] This is the Morrow translation. The relevant Greek here—ἐκ πολλῆς συνουσίας γιγνομένης περὶ τὸ πρᾶγμα αὐτὸ καὶ τοῦ συζῆν—is ambiguous. It's not certain whether there are many associations with *to pragma* itself or many associations with others about *to pragma*. I think the latter makes more sense according to the general context of the letter. For further discussion, see . Hyland, *Plato and the Question of Beauty* (Bloomington: Indiana University Press, 2008): 104.

Friendship and Politics in the Seventh Letter

the recognition that the quality of our interlocutors bears directly on the quality of our practice of philosophy. When intelligent, focused, and concerned people discuss some philosophical topic with us, we see that their insights actually contribute to the refinement and enhancement of our own thoughts. We likewise hopefully provide helpful insights to those interlocutors. The repeated attempts to improve what we and our interlocutors think (and how to live according to those thoughts) contain the seeds for strong friendships to blossom.

A converse of this second lesson is likewise noteworthy (and is exemplified at *Meno* 75c-d).[10] Whoever engages in philosophy for ulterior motives—e.g. to make a grandiose display of one's erudition, to attempt to garner a reputation for being really smart, or simply to engage in a bit of verbal combat—*de facto* treats his or her interlocutors in a way that inhibits the more authentic loving of wisdom. Such a person treats these interlocutors not as equal partners who are needed for philosophizing well, but as instruments through which to attain whatever ulterior goal that philosophy may bring about (e.g. honor or fame).

This kind of behavior stifles philosophy because it stifles a necessary element of practicing philosophy well: earnest and fruitful dialogue with others. Friends engage in discussion not simply to refute one another, but to discuss earnestly and in a way that both participants in the conversation can come to assess and evaluate whatever topic or argument is being put forth. Whatever partial or total refutation ensues from friendly discussion is never the ultimate aim, but rather a necessary and educative step in the attempt to practice philosophy well. The *Seventh Letter*'s emphasis in **T5** on the

---

[10] Here Socrates contrasts for Meno two types of interlocutors, *eristikoi* and *philoi*, in a revealing way: "If my questioner was one of those clever and disputatious debaters, I would say to him: 'I have given my answer; if it is wrong, it is your job to refute it.' Then, if they are friends, as you and I are, and want to discuss with each other, they must answer in a manner more gentler and more proper to discussion. By this I mean that the answers must not only by true, but in terms admittedly known to the questioner." (*Meno* 75c8-d4)

joint pursuit of the subject by teacher and pupil seems to allude to this dimension of friendly discussion as well.

Has Dionysius II understood these lessons? Despite his apparent intellectual abilities (cf. 328a; 338b-c; 339b-e), he conspicuously fails to take up the advice of Plato and Dion to cultivate veridical friendships. This failure becomes manifest in at least two ways. First, Dionysius II fails to philosophize well; he fails to enact, in other words, a proper *philia* for *sophia*. Upon hearing of Dionysius II's renewed desire for philosophy, Plato devises a test to determine if Dionysius II's desire is genuine (340b).[11] Plato explains to Dionysius II the great labor and toil inherent in practicing philosophy well. If Dionysius II acknowledges such labor and proceeds to exert himself continuously in philosophic studies, then his soul is genuinely philosophical and he is a "true lover of wisdom" (ὄντως φιλόσοφος) (340c2). Dionysius II, however, recoils upon hearing the rigor of the philosophical life and claims to already understand philosophy sufficiently well (341a-b). Dionysius II's posture shows that his love of wisdom is rooted in something other than the desire to acquire wisdom and rule well. This is further borne out by the tyrant's odd behavior of publishing and disseminating his discussions with Plato and others as solely his own thoughts (341b; 344e-345d); Plato speculatively attributes this behavior to Dionysius II's shameful love of honor (φιλοτιμίας αἰσχρᾶς) or desire for fame (ἀγαπῶν δόξαν) (344e3-345a1; cf. 338d-e).

The second way this failure can be seen is from how they tyrant comports himself with his peers and colleagues, especially Dion and Plato. Dionysius II displays overt jealousy that Plato and Dion were better friends than he and Plato (330b; 349e). He consistently reneges on promises made to Dion and Plato as well as to Theodotes (345c-d; 347d-e; 348c-349a). In short, Dionysius II shows throughout the letter a dangerous combination of impetuousness and crude self-interest that prevents him from fostering any semblance of amicable relationships, even with those who actively attempt to befriend him.

---

[11] For further discussion, see Filippo Forcignanò's essay in this volume.

A central consequence of Dionysius II's disreputable behavior in philosophy is that whatever relationships ensue, they cannot be the strong friendships that are both characteristic of sincere philosophy and utterly helpful for politics. If they become friendships at all, they will be more like the weak friendships where the other-regarding concerns are accidental and ephemeral. By contrast, those who engage in philosophy (while heeding Plato's advice to recognize that reliable and competent interlocutors are necessary to philosophizing well) will form strong, enduring friendships. The principal reason for this is that the interlocutors' competence and reliability is based on their agreement about philosophy being a cooperative activity necessary to living their lives well. In other words, the competency of competent interlocutors informs their character; it is not an ephemeral feature that may disappear at a whim.

All of this is to say that Plato's repeated advice to Dionysius II is an essential element of his general instructions about how to be a good ruler. Since Dionysius II purports to aim at governing well, Plato's point is that it is only through such friendships that Dionysius II can maintain the stability of his empire and come to realize the proper way to confer sincere happiness upon the Syracusans. Dionysius II's failure to realize this political order is, in turn, attributable to his misapprehension of *philia*—understood both as an orientation toward other people as well as toward wisdom. His choice to cultivate weak and facile friendships with flatterers (e.g. 333b7-c1) attenuates his rule both by creating excessive tumult in Syracuse and by preventing him from coming to see the goals at which the political art should aim. Friendship, as I have attempted to explain in this section, is a legitimate and powerful political principle.

Conclusion

We would go too far in our interpretation of the *Seventh Letter*, however, if we were to infer from the above analysis that friendship is a panacea for all political malaise. Indeed, there is discord between Plato's explicit advice and how he himself behaves in the letter, and this discord is due to Plato's own *philia*-commitments. As a conclusion, I suggest that, instead of undermining the relevancy of

Plato's advice about friendship, this tension actually amplifies it because it shows both that one's political principles, especially one's *philia*-commitments, ought to be informed by the nuances of any specific political situation.

The tension, in brief, is as follows. Plato endorses the principle that one should discontinue advising those who refuse to listen, especially if offering advice is likely to be fruitless or if it puts one in immediate harm (330d-331e). The main justification behind this advice is that it maintains one's sense of self-respect (ἀνδρεία) (330d). Plato's numerous visits to Syracuse to aid Dionysius II apparently violate this principle, since Dionysius II manifestly fails to adopt the advice on Plato's first visit, frequently manipulates Plato and Dion, and endangers the welfare of Plato and his various companions (especially Dion, Archytas, and Archedemus).[12] Per Plato's own advice here, he should not have returned to Syracuse. This advice notwithstanding, Plato obviously does return to Syracuse. There thus arises a tension between Plato's advice to cultivate and nurture friendships and to discontinue advising those who refuse to listen. This tension raises the question of what motivated Plato to return to Syracuse and thereby violate the principle.[13]

---

[12] I thus disagree with the interpretation of this passage found in F. Trabattoni, *Essays on Plato's Epistemology* (Leuven: Leuven University Press, 2016): 268-71, which suggests that Plato does not violate the advice because he only offers *logoi* and performs no *erga*. Plato's actions include *logoi*, but the fact that he makes the voyage to return to Syracuse must be construed unequivocally as an *ergon* that endangers Plato's livelihood (of which Plato must have been well aware, given his previous interactions with Dionysius II). If Plato were to have abided strictly by his own advice, he would never have returned to Syracuse at all.

[13] One objection might be that I've confused the chronology of events. This objector would respond that Plato's principle is formulated in light of his experiences at Syracuse, not before or cotemporaneous with those events. Thus, Plato's behavior does not conflict with his principles, because those principles derive at least in part from reflection on the events that transpired with Dionysius II. Even if this chronology holds up (and it very well might), I don't think this objection addresses the heart of my point. My point is that, conceptually, Plato's advice conflicts with his behavior in Syracuse. Plato's failure to address the conflict (whether potential or actual) suffices for me to show that there is a tension in the letter, and, as long as this tension remains, my point stands.

Surely, he returns not because he is optimistic about Dionysius II's philosophical potential and willingness to accept Plato's instruction (338b-e, 347e), nor because he is unaware of the potential harm inherent in his return (345d-e; 346e-347a). Rather, the clear motivation that spurs Plato to return are his various *philia*-commitments, including his commitment to philosophy (328b-c; 339e-340a) as well as his friendships with Dion, Archytas, and Archedemus (339a-c). Indeed, Plato's following comment about the impetus for his third visit to Sicily captures the motivational primacy of his friendships nicely:

> (**T6**) Now when the summons [by Dionysius II] had taken on this character, with my friends in Sicily and Italy pulling me and those at Athens almost pushing me away with their urging, the same consideration occurred to me as before, that I ought not to betray my friends and followers in Tarentum. (339d6-e3)

Plato's repeated comments about the pronounced role his friendships take in his deliberations about whether to return to Syracuse (coupled with the absence of other motivations) attest that he violated the above principle primarily due to his own friendships.

One reading of this violation may suggest that we ought to cast doubt about the feasibility of Plato's advice in general, particularly the advice to cultivate friendships.[14] If Plato himself cannot act consistently with his own advice, why should we expect anyone else to? This reading, however, construes Plato's advice too rigidly, supposing that no justified exceptions to principles can ever exist.

On my reading, this tension augments and elucidates the appropriate manner to take up Plato's advice. This tension contains two insights about the advice offered elsewhere in the letter. First, political principles ought to be flexible enough to accommodate the demands of any political situation. If Plato were friendless and

---

[14] I disagree with Marina Marren's essay in this volume which suggests that Plato's comments about political friendships will lead to tyranny and cronyism. It is not at all clear to me that Plato shares Euphemus's understanding of political friendship and I think the textual evidence in the *Letter* actually points away from such an understanding.

thereby devoid of any commitments to Dion and the Tarentines, then he could have refused Dionysius II's final summons in good conscience and remained consistent to all of his principles. The context of this ultimate Syracusan voyage shows that such a refusal is, however, unavailable to Plato. Primary among Plato's concerns—and consonant with his suggestions about nurturing strong friendships—is the welfare and wellbeing of his friends, which is threatened especially if Plato refuses to return to Sicily. In the choice between two principles that conflict, Plato's behavior teaches careful readers that during such genuine conflicts, we cannot do otherwise than stand up for our friendships and those whom we view as integral to living well and living philosophically. This decision does not need to be taken as one that undermines the coherency and consistency of Plato's catalogue of advice *per se*. Rather, Plato's decision to aid his friends (and abandon, even if momentarily, his principle to discontinue counseling) exemplifies the judiciousness and care one ought to display in any similarly murky and intricate political situation.

The second and related point is that Plato's conduct towards his friends illustrates that strong, philosophical friendships often demand of us more than just pursuing philosophy together. Such friendships are vital ingredients in the recipe for practicing philosophy well, and we thus should exhibit concern for friends in their entirety. When their lives and livelihoods are threatened, the onus is on us to take their difficulties, at least to some extent, as our own. The constellation of Plato's many suggestions about friendship and his own conduct as a friend to several figures in the *Seventh Letter* work together to illustrate that in the inevitable tribulations our philosophical friends face, it's incumbent on us to come to their aid not as solely as wisdom-seekers but also as friends.

Andrew Hull[1]
Sleepless in Syracuse: Plato and the Nocturnal Council

In *The Pseudo-Platonic Seventh Letter*, Michael Frede argues throughout a series of seminars that the *Seventh Letter* is spurious.[2] The reasons given are multi-facted and interlocking, but I will be focusing on one criticism in particular which is somewhat separable from the others and the most philosophically compelling. To briefly provide a summary of the other arguments, Seminar 1 advances circumstantial considerations on why we should be skeptical of letters attributed to famous classical authors in general. Seminar 2 continues mounting the evidence by showing that Plato's letters (if genuine) would belong to one of the earliest periods we have of "letters" attributed to authors. Scholars (Frede argues) have shown every other set of letters from this period to be forgeries, giving us more reason to be especially suspicious of Plato's letters, even compared to other antique epistles. Seminar 3 shows that other letters related to Plato's political activity are dated to similar times as the *Seventh* but are all spurious. He focuses on one, Speusippus's letter to Phillip II, which is close to the *Seventh* in terms of length and aim. Seminar 5 critiques the plausibility that Plato could have thought Dionysius, Dion, or Hiparinus (335e2-336b4) would have the makings of a philosopher-ruler.

Seminar 4, however, levels a more philosophic charge by accusing the *Seventh Letter* of doctrinal inconsistency with the constitutional recommendations of the *Laws*. According to Frede, the *Letter* writer believes that only a philosopher-led state will be acceptable for Sicily. In contrast, the *Laws* takes the idea of a philosopher-less constitution seriously (739a-e; 875d) while

---

[1] Andrew Hull is a PhD candidate in Ancient Philosophy at Northwestern University, completing a dissertation on 'exactness' in Aristotle's political philosophy under the supervision of Richard Kraut. He received his BA at Emory University with a thesis on Plato's *Seventh Letter* and an MSt from the University of Oxford with a thesis on Atomism.
[2] Myles Burnyeat and Michael Frede, *The Pseudo-Platonic Seventh Letter*, ed. Dominic Scott, First edition. (Oxford: Oxford University Press, 2015), x.

constructing a state that would serve as a goal for most *poleis*, even one as corrupt as Syracuse.³ Frede describes the point of the letter this way:

> The backbone of the apology is an explanation of how Plato came to think that a state had to be a certain way, namely to be ruled by philosophers, and of how he came to be persuaded that Syracuse offered a unique opportunity to bring a state as it should be into being. This, in short, is the answer to why he got involved in Sicilian politics and behaved the way he did."⁴

Assuming this is the correct interpretation, the *Seventh Letter* holds fast to the ideal of the state as advocated in the *Republic* long after the genuine Plato abandoned it.

Could Plato really have still believed in philosopher rulers at this point in his life, and could he really have believed that Dion was the philosopher he had been looking for? The Seventh *Letter* asks us to answer "yes" to both of these questions. However, Frede disagrees, writing:

> I want to attack the question of the authenticity of the Seventh *Letter* head on by trying to argue that (A) Plato at the time that the Seventh *Letter* was written could not possibly have believed that this [constitutional arrangement] is what a state should be like; and (B) that, even if he did believe that this is what a state should be like, he could not possibly have believed that Syracuse offered an opportunity to realize this state."

This essay will disagree with both claims (A) and (B). I will be focusing on claim (A) here, that Plato at this time could not have believed a state should have a philosopher at its head. I will say he did believe philosophers needed special power in a *polis*. However,

---

³ Unless otherwise noted, all translations from the *Laws* are from Thomas L. Pangle, *The Laws of Plato*, University of Chicago Press ed (Chicago: University of Chicago Press, 1988).
⁴ Ibid., 43.

my response to (A) will also mitigate the force of (B).⁵ If I am right, this will mean the *Seventh Letter* is cleared of a major inconsistency between it and the *Laws*.

To rebut (A), I will be focusing on the character of the Nocturnal Council, an organization which occupies an enigmatic position in the constitution. One of the strongest and most commonsensical arguments against the existence of philosophers in the *Laws* is to simply point out that the *Laws* never mentions philosophers. However, while the *Laws* never mentions philosophers, the members of the Nocturnal Council are philosophers in all but name. If so, then Plato thought even an imperfect, law-based constitution like that of the *Laws'* Magnesia should still have philosophers occupy an especially powerful, executive role. But if the *Republic*'s *Kallipolis* is the constitution we pray for while Magnesia is the one we aim for, and if even this constitution contains philosopher-like people as rulers of some sort, it seems reasonable that Plato thought even Syracuse should aim for some kind of philosophic rule.

Plato's continued support of some sort of philosophic rule bears on the believability of Plato trusting Dion because it depends on what sort of philosopher Plato was looking for and thus what sort of candidates he could have had in mind. The view that the *Laws* is devoid of philosopher-calibre people seems false, but one advantage of this view is that it explains why there is so little metaphysics in the *Laws*. There are virtually no mentions of the Forms in Plato's longest work, but there is little reason to mention them. If there is nobody to comprehend the Forms, then they play no actual role in governance.

---

⁵ I sadly do not have the time to delve into the content of Seminar 5, which expands on claim (B). The prospects of Hipparinus becoming a philosopher-ruler (324b2) may seem exceedingly dim in retrospect, and I cannot mount a proper defense of Hipparinus. However, if my position is correct then maybe Plato was simply looking for a young person with a lot of promise and intellect (see esp. *Ep. VII* 330b5-6). Hipparinus may not have been all Plato thought he was, but surely a case of a teacher overestimating the promise of a potential student is a familiar and sympathetic one.

But there is nonetheless a different sort of governing philosopher who never sleeps in Magnesia, an inquiring, critical kind that is eager to learn from all sorts of sources. This is a person who may not necessarily comprehend the Forms. However, they will be a paragon of education and virtue anyway,[6] and just as importantly their actions on the council will reflect these characteristics. They will constantly question what is most just, and in the *Laws* this will include inquiring into the justice of the laws themselves. In other words, it is a Socrates and not a Plato who sits on the council.

But if we think the philosopher at the end of the *Laws* is less demanding and less superhuman than the one found in the *Republic*, then we can imagine Plato the political reformer falling for the temptation of seeing in Dion a young man who might deserve the name of philosopher one day. Dion may not have been perfect, but Plato makes it clear that he at least displayed some significant talent and understanding. My response to (A) thus mitigates the incredibility of the mistake described in (B). Even if Plato made a blunder in thinking Syracuse had a prayer of establishing a non-tyrannical, nonviolent government, it was at least a mistake we can understand Plato making.

The Rule of Law and the *Laws*

The *Laws* is often presented as establishing a state in which the rule of law functions.[7] This is presented as a contrast to the absolutist rule of the philosopher-king in the *Republic*. But there is an ambiguity in the phrase 'rule of law.' We might associate that phrase with the concept of liberal democracy, constitutional government, and so on. We assume the law in a regime under the rule of law is changeable and accountable to the wishes of the people. But a state under an unchanging set of laws would also qualify as respecting the "rule of law," no matter how undemocratic the laws might be, so long as

---

[6] In the *Seventh Letter* 326b we find the familiar claim (cf. *Rep.* 473d, 487e, 499b, 501e) that only a philosopher as a ruler can bring peace to a state, a ruler whom he defines as having learned "by the grace of God, [...] true philosophy," making education a necessary condition for becoming a philosopher.

[7] Ibid., 51, 55; *Laws* 713a1-4.

everybody is subject to them and changes happen according to that law.

What unites these two understandings is the shared conviction that the law cannot be arbitrarily changed or suspended by those with political power, that even they are constrained by the law. Laws are changed in liberal democracies, but they are changed in accordance with procedures set by law as well. Why does this matter for the *Seventh Letter* and Syracuse? Frede appears to argue that the Plato of the *Laws* desires a law-based constitutional government where the people can hold the government accountable and can expect even ministers to obey the law.[8] In contrast, while the writer of the *Seventh Letter* does appear at times to advocate for a law-based *polis* (e.g. 324b2, 326a3-5, 327c, 335d5-7, 336a, 351a), his simultaneous advocacy of a philosopher ruler and insistence on this being the only acceptable constitution (326a7-b4) would seem to limit the rule of law to a secondary, weak place in the state (328c1).

There is certainly some evidence to support this view. For instance, in Book IV, discussing the origins of laws, the Stranger makes the following note about his language: "I have now applied the term 'servants of the laws' to the men usually said to be rulers, not for the sake of an innovation in names but because I hold that it is this above all that determines whether the city survives or undergoes the opposite," (715d1-4). The view that law, and not the wisdom of its ruler, is what most determines a city's success seems contrary to the spirit, if not the letter, of the *Republic*, so 715d seems to reinforce the traditional opposition between the *Republic* and *Laws*. But such argument relies on two assumptions being made about Plato's view of law in the *Laws* which are not necessarily true and which, when not assumed, mitigate the force of this apparent tension:

1) A law and constitution-based city has accountable laws.[9]
2) Philosopher-rulers would not be bound in any way by these laws.

---

[8] Ibid., 55.
[9] Ibid., 55.

If these assumptions are paired with the explicit requirement from the *Letter* that all should obey the law in a just constitution (334d-336a), then the contradiction follows and the *Seventh Letter* is in trouble. I would like to consider these two assumptions in turn.

The first assumption appears dubious when we see that Magnesia's laws are intended to be virtually unchangeable. This is surprising in ways, given Magnesia would contain an assembly, a council, magistrates, and so on. With all these political structures, one would expect a lot of politics and legislating, including amending laws (and even repealing some) to deal with new demands. Yet the Stranger greatly admires Egypt's stability of laws and institutions, many of which had lasted, including on matters like the arts and music, for thousands of years (656d-657a; 798a-b, 799b). Even children's games are to be codified in law and made unchangeable (656e), echoing concerns found in the *Republic* (377b-c, 378d, 391e). There are numerous places where Plato stresses that a number of regulations must remain fixed including complaints, indictments, and handling of witnesses in trials (846b-d, 957d). At 846b The Stranger admits that there will be myriad such regulations to make, but the elder, greater lawmakers should not bother themselves with it. But while these more mundane statutes will take some time and experience to lay down, the Stranger is explicit that even for these, once "all the details seem to have been satisfactorily laid down" (846c6-7) (πάντα ἱκανῶς δόξῃ κεῖσθαι) then the laws should be made totally permanent (846b5-d). This is a remarkably low credence threshold for enacting *de facto* unchangeable statutes.

At 846b-d and 957d the Stranger mentions a number of trial periods. What happens after this one? It is not explicitly stated, but there is reason to believe these laws will eventually become permanent as well. At 772c, when mentioning regulations related to celebrations and festivals, the Stranger says "This done they shall decree them [sc. the improvements] as fixed rules and employ them as well as the rest of the laws originally decreed by the lawgiver"[10]

---

[10] Translated by G. Klosko, "The Nocturnal Council in Plato's Laws," *Political Studies* 36, no. 1 (1988): 74–88, https://doi.org/10.1111/j.14679248.1988.tb00217.x., 82.

The trial period is described as a period of open feedback by which magistrates can note shortcomings of the application of the law in their respective positions of influence. 772c appears to be the first mention of a trial period in Magnesian regulations, and he makes the results unchangeable, in fact comparing them with the primordial laws themselves. Finally, at 846d the Stranger seems open to making even self-admittedly trivial regulations permanent. Given the above, it seems reasonable to conclude that nearly all the laws in Magnesia will be made permanent.

This leads me to the *nomophylakes* or "Guardians of the laws," who may provide an avenue to amending laws. During these trial periods The Stranger assigns the task of making notes of the complaints and reports of the various magistrates to the guardians of the laws (769a-771a), who then make "touch-ups" (769c) to the initial laws. Notice that improvements on the law are not done through some sort of open, democratic process. Instead, magistrates assemble what they take to be questions, ambiguities, and tensions in the law and present them to the guardians who digest the concerns and present a plan to legislators. So even this "trial period" is not especially open to the people.

But notice as well that the Guardians are presented in an assisting role. The Stranger gives an introduction of the guardians of the laws as the "savior of the laws" (770b4) but then says the Guardians of the Laws' only job is to "fill in the outline" (770c1) of laws as they are established by the original painter (the lawmaker). It should be noted that the role of overseeing the success of laws concerning self-described "small" matters only appears diminutive because their work literally "saves" the laws from criticism, defusing the impetus for political change and making the city appear more eternal. However, the Guardians are compared to a "device" that the lawmaker consults (770b5). This does not sound like a political office with its own independent authority, but it is clearly meant to hold some great value despite this, given the rest of the passage. And while there will be strong normative pressure for a lawmaker to accept the advice of this "device," there does not appear to be any clear penalties for ignoring the Guardians' advice.

The Stranger does allow for one political means by which a law could be significantly changed: it requires the entire population of Magnesia (along with the oracles of the gods) to unanimously agree on the changing of the law. But it has to be initiated by the Guardians of the Laws and even a single dissenting voice will scuttle the reform (772c6-d4). The Stranger explicitly includes magistrates and offices of state in the consultation, but these political institutions are considered insufficient to amend a law. Only when these magistrates act in agreement with the entire people can the law be substantially changed. Changing this law *via* this method is of course conceptually possible, but practically speaking it would likely be easier to find a Philosopher-King.

This legal fixedness might appear to be a peculiar position for Plato to take, given his criticism of law as inherently general in the *Statesman*. At 293 the young Socrates compares laws to an absent doctor: "We believe in them where they cure us with our consent or without it, by cutting or burning or applying some other painful treatment, and whether they do so according to written rules or apart from written rules, and whether as poor men or rich," (*Statesman* 293b1-4). Their methods might appear painful and unpleasant, but they are just the established rules designed to treat an average set of conditions. They are designed for anybody but not for any particular person. Yet despite this position, the Athenian Stranger in *Laws* endorse the political gamble of having malformed laws with little recourse to change them. Indeed, for a text supposedly devoid of people with philosopher-level wisdom, the Athenian Stranger seems remarkably optimistic about a group of people within a finite period establishing laws for even bureaucratic and judicial matters that will withstand the test of time.

So, the laws hardly appear popularly accountable, though it is clear that even the Guardians of the Laws have to obey them and they will be highly stable. However, one could imagine the laws' fixedness leading to a sort of proceduralism in application, given that every contingency (ideally) would need to be hammered out. Guaranteeing the goal of these laws is important, and somebody with "intelligence and senses" needs to respect and study these laws (and the society

Sleepless in Syracuse

they govern) well enough to truly steer them towards that end. What makes the Stranger so sure a certain mindless dogmatism will not take over in a constitution with virtually unchanging laws?

Night School: The Education of the Councilors

This leads me to questioning the second assumption underlying the inconsistency charge, that philosophers are not bound by the law, and one way to show this is false would be to demonstrate that Plato establishes a law-based office that relies on people possessing a philosopher-like education in the *Laws*. I think this is the Nocturnal Council.

To see why education matters at all to how we understand the Nocturnal Council, and what this has to do with the rule of law we can simply look at the council's role as described at *Laws* 962a9-c3:

> Then it's likely that in the present case, if our founding of the country is to have an end, there must be something in it that knows, in the first place, this goal we're speaking of (whatever our political goal might happen to be), and then in what way it ought to attain this, and who -- first among the laws themselves, and then among human beings -- gives it advice in a noble or ignoble way. But if some city is devoid of such a thing, it won't be surprising if, lacking intelligence and senses, it acts haphazardly each time in each of its actions.

Even under the rule of law, there needs to be a human element that understands what the *telos* of the laws actually is, something with "intelligence and senses." The Stranger (and Plato elsewhere) makes it clear that he considers the point of the state and the laws to be cultivation of virtue, so it follows that the council members must study the nature of individual virtues (962e-963a) along with their unity (965c-d), the very sort of issues explored in the Socratic dialogues. Related to this, the Council comparatively studies the law by learning from certain authorized foreigners. As described at 950cd, this would entail also sending out distinguished (but not too elderly) citizens as emissaries to these other states.

That there should be an office that studies how to improve public policy may not seem surprising. However, the Stranger adds a number of other subjects that make the Nocturnal Council more than just an ancient think tank. For instance, they must study the philosophic and theological arguments presented in Book X, presumably including the discussion of the soul as self-mover (966c-d). The Stranger also alludes to a constellation of other subjects including psychology, music, and astronomy (also 818c-d), all things that "intelligence is the master of, having arranged the whole in an order."

We see foreshadowing of the special content of the Council's education elsewhere. Earlier in the *Laws* at 818a1-4, Plato restricts advanced mathematics to only an exclusive group (cf. *Rep*. 535a-e), whose identity "we shall say when we approach the end - since that will be the natural place." Elsewhere, at 747b we find mathematics described as the most powerful part of education in a political regime as well, again reserved for the select few (cf. 525d). 809e refers to astronomy and specifically assigns the role of an undefined "lawgiver" to study and explain these matters. These references all make the most sense when seen as foreshadowing the Nocturnal Council, and they also appear very similar to the general curriculum of the *Republic*.

The Athenian Stranger sadly does not develop the curriculum in more detail (968e), but one thing is clear: The Nocturnal Council is meant to study the higher, eternal things that law is supposed to replicate. The Stranger confirms this impression at 966b-c when he says the "true" Guardians of the Law (the Nocturnal Council) must "[judge] by the standard of nature what things come into being in a noble fashion and what things do not," and one of the most noble aspects of nature that the council member has to know is that the gods exist, are interested in us, care for us, and rationally order the universe. Indeed, at 966d the Stranger makes this recognition about the gods a precondition even for consideration for membership on the Council. This is also possibly why one of the dirtier jobs ascribed to the council is the imprisonment of atheists in the "Moderation Tank" (908a, 909a) as the Council is the authority most keenly aware of the importance of belief in a rational, benevolent creator.

The Nocturnal Council is clearly interested in pursuing intellectual discovery and contemplation, and their education contains many of the same subjects that the Kallipolis' curriculum does, including the priority set on mathematics (whose truths are eternal) and astronomy (whose movements are mathematically predictable and eternal). However, dialectic and by extension the grasp of the Forms are both absent in the Nocturnal Council's curriculum. What we end up with is a Council composed of extraordinary people devoted to the philosophic life but none of whom is quite in possession of the perfect knowledge (direct knowledge of the Forms, particularly the Good) which would render any sort of discussion or collaboration with other members unnecessary. Throughout all this, however, the Nocturnal Council's primary goal is to serve the laws, making sure their *telos* is truly carried out and that the laws are enforced sensibly.

The Possibility of Philosophers

So, it seems the Nocturnal Council does in fact have philosopher-like people, but perhaps I have only demonstrated the *Laws* has a philosophic curriculum for the Council. I have not yet shown something stronger, that people who reach the divine level of virtue attributed to the Philosopher-King actually exist in Plato's view. Supreme gold souls remain to be found. I believe I have found them at 951c:

> The fact is, there are always among the many certain divine human beings -- not many -- whose intercourse is altogether worthwhile, and who do not by nature grow any more frequently in cities with good laws than in cities without. These, the inhabitants of cities with good laws, if he's uncorruptible, must always seek and track down, by going over sea and land, in order to place on a firmer footing those legal customs that are nobly laid down, and correct others, if they are lacking something. (951b4-c3)

This is a fascinating passage that does not receive the attention it deserves. It takes place in the description of the Nocturnal Council's powers and appears to commit the Stranger to the proposition that exemplary people who would clearly qualify as philosopher-rulers do exist. Furthermore, even in bad constitutions (e.g. Syracuse) these people will arise, possibly at the same rate as in good constitutions. Such a possibility is also presupposed by the *Republic*'s argument that philosophers arising in a bad constitution would understandably not have to engage in state affairs (520a9-b4). Between these two passages, the only difference is that the *Republic* describes the philosopher ruler as arising "against the will" of a constitution, while the *Laws* is not phrased in such oppositional terms. The basic commitment to the possibility of philosophers existing in bad constitutions remains.

Aristotle also makes mysterious references to such "divine people" (*NE* VII.6 1145a17-30; 1150a1-3; *Pol.* I.2 1253a3-9, IV.2 1289a38-b2), but he characterizes them similarly to how Frede thinks they function in the *Laws*, as interesting counterfactuals but irrelevant to the interests of the *Politics*. In contrast, The Stranger believes they do exist, even in the world of the *Laws*, and are very relevant. Moreover, finding these extraordinary people is worth sacrificing the time and comfort of an "incorruptible" (ἀδιάφθαρτος) citizen (951c1-3). Why? Because these divine people are vital to providing input on their laws and their own ideas of how a city should live, and there is an actual chance Magnesia will locate them. Needless to say, Aristotle's ideal *polis* in *Politics* VII-VIII has no such emissaries.

Recall the political route by which laws in Magnesia can be changed. It required unanimity among the citizens, yet the thoughts of one non-citizen is enough to spur any sort of reform. One presumes Plato would not want his constitution to accidentally leave out divine people who have a reasonable chance of appearing in Magnesia. Frede may be right that a philosopher in the *Republic's* sense of the word - somebody who has true access to the Forms including the Good - does not exist in the *Laws*. But there can be two reasons such people do not figure in the *Laws*: 1) because there is nobody of such high virtue that they may be able to be educated enough to reach the Forms directly, but also 2) Plato wants to see how far he can build a feasible law-based state without positing these superior people as political agents.

Given the above passage, it would seem 1) is false; while the Nocturnal Council itself does not receive an education in the Forms, this does not imply there is nobody who can comprehend the Forms.

But we can also affirm these peoples' existence while preserving the truth of 2) if putting philosophers on the council represents Plato's conclusion about just how plausibly a state based on laws can be founded. He thinks laws can handle the vast majority of societal problems and even overcome widespread, near universal social conditioning (781a-c). But these laws necessarily require the input, if not the direct administration, of philosopher-caliber people.

I turn to my last piece of evidence, which is that the Nocturnal Council is described in the same language as these divine people. They are given various superlatives: at 961c, they are the "anchor" of the city; at 960e8 they are its "savior." Most important, at the very end of the dialogue, the Stranger says:

> Now if, indeed, this divine council should come into being for us, dear comrades, the city ought to be handed over to it; (ἐάν γε μὴν οὗτος ἡμῖν ὁ θεῖος γένηται σύλλογος, ὦ φίλοι ἑταῖροι, παραδοτέον τούτῳ τὴν πόλιν) of the present day lawgivers, none, so to speak, have any quarrel with this. (969b1-b3)

This is a strong statement to make, as shown by the present general construction. The council is described as divine, the same language used to describe the extraordinary people whose wisdom specially guides Magnesia's legal development. It has to be admitted that Plato is sometimes loose in his language, but the divine predicates function similarly here: their personal wisdom and virtue are so great as to afford them special say over Magnesia's laws. It does not matter if they are citizens; their excellence is sufficient to afford them influence. Further, 951 clearly implies such people likely exist in Magnesia already, making the construction of a Nocturnal Council with people like these feasible through proper education and cultivation, enough to become φύλακες ἀποτελεσθῶσιν, "perfected guardians," (969c3). This explains why the Nocturnal Council accepts some young citizens on the basis of great merit (951e-952a; 961a-b), those already good enough to be Guardians of the Laws (957a-b).

This may make the *Laws* seem inconsistent. The rest of Magnesia's constitution (and Books I-XI generally) is a complex, legally ossified structure. The Nocturnal Council is in contrast a small body that is always inquiring into the laws and possessing a plenitude of power. Furthermore, at 966b the Stranger refers to the council as the "real" guardians of the laws, leaving the other Guardians of the Laws' place in question. In order to overcome this incoherence, some describe the council more as a nonpolitical advisory body that the state would simply listen to as a matter of course. In effect, the Academy. This idea is most influentially advanced by Glenn Morrow.[11]

But there is reason to think that this does not capture the strength of the text's emphasis on the Council's role. Under the "institutional" interpretation of Klosko, they truly will hold dominating political power inside the constitution. This would square with some of the council's coercive duties such as its maintenance of the atheist prison. It would also account for how the Stranger takes it as obvious among the three speakers that the "divine" Nocturnal Council's very composition would warrant it unique power. However, it would prove Aristotle (*Pol.* 1265a2-4) correct when he accuses Plato of rehashing the philosopher-king in a collaborative form. Deciding whether this is how the Nocturnal Council functions, or whether there is an actual contradiction at the end of the *Laws* like the one Klosko proposes,[12] is beyond the scope of this chapter.

Whichever it is, however, at the end of the *Laws* we still find an embrace of philosophic rule of some kind. If there is a contradiction at the heart of the *Laws*, then the similar confusions found in the *Seventh Letter* are not so incriminating with regards to authenticity. On the other hand, if there is no contradiction and the council holds some sort of consistent advisory role inside Magnesia like a state-sponsored Academy, then that undercuts ascribing such a confusion

---

[11] Glenn R. Morrow, *Plato's Cretan City: A Historical Interpretation of the* Laws (Princeton, N.J.: Princeton University Press, 1960).

[12] Klosko, "Nocturnal Council," 84 ff.

Sleepless in Syracuse

to the *Seventh Letter*. Under Morrow's "informal model," Plato has provided us with such a stable constitution based on laws but with an element of non-political philosophic rule. Frede's argument proceeds on the basis that philosophers and laws do not mix for Plato, while Morrow's model shows they can. Whichever is the case for the Nocturnal Council (all-powerful contradiction or collaborative advisor), the charge of incoherence in the *Seventh Letter* is no longer so threatening. The *Letter* may fall for other reasons, but it is acquitted on this one.

Doctrinal Consistency and Plato's Political Life

Now, one final objection that could be levelled against my interpretation is that my argument is founded on the false premise that we should expect Plato to have doctrinal consistency at all between the *Laws* and *Letters*. The *Laws* is a massive work which Plato spent years carefully writing. In contrast, *Seventh Letter* presents itself as being composed in the heat of political upheaval. Why should we expect that the authentic Plato stay consistent between these two works given the radically different circumstances of their compositions? This is the "Consistency Assumption," (CA) and it may be false. The *Seventh Letter* may still be genuine, so this argument would go, but not because of the reasons I give.

It is possible that Plato is just inconsistent and my explanation itself is merely a likely story that is simply not the case. However, we should consider closely what we are rejecting when we dump the CA. It is not to deny that, when there is consistency, that this is a sign of authenticity (though not a sufficient one). Such a conditional seems true. Rather, rejecting the CA is to deny consistency as a necessary (or practically necessary) condition of authenticity.

However, one can deny the CA and also believe my interpretation is still correct, that nothing in the *Laws* appears to seriously undermine the stated mission in the *Seventh Letter* on the matter of the philosopher. If one does so, then one is acknowledging there is consistency, or enough consistency such that conflicts are minor enough so as to be understandable.[13] But if so, then that means I have provided a strong sign of authenticity, even as I acknowledge it is not quite enough to ensure genuineness.

My interpretation does, at least, seem to relieve the burden of proof Frede convincingly argues should rest on any ancient letter. Plato should maybe not be expected to have stayed consistent between the *Laws* and the *Letter* given the circumstances, but it is to his credit as a philosopher that there does in fact appear to be serious conceptual continuity between these works if my interpretation is right. Dion may have been a rather poor candidate for the role of philosopher-ruler, but I hope to have shown Plato was looking for candidates nonetheless.

---

[13] In fact the same intuitions about human reactions to political upheaval that leads to a rejection of the CA would require us to adopt a broad tolerance on inconsistencies generally.

Philosophical Reception

Karen Sieben[1]
Plato and Diogenes in Syracuse

In turbulent times it is no mean feat for a moral or social critic to attempt to effect change and still keep his head, both literally and figuratively. As it happens, Syracuse is the backdrop for an exchange between two ancient philosophers over this problem. One of them was the most famous philosopher of all, Plato, and the other was his arch-nemesis Diogenes of Sinope. Their relationship was not a congenial one. The rapport between them alternated between contempt (Diogenes's view of Plato), and strained civility (Plato's view of Diogenes), which was caused by their fundamental disagreement as to the nature of philosophy itself, and, more specifically, by a dispute over Plato's activities in Syracuse.

In ancient Athens how a philosopher handled himself in the public arena was a matter of concern to him since how others viewed his behavior was a means to judge his character. Both Diogenes and Plato were well aware of this public display of oneself, and in the case of Diogenes, he used his confrontational style to his advantage to win over the likes of Alexander the Great[2] and his father, King Philip.[3] In the case of Plato, however, we find that even the wisest among us can become conflicted and succumb to dissembling when our philosophical theories meet harsh reality as was the case in Syracuse when Plato engaged the tyrants Dionysius I and Dioysius II. It is to this issue that the lesser known philosopher, Diogenes, confronts the

---

[1] Karen Sieben is an Adjunct Assistant Professor of Philosophy at Ocean County College, Toms River, N.J., teaching courses in Metaphysics, Logic, Ethics and World Religion. She earned her PhD in Philosophy from the University of Wales Trinity St. David. Currently, she is writing on topics concerning Cynicism and is researching ancient Indo-European concepts of human nature.

[2] Diogenes Laertius, *Lives of Eminent Philosophers,* trans. R. D. Hicks (Cambridge MA, Harvard University Press, 2005), VI. 38. When Alexander came to speak with Diogenes in Corinth, Diogenes famously said, "Stand out of my light".

[3] Ibid. VI 43. When Diogenes was dragged off to see Philip, when he was asked who he was, Diogenes said, "A spy upon your insatiable greed". He was so admired for this, he was set free.

erstwhile philosopher, Plato, and wins the discussion. How he does so sheds light on the early beginnings of philosophy and shows how, in the aftermath of Socrates's death, individuals faced challenges to their reputations and even to their lives when they lost or gained the favor of powerful men.

Plato and Syracuse

What happened to Plato in Syracuse is the place to start our contrast between the two philosophers. We have two sources of information concerning what went on there. In addition to Diogenes Laertius's account,[4] Plato himself reveals the particulars of his intervention in Syracuse in his *Letters*.[5] The *Letters* reveal a great deal about the complicated relationships Plato formed in Syracuse and the motivations for his political activity there. In his introduction to the *Letters*, Bury explains that Plato found himself in Syracuse at the age of 40 after leaving Athens upon the death of his teacher, Socrates.[6] In his *Seventh Letter* Plato explains that Socrates was tried for impiety and condemned (325c). As a consequence, Plato found that he no longer had the heart to engage in Athenian public life and politics, since, to use the words of Socrates in the *Republic* "he would be as a man who has fallen among wild beasts, unwilling to share their

---

[4] Diogenes Laertius. *Lives of Eminent Philosophers,* ed. James Miller, trans. Pamela Mensh (Oxford: Oxford University Press, 2018).

[5] Plato, *Epistles,* trans. R. J. Bury (Cambridge, MA, Harvard University Press, 1929). Bury suggests that only the *Seventh* and *Eighth Letters* are Plato's own work for the reason that they are, as he argues, "open" letters available to everyone, especially Athenians who Bury believed were his primary audience. He suggests that as open letters they would be available for public scrutiny and are therefore unlikely to be forgeries. In the newest translation of Diogenes's *Lives*, cited above, Pamela Mensch says concerning the *Seventh Letter* that "the majority of modern scholars regard [it] as genuine" (142-43). There are opposing views; such as M. Burnyeat and M. Frede, *The Pseudo-Platonic Seventh Letter,* ed. Dominic Scott (Oxford: Oxford University Press, 2015). For an earlier account of the *Seventh Letter,* see P. Shorey, *What Plato Said* (Chicago: U. of Chicago Press, 1933). K. J. Dover's use of linguistics in his *Greek Word Order* (Cambidge: Cambridge University Press, 1960) is inconclusive. Of all the views, Bury's seems the strongest, and is in favor of acceptance.

[6] Bury. *Epistles*, 386.

misdeeds and unable to hold out singly against the savagery of all, and he would thus, before he could in any way benefit his friends or the state, come to an untimely end without doing any good to himself or others" (*Republic* 496d).[7]

Grieving for his teacher, Plato travelled widely and conjecture is that he came to Syracuse the first time to learn from the Pythagoreans.[8] Instead, as Plato recounts in his letter, he met Dion, nephew to the local tyrant Dionysius I. Dion introduced Plato to Dionysius I, who at the time was attempting to make Sicily into a seat of learning in addition to attempting to make Syracuse a great military power. Plato shared his political ideas with those in Dionysius I's court and Dion became an apt pupil (*Seventh Letter* 327). Plato came to love Dion and their relationship lasted until Dion's death thirty-three years later.[9] Plato stayed only a short time on this visit and then returned to Athens. (Diog. Laert. 3.23)

Upon his return to Athens, Plato founded his school, the Academy, with a loan from Dion[10] and decided to devote his life to educating Athenian youth. Five years later in 367 BCE, Dionysius I died and rule fell to his son, Dionysius II. Dion, also a legitimate claimant to the tyranny, aided Dionysius II in his early reign.[11] In the letter, Plato claims that Dion suggested that his ideas might be of benefit to the new tyrant and so Dion encouraged Plato to return for

---

[7] P. Shorey (trans.), Plato. *Republic*, ed. E. Hamilton, (Princeton, NJ: Princeton University Press, 1961).

[8] R.W. Hare, *Plato*, (Oxford, Oxford University Press, 1996), 7.

[9] J.M. Edmonds (ed.), Plato, "Epigram 3," in *Elegy and Iambus,* v. II, www.perseus.tufts.edu. The poem reads, "The Fates once decreed tears unto/ Hecuba and the women of Troy at their/ birth; Thy widespread hopes, Dion, the/ Gods did spill upon the ground when/ thou hadst triumphed in the doing of/ noble deeds; and so in the spacious city/ that bares thee liest thou honoured by they/ fellow countrymen, O Dion who didst/ make my heart mad with love of thee."

[10] Mensch. *Lives*. III 20. In the biographical section of the book, Laertius recounts that Plato had been sold into slavery by Dionysius I, and was ransomed by Annceris. Dion remitted the sum to Annceris, who refused to accept it and gave the money to Plato instead to buy land for the Academy.

[11] Hare, *Plato*, 7.

a second visit to instruct Dionysius. (*Seventh Letter* 328b). Plato did return, but rather than help the young tyrant, his political views stirred controversy. When Dion attempted to implement Plato's ideas on behalf of the tyrant, he created enemies within the court and created factions who meant to thwart him. Once details of Plato's ideal government were revealed to the city's citizens, factions grew up ready to discredit Dion (*Seventh Letter* 329c).

In the end, Dionysius II agreed with the factions and exiled Dion (*Seventh Lettter* 329d). Plato went home to Athens, but he continued "to interest himself in Sicilian affairs."[12] Subsequently, Dionysius II attempted to restore the kind of court presided over by his father. To that end, within a few years, he invited sophists and scientists to the court and that invitation included Plato (*Seventh Letter* 327d). Plato resolved to travel there on his third trip in the hopes of reconciling Dion to Dionysius II. It was a false hope because Dionysius II, in the end, found Plato to be disloyal to him and loyal to Dion whom he considered a threat. Plato was put under close scrutiny and not allowed to leave the palace and Dion's property was confiscated. Plato's efforts to reconcile Dion and Dionysius II came to nothing (*Seventh Letter* 345-350).

Knowing the die was finally cast, Plato, with the help of his friend Archytas, escaped from Syracuse and travelled to Olympia to meet Dion. While there, Dion revealed his intention to unseat Dionysius II (*Seventh Letter* 350-351). He did so in 357 BCE and with those loyal to him took control of the city. However, when Dion again attempted to implement Plato's political ideas, the population revolted against him under Heracleides. In response, Dion executed Heracleides and this increased the tension further. Eventually, Dion was assassinated by Callipus (one of Plato's students) triggering turmoil that continued long after Plato's death in 347 BCE.[13]

The account of Plato's activities in Syracuse in the *Seventh Letter* differs from the account by Diogenes Laertius. Laertius claims Plato

---

[12] Bury, *Epistles*, 387.
[13] Ibid., 388-89.

was sent away to be sold into slavery by Dioysius I and was eventually ransomed. This event is well attested to by Laertius's source, Favorinus's *Miscellaneous History*.[14] Laertius also includes the information that Plato asked Dionysius II for "territory and men" so that he could implement his ideas from the *Republic*.[15] More importantly, Laertius claims that Plato encouraged Dion to liberate Syracuse, but in the *Seventh Letter* Plato avows he was not involved in any plans for a coup.[16] Finally, in Laertius's account, on this third trip to Syracuse, when he realized he could not reconcile Dion and Dioysius II, Plato returned to Athens and devoted himself to teaching at his Academy. In the *Seventh Letter,* as mentioned above, Plato needed Archytas's help to escape from Syracuse, and Plato did not go right home to Athens. He went to Olympia to meet with factions trying to unseat Dionysius II. These bits of information dramatically change one's perception of what actually happened in Syracuse, and naturally lead to questioning why Plato omitted them from his own account.

Criticism of Plato

What actually happened in Syracuse, while unclear to us, was openly discussed in his own time. Thirty-three years of Plato's activity in Syracuse did not go unnoticed by the Athenians and they were quick to judge him harshly.[17] So Diogenes was not alone in his condemnation. It was Diogenes, however, whose criticism was most pointed. Diogenes Laertius relates many encounters between the two in his history of Diogenes of Sinope, two of which deal specifically with Syracuse and Plato's actions there, and they reveal much about their ideological differences. In the first encounter Plato saw Diogenes washing lettuces and said to him "Had you paid court to Dionysius, you wouldn't now be washing lettuces." Diogenes replied, "If you had washed lettuces, you wouldn't have paid court

---

[14] Mensch, *Lives* III, 19-20.
[15] Ibid. III 21.
[16] Ibid. III 21 and related footnote.
[17] Bury, *Epistles,* Introduction, 474.

to Dionysius" (Diog. Laert. 6.58). One of the fundamental ideas upon which Athenian democracy was based was the idea of equality and that no man should debase himself by being held accountable to another, nor be subservient to another.[18] Plato's subservience to Dionysius II in his court broke that time-honored principle. It was an unpardonable sin in the eyes of all Athenian citizens and especially to Diogenes who advocated self-sufficiency as the means to be a totally free individual.

Another encounter between Plato and Diogenes related by Diogenes Laertius is this:

> Observing Plato one day at a costly banquet taking olives, "how is it," he said, "that you the philosopher who sailed to Sicily for the sake of these dishes, now when they are before you do not enjoy them?"
>
> "Nay, by the gods, Diogenes," replied Plato, "there also for the most part I lived among olives and such like."
>
> "Why then," said Diogenes, "did you need to go to Syracuse? Was it that Attica at that time did not grow olives?" (Diog. Laert. 6.25)

Both Plato and Diogenes were followers of Socrates and his way of life. Socrates lived and dressed simply and usually walked about Athens shoeless. He was a teacher who gathered students around him as he asked pointed questions about truth, justice, and human life. His questioning technique eventually provoked the ire of powerful Athenians who suffered under some of Socrates's withering criticism. Victims of Socrates's questioning eventually accused him of undermining the Athenian polis and took him to the Athenian court for this. Refusing to back away from his arguments and ideas, he would be found guilty and was ordered to be put to death.

---

[18] G. Robert, *Daily Life of the Ancient Greeks* (London, Greenwood Press, 2009), 231. It is for this reason that Athenians were so dependent upon slaves to do the work. Citizens could manage others in doing work, but they could not do any work dictated by others.

The *Seventh Letter* suggests that Plato left Athens thinking he could no longer find a future there. At least, that is what Plato says, as we noted above. Diogenes alludes to something else in the conversation. If Plato was willing to confront the danger of promoting his ideas in Sicily, why wasn't he willing to do the same thing in Athens? Additionally, if Socrates knew the danger in pursuing the life he led there and yet continued to teach the Athenian people, how could Plato think he was following in Socrates's footsteps by escaping to Sicily? Since Diogenes did follow Socrates's path in this regard, he is questioning Plato's courage.

Assessment of Plato's activities in Syracuse

If we expand on Diogenes's criticism, we have good reason to claim that Plato's intrusion into the politics of Syracuse in the 4th c. BCE was a debacle. Not only did it destabilize the city by inciting different factions, some loyal to Dionysius II and some to Dion, but it also proved a testing ground for the implementation of Plato's political ideal. The gist of Plato's theory was his belief that democracy is wrongheaded in that it allows the uneducated masses to rule. Instead, Plato proposed (mainly in the *Republic*) that society should be organized into two classes—an educated class and the working class. The educated class would be further divided into the educated elite and soldiers. Of the educated elite, some would fill the ranks of administrators of the city and some, the best of them, would take turns ruling as philosopher-kings. In this system "the masses in the lowest of the three classes are excluded from any part in government; their role is to obey, and to supply the community's needs by engaging in useful trades."[19]

Plato himself admitted that his experience in Syracuse proved the impracticality of his ideal political system as expressed in *the Republic*. He defends his actions, however, by saying,

> For this course of actions is closely akin to that which Dion and I together, in our plans for the welfare of Syracuse, attempted to carry out, although it is but the second-best; for the first was that

---

[19] Hare, *Plato,* 59.

> which we first attempted to carry out with the aid of Dionysius himself—a plan which would have benefited all alike, had it not been that some Chance, mightier than men, scattered it to the winds (337c).

Was it really chance that upset the plans that Plato and Dion had in mind, or something else? Scrutiny of the *Republic* reveals that it is long on theory and fails, as Hare says, because "hardly any detail is given in the *Republic* of how the government of the ideal state is actually to be carried on."[20] Hare is correct about this. One of the mistakes was the problem of getting the citizens to go along with it. Plato's reliance on an educated class to govern did not allow for a society in which an educated class did not exist, as was the case in Sicily. One would have to educate the working class or ruling class enough to accept the fact that the educated class should rule! Without the cooperation of the citizens in implementing his plan in the first place, dissent should have been expected, if not outright revolt. And revolt is what happened in Syracuse.

Bury's view of this aspect of Plato's life in Syracuse is that Plato was very serious about implementing his political theory there and that part of the rationale for the *Seventh Letter* was to explain "the particular measures he took with Dion as his colleague to realize that Ideal."[21] However, Bury claims the situation made clear to Plato "how in default of the Ideal, he was led to fall back upon the rule of Law."[22] Bury concludes that the failure to implement the Ideal is the reason that the *Laws*, rather than a reworked *Republic*, was the main work of Plato's declining years.[23] The criticism of W. Guthrie is also to the point of the Republic's flaws. In his mind,

> [T]he individual is to be subordinated to the common weal with what appears to our eyes an excessive relentlessness. The taking

---

[20] Ibid., 60. In particular he mentions "the relation of the rulers to the laws remains somewhat obscure."
[21] Bury, *Epistles*, 390.
[22] Ibid., 390.
[23] Ibid., 390.

away from these, the most valuable citizens of the state, of property and family life...all this seems shocking to our eyes.[24]

It should have been obvious to Plato that various interests within the tyrant's government would be impacted by any sort of change, and that those groups would not sit idly by while their lives might be negatively impacted. From Plato's point of view, Dion's exile and the confiscation of his property in support of Plato's theory was unjust (347d). But was it? Let's imagine what would have to happen to implement Plato's politics in Syracuse. If Dionysius II adopted Plato's political views as expressed in the *Republic*, he would have had to reconstruct Syracusan society. He would have to establish an educated class and even establish a basis and rationale for the education. He would need to segregate all other Syracusans from any type of leadership and participation in the government and reduce most of the population to subservience to the educated class. Sensible people would not vote for their own disenfranchisement. Dionysius II needn't have been a brilliant leader to figure that out and to figure out that even an attempt to do as Plato suggested would lead to outright revolt, and that is precisely what happened when Dion attempted to implement some of Plato's ideas.

So a tyrant as modestly educated as Dionysius II was, who showed no enthusiasm for education, would not reason to a judgment about Plato and his intentions. He, like most Greeks, would judge a person and what they said by their actions. The logic for Dionysius II might have gone like this: "Dion accepted Plato's views. Dion attempted to implement them and the Syracusans reacted against him. His actions were not the type of system my father put in place. So Dion and Plato were not loyal to the Syracusan system. I represent the system. Are Dion and Plato loyal to me? No, not if they try to implement ideas not in keeping with the policy we have here."

Diogenes's Reaction

The two episodes mentioned here may give us pause in our overall evaluation of Plato and his actions in Sicily, but probably do

---

[24] W.K.C. Guthrie, *The Greek Philosophers* (New York: Harper Perennial, 1975), 85.

no serious harm to his august reputation. However, if we shift our gaze from Plato to Diogenes, these two events take on more significance. Diogenes's background led him to think about himself and society differently. Diogenes was not originally from Athens. He was a banker in Sinope, a Greek colony on the southern coast of the Black Sea. In his later years, he and his father, who was also the banker for the city, defaced some of the currency in circulation there. The full details of this are not clear, but it may have been that it was an attempt by Persian satraps to undermine the city, which was loyal to Greece, by flooding the city with counterfeit currency. When the satraps gained power in the city, they charged Diogenes and his father with altering currency. Diogenes's father was imprisoned and Diogenes fled (Diog. Laert. 20-21). One thing is clear from the details of his early life, Diogenes was a powerful figure within Sinopean society and as we read Diogenes Laertius stories about him, we see in him a sense of autonomy and dignity which stayed with him all of his life. He was not a person who could be intimidated or subjugated. He remained very much his own person.

Later, in exile in Athens, Diogenes found that the house he was to rent was not ready (Diog. Laert. 23). With nowhere else to go he took up residence in his famous tub or wine jar and dedicated himself to philosophy after a meeting with Antisthenes, a follower of Socrates (Diog. Laert. 22). Like Antisthenes's, Diogenes's approach to philosophy was decidedly different from that of Plato. Both Antisthenes and Diogenes focused on the moral aspect of life and both exhorted Athenians to follow the traditional moral perspective, which was being undermined at that time by increased trade and the allure of wealth and class distinctions. But it was Epictetus in late antiquity who picked up on one particular aspect of Diogenes's philosophy as important. Epictetus noticed the aforementioned passage in Laertius's life of Diogenes where Diogenes was brought before King Philip of Macedonia. Philip asked him why he was brought before him, and Diogenes answered, "to spy upon your insatiable greed" (Diog. Laert. 43). Philip was so impressed with him, that he let Diogenes go. But it was the word "spy" that caught Epictetus's attention. He took up the idea of the spy as characteristic of Cynicism and he tied it to the Greek value of *parrhesia* or freedom of speech. Epictetus's conclusion is that

> A Cynic is a messenger sent from Zeus to men, concerning good and evil, to show them that they are mistaken, and seek the essence of good and evil where it is not, but do not observe it when it is, that he is a spy like Diogenes, when he was brought to Philip after the battle of Charonea. For, in effect, a Cynic is like a spy to discover what things are friendly, what hostile, to man; and he must, after making an accurate observation, come and tell them the truth; not be struck with terror, so as to point out to them enemies where there are none; nor, in any other instances, be disconcerted or confounded by appearance. (*Discourses* Bk. 3)

In regard to Plato's activities in Syracuse then, Diogenes's responsibility was to speak the truth to Plato as he did to Philip and to castigate him for his moral lapses. In Diogenes's mind, enduring the indignity of being a servant in Dionysius's court was one lapse of judgment, and not following in the steps of his revered teacher by teaching in Athens was another.

Plato's Defense

There is also a more serious lapse, which Plato reveals himself. In the *Seventh Letter*, he spends a good deal of time justifying his actions and encouraging the faction that supported Dion. He places the blame for all that happened on Dionysius II's and Dion's enemies within the Court. It is a lengthy self-justification for his actions, and as Bury recounts, not intended for the people to whom it is addressed. Bury shows that the letter was a public letter intended not for the people of Syracuse, but rather for the people of Athens and to the severe criticism from there. In fact, says Bury, "Plato wrote the letter to counter what he considered to be the ignorant gossip, malicious rumors and damaging misrepresentations current in Athens" in his time.[25]

It is probably the case that, of the rumors spread about Plato and Syracuse, many were ignorant and malicious, but it also appears that

---

[25] Ibid., 474. In the letter Plato refers to it as "absurd and irrational stories" (352).

Plato's justification of himself led to some misrepresentations of his own. The tone of his letter is off-putting as Plato points fingers at others concerning the unrest in Syracuse. He begins by painting a picture of life in Syracuse as sordid. In the *Seventh Letter* he says,

> And when I came I was in no wise pleased at all with "the blissful life," as it is there termed, replete as it is with Italian and Syracusan banquetings; for thus one's existence is spent in gorging food twice a day and never sleeping alone at night, and all the practices which accompany this mode of living. For not a single man of all who live beneath the heavens could ever become wise if these were his practices from his youth, since none will be found to possess a nature so admirably compounded; nor would he ever be ever be likely to become temperate; and the same may truly be said of all other forms of virtue. (326bc)

As a rationale for introducing the people of Syracuse to philosophy, this passage is reasonable. However, the issue is Plato's activities in Syracuse and his culpability in the tragic events that unfolded because of his meddling in the governance of the city. What he needed to do was defend his political views and how the citizens reacted to them, and there is no evidence of that in the entire letter. Instead, Plato constructs an *ad hominem* attack on the character of the people of Syracuse, including Dionysius II, and even the character of Dion. His criticism of Dion is this:

> And Dion's downfall was, in fact, due to the same cause; for while he most certainly did not fail to notice that those who brought him down were evil men, yet he did fail to realize to what a pitch of folly they had come, and of depravity also and voracious greed; and thereby he was brought down and lies fallen, enveloping Sicily in immeasurable woe. (351de)

Plato explains that Dion was killed by two of his friends, Callipus and Philostratus, brothers whom he met returning from exile. Plato is quick to remark that they did not have philosophy in common; rather the friendship was derived from "mutual entertaining and sharing in religion and mystic ceremonies" (*Seventh Letter* 333e). In the end the brothers turned against Dion because Dion executed Heracleides, the same Heracleides exiled by Dionysius II, who also wished to reform Syracuse. It was when Dion began to institute political reforms in conformity with Plato's theories that Heracleides united the people against him.[26] What Plato also does in his discussion of Dion's assassination is try to defend Athens as the culture which nurtured them. Plato omits that they were his own students, thereby shifting the blame to Athens instead of himself and the teachings in his own Academy.[27]

Plato demurs from casting blame at Dion's death. Instead, his move is to defend the charge that the death was Athens's doing (*Seventh Letter* 334, 335c). Plato admits that he had a right to be angry because those who slew him deprived mankind of an opportunity to implement a society based on justice (335c). It is here that the ire of the truth-teller Diogenes would rise to the occasion (and did) with a resounding "no" to Plato's explanation.

Thus, Diogenes's exchanges with Plato reflect more than a mutual dislike. They are indicative of different views of the nature of philosophical life. Diogenes would say, philosophy can't be about utopian theories; it must be a showing of how life is best lived, and in his mind, best lived for all citizens since he was a believer in democracy. That showing is displayed in one's actions, which reveal the character of the man doing those actions, and in Diogenes's mind, Plato came off this Syracusan episode very badly indeed.

Conclusion

What we find in Plato's activities in Syracuse is his attempt to implement his political ideas. He finds a receptive member of the Dionysian court, Dion, who also establishes a relationship with Plato that lasts until Dion's death thirty-three years later. Upon the death of Dionysius I, his son Dionysius II became tyrant with Dion assisting him in the early years of his reign. Attempts by Dion to implement Plato's political ideas caused the rise of factions against both Dion

---

[26] Hare, *Plato*, 8.
[27] Ibid., 8.

and Plato, and Dion was exiled as a consequence. Eventually, Dionysius confiscated Dion's lands and income and that resulted in the coup in which Dion replaced Dionysius II as tyrant. When Dion again attempted to implement Plato's ideas, factions under Heracleides revolted. Dion had him executed, and in turn his own friend, Callipus, assassinated him.

Plato's reactions to these events expressed in his *Seventh Letter* are the basis of the thesis here that his ideas were impractical to implement and they caused Syracuse to become destabilized. Instead of defending himself against this accusation, Plato blamed the turmoil and chaos that resulted in the licentiousness of Dionysius II and of the Syracusans themselves. It was Diogenes the Cynic who called Plato to account concerning his activities in Syracuse and Diogenes found Plato wanting in common sense and duplicitous. In Diogenes's eyes, Plato debased himself by his behavior in Dionysius II's court, and he failed to courageously follow the path of his teacher, Socrates. Also, a careful reading of the *Seventh Letter* shows that Plato misdirects the reader by focusing on Dionysius II's behavior rather than his own in answer to the accusation that he and his political ideas caused the turmoil in the city, which led to revolt and to the death of Dion and others.

It was Isocrates, also charged as Socrates was with undermining the youth, who explained in his defense that words alone are not enough to exonerate one's life against unjust charges.[28] There are words and then there is the character of the individual who says them. Character is judged by one's actions. The same is true of the Cynic's approach to truth-telling. One believes what another says because one believes in the character of the man who recounts what is purported to be true. From this study, we must conclude that Plato in his activities in Syracuse can be accused of duplicity in terms of what he said and what was the case. Thus, Diogenes was correct at least in this respect to bring Plato to account concerning his character and find it wanting.

---

[28] Isocrates, *Antidosis*, 88.

Jill Gordon[1]
Power/Knowledge in Syracuse or
Why the Digression in the *Seventh Letter* is Not a Digression

Introduction

Scholars presumably believe that the *Seventh Letter*'s discussion of names, definitions, image, knowledge and the thing itself (*onomata, logoi, eidolon, epistēmē, auto*, 342a-345b) takes the narrator's attention away from the letter's political concerns, and so consider it a "digression."[2] Perhaps, however, the digression is not a digression at all. The letter itself describes the discussion as a story and a wandering (*tōi muthōi kai planōi*, 344d), and it warrants investigation whether the passage is integral to the surrounding themes of the *Letter*. This exploration of *Seventh Letter* is inspired, in part, by Foucault's insights into knowledge and power, or more specifically, what he calls regimes of discourse and regimes of truth. It will address some of the views proffered in his 1971 *Lectures on the Will to Know*,[3] which provide a lens through which to view the *Letter* and to understand the function of the so-called digression as part of a continuous whole, comprising the political, the epistemic, and the discursive. The entire letter is a battle against false *logoi*, an attempt

---

[1] Jill Gordon is the Charles A. Dana Professor of Philosophy at Colby College. She is the author of *Plato's Erotic World: From Cosmic Origins to Human Death*, (Cambridge University Press, 2012); *Turning Toward Philosophy: Literary Device and Dramatic Structure in Plato's Dialogues*, (Penn State Press, 1999); and several journal articles in ancient Greek philosophy. She also publishes on philosophy of race, social philosophy, and economic justice.

[2] I take no position here on the authenticity of the letter, but will refer to its narrator; when I do refer to "Plato," I intend the personae of that narrator. My argument here does not depend on the authenticity of the letter as penned by Plato himself, but relies only on the letter's origins in the late classical period and its author's familiarity with Platonic work. There is a vast literature on the letter's authenticity, but I direct the reader to the most recent work on the issue which is a lively, thorough, and erudite resource, if slightly grouchy: Myles Burnyeat & Michael Frede, *The Pseudo-Platonic Seventh Letter*, edited by Dominic Scott, (New York, Oxford University Press, 2015).

[3] Michel Foucault, *Lectures on the Will to Know: Lectures at the Collège de France, 1970-1971*, edited by Arnold I. Davidson, (Palgrave McMillan, 2013). All page references to this text appear parenthetically in the text.

to persuade with true *logoi*, the inherent difficulty of each task, and the political stakes of that situation. In short, Foucault's work can help us see that the digression is not a digression after all.

In order to demonstrate that the so-called digression in the *Seventh Letter* is integral to the letter as a whole, I first present Foucault's genealogy of truth and explain how it bears on the *Letter*. Foucault's genealogy begins with the Homeric oath and ultimately links truth to discourse, and both truth and discourse to political power and justice in the classical period. In the second section of the essay I turn to the letter itself and show what type of document it is: a truth-telling document, as Foucault accounts for truth in the classical period. Then in part III I show that the "digression" addresses certain obstacles to truth telling and thus to power, rooting these obstacles in the limitations of discourse itself. In the final section, the argument turns to the rhetorical and sophistic regimes of truth that originate in Sicily, and the manner in which these are unstable *logoi* that challenge the narrator's vision of truth and power. The *Letter*, which can thus be read as a continuous whole, works against this instability, gesturing at establishing truth and power by way of a stable *logos*. At the same time, however, the *Letter* indicates that instability is inherent in word, definition, and image. The *Letter* thus raises challenging and perhaps paradoxical issues for knowledge, truth, power, and stability.

Genealogy of ancient regimes of truth

In his 1971 lectures, Foucault is beginning to formulate ideas about truth and power that appear later in his better-known work from the mid-1970s and early 1980s, though in a slightly different idiom. In this earlier work, Foucault traces two transitions in Greek institutional systems of truth: first, a transition from the archaic period to Solon, and second, a transformation from those early years of Athenian democracy into the late classical period. I situate the *Letter* against the background Foucault establishes regarding truth regimes, mindful of the concern in the classical period about the epistemic commitments and discursive practices of sophists and rhetoricians. This necessitates paying attention to what the *Letter* tells us about truth, which in turn, if Foucault's insights are correct, reveals something about what it has to tell us about power. Most importantly, it tells us something about the integral nature of the *Seventh Letter* and its "digression," which is my primary concern.

According to Foucault's genealogy, truth in the archaic period emerges from an *agōn,* or struggle, in which one party swears an oath as a challenge to another. By accepting or not accepting that challenge, the truth emerges through the struggle. "…[T]he assertion assumed or conceded does not fundamentally concern the truth of the proposition, but the speaking subject's will to hold to what he has said. The assertion belongs to the realm of the oath rather than to that of the factual observation" (62).

Foucault illustrates his view through two examples, both from the *Iliad*: the dispute regarding whether Antilochus cheated in a chariot race to overcome Menelaus, despite having weaker horses (23.565-614); and the scene on Achilles's shield depicting a dispute (18.497-509). I shall limit myself to his analysis of the first, which is representative of his fundamental point that truth is established in this archaic period through swearing an oath and making a challenge.[4] In this scene between Menelaus and Antilochus, Foucault tells us that, at first, Menelaus proposes to bring the case before the "guides" of the Argives for them to judge in front of the people. But

---

[4] The shield depicts two men in dispute, and Foucault says it includes these important characteristics: "Each judge is linked to sovereignty when he speaks [holding the scepter]. To give his view is to be, for a time at least, sovereign… Nevertheless, we can see that this is a very limited and partial sovereignty… Sovereignty intervenes only indirectly since it only judges the judges and is present only symbolically in the scepter held by the judges"; "the matter of the murder itself is not submitted to the judges… [They] do not intervene with regard to the offence; they intervene with regard to the application of the legal customs put to work by private individuals in order to regulate their disputes"; "the judges are in a secondary position…they do not have to tell the truth: they do not have to establish the truth of the facts, they have to say what must be done"; and finally, "Supporters of the two adversaries are pressing around the scene where the dispute unfolds… It is a whole group of which he [the litigant] is a part. It is this group, as a whole, which will win or lose. The individual is not a subject of right" (79-80).

then he immediately changes his mind and gives the judgment to himself. "And 'according to rule,' he proposes that Antilochus swear 'by he who holds up the earth, who shakes it' that he did not impede Menelaus's chariot… Antilochus gives way, acknowledging his fault (74)."[5] Foucault understands this episode as a kind of truth procedure in which "The truth is not what one says (or the relationship between what one says and what is or is not the case in fact). It is what one confronts, what one does or does not accept to face up to. It is the formidable force to which one surrenders. It is an autonomous force" (75). Even more vividly, he claims that in the archaic world,

> Truth does not have its seat in discourse…One approaches it through discourse; discourse, in the form of the oath and the imprecation, designates the person who has exposed himself to its unbearable gaze. If something is disclosed in the oath of truth, it is not what happened, it is not things themselves, but rather the defenseless nakedness of the person who agrees to being seized by it, or on the contrary the evasion of the person who tries to escape it…The power of the truth is not introduced by an arbitral intervention. One of the two parties throws down a challenge to the other…This means that the oath in which the truth is asserted always arises from the series of rivalries. It is a phase of the *agōn*, one of the faces of struggle. (75)

Foucault summarizes the elements of archaic truth as struggle, confrontation, challenge to make the oath of truth, and finally, confrontation with the gods (77).

> Truth is not observed; it is sworn: oath and imprecations. — The word of truth does not rest on what has been seen or experienced; it exposes itself to the possible future anger of the gods. — The word of truth does not disclose what has happened; although directed at the facts, it indicates the person who takes

---

[5] In his discussion of the depiction of an oath challenge on Achilles's shield, Foucault sees signs of the transition to come in which the power of judgment, truth, and discourse are transformed: the identification of political and juridical power; the substitution of written law for the *histōr*, or wise judge; and judgments based on established fact (81).

the risk, by excluding the person who declines the risk. — Finally, it does not found a just decision; through its specific effectiveness, it wins the day. (84)

As Foucault works to establish the points on which he will contrast archaic truth with truth in the classical period, he tells us that

> The non-verbal equivalent for the word of truth is the ordeal, the test, or being exposed or exposing someone to undefined danger. Taking the oath of truth or exposing oneself to the danger of blows, the thunderbolt, the sea, wild beast...In archaic judicial practice, the word of truth is not linked to light and looking at things; it is linked to the obscurity of the future and uncertain event. (85)

Hesiod's texts prove crucial, according to Foucault, in bridging the archaic and the classical modes of truth, moving the Greeks from truth as oath and ordeal in the archaic period, to truth as independent arbiter in the classical period. The fulcrum for this shift from this archaic to the classical notion of truth is *krineîn*, a particular kind of judgment that relies on deciding and discerning. Foucault sees in Hesiod two forms of "judgment," *dikazein* and *krineîn*, which he says are "correlative" (94), and most significant to his genealogy, *krineîn* "gradually occupies the whole space of Greek judicial practice" (90). The transition from the truth of the archaic period — truth rooted in *agōn* and the swearing of oaths to the gods, including *Dikē* and Zeus — relies on the emergence of *dikaion* from *Dikē*. In *dikaion*, as opposed to the god *Dikē*, justice and good judgment are now rooted in measure, balance, and order. In Hesiod's texts, these are evident in time cycles in human life and in cosmic movement; in planting and sowing; indebtedness and paying back; moments of promise and remittance. In short, *dikaion* is found in the cosmic order and the reflective order of the "works and days" of human life. "The decisive oath is replaced (or at least begins to be replaced) by the judgment-measure. At the same time, the truth-challenge, truth by ordeal is replaced by truth-knowledge" (108). The truth knowledge here in Hesiod is rooted in discerning the measure of time, in discerning the measure of labor, the measure of growing, and so forth. As an intermediate figure, then, Hesiod points the way forward in the long genealogy from the invocation of the divine *Dikē* to *dikaion*, from *dikaion* to *krinein*, and finally in the classical period, from *krinein* to *alētheia*, that is to say, a genealogy, beginning from Justice, then justice, then discernment, and finally truth.

Foucault turns to judicial institutions to find that in classical judicial practices truth emerges as a third entity, separate and independent of either of the two parties to a dispute. It is spoken by a literal third party, the witness, who is on neither one side nor the other (75). The witness conveys factual observation through speech, and truth decides between people (77).

> The decision of justice will have to be right (*juste*), the sentence will have to express *dikaion* and *alēthēs*, the just and the true, that which is fitted to the order of the world and things, and which restores this very order when it has been disturbed…[T]he knowledge which was linked to power…will now be linked to *dikaion*. Its primary role will be to ensure relations of justice, to help restore order, to put things back in their place and time. Knowledge will not be produced [in order] to triumph, master, and govern, so much as to enable and even constrain repayment of what is due. To be in the truth will be more to be in the just than to be in power. (120)

What we see developing in the Athenian court system is paradigmatic of this regime of truth, and knowing and telling the truth are bound up with justice.

Truth and Justice in the *Seventh Letter*

The *Seventh Letter* reflects this classical regime of truth in which judgment of truth is made on the facts of the matter as told by a witness. It makes truth claims, it presents its narrator as a witness and its audiences as judges of the truth, and it links judging and truth to justice.

> Plato to Dion's associates and friends, Greetings. You wrote to me that I ought to consider that your policy was the same as that which Dion had; and moreover you charged me to support it, so

far as I can, both by deed and word. Now if you really hold the same views and aims as he, I consent to support them, but if not, I will ponder the matter many times over. And what was his policy and his aim *I will tell you, and that as I may say, not from mere conjecture but from certain knowledge*... Dion... believed that the Syracusans ought to be free and dwell under the best laws... Now the manner in which these views originated is *a story well worth hearing for young and old alike, and I shall endeavor to narrate it to you from the beginning*; for at the present moment it is opportune. (323-324b, my emphasis)[6]

The letter announces in these early lines that it is based on the narrator's knowledge of events and that it is something worth hearing.[7] Its narrator bears witness to facts that will adjudicate the truth for the hearers of the letter, and the letter aims to convey a truth over against rumors or falsities that are circulating among Dion's friends.[8] These introductory themes resonate with Foucault's understanding of changes in Greek notions of truth and justice, and they will help to shed light on the "digression," which raises concerns about the limitations of names, definitions, images, and knowledge. The inherent limitations of these likewise limit justice.

Before saying anything about his voyages to Syracuse or the righteousness of Dion, the narrator begins with Socrates's treatment at the hands of the Thirty, which grounds the connections between truth and justice. He says that in his youthful mind, he assumed that the Thirty would lead the city from an unjust way of life to a just way of life (*ek tinos adikou biou epi dikaion*, 324d). In a short time, however,

---

[6] R.G. Bury, Translator, *Epistles*, "Seventh Letter," Loeb Classical Library, (Harvard University Press, 1989). All quotations come from this edition.

[7] Hearing is the counterpart to witnessing, and thus we and the audience of the letter shall know the truth by hearing it from its author. Hearing and listening are clearly thematized in the letter, as evidenced by their frequent appearance: 335a ff.; 337e; 338e, 339a; 339e; 340c; 341b ff. Though listening could arguably be considered different from hearing, see Sophie Hartounian-Gordon, "Listening —in a Democratic Society," *Philosophy of Education Yearbook* (2003): 1-18.

[8] This project does not address Foucault's work on *parrhesia*, "plain speaking" or "truth-telling," which he develops later, in the early 1980s.

Jill Gordon

he saw that this was not true, and above all, he saw the previous regime in the city as a golden age, by comparison, when he saw how the Thirty treated Socrates, who is described here as "the most just" (*dikaiotaton*, 324e). Plato thus makes it clear here that he is testifying about the just and the unjust. The Thirty Tyrants constituted a regime that could treat the most just unjustly. Plato moves quickly from the regime of the Thirty, whose demise led him to believe again that he might participate in politics, to the indictment and execution of Socrates under the democracy, which forever convinced him that the tribes of humanity will have no freedom from evils until the correct and true philosophers rule or those in power in the cities have a divine share in philosophy (326a-b). This, he tells us, was his mindset when he arrived for the first time in Sicily. These opening pages of the letter thus establish Plato's purpose—to tell the truth or bear witness—and his state of mind—convinced that the wrong people were in power everywhere and that he did not, as a result, wish to participate in politics.

The narrator then introduces the connection between *logos* and politics, thus unveiling a regime of truth, which enriches the narrative leading up to the so-called digression:

> How can I say that my coming to Sicily then was the beginning of all these disasters? Dion was a young man at that time, and in our conversations I imparted to him (*mēnuōn dia logōn*) my ideas of human welfare and urged him to put them into practice; and in so doing I was secretly, and all unwittingly, working for the future destruction of the tyranny. (326e-327a)

Tracing this link between *logos* and politics through the first half of the *Letter* highlights its thematic role and consequently puts the digression in a new light. Just after the passage cited above, Plato emphasizes that the quick-witted Dion grasped his arguments (*logous*, 327a) and that he came to embody in action what he had grasped from right argument (*orthōn logōn*, 327c). These passages convey clearly that instruction through *logoi* can lead to the overthrow of tyranny. The particular *logoi* that Dion heard and acquired under Plato's tutelage led to his desire for the noblest and best life and, ultimately, to attempt to overthrow the tyrant. Before that happened, however, Dion and Plato made several attempts to get that future tyrant, Dionysius II, to hear the correct *logos* from Plato. Plato also tells us that Dion urged his visit to Syracuse because the time was right because of his (Dion's) own power (*tēn hautou dunamin*, 328a) in Syracuse, the youth of Dionysius, and the extent of the empire in Italy. Now, if ever, Dion urged, was the time to see philosophers rule in the great cities (327e-328a). The *Letter* conveys that *logos* plays a central role in that possibility.

Plato takes on the task with some trepidation of failure, and in his dreams he is urged to bring *logos* in the form of arguments and persuasion to Dion and to Syracuse. At one point he imagines the voice of Dion, saying, "O Plato, I come to you as an exile not to beg for foot-soldiers, nor because I lack horse-soldiers to ward off mine enemies, but to beg for arguments and persuasion (*logōn kai peithous*), whereby you above all, as I know, are able to convert young men to what is good and just and thereby to bring them always into a state of mutual friendliness and comradeship" (328d-e). Upon his arrival, Plato finds that Dion's name is mired in slander (*diabolōn*, 329b), and his fear increases now, lest Dionysius take him as a further threat because of his associations with Dion. One cannot help but think of the same slander that undoes Socrates, as described in Plato's *Apology* (18d, 20c, 20d, 20e, and 28a), a poignant case of *logos* aimed at truth and justice. Clearly the *Letter* indicates that Plato must bring true *logos* to Syracuse to prevent another injustice from happening. And further, he must undo another *logos*, the false *logos* circulating about Dion's intentions.

After describing Dionysius's disguised abduction of him in Syracuse, Plato reports the need to expose the truth of what was really happening: "But what were the facts? For the truth must be told" (*to d'eiche dē pōs? To gar alēthes dei phrazein*, 330a). This narration typifies Foucault's description of the new regime of truth ushered in to classical Greece. Plato thinks the best way to convince Dionysius that he was his special friend, and closer to him than to Dion, was to occupy the young tyrant with learning and listening to Plato; nonetheless, Dionysius continued to be distracted by the talk of the slanderers (*tous tōn diaballontōn logous*, 330b) and fearing the success of Dion's designs against him. Plato carried on nonetheless, hoping Dionysius might develop a genuine desire for philosophy.

On Plato's second visit to Syracuse, the concerns with words, language, and political power continue. He prefaces the tale of his second visit with an apt analogy that again highlights the political role of *logos* (330c-331d). The doctor would only counsel the patient who could listen to the advice and benefit from it by changing her actions accordingly; likewise, with diseased regimes, the good man knows when to stop giving counsel to a regime or ruler that will not listen to the advice.

> So likewise it behooves the man of sense to hold, while he lives, the same view concerning his own State: if it appears to him to be ill governed he ought to speak (*legein men*), if [it] so be that his speech is not likely to prove fruitless nor to cause his death (*ei melloi mēte mataiōs erein mēte apothaneisthai legōn*)... (331c-d)

Speaking the truth can right the city, but not always. Anticipating the themes introduced by the "digression," we can see here that there are limitations to *logos*. It is possible that a true *logos*, such as sound advice to a ruler, can go unheeded, and a false *logos*, such as the false rumors that circulate about Dion, can be persuasive.

A central aim of Plato's counsel to Dionysius—expressed in unclear and veiled *logos* (*legontes ouk enargōs ho'utōs, ou gar hēn asphales, ainittomenoi de kai diamachomenoi tois logois…*, 332d) for reasons of safety—was that the tyrant needed to cultivate more loyal friends in order to create and sustain lasting political power. "And if he had pursued the course we described (*legomen*) and made himself right minded (*emphrona*) and sober minded (*sōphrona*)," then he could have united the cities of Sicily against the barbarians and had twice the empire of his father (332d-333a).

The letter goes on to relate what one might describe as Dionysius's inability to discern (*krinein*) the true from the false. He listens to the slanderers and what they say (*ho de tois diaballousin hupēkousen kai legousin…*, 333b) about Dion and Dion's motives instead of seeing Dion's acts as an attempt to improve the power of

Power/Knowledge in Syracuse?

Syracuse, and Dionysius himself (333b-c). The contested ground here is most assuredly things said and whether they attach to some truth or not. And, Dionysius's failures, even those we might consider his moral failures, are attached to this failure at hearing the correct *logos*, hearing *logoi* correctly, and getting the truth. The problem, of course, was that these slanderous *logoi* triumphed in Syracuse (*tauta tote enikēse kai to deuteron en Surakosiois legomena...*, 333c), Plato failed in his attempts to persuade, and Dionysius acted against Dion.

The narrator concludes this segment of the letter saying emphatically "This is my *logos*" (*ho g'emos logos*, 334c). Stressing the point, he says again that "these are the words I said" (*ego legōn tauta*, 334c), and had Dionysius or the slanderers listened and been persuaded by these *logoi*, perhaps justice, power, and philosophy might have been joined together in the same person (335c-d). There is power in words and arguments, and their power can upset a tyranny. Perhaps.

In the final segment of the *Letter* preceding the so-called digression, the narrator again says he is bound by justice to tell the truth (*Dikaios dē legein eimi t'alēthes*, 339a), reconfirming the *Letter* as a truth telling *logos*, a witness's testimony to matters of fact. The narrator tells the reader that once again the recurring argument (*palin ho logos*, 339a) was that Plato should not betray Dion and so must go again to Syracuse to see whether any of the reports were true that Dionysius had great desire for philosophy (339d-e).

He investigates the rumors that Dionysius is keen on philosophy and finds out the truth of the matter by way of a test (*elenchon*, 340b). There exists a method for testing (*esti dē tis tropos tou peri ta toiauta peiran lambanein*), he tells us, which is not ignoble (*ouk agennēs*, 340b) and which works well with tyrants: show them how arduous will be the task, what many things will need be done, and then see whether they are still enthused for the task (340b-341a). This test, he says, is most clear and most infallible in separating out those ready, and those not ready, to study philosophy. When he told Dionysius that there was this test, the young tyrant simply replied that he already was sufficiently informed about Plato's doctrines (341a). The narrator famously tells his readers: "There does not exist, nor will there ever

Jill Gordon

exist, any treatise of mine dealing therewith." (*oukoun emon ge peri auton esti suggramma oude mēpote genētai*, 341c). The digression begins here with its discussion of word, argument, image, and knowledge.

The So-Called Digression

The digression is itself a demonstration of the very test the author of the letter is referring to. If the audience of the letter can get through this difficult passage, then the narrator may know whether they are serious about grasping the truth and creating justice in Syracuse. In this way already, the digression seems more of a piece with the rest of the *Letter*, but there are deeper reasons for viewing the digression as an integral part of the rest of the *Letter* and its concerns about truth and *logoi*.

The arduous piece of philosophizing, looks like this in a simplified form:[9] There is a true argument (*tis logos alēthēs*, 342a) that the narrator has frequently laid out in the past, and it points to the weakness of language or *logos* (*dia to tōn logōn asthenes*, 343a). In order to have perfect knowledge (*teleōs epistēmēs*, 342d) of any thing in-itself, one must grasp four other things: its name, its definition, its image, and then knowledge—a knowledge of these three preceding things. The soul endeavors to know the thing itself, which the *Letter* emphasizes is fixed and stable (*bebaios*, 343b),[10] but the instruments of

---

[9] I do not intend this to be a detailed analysis of the "digression," but rather an argument for its being continuous with the whole of the letter on philosophical and political grounds. There are, of course, many fine works on the Seventh Letter's "digression," and I consulted the following: Giorgio Agamben and Julia Schiesari, "The Thing Itself," *Substance* 16:2 (1987): 18-28; Francisco J. Gonzalez, "Nonpropositional Knowledge in Plato," *Apeiron* 31:3 (1998): 235-84; Andrew Hull, *The Mystery of the Seventh Platonic Epistle: An Analysis of the Philosophical Digression*, Doctoral Dissertation, Emory College of Arts and Sciences (2012); V. Bradley Lewis, "The Rhetoric of Philosophical Politics in Plato's 'Seventh Letter,'" *Philosophy and Rhetoric* 33:1 (2000): 23-38; Eric W. Robinson, "The Sophists and Democracy Beyond Athens," *Rhetorica* 25:1 (2007): 109-22; and Harold Tarrant, "Middle Platonism and the Seventh Epistle," *Phronesis* 28:1 (1983): 75-103.

[10] Cognates of this term appear four times in just this portion of the Stephanus page at 343b. One could perhaps make the argument that the inherent instability in *logos* corresponds to an inherent instability in political power, both as depicted in the *Seventh Letter* and in other Platonic texts.

knowledge (name, definition, and image) give the soul what it is not seeking, namely stability, and instead fill everyone with the utmost perplexity and confusion (*aporias te kai asapheias epimplēsi pasēs hōs epos epein pant'andra*, 343c). We prove capable of using and testing the four components of knowledge, but we do not do so well grasping the real thing itself. "And so with each of the Four, their inaccuracy is an endless topic..." (343b). When it comes to answering questions or making explanations about the thing itself, the *Letter* tells us:

> [A]nyone who is able and willing to upset the argument gains the day, and makes the person who is expounding his view by speech or writing or answers (*en logois hē grammasin hē apokrisesi*) appear to most of his hearers to be wholly ignorant of the subjects about which he is attempting to write or speak; for they are ignorant sometimes of the fact that it is not the soul of the writer or speaker that is being convicted (*hē lexantos elenchetai*) but the nature of each of the Four, which is essentially defective (343d-e).

The names, definitions, and images are essentially defective, and can thus be manipulated in such a way as to be refuted, but the speaker's soul, or perhaps the things themselves, have not necessarily thus been refuted. This is a rhetorical outcome one might commonly see in sophistic, and it resonates with the concerns expressed in the early passages of the *Letter* that the friends of Dion will believe the rumors and not know the truth that the *Letter* is trying to convey. It matters very much then that names, *logoi*, images, and knowledge attach to stable things.

Mirroring Foucault's account of the classical view of truth in which *dikaion* is central, the *Letter* then claims that neither quickness in learning nor good memory makes someone capable of knowing the thing itself. Rather, only the person who is naturally akin to justice and all other forms of beauty (*hoste hoposoi tōn dikaiōn te kai tōn allōn hosa kala*, 344a) can attain truth. And even in those instances, only after much labor, after names, definitions, images and other things have been rubbed together, kneaded over time (*tribomena*), asking and answering questions, directing all their human powers—

only then can the spark of illumination come to the nature of anything (344b). The narrator concludes by saying that every serious man avoids putting his most serious work in writing, but instead it "abides in the fairest regions he possesses" (*keitai de pou en chōra tai kallistē tōn toutou*, 344c). This cryptic, but utterly Platonic, claim is fitting. Even those naturally akin to justice will still need to engage in serious dialectic in order to spark any illumination about reality, and due to the inherent limitations of names, definitions, and images, writing will not capture or convey that reality.

Immediately after his discussion of the inherent limitations of names, definitions, images, and knowledge, the narrator appeals to those who are following along (*ho sunepispomenos*, 344d), and calls what the followers have been following a "story and wandering" (*tōi muthōi te kai planōi*, 344d). This particular description of the passage surprisingly furthers the case that the so-called digression is integral to the rest of the *Letter*.

While the Greek term *planō* is now canonically translated as "digression," it has various meanings. It is, first of all, a different term than what is used in the *Theaetetus*. There, the word translated as "digression" is *parergon*, which refers to something that is beside the main subject, subordinate to what is central, a secondary concern, an appendix, an ancillary purpose.[11] In *Theaetetus* Socrates declares somewhat abruptly, "But this is a digression. —Let us turn away from these matters." (*Theaetetus*, 177b). The term, *planō*, in the *Letter* means a wandering, a roaming. It can indicate continuity among the *Letter*'s themes, not discontinuity. The limitations of names, definitions, and images—that is to say, the limitations of *logos*, broadly construed—are central not peripheral to the narrator's political concerns in the *Letter*, and the *Letter* wanders through these subjects. The links between the limitations of *logos* and the narrator's political concerns echo similar concerns expressed in Plato's dialogues. We have seen already the degree to which the *Letter* aims

---

[11] Liddell-Scott-Jones, *Greek-English Lexicon*, accessed through Perseus Project, www.perseus.tufts.edu. *Planō* can also mean deception, but that meaning is unlikely in this context. See also *Phaedrus*, 274a where a cognate of *parergon* is again used. See also *Republic* 411e, 477b, and 498a. See also *Phaedo* 91a.

to speak out against rumors, to establish stability (*bebaios*) and truth, and to link these to stable and true politics. The attitude of the *Seventh Letter* is consistent with the *Apology's* portrayal of the power of the rumors that helped to undo Socrates and with the anxiety over sophistry that animates Plato and other thinkers in the late classical period, especially the anxiety over unstable meaning of words and unstable objects of knowledge.[12] This highlights exactly what is at stake in the *Seventh Letter* and what power underlies the new regime of truth defended in the *Letter*. Name, definition, and word are all powerful, despite their limitations; they can be used to persuade one of false rumors or create paranoia in a ruler about those who aim to help the city, but they can also be used to persuade a young tyrant to practice philosophy or to persuade the friends of Dion that he aimed to benefit Syracuse and her allies.

Lest we think in terms of a clean binary of truth and falsity, things in themselves and images of them, however, the *Letter* quite muddies these waters. Yes, the narrator aims to expose the truth, and yes the narrator is concerned about the power of the false rumors, and yes he links truth to justice. But he is also saying that there is something inherent to the *logos* that will always prevent our fully grasping truth, and hence will prevent perfect justice.

Knowledge/Power in Syracuse

Sicily is the birthplace of the self-conscious use of unstable discourse in the exercise of political power. There we see the origins of a certain kind of unstable *logos*. Tisias and Corax are taken to have invented rhetorical techniques that make their way into the public or political sphere.[13] Though uncredited, Marcel Detienne's 1967 work,

---

[12] For example, Book 4 of Aristotle's *Metaphysics* Γ.

[13] See, for example, D.A.G. Hinks, "Tisias and Corax and the Invention of Rhetoric," *Classical Quarterly* 34:1/2 (1940): 61-69; and Thomas Cole, "Who Was Corax?" *Illinois Classical Studies* 16:1/2 (1991): 65-81. Of course there are examples of unstable *logoi*, and of authors' self-conscious reliance on them before Tisias and Corax. The particular type of political uses of their rhetoric, however, place them at the beginning of the kind of rhetoric that poses political and epistemic anxiety among the philosophers of the classical era.

Jill Gordon

The Masters of Truth in Archaic Greece, supplies much of the theory behind Foucault's 1971 lectures, focusing on this unstable *logos*.[14]

Detienne tells us that "Both sophistry and rhetoric, which appeared with the advent of the Greek city, were forms of thought founded on ambiguity. This is not only because they developed in the political sphere, the particular world of ambiguity, but also because they defined themselves as instruments that formulated the theory and logic of ambiguity and made effective action on that same level of ambiguity possible" (116). As Foucault echoes in his own lectures,[15] Detienne indicates that sophistry and rhetoric threaten or perhaps destroy stable truth discourse. "In a fundamentally ambiguous world, these mental techniques allowed the domination of men through the power of ambiguity itself" (118). Detienne locates power in the very aspect of the *logos* that worries the narrator of the *Letter*, namely, the political use of ambiguity: "Discourse was certainly an instrument, but not a way to know reality. *Logos* was a reality in itself, but not a signifier pointing to the signified. In this type of speech there was no distance between words and things" (118). Detienne explains how Sicilian rhetoric disrupted the type of truth that the narrator of the *Letter* wishes to defend: "The power of *logos* is immense: it brings pleasure, dispels worries, fascinates, persuades, and changes things as though by magic. At this level, *logos* never attempts to tell *Alētheia*... Sophistry and rhetoric were thus beyond the scope of *Alētheia*" (118- 119).[16]

---

[14] Marcel Detienne, *The Masters of Truth in Archaic Greece*, with a forward by Pierre Vidal-Naquet, translated by Janet Lloyd, Zone Books, New York, 1996. I will cite this text parenthetically in the main body of the chapter. Detienne's influence is telegraphed by Foucault, *Lectures on the Will to Know*, 96, where he refers to Solon and Empedocles as "masters of truth," and it is evident in substantive theoretical ways throughout the lectures. The translator and editors of Foucault's lectures note various connections to Detienne's work, and Daniel Defert also discusses Detienne in his essay, "Course Context," included in the Foucault volume, 262-86.

[15] Foucault, *Lectures on the Will to Know*, 62 ff.

[16] See also Detienne, *The Masters of Truth in Archaic Greece*, 133-34 on Parmenides and the Eleatic effect on *alētheia*, which also causes this same kind of anxiety; and see Vidal-Naquet's foreword, in that same volume, 11.

Power/Knowledge in Syracuse?

What the *Letter* aims to do is to tether justice (*dikaion*) to truth (*alētheia*). What is needed for that is a stable *logos*—a way for names, definitions, arguments and knowledge to attach to justice itself, and for justice to be true justice. Such a knowledge regime, whether discursive or political, might combat the slanderers and sophists, and secure a place for those who give witness to truth and justice. Although in a manner true to Platonic ambiguity, it might not. The so-called digression is therefore an integral part of the narrator's attempts to bring truth and justice to Syracuse and, at the same time, to recognize the inherent limitations of the means to do that.

Francisco J. Gonzalez[1]
Did Heidegger go to Syracuse?

Martin Heidegger's involvement with National Socialism in the 1930s has been often compared to Plato's trip to Syracuse supposedly to put into practice his ideal of 'philosopher-kings' by converting the tyrant of Syracuse, Dionysius II, to philosophy. In both cases we are meant to see nothing more than the disastrous consequences of philosophers getting involved in politics. The argument of this essay, however, is that the comparison is a complete misrepresentation of the politics of both Plato and Heidegger. The differences between the views of these two thinkers on the relation between politics and philosophy are so great as to allow for no meaningful parallel between their two stories of political engagement. Heidegger did not go to Syracuse, never pursuing a project even remotely similar to that of Plato, and Plato would have found Heidegger's own politics utterly incomprehensible, even deeply repugnant.[2]

Before turning to this argument, we should note that the connection between Heidegger and Syracuse is often made with the purpose of *defending* Heidegger.[3] Thus Gadamer chose "Back from Syracuse?" as the title for his response to the book by Victor Farias[4],

---

[1] Francisco J. Gonzalez is Professor of Philosophy at the University of Ottawa. His publications include *Dialectic and Dialogue: Plato's Practice of Philosophical Inquiry* (Northwestern, 1998) and *Plato and Heidegger: A Question of Dialogue* (Penn State, 2009); Email: fgonzal2@uottawa.ca

[2] In an earlier article, "Heidegger's 1933 Misappropriation of Plato's Republic," in *Ermeneutica e Filosofia Antica*, F. Trabattoni and M. Bergomi, eds. (Milan: Cisalpino, 2012), 63-119, I defend a similar thesis, though there through a reading of the *Republic* and of Heidegger's writings as published at the time, i.e., not including the *Schwarze Hefte*.

[3] Though not always. Hugo Ott, certainly no apologist for Heidegger, finds the parallel between Heidegger's rectorship and Plato's trip to Syracuse so obvious that, without any explicit reference to Plato and therefore any justification, he simply entitles his chapter on the aftermath of Heidegger's rectorship, "Back from Syracuse" (*Martin Heidegger: Unterwegs zu seiner Biographie* [Frankfurt am Main: Campus Verlag, 1992], 249-54).

[4] Published in English as *Heidegger and Nazism* (Philadelphia: Temple U. Press, 1989).

which made the case that Heidegger's involvement with National Socialism, far from being a naive or innocent mistake, had deep roots in his philosophy. Gadamer explains his choice of title as follows:

> That Heidegger's revolution in the universities failed, and that his involvement in the cultural politics of the Third Reich was a sad story we watched at a distance with anxiety, has led many to think about what Plato came up against in Syracuse. Indeed, after Heidegger resigned from the rectorate, one of his Freiburg friends, seeing him in the streetcar, greeted him: 'Back from Syracuse?'[5]

The clear suggestion here is that Heidegger's involvement with National Socialism was simply unfortunate in the same way as was Plato's trip to Sicily: like Plato he entered politics with the good, if naïve, intention of political reform (in particular, reform of the university) and was defeated by the hard facts of political reality. In both cases we have nothing more than a 'sad story'.

The same apologetic purpose of tying Heidegger to Syracuse is even more explicit in Hannah Arendt's celebratory text, "Heidegger at Eighty":

> Now we all know that Heidegger, too, once succumbed to the temptation to change his 'residence' and to get involved in the world of human affairs. As to the world, he was served somewhat worse than Plato because the tyrant and his victims were not located beyond the sea, but in his own country. As to Heidegger himself, I believe that the matter stands differently. He was still young enough to learn from the shock of the collision, which after ten short hectic months thirty-seven years ago drove him back to his residence, and to settle in his thinking what he had experienced ...

Arendt here manages to use the comparison with Plato to Heidegger's advantage. First, Heidegger's story was even sadder than Plato's because he had to endure the tyrant and his victims at

---

[5] Trans. John McCumber, *Critical Inquiry* 15, vol. 2 (Winter 1989): 429.

home rather than across the sea. Secondly, he nevertheless managed better than Plato, perhaps because of his greater youth, to learn from his mistake. Despite these differences, what they both share, according to Arendt, is being victims of the perennial opposition between the residence of the thinker and the world of political affairs. This enables her to characterize Heidegger's involvement with the Führer as *"a déformation professionelle"* therefore shared by Plato and every other philosopher.[6]

This strategy is still employed by apologists for Heidegger today. In the context of a contribution to a volume on Heidegger and the Jews, Gérard Guest suggests that the motivation for the *Rektoratsrede* was 'Platonic' and could be attributed to what he calls the "Syracuse complex."[7] Barbara Cassin, faced with the revelations of the *Black Notebooks* to be discussed below, has echoed Arendt's 'apology' in commenting: "Philosophers love tyrants, it's a déformation professionelle."[8] We can articulate as follows the assumptions being made here: 1) Plato's failure in Syracuse was the result of naively believing that the ideal republic existing only in the sky of his philosophical theory could be realized here on earth and that philosophical knowledge could be an adequate substitute for political judgment; 2) Heidegger's failure in Nazi Germany was the result of naively believing that his philosophy of being could be translated into politics and that the philosopher could be the real Führer of a political movement. Both of these assumptions, I wish to argue here, are false.

Plato as Political Realist in the Seventh Letter

The first point to make with regard to Plato is that, contrary to what is often assumed, the project of Plato, Dion and his followers had nothing to do with 'wiping the slate clean' and imposing on Syracuse

---

[6] Hannah Arendt, "Martin Heidegger at Eighty," *New York Review of Books*, October 21, 1971.
[7] *Heidegger et les 'Juifs'*, *La Régle du Jeu* 58/59 (September 2015): 140.
[8] Cited in François Rastier, *Naufrage d'un prophète: Heidegger aujourd'hui* (Paris: PUF, 2015), 172. To this Rastier rightly retorts: "Or, les philosophes victimes des tyrans sont cent fois plus nombreux que ceux qui les ont servis" (173).

Francisco J. Gonzalez

something like the state described in the *Republic*.⁹ Plato indeed explains his trips to Syracuse by expressing his shame at appearing to himself to be nothing but empty words (παντάπασι λόγος μόνον ἀτεχνῶς τις), unwilling to undertake any deed (ἔργον, 328c7-8). He could therefore be said to have gone to put his ideas into effect. But what ideas? Plato speaks of τὰ διανοηθέντα περὶ νόμων τε καὶ πολιτείας (328b10-c1). So what are these thoughts on laws and the constitution?[10] One political doctrine Plato articulates in the letter, what he calls the thought about the city (διανοούμενον περὶ πόλεως, 331c8) that the man of sense must live by, is the following: if one finds a city badly governed, to speak out if one's words will be neither vain nor suicidal, but not to impose a political change on the city with violence in a case where it cannot become better without expulsions and massacres, keeping in this case quiet while praying for the best for oneself and the city (331c9-d6). These are hardly the words of an ideological revolutionary![11] The other political doctrine that Plato

---

[9] I reject both Michael Frede's argument against the letter's authenticity based on the political content (for reasons presented below), as well as Myles Burnyeat's argument based on the philosophical content (because it depends on an idea of what makes philosophical sense that is apparently peculiar to Burnyeat; for a different idea, see my reading of the philosophical digression in ch. 9 of *Dialectic and Dialogue: Plato's Practice of Inquiry* [Northwestern, 1998]), both found in *The Seventh Platonic Letter: A Seminar*, ed. Dominic Scott (Oxford University Press, 2015). Nevertheless, I find quite persuasive the general historical objections to authenticity outlined by Frede (3-40) (the letter is suspect, in short, because of the company it keeps) as well as the stylistic objections, some of which are presented by Burnyeat in the same volume (193-95). So all references below to 'Plato' are to the character thus presented in the letter and make no claim concerning Plato's authorship of the letter.

[10] M. Isnardi Parenti rightly comments that Plato is not speaking here of the ideas presented in the *Republic* (*Platone: Lettere* [Mondadori, 2002], 220-21).

[11] One must therefore wonder how Luc Brisson can suggest that Plato is the kind of advisor "qui pretend changer radicalement l'équilibre des forces en presence, sans se plier à quelque négociation et à quelque compromis que ce soit" (*Platon: Lettres,* 4th ed. [Paris: Flammarion, 2004], 55). As Isnardi Parenti notes, many have seen in this prohibition of violent revolution evidence of the dialogue's inauthenticity since they see it as inconsistent with Plato's position in the *Republic* (220, 223).

claims to form part of his advice is that neither Sicily nor any other city should be subject to despotic rulers, but only to laws (334c7-9).[12] Despotism can appeal only to people who are servile and who know nothing, neither in the present time nor the time to come (*kairos*), about what is good and just, either human or divine (334d2-6). As for the reform Dion sought in acceding to power,[13] Plato describes it as simply the introduction of good order by making good laws for his citizens, freeing the rest of Sicily from barbarians, and through such acts showing what the virtues of a just, courageous, temperate and philosophical man can achieve (335e-336b). Another related principle the letter articulates is that the victors should show themselves even more submissive to the laws than the vanquished (337c8-d2). In short, what Dion wanted is what Plato himself wanted: a constitution of just and noble laws obtained without any assassinations or expulsions (351c4-6). There is therefore no suggestion here of 'wiping the slate clean'.

If Plato does not have the naiveté of thinking that he can realize his ideal republic in Syracuse, this is because the letter shows him to be fully aware of the fact that good governance depends on factors over which philosophy has no control. First, a central idea here is that one must always wait for the 'opportune moment' (καιρός) to speak and act. Plato would not now be writing this letter to Dion's companions if it were not the opportune moment for what he has to say (324b7-8). In the political upheavals of his youth, he always looked for the opportune moment to act (326a1). He is first persuaded to come to Syracuse in part by Dion's claim that this is the opportune moment Plato has been waiting for (327e3). But there is also the

---

[12] Isnardi Parenti characterizes Plato's advice here as being only as much as he considers possible for a city that already exists and has a complex history (226).

[13] Jürgen Sprute assumes that Plato's aim in going to Syracuse was the realization of his political ideals in the *Republic*, but he argues that *Dion* in contrast acted out of purely private interests ("Dions Syrakusanische Politik und die Politischen Ideale Platons," *Hermes* 100, no. 3 [1972]: 299, 301) and that Plato's personal attachment blinded him to this fact (312). The opposite conclusion regarding Dion's motives is reached by Kurt von Fritz (*Platon in Sizilien und das Problem der Philosophenherrschaft* [Berlin: Walter de Gruyter, 1968], 63-108).

recognition that one must contend with chance as well as with the character of the Sicilian people and the power structures currently in place.¹⁴ This is why Plato goes to Syracuse not with naive optimism, but with *fear*, both the second time (φόβος, 328b3)¹⁵ and even more the third time (πολλὰ δεδιώς, 340a3), despite in the last case not considering it impossible for a young man like Dionysius II to be possessed with ἔρως for the best life (339e3-6). Fear is the proper disposition of a politics that recognizes its dependence on chance.

It is important in this context to note that Plato does not need Sicily to dispel any illusions he might have had with regard to politics, having been disillusioned much earlier by Athenian politics. Furthermore, philosophy is the *consequence* of his disillusionment with politics rather than the cause. The letter does not depict Plato as someone who starts with philosophy and then makes an ill-advised foray into politics. He begins with politics, deciding early on to dedicate himself to "the common matters of the city" (τὰ κοινὰ τῆς πόλεως, 324b10). After the fall of the Thirty he is once again possessed by "the desire to practice those things that are common and pertain to the city" (ἡ περὶ τὸ πράττειν τὰ κοινὰ καὶ πολιτικὰ ἐπιθυμία, 325a10-b1). He soon saw the difficulty, however, of correctly managing political affairs (325c10-d1). Indeed, his head started spinning (ἰλλιγιᾶν) with all the political upheaval, but he kept always on the lookout for the opportune moment to take action (τοῦ δὲ πράττειν αὖ περιμένειν αἰεὶ καιρούς, 326a1). He soon came to see that all cities were so badly governed that a great amount of work *along with chance* (μετὰ τύχης, 326a5)¹⁶ would be required for

---

[14] Raül Garrigasait Colomès has rightly drawn attention to the emphasis the letter places on the importance of chance in every political endeavor (*Cartes* [Barcelona: Fundació Bernat Metge, 2009], 31).

[15] On the significance of these apprehensions, see V. Bradley Lewis,"The *Seventh Letter* and the Unity of Plato's Political Philosophy," *The Southern Journal of Philosophy* 38 [2000]: 233.

[16] The necessity to contend with chance in politics is a theme that runs throughout the letter. This is why it seems simply wrong to assert that Plato was convinced of the "absolute efficacy" of his counsels (Brisson, *Platon*, 54-55).

change.[17] It is at this point that Plato introduces the need for philosophy, claiming that it is what enables us to see what is just, both in the political sphere and in the individual (326a7-8). There will be, he concludes, no end to evil for the human species until true philosophers assume political power or current rulers begin to philosophize through some divine dispensation (326a9-b3).[18]

Kings becoming philosophers?

But is it not clear that what Plato therefore seeks to do in Sicily is realize his idea that philosophers should be kings and kings philosophers and is it not this that entitles us to speak of his political naiveté? Plato indeed appears to go to Syracuse with the hope of the same people becoming philosophers and rulers of great cities (328a-b). But did Plato really go to Syracuse with the truly naive intention of turning Dionysius II into the kind of expert philosopher idealized in the *Republic*?[19] This is often simply assumed and common translations of what Plato says at 330a8-b1 indeed make this assumption quite natural: "How this best could have come about [winning Plato's praise and friendship], if at all, was through his becoming my disciple and associating with me in discourse about philosophy" (Glenn R. Morrow).[20] But this talk of Dionysius II becoming Plato's disciple is not there in the Greek, which is indeed much more ambiguous: "He shrank from the best way in which this

---

[17] See Lewis, "The *Seventh Letter*," 236.

[18] Colomès notes that the sequence of facts recounted by the letter enables us to see "a Plato very different from that daydreamer and constructor of ideal cities that certain views today tend to present him as. The desire to participate in public matters does not take its initiative from a prior conception of the 'perfect city'; Plato does not approach the city with his vision resting on a celestial model; the philosopher, in fact, does not approach the city because he is already there" (29; my translation).

[19] Isnardi Parenti speaks of Plato's great imprudence in trying to turn Dionysius into a philosopher (xviii).

[20] Likewise: "Mais il hésitait à prendre pour cela le meilleur moyen, à supposer que ce moyen existait, c'est-à-dire, bien sûr, se familiariser avec moi et me fréquenter comme élève et comme auditeur de mon enseignement philosophique" (Brisson); "frequentarmi, ascolatare le mie lezioni, imparare le mie dottrine filosofische" (Isnardi Parenti).

could come about, if it could come about: to associate and become familiar with me as would one listening to and learning what I have to say about philosophy." Plato says simply that Dionysius II could best win his friendship by associating with him in conversation; as for what Plato would have to say in such conversation, its philosophical content would comprise no more than talk *about* philosophy. Indeed, what Plato in the end had to say to Dionysius II about philosophy appears to have been no more than what was required by "the anti-tyrant test": a simultaneously protreptic and apotreptic description of both the great rewards and the great difficulties of studying philosophy. What awakened earlier in Dion a desire for the best and most beautiful life (327c9-d2) is precisely this kind of συνουσία with Plato. What Dionysius II's failure of the anti-tyrant test is said to show is that he, in contrast, is not capable of "living with care for intelligence and virtue" (φρονήσεως τε καὶ ἀρετῆς ζῆν ἐπιμελούμενος, 345b4-5).

As for Dionysius II's book, Plato makes it clear that Dionysius II based it on what he heard *from others*, not from Plato. Here too translations are misleading. A literal translation would read as follows: "Many things I neither discussed nor Dionysius sought to hear. For he pretended to know himself many and the most important things and to possess them sufficiently *on the basis of what he had heard from others* (διὰ τὰς ὑπὸ τῶν ἄλλων παρακοάς). I hear that afterwards he wrote about the things he had heard at the time (περὶ ὧν τότε ἤκουε), presenting it as his own work (τέχνη) and nothing of (the things, the people?) he had heard" (341a10-b6). Now consider Morrow's translation: "Later, I hear, he wrote a book on the matters *we talked about*, putting it forward as his own teaching, not what he had learned *from me*." What is in italics is inserted into the text by Morrow and with no justification. The natural way of understanding the passage is that the things Dionysius II heard at the time and on which he based his book are the things he heard from others, not from Plato.[21] The rest of the letter shows that the only hope Plato had for Dionysius II—and even that was a faint hope—is that

---

[21] Brisson and Isnardi Parenti translate accordingly.

he had a desire for virtue and thus could be converted into a just ruler. The advice he therefore describes himself as giving to Dionysius II is that he be master of himself and possess reliable friends: advice that is far, in short, from any kind of teaching on the ultimate principles of reality![22]

So while we have the idea of philosopher-kings here, what the unity of philosophy and power 'in the same' (ἐν ταὐτῷ, 335d1-2) would show to all, according to the letter, is simply the true opinion (ἀληθής δόξα) that "neither city nor man can be just when they do not carry out their life with prudence and under justice" (335d5-8).[23] The connection made in the letter between philosophy and politics is therefore that philosophy is required for the kind of life and character we need to see in the rulers of a just society. Thus, as we have seen, the advice Plato claims to have given Dionysius II, the same he is giving now to the friends of Dion, is to be master of himself and possess reliable friends (331d9-e1). If we have the suggestion that rulers would ideally be philosophers, we have nowhere the suggestion that they would apply their philosophical knowledge to politics, that political decisions would be derived from philosophical truths. Such truths are eternal and unchanging whereas we have seen the letter emphasize that political decisions must respond to chance, circumstance, and the opportune moment.

Foucault's reading of the letter is of a great value for recognizing this key point: "this philosophizing should not define for politics what it has to do. It has to define for the government, for the political man, that which he has to be. It is a question of the being of the political man, of his mode of being."[24] And here the act of the letter itself is revealing: the advice Plato gives the friends of Dion is, first of all, not derived from any philosophical theories but completely

---

[22] Lewis, "The *Severnth Letter*," also casts doubt on the common assumption that Plato was trying to turn Dionysius into a philosopher (242-43 & 249 n. 38).

[23] Lewis, "The *Severnth Letter*," argues that what we have here is simply the view that "Philosophical rule is an answer to the problem of *stasis*" (239). See also Colomès (32).

[24] *Le gouvernement de soi et des autres* (Paris: Gallimard/Seuil, 2008), 273. Translations are mine.

focused on the practical and narrowly political issues they must resolve (restoring order after civil war, taking steps to prevent further dissension, etc.); secondly, as Foucault also notes, Plato does not even propose any specific laws but leaves that entirely to them (251). Foucault furthermore perceptively notes the striking fact that when Plato's counsel makes reference to the immortality of the soul, a perfect opportunity for introducing his own theories on the matter, he instead advises Dion's friends to place their trust in "the ancient and holy accounts" (τοῖς παλαιοῖς τε καὶ ἱεροῖς λόγοις, 335a2-3). Foucault remarks: "These non-philosophical accounts, these accounts of religious beliefs and of sacred traditions, are what ought to constitute the theoretical backdrop to which the political man refers" (253). It is, in short, completely mistaken to see Plato in Syracuse as attempting to implement his philosophical theories and being defeated by a recalcitrant reality he did not anticipate.

It is therefore surprising that Michael Frede's case against the authenticity of the *Seventh Letter* is based on the premise that "the author of the Seventh Letter clearly presents Plato as trying as well as he can to turn Syracuse into the ideal state of the *Republic*" (75; see also 48), an aim, Frede argues, that Plato cannot possibly have had at the time he was writing the *Laws*.[25] Frede's justification for this premise appears to amount to this: 1) the idea of philosopher-kings is quoted from the *Republic* as the solution to political evils and 2) Plato's hopes for Syracuse appear to depend entirely on turning Dionysius II into a philosopher and on Dion's already being a philosopher. But what Frede needs to show is that the Plato of the letter seeks to make them into philosopher-kings in exactly the sense articulated in the *Republic*; indeed, on this claim depends his other argument against authenticity, i.e., that even Dion fell far short of this ideal, and that Dionysius II could never have been considered capable of reaching it (59-65, 78-84).

---

[25] See on page 52. Frede's surprise that the Syracusan project does not follow the program of the *Laws* is itself surprising: is there not a major difference between a colony to be founded from scratch and a city like Syracuse with existing laws and power structures?

Did Heidegger go to Syracuse?

That the Plato of the letter sought to realize the ideal of philosopher-kings exactly as presented in the *Republic* is something we must assume only if we have evidence for believing that he sought to turn Syracuse into exactly the ideal republic described in that dialogue with its guardian class, its abolition of private property, its holding of women and children in common, etc. But as noted by Myles Burnyeat in the same volume: "There is not a word about the other controversial institutions of the *Republic*: cultural reform, abolition of the family and private property for the ruling class, a full-time citizens' militia. Some scholars supposed that Plato hoped to turn Syracuse into the ideal city of the *Republic*. But that is not the message of VII, which restricts itself to promoting the rule of a philosopher" (141). Against this Frede appears to rest everything on the claim at 327c5-6 that Dionysius II's conversion to philosophy and the life of virtue will grant him and all his Syracusan subjects 'immeasurable bliss' (*amêchanon makariotêti*); surely, Frede reasons, only a city exactly like that of the *Republic*, and therefore philosopher-rulers exactly like those required for such a city, could provide immeasurable bliss (54)! But can so much be read into what in context is likely to be an exaggeration for rhetorical effect? The sole reason given in the letter for wishing to turn Dionysius II into a philosopher, as we have seen, is to make him a just person who will therefore enact, without having to resort to violence, just laws that apply equally to ruler and ruled, where all the emphasis is on the importance of such laws.[26] Frede is only the most recent example of a common misreading of the letter, though scholars are increasingly, like Burnyeat, rejecting this misreading.[27]

---

[26] Frede himself must recognize this emphasis as an important difference between the letter and the *Republic* (51).

[27] In addition to Colomès (36-37), Isnardi Parenti, and Lewis, already cited above, see Susan Sara Monoson, *Plato's Democratic Entanglements* (Princeton University Press, 2000), 147-50, and Mark A. Ralkowski, who asserts succinctly: "The *kallipolis* simply wasn't part of their plans" (*Heidegger's Platonism* [Continuum, 2009], 149). Even the editor of Frede's seminar notes, Dominic Scott, while agreeing, wrongly in my view, that Plato set out to create the philosopher-rulers of the *Republic* (an agreement that makes him find Frede's second

Francisco J. Gonzalez

What, then, was Plato's error? It is significant that his harshest Ancient critics, unlike modern critics, never thought of accusing him of naive idealism or political blindness. Their accusation, instead, is that Plato was the parasite and flatterer of a tyrant and thus that he sacrificed his principles to gain power. What they accused Plato of, in short, was moral corruption.[28] The response of the *Seventh Letter* to such an accusation is to describe Plato's Sicilian adventure as πλάνη and ἀτυχία (350d7).[29] It was not a political or moral error, not a philosophical error, but simply a result of that 'chance' on which, as Plato knew full well, all political success depends. Plato was not surprised by the events in Syracuse. He knew the risks and therefore went to Syracuse on both occasions with fear. There he met with the mischance of what he feared coming to pass.

Heidegger's amoral and apolitical politics

There is a close parallel to Plato's *Seventh Letter* in the case of Martin Heidegger: it is a text he wrote after the war entitled, "The Rectorate 1933/34: Facts and Thoughts." This text has been much

---

argument against authenticity as noted above compelling, 97), takes issue with Frede in noting, on the basis of 337c6-d8, that the Plato of the letter comes to recognize and settle for the 'second-best' solution of a rule of law to which both rulers and ruled are subject, even if there is no philosopher ruling (95). Von Fritz seems to need no evidence that Plato sought to realize his ideal republic in Syracuse since he appears to think that such a project follows a apriori from Plato's having written the *Republic* (33).

[28] See pages 26-27 of Colomès for Ancient criticism of Plato's involvement with Dionyisus: specifically, his characterization as the parasite of a tyrant by Aristoxenus of Tarent (pupil of Aristotle) and the characterization of the Platonists as διονυσοκόλακες by Epicurus.

[29] Von Fritz believes that the facts of Plato's lack of success in Sicily by themselves show him to have been guilty of "politically an extremely poor judgment" (17). But how does it show poor political judgment to recognize, as Plato did, that success depends largely on chance and circumstance and then to be proven *right* rather than wrong when chance and circumstance turn out to be unfavorable? Even if a sense of obligation to his friends led Plato to engage in a project he saw as having little prospect for success, this could not be described as *politically* poor judgment. Von Fritz himself (53-54), as well as Monoson (149), note the importance of this non-political motive.

discussed since its publication, provoking very different reactions; it is fair to say, however, that given what we know today, it has come to appear at best misleading, and at worst dishonest.[30] With the recent publication of the notebooks Heidegger kept during the 1930s and 1940s[31] we have what is at least a more candid and less reserved presentation of his view on political matters at the time. These notebooks are not simply a private diary but were clearly meant to be read by others, so that they are in this way similar to the *Seventh Letter*, which has the form of a private document while really being intended as a public document. The fact that Heidegger insisted on these notebooks not being published until well after his death suggests, however, that he reveals more here than in the text published during his lifetime.

In the notebooks Heidegger repeatedly describes his position in 1933, when he became rector of Freiburg University and joined the National Socialist party, with a word akin to the word Plato used: *Irrtum* or *Irren*, which could be a direct translation of the Greek πλανή and means 'erring' in the sense of 'going astray'. But how does Heidegger understand his error?

In 1938/39 Heidegger characterizes his mistake as follows: "Thinking purely 'metaphysically' (i.e., in terms of the history of being), in the years 1930-34 [note the dates!] I took National Socialism

---

[30] Die Selbstbehauptung der deutschen Universität : Rede gehalten bei der feierlichen Übernahme des Rektorats der Universität Freiburg i. Br. am 27.5.1933 ; Das Rektorat 1933/34 : Tatsachen und Gedanken (Frankfurt am Main: Vittorio Klostermann, 1983). Translated by Karsten Harries as "The Self-Assertion of the German University: Address, Delivered on the Solemn Assumption of the Rectorate of the University of Freiburg; The Rectorate 1933/34: Facts and Thoughts," Review of Metaphysics 38 (1985): 467-502.

[31] *Überlegungen II-VI (Schwarze Hefte 1931-1938), Gesamtausgabe* 94 (Frankfurt am Main: Vittorio Klostermann, 2014); *Überlegungen VII-XI (Schwarze Hefte 1938-1939), Gesamtausgabe* 95 (Frankfurt am Main: Vittorio Klostermann, 2014); *Überlegungen XII-XV (Schwarze Hefte 1939-1941), Gesamtausgabe* 96 (Frankfurt am Main: Vittorio Klostermann, 2014); *Anmerkungen I-V (Schwarze Hefte 1942-1948), Gesamtausgabe* 97 (Frankfurt am Main: Vittorio Klostermann, 2015). All translations are my own.

Francisco J. Gonzalez

to be the possibility of a transition to a new beginning and gave it this interpretation" (GA95, 408). But Heidegger then proceeds to describe this as an *under-estimation* rather than over-estimation of the movement. This is because what he now recognizes the movement as carrying out is "the completion of modernity [die Vollendung der Neuzeit]." This is clearly what Heidegger notoriously describes in the 1935 course "Introduction to Metaphysics" as the "inner truth and greatness" of National Socialism.[32] But then the movement is to be affirmed now even more essentially, rather than criticized. "The result of full insight into the earlier deception about the essence and the historical essential power of National Socialism is first the necessity of its affirmation and indeed on *philosophical* grounds" (408). Heidegger then asks how such an "essential affirmation" could be valued less than a merely superficial and blind agreement (408-9). The implication is clear. Heidegger no longer loudly applauds National Socialism, but he affirms it in a much more essential way, indeed, *on philosophical grounds*.[33] This is how we are to understand Heidegger's characterization of the denazification process he underwent after the war: "One is now finally stamped as a Nazi, something that one was not at all *in the way in which the world understands this*" (Letter to Fritz, September 21, 1949).[34] He continues to think of National Socialism purely metaphysically: the difference is that while he earlier thought it represented a new beginning, he

---

[32] *Einführung in die Metaphysik* (Tübingen: Max Niemeyer, 1953), 152; *Gesamtausgabe* 40 (Vittorio Klostermann, 1983), 208.

[33] Ingo Farin can maintain his view that Heidegger by 1934 no longer supported National Socialism only by interpreting the cited passage as Heidegger deluding himself into thinking that he still supports it ("The Black Notebooks in Their Historical and Political Function," in Reading Heidegger's Black Notebooks 1931-1941, eds. Ingo Farin and Jeff Malpas [Cambridge, MA: MIT Press, 2016], 306). As we will see, Farin would need to apply this questionable hermeneutics to many more passages to sustain his view. Fortunately, others in the same volume, such as Jean Grondin (96) and Thomas Rohkrämer (246-47), rightly reject this view on the basis of the overwhelming evidence.

[34] In *Heidegger und der Antisemitismus: Positionen im Widerstreit: mit Breifen von Martin und Fritz Heidegger*, eds. W. Homolka and A. Heidegger (Freiburg: Herder, 2016), 142. Translations are my own.

now sees it as the full realization of the first beginning and therefore in a sense as even greater than he thought: there could be no new beginning without the completion of the first beginning carried out by National Socialism.

This is borne out by what is perhaps Heidegger's clearest and most consequential analysis of his 'error' offered after the war: "The error did not consist in the fact that an attempt was made with 'National Socialism' . . ." To make this attempt was only to be near to "what 'is', still is" since National Socialism was "a form of the unavoidable realization and instituting of the absolute metaphysics of the will to will" (GA97, 147). Heidegger therefore maintains that his decision in 1933 was *and remains* (*"war und bleibt"*) a decision more essential (wesentlicher) than all the standing-by and wrinkling of noses on the part of those who, from the perspective of whatever other party, claimed to know 'better'. Heidegger can therefore also maintain that "politically in the world-historical sense the decision was not an error" (148). National Socialism was rightly thought as the end of metaphysics and therefore as a transition that could be overcome only from and through a new beginning. The 'error' was only in thinking that this could at the moment be directly established and demanded (148).

What emerges here with a clarity that cannot be denied is that Heidegger in 1946 does not in any way retract his explicit support of National Socialism in 1933, much less his silent and therefore 'more essential' support in the years since. In a later and even more revealing note Heidegger speaks of the few who already in 1932 thought, "in a genuine and not at all destructive sense," "that, namely, the technical world of modern man is not to be overcome by half-measures, but only by going through its full essence . . . " (GA97, 249-250). Anticipating that he will be branded a Nazi for these reflections, Heidegger denies that the catastrophe that befell Europe was Hitler and let spill onto the page all his contempt *for Hitler's opponents*:

> No—you prigs, [the catastrophe was] your cluelessness and shortsightedness. These kept you from seeing beyond the

marches and the somewhat bad appearances that disturbed you and your indolence. These kept you from thinking beyond yourselves and beyond Hitler, himself only a sign of the age, and seeing why it was that he became a disaster, [namely], because people stood on the sidelines or felt a quaint revulsion that wished to avoid him (250; see also GA96, 172).[35]

But why this support of National Socialism in particular?[36] The answer is made clear in the following comment: "In what one calls, geographically and politically, the 'Western democracies', modernity has long ago come to a standstill and indeed in its explicit and implicit *'metaphysics'*; the power, and above all the essential calling, is lacking for the step towards completion" (GA95, 405-6). The western democracies lack the strength to carry out the *Vollendung* that Heidegger sees National Socialism as carrying out. And the undemocratic, dictatorial character of the latter is key to the required power, as Heidegger makes clear in the following passage:

---

[35] In a letter of May 4, 1933, to his brother Fritz, who still hesitated to embrace fully the National Socialist movement, Heidegger advises him "in no way to pay attention to what is taking place around you in the form of vile and less pleasant things" (36). It is astonishing that after the horrors of the subsequent thirteen years (including the Holocaust!), Heidegger's advice remains the same.

[36] This support must be distinguished from a 'National Socialist Philosophy' which Heidegger dismisses as a superficial philosophy that "with the help of dolled-up expressions and slogans pretends to have overcome 'Christianity' and puts forth supposed 'decisions', after having first brought about a 'sacrifice of thought' in comparison to which the 'thought' of a Catholic vicar must be called 'free-spirited'" (GA95, 339). That 'National Socialism' and philosophy no more 'mix' than do Christianity and philosophy is a constant theme in the notebooks: see also GA96, 214, 233, and GA97, 157-58. In the one passage in which Heidegger speaks of any relation at all, it is to insist that National Socialism must be placed *under_*philosophy and recognize its own limits (GA94, 190). The notebooks therefore not only completely invalidate the central thesis of Emmanuel Faye's book, *Heidegger, l'introduction du nazisme dans la philosophie* (Paris: Albin Michel, 2005), but show that its very title represents an absurdity for Heidegger. The prosecutorial style of Faye is not, however, bothered by counter-evidence; he can even himself cite the last passage cited above without acknowledging its inconsistency with his thesis ("Antisémitisme et extermination: Heidegger, L'*Oeuvre intégrale* et les *Cahier noirs*," *Cités* 2015/1 [no. 61]: 119).

> Those who carry out the completion of modernity towards its highest essence are misleadingly called 'dictators' and only from the superceded position of the democracies—their greatness lies in the fact that they are capable of being 'dictatorial', that they sense the hidden necessity of the machination of being and do not let themselves be forced off course by any temptation (404).

Heidegger makes it clear that any moral criticisms here are completely beside the point: "Never, however, should these supports of violence be 'morally' devalued…" (404).

Heidegger in these pages begins to speak of "the brutality of being" that names the "unconditionality of the machination of being [*Machenschaft des Seins*]" and that, he insists, has nothing to do with some *bürgerlich* moral judgment (394). This brutality of being has as a consequence the brutality of man, by which is meant man taking himself to be a *factum brutum* and 'grounding' his animality (*Tierheit*) through a doctrine about race (396). It is not too hard to imagine the brutality in deed that will result from this metaphysical brutality. "But the predator, outfitted with the means of the most advanced technology—completes the realization of the brutality of being, and indeed in such a way that all 'culture' and historically calculated history—the image of history—is placed in its dust…" (397). Heidegger did not simply overlook the brutality of National Socialism in seeking something else of value in it; he considered its brutality to be essential to its inner truth and greatness. "Therefore, every 'political', every 'moral', every 'religious' critique and every critique concerned with 'culture' not only is short-sighted, but is already as a 'critique' a misunderstanding, because the unconditional brutality of mankind corresponds and must correspond to the completion of the machination in being itself" (402). Furthermore, if the brutality of the Nazis at least held the promise of a new destiny for the German people, Heidegger after the war sees this brutality as simply being replaced by the greater brutality of the Allies in making the German people betray their historical essence and destiny (GA97, 83). When he at one point refers to "the machinery of death that is now being brought on its way in Germany" (GA97, 148), he is not writing during the war in reference to the actions of the Nazi's, but after the war in reference to the actions of the Allies. The destruction of Europe, Heidegger maintains, has been brought about not by Hitler, but by the Americans; Hitler was only a pretext (*Vorwand*) (230; see also 390). What has thrown man into the extreme depravity of a rigidified forgetfulness of being is not mass murder (i.e., not what the Germans did), but rather the unconditional objectification of the world by 'American man' (309). Moral indignation is dismissed as a tired old joke, the biggest joke being those who just hung their cruder criminal precursors (apparently a reference to the Nuremburg trials). So if Heidegger now acknowledges "the massive brutality of a National Socialism that lacked destiny [*geschichtslos*]," it is only to insist that this brutality was "pure harmlessness [*die reine Harmlosigkeit*]" compared to "the planetary terror of world opinion" (87), the destructive power of which is, he repeatedly insists, much greater than that of the atomic bomb (151, 154; see also 413 & 426).

The result of all this is that, in contrast to Plato's emphasis on virtue as the condition of all politics, Heidegger's politics is characterized by 'brutality' and 'barbarism'. Heidegger in a note written as early as 1932, and therefore before his assumption of the rectorship, explicitly characterizes National Socialism as a 'barbaric principle' only to claim that in this lies its essence and possible greatness. The danger, Heidegger claims, lies not in the barbaric principle itself, but in the possibility that it will be rendered harmless through the preaching of what is true, good, and beautiful! (GA94, 194) We see here why Heidegger will never object to the ugliness, the evil, the mendaciousness of National Socialism. This he takes to be essential to the greatness of the movement, whether this greatness is understood as the possibility of a fundamental transformation in our relation to being and thus of another beginning or as the completion of the first beginning and thus as the completion of the metaphysical, technological relation to being understood as machination.

As for 'culture', all of Heidegger's references to this notion positively drip with contempt. 'Culture' is conservative, is nothing but "the cobbling together of what has been" (GA94, 195) and should be translated '*Vergnügungsbetrieb*' ('entertainment', GA96, 229).

Barbarism and collapse are not, Heidegger insists, the greatest danger "because these conditions can impel us towards an extreme situation and thus bring forth a need" (330); the greatest danger is instead "mediocrity" (a point made repeatedly: see also, e.g., GA96, 145, 195). This is why, writing on the eve of the war, Heidegger can chillingly comment that if understanding and compromise could avoid much horror and suffering, they would only drag man deeper into the 'humanization' [*Vermenschung*] of himself and of beings and into the stupidity of a domination of all beings blind to the history of being (GA95, 194). War, as he goes on to say, is not what is most frightening (GA95, 202). Even at the war's end, Heidegger looks upon its catastrophes with cold indifference, criticizing those who see anything essentially historical ending or beginning with the entrance into Germany of Russian troops (GA97, 53). Heidegger furthermore insists that the 'justice' of the victors is a greater presumption and a more twisted [*verfänglichste*] form of the will-to-power than any of the crimes committed during the war (64; see also 117). In a revealing note further developing this point, Heidegger grants that the terror that wipes out 'life' (the disturbing quotation marks are Heidegger's) is dreadful (*grausig*), but insists that there is another kind of terror that is more dangerous because cleverer: the terror of 'truth-possession [*Wahrheitbesitzes*]'(74). Even after the war the catastrophe of the West is still in the future for Heidegger (375), since we have yet to pass through the stage that he presumably had initially expected the Nazis to accomplish: "the rising up of man into the superman (in a negative as well as a positive way)" (367) through which being will collapse into completed subjectivity (384). This, he now believes, could take several centuries (512).

Heidegger's political nihilism

In the notebooks of 1938/39, at the height of Nazi power, one therefore finds Heidegger defending a completely amoral conception of politics well suited to the Nazis. He describes the gullibility [*Gutgläubigkeit*] of the people as a powerful weapon. The ruler will reveal his true aims only once his success is guaranteed; then his task will be to make the people recognize their own will in the fulfillment

Francisco J. Gonzalez

of the ruler's will. The value of such concealment and deception cannot be minimized by any 'moral' (Heidegger's quotes) points of view (GA95, 190). Heidegger here also hints at a higher politics, though not higher because it is any more moral. Heidegger imagines the possibility of Da-sein being sustained by a truth that, rather than goals or success, knows other sources of rule. Here Heidegger is presumably alluding to the rule of being itself. But such rule is, if anything, even *more amoral*: "But then does 'morality', as a supplemental teaching, first become truly impossible" (190).

Heidegger later makes his suggestion even more explicit: "Political action should not be measured by the standard of sensitivity and moral uprightness (*Sittenrichterei*)" (GA95, 232). But then from where should such action derive its law? We get this extraordinary response:

> Political action, *which is indeed nothing in itself* but is fully built into the essence of contemporary man and his history, finds *its* law in the *ruthless* [rücksichtslos] development towards an unrestrained and absolute reckoning with the putting into motion of masses as a whole--, all appeals to the preservation of the substance of the people and the like are necessary, but they always remain only pretexts for the unlimited domination of the political..." (my emphasis)

We find here perhaps the most important claim for understanding Heidegger's 'politics': 'political action' is nothing in itself because it is simply what we have seen Heidegger describe as "the completion of modernity" and as such it must be utterly ruthless and amoral. As he also asserts, making the contrast with Plato even clearer, "Politics has nothing more to do with the πόλις, just as little with morality [Sittlichkeit] and even less with 'becoming a people' . . . 'Politics' is the executor of the machination of beings; it is to be grasped only metaphysically; any other assessment falls short" (GA96, 43).

For Heidegger it would therefore be the greatest stupidity to raise any political objections, much less moral objections, to National Socialism or any other political worldview, whatever its horrors.

To want to combat political worldviews politically, indeed to want to burden them with arbitrary and isolated scruples, is to fail to understand that what comes to pass in them is something of which they themselves are not master, of which they are only the passive and shackled executors--; namely, the forgetting of being (*Seinsverlassenheit*) that being (*Seyn*) itself has bequeathed to beings, the hidden refusal of the commencement and of the sites of originary decisions. Therefore, it can never occur to reflection (*Besinnung*) to take seriously common short-sighted objections against those political movements. (GA95, 317-318)

The view that Heidegger became a critic of National Socialism after his initial 'error' is therefore unsustainable. Certainly no other political ideal is to be preferred, as reflections written at the end of the war make perfectly clear: "We need neither democratic nor fascist 'ideals'; we need no political ideals whatsoever, least of all moral preaching and political education through others" (GA97, 44). He then explains that there can thus be no question of opposing democracy to fascism:

> the confrontation between 'democracy' and its opposite [*Gegenspiel*] is never an essential one because, remaining in the political, it fails to see that what is to be decided is metaphysics and its essential dominance. What presses forward in political power structures is our own modern Western essence: humanity, nationality and bestiality—these are the essential steps in the unfolding of the subjectivity that reaches completion in the brutality of the will to will (44-45).

Indeed, after the war Heidegger will simply obliterate the opposition in asserting that the anti-Fascist democracies represent fascism in its massive form (*der Großfascismus*, 247, 249). The same obliteration occurs when Heidegger, again suggesting that those intellectuals who opposed Hitler early on did so only because they felt their idleness and lust to rule threatened, not only asks if those who were for Hitler "did not precisely see something else, something broader and more essential, not remaining fixated on the superficial" (460), but even suggests that "perhaps some of these were in a sense against Hitler already and earlier than those [who opposed him] later" (460). That is right: Heidegger is suggesting that if he supported Hitler, this was perhaps the most genuine way of being against Hitler. If that suggestion is not shocking enough, Heidegger proceeds to ask why his support of Hitler should be considered an error when Churchill's early support of Stalin is not (461), though Heidegger thankfully goes on to assure us that he does not really mean to compare himself to Churchill (462). When enthusiastically and aggressively supporting Hitler, in both words and actions, can be turned into the most genuine way of being against Hitler and can be treated as equivalent to Churchill's reluctant but practically necessary alliance with Stalin, we have arrived at a point where all political distinctions and considerations are simply obliterated.

It becomes especially clear in Heidegger's notes after the war that for him the only imperative is to meditate on *what is*, where this excludes any moral or political judgment about what ought to be. Thus, against those who want a return to the time before 1933, Heidegger asserts that what was willed between 1918 and 1933 *was blind to what genuinely is* (GA97, 127). He adds: "But what is at issue now is not whether Hitler or Mussolini or anyone else was 'right' or not, but rather that we experience *what is* . . ." (128). The problem, according to Heidegger, was that "everything was seen only 'politically', not even metaphysically, not to mention in terms of the history of being [*seynsgeschichtlich*]" (130). While Heidegger goes on to assure us that he is not thereby 'justifying' (his quotation marks) criminal activity (*das Verbrechertum*, 134) or 'National Socialism' (136; his quotation marks again), he also considers critique pointless:

> One turns up one's nose at the 'Nazis' and their terror and hangs onto everything superficial and undeniably ghastly on the part of individual party functionaries and arrangements and one deceives oneself about what here, without the proper knowledge of National Socialism itself, was *willed* and had to be willed—with the help of indignation and moral clarifications one deceives oneself about what genuinely is and one takes refuge where possible still in the 18th century or wherever else and does

not see what is already there and will not merely perhaps 'come' (136-37).

This insistence on understanding *what is* as the only imperative continues throughout the notes written after the war, as well as the complaint that any such attempt to reflect on "what genuinely *is* in a world-historical sense" is branded as "fortified 'Nazism' [Heidegger's quotation marks]" by [Allied] propaganda (136). We should recall that the 1949 Bremer lecture series, in the course of which Heidegger makes his notorious comment that the production of corpses in gas chambers is in essence the same as the modern agricultural industry,[37] was given the title: "Insight into what is [*Einblick in das was ist*]." The essential assumption is most clearly and brutally expressed when Heidegger asserts that "Science and morality have destroyed thinking" (234) and that, conversely, "Thinking holds onto neither science nor morality" (237).

Conclusion

The above should make clear that Heidegger's relation to National Socialism, rather than in any way reenacting Plato's trip to Syracuse, is the utter negation of everything such a trip represented. If for Plato the trip was about morally educating the ruler, encouraging the creation of just laws, and putting an end to political faction and violence, Heidegger not only accepts the brutality and barbarism of National Socialism, but gives it metaphysical justification as a result of the brutality and barbarism of being itself. Whether he sees the greatness of National Socialism as lying in its transition to a new beginning, as he did in 1930-34, or as lying in its culmination of the modern technological age in such a way as to call for a new beginning, as he did afterwards, what Plato and we would object to in National Socialism is for Heidegger of such triviality and

---

[37] "*Bremer und Freiburger Vorträge*, *Gesamtausgabe* 79 (Frankfurt am Main: Klostermann, 1994), 27. As Rastier generally observes, "Alors que le principe de la pensée analytique—et déjà de la dialectique selon Platon—consiste à distinguer pour articuler, il s'agit ici de confondre tant les formes que les fonds sémantiques et les moments, par l'intervention providentielle d'une identité métaphysique qui réside dans l'Essence, *im Wesen*." (100).

vacuity as not to be worthy of serious philosophical reflection, much less self-righteous bourgeois moral-indignation at the violation of human rights and the loss of life.

Plato's trip to Syracuse is a recognition that political action is something in itself, making special demands and subject to conditions outside the control of philosophy, such as circumstance, chance, and the opportune moment. Furthermore, the project of such a trip is not to substitute philosophy for politics (which would involve confusing a philosophical ideal with a real city), but to have philosophy influence politics by way of morally improving the character of the ruler and lawmaker. For Heidegger, in contrast, any critique of the politics of National Socialism, any attempt at morally improving it, is an absurdity because such politics, being nothing in itself, is only the completion of the modern technological age to which both brutality and barbarism are indispensable. And while Heidegger agrees with Plato that "philosophers should be rulers and guardians," it is only with the qualification that "the rule of these rulers is no public possession of power by the powerful" (GA96, 35). As for the idea, therefore, that philosophers should *descend* from the contemplation of being *back* into the Cave, Heidegger calls it "comic" because it "is uttered at the moment that philosophy has given up thinking" (GA97, 343). There is no bridge between thinking and politics. Heidegger therefore expresses as follows the *choice* that faces the "spiritual, active" man around 1940: "either to stand outside on the commando bridge of a minesweeper or to turn the ship of the most extreme questioning against the storm of beyng" (GA96, 160). Heidegger is simply expressing his choice to remain outside the Cave when he writes to his brother Fritz on December 29 of the same year: "Since beings [*ein Seiendes*] never reach Beyng [das Seyn], much less are able to replace it, no matter with how much noise and how broadly they might conduct themselves, it is good to stay with Beyng [my emphasis]" (69).

In conclusion, to lump Plato and Heidegger together as both symptoms of the same old problem philosophers have always had with politics does justice to neither;[38] if it serves, as we have noted, the apologetics of some Heideggerians, such apologetics does Heidegger himself less justice than confronting what is genuinely problematic and even shocking in his relation to politics.[39]

---

[38] Cf. "One of Heidegger's mistakes was surely to think, like Plato, that philosophy offered a surer basis for political engagement than is available to others—that the philosopher in politics is less prone to failure than the mere politician (which is perhaps why Heidegger could imagine that he was capable of guiding even Hitler—*Den Führer führen*). This is surely one of the vanities of philosophy—that philosophy can guide politics, that it can provide the ground for political decision" (Jeff Malpas, "On the Philosophical Reading of Heidegger: Situating the *Black Notebooks*," in *Reading Heidegger's* Black Notebooks *1931-1941*, 19). I hope this article shows that this conclusion is wrong about both Plato and Heidegger, though for very different reasons, and that the common trope of the 'vanity of philosophy' (Arendt's *'déformation professionelle')* is of no help in understanding the politics of either.

[39] For why I see none of the above as an excuse for not taking Heidegger seriously as a philosopher, see my "Heidegger's Remains," *Acta Philosophica* 25.2 (2016): 339-42.

Epilogue

Nickolas Pappas[1]
Toward and from Philosophy

In Syracuse lay the hope of joining philosophy to power, folding philosophical knowledge into established political strength as if according to a recipe for producing the good city. Philosophy and power could mix together in the opposite order too, when someone antecedently a philosopher chances to occupy a king's place in the city.[2] But chance is something you can't plan for (by definition) and shouldn't trust. The more practical option is to go where power already exists and educate the king or tyrant in philosophy. If you believe the *Seventh Letter*, that's what Plato was doing.

The premise of the Academy, and the implication of early anecdotes we hear about it, is systematic education in philosophy.[3] Instead of the Socratic examinations that responded to what someone else said, instruction in the Academy could begin with first principles and proceed to describe the whole enterprise. The *Seventh Letter* was either written by Plato, or (what I suspect is more likely) written in order to sound like Plato,[4] and either way it brings together a young

---

[1] Nickolas Pappas is professor of Philosophy at the CUNY Graduate Center, New York. He is the author of the *Routledge Philosophical Guidebook to Plato's Republic*, now in its third edition (2013) and, with Mark Zelcer, *Politics and Philosophy in Plato's Menexenus* (2015), both Routledge, along with other books and numerous articles, mostly on subjects in ancient philosophy and aesthetics.

[2] Plato *Republic* 5.473c-d, 6.499b-c.

[3] Thus the parody reported by ancient comedy, according to which Plato guided students toward a definition of "pumpkin." The scene, written by Epicrates in fourth-century Athens, is reported in Athenaeus *Deipnosophistai* 2 59d, and provides some of the earliest evidence for what took place in Plato's Academy. That the scene occurs in comedy with intent to ridicule implies that Plato would not have been after his students to discover what a gourd or pumpkin is; that sounds like a mocking version of what could have been the effort to define "human being" or "justice." I discuss this evidence in *The Philosopher's New Clothes: The* Theaetetus, *the Academy, and Philosophy's Turn against Fashion* (London: Routledge, 2016), 18-21.

[4] For a very recent discussion of the *Letter*'s authenticity (one argument after the other *against* its authenticity) see Myles Burnyeat and Michael Frede, *The Pseudo-Platonic Seventh Letter*, edited by Dominic Scott (Oxford: Oxford University

tyrant and an established teacher. This teacher has a method for bringing students into philosophy. What could go wrong?

According to the *Letter*, though, Dionysius II responds to Plato's instructions in every respect as unphilosophically as possible. He avoids the work of philosophical training; settles for secondhand talk about Plato's teaching from men who had heard or overheard others talking about it; violates the rule against writing down that teaching for widespread consumption. In fact nothing makes the *Seventh Letter* seem like a forgery as much as this portrait of Dionysius II does, saddling him with all the failings that philosophy's students can have as if for the purpose of making the narrator sound like Plato.

How did the attempted instruction misfire? Aside from his vanity or craving for glory, Dionysius II is said to be "otherwise bestowed with the ability [*dunamin*] to learn." He could have mastered the material. In this narrative's well-known image of the ineffable transmission of philosophy, "like light sparked by a leaping flame," the spark eluded Dionysius II. Plato says he tested the tyrant with an overview of philosophical learning and all its obstacles and hazards, and Dionysius II failed the test, as potential students do when they are not truly philosophical and *idontes* "they see" the extent of study required. The philosophical spark does not show itself to souls in a corrupted condition; "not even Lyncaius could make such people see [*idein*]."[5]

Even if not a Platonic work, the *Seventh Letter* qualifies as nearly Platonic, by which I mean that its author knows the Academy and its teachings, enough so that Plato's alleged predicament with Dionysius II reflects a question latent in the Platonic philosophy: How does one first come to study, let alone to value the study of philosophy? The spark lights up truth in the soul, but only if the soul already stands able to see the spark.

Press, 2015). As I made clear when reviewing this book, I find it largely persuasive: *Philosophical Forum* 47.1 (2016): 39–45.

[5] Plato *Seventh Letter*: Dionysius "otherwise bestowed," 338d; "leaping flame," 341c–d; seeing the study required, 340d; "not even Lyncaius," 344a.

Toward and from Philosophy

Indeed the very idea of an overview as a test, such as the one Plato tries out on Dionysius II, problematizes the fantasy of an illuminating insight. Seeing philosophy writ large inspires students to pursue it, or else discourages them to such a degree that "they become unable to pursue it."[6] Thus the *Letter* leaves us with a most equivocal advertisement for the Academy's pedagogy. Our course of study will heighten your capacity for philosophy in a manner that no course of study can do in any other subject – or else will leave you utterly inept at it.

It is at least possible that someone other than Plato wrote the *Seventh Letter* – I consider this the minimal claim of its inauthenticity; and a greater claim than one can make about, for example, the *Republic*. And because this might not be Plato's writing, we should not accuse him and his school of the pedagogical equivocality found in this document.[7] Thus, as a statement about Plato the teacher, it falls short of a serious indictment. Even so, the predicament of Plato's tutorial with Dionysius II gives us a question we will want to bring back to the Platonic dialogues and interrogate them with: How do non-philosophers begin to move toward philosophical knowledge? Do the phenomena that inspire philosophical thinking carry one surely toward knowledge; or are there elements in non-philosophical perception that while instigating inquiry also obstruct it?

If some particular experience made everyone a philosopher, then it's a wonder we don't have more philosophers walking the earth. If *no* experience had that effect, it would be a wonder we have any.

To my mind the story about Plato in ancient Syracuse belongs with discussions of beauty in Plato, despite the *Letter*'s saying almost nothing about the Greek words *kallos* or *to kalon*, and having almost nothing that it needs to say *with* those words, because the dialogues sometimes put a literally visual experience forward as significant to

---

[6] Plato *Seventh Letter*: students inspired, 340c; unable to pursue, 341a.

[7] Needless to say, even if authentic the *Letter* may be deliberately evasive about the Academy's methods, being as it claims to be a communication with the relatives of Dion, after his assassination, in reply to their suspicions about Plato's role in that affair. If Plato wrote it he had every reason to write cagily. The document does not become reliable evidence just because it is authentic.

incipient philosophical study; and yet let such an experience shoulder the blame, insofar as it's visual, for the failure of inquiry. And at its most visual, the experience may be called beauty.

The ambiguous effect of eyesight

We don't need the figurative visions described in the *Seventh Letter*, or the mystical imagery of a leaping spark, to show how a sight can inspire higher thinking. The *Timaeus* credits the sight of astronomical phenomena with making a soul philosophical, in both senses of that overused word, so that the soul engages in philosophical theorizing and also comports itself virtuously. Intellectually speaking, the soul governed by philosophy arrives at number and geometrical order through its *opsis* "vision" of day, night, months, and cycles of years. Morally speaking – as when we attribute virtues above all *sōphrosunē* to philosophers – the soul governed by philosophy stabilizes itself when it calculates the patterns and rhythms of astronomical motions. The errant and eccentric revolutions in a soul grow to resemble the "steady motions of the god" as those motions appear in the night sky.[8]

The *Timaeus* almost promises that looking at the stars will make you the complete philosopher. Meanwhile a companion passage in the *Republic* identifies the limit of the astronomical effect.[9] In that passage from Book 7 Socrates has proposed that the new city's guardians study astronomy, and not for the practical benefits that Glaucon initially thinks of (calculating seasons etc.). Having been corrected, Glaucon tries again to say why astronomy matters and to sound like a philosopher when he does so. It gets you looking upward, he says.

But that answer is wrong too. Glaucon is describing the act of looking spatially upwards, or as you might say, toward what the body considers the up direction. Looking at the stars that way amounts to looking down, Socrates says; he means that it privileges the visible over the intelligible.

---

[8] Plato *Timaeus*: vision of day and night, 47a; "steady motions of the god," 47b-c.
[9] Plato *Republic* 7.527d-529b.

Toward and from Philosophy

Socrates's philosophical act of rectification in *Republic* 7 follows the same reasoning found in Book 6 in connection with the Divided Line. Visible geometrical patterns inspire people to abstract from those patterns in their visible forms and to contemplate the intelligible order behind them – but only given a geometrizing bent in those who see the patterns.[10] Vision may well inspire thought, but vision alone won't do it. The second and third portions of the Divided Line can be seen either as mere visual appearances or as signs of some greater reality. So the sight of them doesn't suffice to turn the soul to greater visions.

The sight of the new gymnasium

Vision as both impetus to wisdom and impediment to philosophy makes no entry more remarkable, to my mind, than in the *Republic*'s proposal for coeducational exercise. In a single passage the length of one Stephanus page, Socrates asserts the epistemic worth of looking even as he condemns the folly of the eyes.[11]

Socrates has been saying that in the good city women will govern and battle alongside the men. Able soldiers need regular exercise at the gymnasium.[12] Greek gymnasia being, as their name implied, places where one was *gumnos* "naked," women's equal role alongside men in the city's ruling classes is going to create the risible scenario of their open nudity in public exercise.[13] And because Socrates has spoken of women guardians by way of imagining how the hypothetical city will actually operate, the laughter greeting the women means that the new city's inhabitants will not after all be consenting to its revolutionary regime.[14] This will be not a welcoming smile but the belittling laughs we also hear in the cave.[15]

---

[10] Plato *Republic* 6.510c-d.

[11] Plato *Republic* 5.452.

[12] The Greeks justified their preoccupation with the gym this way even though dissenters questioned the culture's athleticism and military effectiveness.

[13] Plato *Republic*: proposal sounds ridiculous, 5.452a4-6.

[14] I develop the implications of this passage in "Women at the Gymnasium and Consent for the *Republic*'s City," *Diálogos* 98 (2015): 27-54.

[15] Plato *Republic* 7.517a.

The danger and the nature of the laughter heard in the new city's gymnasium emblematizes the worry of generating consent for the good city among its population. The change in how citizens can see therefore speaks to the very pressing problem that Rachana Kamtekar raises about concord in the *Republic*'s city, in her article "What's the Good of Agreeing?"[16]

Given what is at stake, it is understandable that Socrates rebukes the laughing response. As the nudity of exercising men had also been when that practice originally came to Athens, the nudity of the new city's women at the gym will only be funny "to the eyes." People laughed when male athletic nudity arrived in Athens, but then (says Socrates) *ephanē* "it appeared, it seemed" that this new practice was better. You want to show such things not *sugkaluptein* "cover, veil, or hide" them. Shameful behavior is the only *opsis* "sight, spectacle" that deserves to be responded to with laughter.[17]

I call this passage remarkable because it appeals to visual access and transparency even as it demonizes the eyes for standing in the way of social change. On the one hand, what justifies athletic nudity is its unembarrassed frankness. The guardians' bodies will be open to inspection as their living quarters are open for all citizens to enter and look into, and as the battles they fight in are open for the guardians' children to watch and learn from. The complementary condition, which affirms the link between what's good and what's visible, is the grim fate of infants born to undeserving warriors, births that the rulers hide away.[18]

Plato follows Greek tradition in equating nudity with ease of being known. Not to say the practice really began this way, any more

---

[16] Kamtekar, "What's the Good of Agreeing? *Homonoia* in Platonic Politics." *Oxford Studies in Ancient Philosophy* 24 (2004): 131-70.

[17] Plato *Republic* 5.452: nudity only funny "to the eyes," d; people laughed at Spartan and Cretan male nudity, but then stopped, c-d; it *appeared* that it was better not to *veil* or *hide*, d; bad behavior the only undesirable *opsis* "sight," d.

[18] Plato *Republic*: living quarters open, 3.416d; battles open, 5.466e, 5.467e; births of the undeserving hidden, 5.460c. I am grateful to Adi Ophir, *Plato's Invisible Cities: Discourse and Power in the Republic* (London: Routledge, 1991) for exploring this theme and pointing out its significance to the *Republic*'s thought.

Toward and from Philosophy

than gymnastics began as military training; but the Greeks understood and (after the fact) justified their practices this way. In this spirit we are told that the Spartans made their men strip to confirm they were staying in shape. Even trainers at the Olympics – so the story goes – had to strip for inspection, in their case to keep women from cross-dressing to train the athletes, after one enthusiastic mother came to the Olympics dressed in drag as her boy's trainer.[19]

Thus we are obliged to prize nudity for the visual access it offers, openness to inspection representing knowledge; and we condemn the laughter that stands in its way, that laughter representing the bodily reaction that really betrays nothing other than the fact of its own ignorance.

Seeing resembles knowing, typically signifying a first movement in the direction of knowledge. In English we say "I see" meaning "I know" and the Greeks did the same. Nevertheless as one of the senses, seeing keeps company with the impulses that keeps human beings ignorant. Seeing is the name for knowing that those who exercise should strip. It is also the diagnosis for a failure to know.

Curiously enough the eyes win respect for knowing the human body even as their partnership with the other bodily senses personifies the eyes as juvenile bullies. The body at the gym being seen evidently differs from the body that engages in looking, the visible body rather something like an idea of the body, while the

---

[19] Inspection of Spartans, Aelian *Varia Historia* 14.7; of trainers (after Kallipateira), Pausanias *Description of Greece* 5.6.7-8. The essential first discussion of Greek athletic nudity is Larissa Bonfante, "Nudity as a Costume in Classical Art," *American Journal of Archaeology* 93: 543-70. Bonfante identifies inspection as after-the-fact justification for nudity. Also see James Arieti, "Nudity in Greek Athletics," *Classical World* 68: 431-36; Mark Golden, *Sport and Society in Ancient Greece* (Cambridge: Cambridge University Press, 1998); John Mouratidis, "The Origin of Nudity in Greek Athletics," *Journal of Sport History* 12 (1985): 213-32. On the *Republic* passage's claim about when nudity entered Athenian gymnastic practice see Myles McDonnell, "The Introduction of Athletic Nudity: Thucydides, Plato, and the Vases," *Journal of Hellenic Studies* 111: 182-93.

body that houses vision and the other senses goes wrong in its presumption that it can function without reference to the ideas.

The ambiguous sight of beauty

Beauty promises a way out of ignorance unlike any other enticement to philosophy to be named in Plato's dialogues. The long and mostly mythical speech in the *Phaedrus* that is known as its palinode contrasts the motivational effect of beauty with that of other objects of knowledge. "There is no glow [*pheggos*] in the things of this realm named after justice, self-control, or the other things valued by souls." Socrates is referring to objects and actions in the visible domain that participate in the Platonic Forms. Lacking this luster that beauty possesses, the other Forms inspire only a few (*oligoi*) minds to advance and gaze at what is represented by just or temperate images. *Kallos* "beauty" by comparison "gleamed where it was among those beings there, and when we came here we found it to be the most manifest to the most manifest of our senses." That sense, the sharpest most clarificatory sense, is sight. But for all its epistemological virtues eyesight fails to reach most intelligible objects, perceiving as it does only beauty.[20]

This emblem of visibility as such, *pheggos*, that explains beauty's unique availability to eyesight – call it glow or light or shining – seems to account for the bifurcated effect of vision that is left mysterious in other discussions within the dialogues. Justice will not induce a mind to think of the Forms unless that mind is already philosophizing; so if you see a just action and work your way up toward justice itself, but someone else remains visually encumbered, not reasoning toward Forms – well, that is the most anyone can expect. It is not the fault of vision. Beauty alone can work through the eye alone.

Compare this promise of philosophical happiness to the ascent that Diotima speaks of in Plato's *Symposium*. She pictures the philosophical novice guided by an expert teacher, recapitulating the

---

[20] Plato *Phaedrus*: luster, 250b; few minds drawn by other realities, 250b; beauty "gleamed where it was," 250d; sight the sharpest sense, 250d.

Eleusinian Mysteries, which took place only with the help of a guide.[21] As an equivalent to the Mysteries' initiation, or more rightly as the putative true version of what Eleusis accomplished in its murky and trivializing way, Diotima's voyage upcountry to the great sea of beauty takes the initiate somewhere new and even unexpected. This is not a sea you find by yourself and while looking for something else. Most people never reach this shore.

Socrates's speech in the *Phaedrus* also invokes the Mysteries. We see the young as those who are recently initiated, entering bodily form still freshly remembering the great insights they received. But here is the telling difference between the two narratives of ascending with (or to) beauty, that the *Phaedrus*'s soul underwent its initiation before its embodiment and apart from other (embodied) human beings. Seeing beauty now will lead it not to new philosophical understanding but back to the philosophy it had once lived in.[22] This trek upcountry leads the soul back home, as that other trek made during Plato's younger days had led Xenophon's men to the sea they hailed and cheered for, not because of its newness but because it presaged their return to a better previous state.

Does the *Phaedrus* therefore possess the potential to correct the *Seventh Letter*? Should we point the difference out to the *Letter*'s narrator? Plato tested Dionysius when he should have been teaching him. Not a panorama of philosophy in all its detail and with all its arcana, but something beautiful, should have been spread out before the young tyrant. He might have followed that vision and persevered instead of throwing up his hands to sink back into the unphilosophical hopelessness in which Plato evidently left him.

---

[21] Plato *Symposium*: Diotima refers to the *hêgoumenos* "leader, guide" who leads a lover to higher kinds of love, 210a. Socrates describes her as a teacher, 201d, 207a. On initiatory language see Nancy Evans, "Diotima and Demeter as Mystagogues in Plato's *Symposium*," *Hypatia* 21.2 (2006): 1-27; and especially Anne M. Farrell, *Plato's Use of Eleusinian Mystery Motifs* (Ph.D. dissertation, University of Texas at Austin, 1999).

[22] Plato *Phaedrus*: the lover initiated, 251a; returning to heavenly existence and the philosophizing done there, 248c-249b.

Surely this is hard to believe about a tyrant, though, that beauty of all things will guarantee his philosophical activity. The *Republic* identifies tyrants with unbridled manifestations of *erōs*, and if anything Plato is not challenging but echoing Greek culture when he speaks of tyranny in such terms. Periander of Corinth was a tyrant, like Oedipus, said to have committed incest with his mother. Athens' own Pisistratus was rumored to have practiced unlawful sex of some kind, and his heirs' affairs brought down his dynasty. Gyges of Lydia, very possibly the first man the Greeks called by the name "tyrant," took power in connection with some sordid palace affair. Closer to home, in Syracuse, the father of Plato's would-be charge, Dionysius I, had married two women on the same day and given two of his daughters as brides to his two brothers, the third one to his son.[23] Show beauty to this type and you can expect the worst, a decisive turn away from intelligible being rather than the pursuit of it.

The *Phaedrus*'s palinode recognizes the fate of beautiful sights around a tyrant. Everyone notices the sight of beauty and everyone is struck by the sight, but not all in the same way. "One who is not just initiated," Socrates says, "or who has been corrupted [*diephtharmenos*, from *diaphtheirô*]" will not respond to a beautiful appearance with dialectical recollection that takes him to that other beauty. He will respond lustfully and try to have intercourse as animals do.[24] The language comes close to what the *Seventh Letter* said about the type who is blinded to philosophy, "of a bad nature or corrupted [*diephthartai*, again from *diaphtheirô*]."[25] In one case the sight of philosophy lures you in of its own enchantment unless, thanks to a corruption already achieved in the soul, it fails to lure you. In the other case the particularly visible sight of beauty turns the

---

[23] Tyrants and *erôs*: Plato *Republic* 9.573a-c; Periander of Corinth, Diogenes Laertius *Lives of the Eminent Philosophers* 1.96; Pisistratus and unlawful sex, Herodotus *Histories* 1.61.1; and affair by heirs, Thucydides *The Peloponnesian War* 6.56-59; Gyges and palace affair, Herodotus *Histories* 1.8-12, Plato *Republic* 2.360a; Dionysius I, Plutarch *Life of Dion* 6.1.

[24] Plato *Phaedrus* 250e.

[25] Plato *Seventh Letter* 343e-344a.

soul to thoughts of its pre-embodied life; unless corruption in the soul makes it turn to the worse.

Philosophy still in need of a beginning

If these passages failed to describe the mechanism that draws someone assuredly into philosophy, we could observe that they do not provide the first stage of study. The right sight works sometimes, falls flat otherwise. Other passages might supply a more reliable mechanism: the speech of Diotima, or the *katharsis* by interrogation that the *xenos* describes in Plato's *Sophist*, and that Socrates enacts all over the place. If these don't work we can express regret. How much nicer it would have been if *Platōn didaskalos* had offered some usable inducement.

Things are worse than that, though. The hyperuranian birth of beauty as lambent visibility repeats the visual conundrum that we've been promised in the new city's gymnasium. Seeing, which was going to amount to, or would harbinger, acceptance of the new city, also accounts for the new order's being a laughingstock.

The besotted lover likewise either flies upward to philosophical insight or remains below incapable of it, in both cases because of that sight of beauty. Failure in the flight upward is not a lapse in the way eyesight works, or chance effect or malfunction, but represents eyesight's doing its job, just as surely here as in the cases we call successful. *Both the ascent to philosophy and the non-ascent reflect the functioning of eyesight.* Where there is (really *wherever* there is) a visuality capable of bringing the newcomer into philosophy, you will also find a positive contrary, obfuscatory capability, latent in the same phenomenon, that not only does not rise toward knowledge but refuses to, rather abetting ignorance.

Here is the lingering cause for worry in the *Seventh Letter*'s tale of testing the tyrant. The *Letter*'s narrator reveals that although this glimpse of philosophy as a whole inflames those with talent for the subject to study more and persevere, the rest will glimpse their incapacity for such sustained industry; *oute epitēdeuein dunatoi gignontai* "nor do they become capable of pursuing the subject."[26] On

---

[26] Plato *Seventh Letter* 341a.

the contrary, having mistaken the preview for the conclusion, they believe that they pretty much know all there is to know about philosophy. In the language of the *Phaedrus*, it is as if they tried to beget young upon philosophy after the manner of beasts, instead of getting by for three lifetimes on abstinence. All thanks to the test they've just failed.

The *Seventh Letter* insists that the test absolves the teacher of all blame for instruction gone bad. They can't call the one who revealed their incapacity for learning the *aitia* "cause" of that incapacity.[27] That would have been a tolerable excuse had Plato done no more, or nothing worse, than fail to turn Dionysius II toward philosophy. But despite the *Letter*'s embarrassed claim about the instructor's being freed from blame, in fact he is telling us that he helped to set Dionysius against higher learning. You can't even test for the philosophical aptitude without sometimes driving it away. In light of this danger, philosophical education needs to become systematic and yet never can do so. Does beauty possess the same loose-cannon power of malevolence, testing for the souls of philosophers and along the way turning most people against philosophy?

---

[27] Plato *Seventh Letter* 341a.

General Index

Achilles, 249-50
Alcibiades, 82, 95-6
Anaximander, 175, 184
Antikythera mechanism, 170, 182-83
Antilochus, 249
Antisthenes, 242
Apollocrates, 105
Apuleius, iv, 82
Archedemus, 41, 67, 201, 212-13
Archimedes, viii, 167-71, 174-75, 180, 182-83
Archytas, 39, 41, 43, 69, 86-7, 92, 149, 169, 171, 184, 195, 196, 201, 212-13, 236-37, 309
Arendt, Hannah 266-67, 289
Aristotle, ii, 101-2, 153, 157, 163, 173, 184, 187, 192, 215, 226, 228, 261, 276
Athenian Stranger, 222, 224
Athens, ii, iv, v, 25, 27, 35, 43, 59, 69, 77, 80, 85, 88, 91, 93-8, 100-1, 129, 150, 153, 169, 171, 174, 183, 187, 191-92, 198, 204, 213, 233, 234-38, 241-43, 245, 258, 293, 298, 302
Brisson, Luc, 268, 270-72
Burnyeat, Myle,s ii, 92, 161, 169, 179, 215, 234, 247, 268, 275, 293

Bury, R. G., 234, 236-37, 240, 243, 253
Callipus, vi, 88, 236, 244, 246
Cicero, i, 129, 167-70, 172, 183
Cornelius Nepos, 109, 110
Cosmology, 175
Ctesibius, 180-81
Darius, 21, 85, 98
Demetrius, xi, xii
democracy, 7, 89, 95, 100, 121, 190, 218, 238-39, 245, 248, 254, 285
Demosthenes, 93, 112-14
Dialogue, iii, 145, 164, 265, 268
Digression, 8, 247, 258, 309
Diodorus Siculus, iv-v, 83, 107, 108, 111, 113, 124
Diogenes Laertius, iv-v, 77, 80, 82-3, 169, 233-34, 236-38, 242, 302
Diogenes of Sinope, ix, 77, 80, 233, 237
Dion, iv-vii, ix, 3, 9, 11-13, 15, 21, 23, 25-7, 29, 31, 33, 35, 37, 39, 41, 43, 57, 59, 61, 63, 67, 69, 71, 73, 78-9, 81-9, 92-4, 97-102, 105-17, 119-21, 124-26, 149, 153, 187-88, 190-99, 201-6, 208, 210, 212-18, 230, 235-37, 239-41, 243-46, 252-57, 259, 261, 267, 269, 272-74, 295, 302, 309

Dionysius I, iii-viii, 21, 82, 84, 92-4, 97-8, 105-8, 120, 123-24, 129-30, 149-51, 153-54, 156, 159-61, 187-88, 191-97, 201-2, 204-6, 208, 210-14, 233, 235, 236-39, 241, 243-46, 255, 265, 270-75, 294-95, 302, 304

Dionysius II, v-viii, 21, 84, 92-4, 97-8, 105-8, 120, 123-24, 129-30, 149-51, 153-54, 156, 159-61, 188, 191-97, 201-6, 208, 210-14, 235-39, 241, 243-46, 255, 265, 270-75, 294-95, 304

Diotima, 301, 303

Divided Line, 297

Edelstein, Ludwig, ii, 79, 94, 129

Ephorus, 109-10, 112

Epictetus, 242

Eratosthenes, 175

Eudoxus, 171-74, 177, 184

Euphemus, 98, 213

Finley, Moses, 130, 134

Forms, 177, 217-18, 225-27, 300

Foucault, Michel, ix, 247-53, 255, 259, 262, 273

Frede, Michael, ii, ix, 92, 145-46, 161, 215-16, 219, 226, 229-30, 234, 247, 268, 274-75, 293

Gadamer, Hans G., 155, 265

Gonzalez, Francisco, iii, ix, 164, 258, 265

Guardians, 221-22, 224, 228

Heidegger, Martin, ix, 129, 175, 265-67, 275-89

Heracleides, vi, 65, 67, 120, 196, 236, 245-46, 309

Heraclitus, 168, 176, 184

Hermocrates, 96, 169

Hero of Alexandria, 180, 184

Hesiod, 168, 183, 251

Hipparchus, 174, 183

Homer, 168, 183

Ibn Isma'il al-Jazari, 182

Irwin, Terrence, ii, iv, vii, 79

Isocrates, 246

Kahn, Charles, ii-iii

Kallipolis, iii, 132, 217, 225

Klosko, George, 221, 228

Knowledge, 8, 103, 145, 169, 182, 247, 252, 258, 261

Leon of Salamis, 80

Lewis, Bradley ii, iv, vii, 82-3, 89, 92, 94, 99, 101, 103, 201, 205, 258, 270-71, 273, 275

life-structuring practice (*epitēdeuma*), viii, 130-37, 146-47

Machiavelli, 206-7

Magnesia, 77, 217-18, 220-21, 222, 226-29

Marcellus, 170, 172

Menelaus, 249

Morrow, Glen, ii, iv, 92, 110, 129, 150, 157, 159-60, 201, 208, 228-29, 271-72

Nails, Deborah, 82, 88, 92-93, 96, 169-71

National Socialism (Nazism), ix, 265-66, 277-82, 284-88
Nocturnal Council, 8, 215, 217, 221, 223-29
Olympiodorus, iv, 82
Philistion, 171, 184
Philistus, 115, 191, 194
Philo of Byzantium, 180, 182
Plato,
    Apology, 80, 137, 189, 261
    Charmides, 150
    Eighth Letter, 82, 130 n3, 188, 234
    Euthydemus, 149
    Gorgias, iii, 134, 141,
    Laches, 149-50
    Laws, iv, ix, 77, 99, 188, 198, 215-30, 240, 274
    Phaedrus, viii, 130, 140-46, 260, 300-4
    Protagoras, 139, 149, 151, 153, 155
    Republic, iii, iv, vii-viii, 97, 130-35, 137, 155, 157, 169, 178-79, 216-18, 224, 235, 260, 265, 268, 269, 275, 276, 293, 296, 297, 298, 299, 302
    Second Letter, 141, 144, 175, 194-95
    Sophist, 139, 140, 303
    Statesman, iv, viii, 130, 140-42, 146, 188, 222
    Symposium, 96, 193, 301
    Theaetetus, 139, 141, 260, 293

Timaeus, viii, 96, 167-84, 296
Plutarch, i, iv-vi, viii, 26, 83-4, 88, 99, 105-21, 123-26, 153, 170, 189, 191, 193-94, 197, 302
Pythagoras, 172, 184, 187
Riginos, Alice, iii, iv
Sicily, i, iv-v, vii, 7, 9, 11, 17, 21, 23, 27, 29, 33, 35, 39, 41, 63, 65, 73, 82-83, 86, 88-9, 91, 97-8, 100, 105-17, 119-22, 124-26, 129, 133, 146, 169, 171, 184, 187, 188, 190-93, 195-98, 205-6, 213-15, 235, 238-41, 244, 248, 254, 256, 261, 266, 269-71, 276, 311
Simplicius, 173, 175
Socrates, iii, 5, 78-80, 97, 131-32, 135, 137-39, 141, 143-44, 146, 149, 151, 169, 178-79, 187-89, 209, 218, 222, 234, 238-39, 242, 246, 253, 255, 260, 296-98, 300-3, 309
Solon, 187, 248, 262
Speusippus, vi, 113, 115-16, 215
Syracuse, v-vii, xi, 3, 9, 13, 15, 33, 37, 39, 41, 77-8, 82-9, 91-2, 96-8, 100-1, 105-7, 110-11, 113-19, 122, 126, 130, 134, 149-50, 153, 169-70, 174-75, 183, 187-92, 194-96, 198, 200-4, 211-13,

216-19, 226, 233-41, 243-46, 253-58, 261, 263, 265-67, 269, 271, 274-76, 287-88, 293, 295, 302
Thales, 168, 171-72, 184, 187
Theodotes, 65, 67, 196, 210, 309
Theon, 175
Theophrastus, 175
Thucydides, 95, 96-8, 299, 302
Timaios, 110
Time, 7, 167, 176, 181

Timoleon, iv, viii, 82, 84, 88, 99, 100, 105-8, 110, 114, 118, 121-26
Tisias and Corax, 261
Truth (*alētheia*), 15, 250, 252, 262
Tyranny, 94, 309
Writing (*syngrammata*), 138, 143
Zeus, 12, 13, 29, 57, 69, 192, 196, 243, 251

Index of Topics/Passages in the *Seventh Letter*

Archytas of Tarentum
    338c-d, vi, 84, 210, 213, 294
    339a, 213, 257
    339d, 87, 149, 213, 257
    350a, 87

Athenian Revolution
    324c-325b, 80, 93, 189, 253-54, 99-100, 189, 270

Captivity
    329e-330a, v
    338a-b, vi
    347a, 213
    347e-348a, 213
    349d, 196

Civil war
    336e-337b, 81-2, 102
  solutions for
    337b-d, 82, 240, 269, 275-76

Critique of writing
    341c-344e, 103, 130, 138-41, 154, 162-63, 208, 247, 258-60, 294, 303

Dion
  appeals to Plato
    328d-e, 83-5, 255
  as a student
    327a-b, 84, 191, 254
  character and opinions
    324a-b,
    327a-c, v, 83-4. 15, 191, 207, 219, 254, 272, 275
    328b, v, 84, 129, 192, 213, 235, 268, 270
    336a-b, 81, 83, 97, 126, 215, 219-20, 269
    351a-e, 88, 198, 207, 219, 236, 244, 269
  exile of
    329c, 236
    333a-b, 84, 256-57
    333d, 86
    338a-b, v-vi, 86, 210, 213
    339b-c, vi, 195, 210
    346b-c, v, 87
    350b-c, vi, 87-8, 197
  friendship with
    328d-329a, 83-5, 255
    330a, 86, 193, 208, 255, 271
    339c, vi, 86
    339e, 87, 213, 253, 270
    346e-347b, 213
    350d, vi, 88, 276
  loss of asssets
    345c, 87, 196, 210, 236
    347b-e, 87, 152, 210, 241
    349c-e, 196, 210
  murder of
    333e-334c, 88-9, 201-3, 244
    335e, 97, 215, 269
    351d-e, 88, 236, 244

Dionysius
  advising of
    331c-333a, 81, 85-6, 97-100, 201, 205-7, 212, 256, 268, 273

333d, 86
335c, 85, 257
court of
   329b-d, 85-6, 236, 255
   333b-c, 211, 256-57
father of
   331e-332a, 85, 205
   332c-d, 85, 205-6
interest in philosophy
   328a, 84, 210, 255, 271
   330a-b, 193, 208, 255, 271
   338b-c, vi, 210, 213
   338d-e, 84, 210
   339e-340a, 87, 150, 195, 213, 253, 270
   340b, 87, 144, 149, 201, 210, 257
   341a-b, 154-55, 162, 201, 210, 257, 272, 295, 304
   345d, 196, 210, 213
Gelon
   333a
Heracleides
   348b-349c
   349e
Hieron
   336a
Laws
deterioration of
   325c-d, 80, 129, 189, 234, 270
   326a, 79-81, 93, 190, 207, 219, 254, 269-71
   326c-d, 79-80, 190
   336b, 79-80, 97, 190, 269
importance of
   324b, 81, 219, 253, 270
   332b, 85
   332e, 85, 205
   334c, 81, 99, 269
   336a, 81, 83, 97, 102, 219-20
   336d
   337c-d, 81-2, 102, 239-40, 269, 275
Philosophy
and politics
   326b, 79, 218
   330a-b, 193, 208, 255, 271
   335d, 82, 84, 207, 219, 273
   336a-b, 81, 83, 215, 219-20, 269
misconceptions about
   338d-e, 84, 210
   340b-341a, 87, 137, 149, 158, 163, 201, 210, 257, 294, 295, 304
   341c-342a, 130, 138-39, 154, 162-63, 208, 247, 258
Political engagement
   325c-326b, 79-81, 84, 99-100, 129, 189-90, 234, 270
   330c-331d, 256
   337d
Socrates
   324d-325c, 79-80, 99-100, 189, 234, 253-54, 270
Syracusan lifestyle
   326b-d, iii, 79-80, 83, 133-34, 155, 190, 218, 244

336d
Test (*peira*)
    340b-341b, 87, 144, 149,
        201, 210, 257
Theodotes
    appeal for Heracleides
        348c-349b, 210
    relations with Plato
        349d-e, 196, 210

Theory of knowledge
    342a-343c, 140-41, 162,
        247, 258,
    344b-c, 259, 103, 141, 162,
        260
Tyranny
    326d, 80, 134
    327a-b, 84, 190-91, 254
    329b, 85, 139, 255

About the Editors and Translator

Heather L. Reid (editor) is Professor of Philosophy at Morningside College in Sioux City, Iowa USA and Scholar in Residence at Exedra Mediterranean Center in Siracusa, Sicily. She is a 2015 Fellow of the American Academy in Rome, 2018 Fellow of Harvard's Center for Hellenic Studies, and 2019 Fulbright Scholar at the Università degli Studi di Napoli Federico II. As founder of Fonte Aretusa, she promotes conferences and research on Western Greece. She has also published books and articles in ancient philosophy, philosophy of sport, and Olympic Studies, including *Introduction to the Philosophy of Sport* (2012), *Athletics and Philosophy in the Ancient World* (2011), and *The Philosophical Athlete* (2002, 2nd ed. 2019).

Mark Ralkowski (editor) is Associate Professor of Philosophy and Honors at George Washington University. He is the author of *Plato's Trial of Athens* (2018) and *Heidegger's Platonism* (2009), and he is the editor of *Time and Death: Heidegger's Analysis of Finitude*.

Jonah Radding (translator) is Visiting Assistant Professor of Classics at Northwestern University. His research focuses primarily on ancient drama and on intersections between politics and poetry in the classical Greek world. He has published articles on Euripidean tragedy in the *American Journal of Philology*, and *Greek, Roman, and Byzantine Studies*, and has another article forthcoming in *Erga-Logoi*.

Made in the USA
Columbia, SC
11 March 2019